Lecture Notes in Comput

T0230273

9

Commenced Publication in 1973
Founding and Former Series Editors:
Gerhard Goos, Juris Hartmanis, and Jan van Leeuwen

Editorial Board

Henk Schepers (Ed.)

Software and Compilers for Embedded Systems

8th International Workshop, SCOPES 2004
Amsterdam, The Netherlands, September 2-3, 2004
Proceedings

 Springer

Volume Editor

Henk Schepers
Philips Research
Prof. Holstlaan 4, 5656 AA Eindhoven, The Netherlands
E-mail: Henk.Schepers@philips.com

Library of Congress Control Number: 3540230351

CR Subject Classification (1998): D.3, D.4, D.2, D.1, C.3, C.2

ISSN 0302-9743
ISBN 3-540-23035-1 Springer Berlin Heidelberg New York

Springer is a part of Springer Science+Business Media

springeronline.com

© Springer-Verlag Berlin Heidelberg 2004
Printed in Germany

Typesetting: Camera-ready by author, data conversion by Olgun Computergrafik
Printed on acid-free paper   SPIN: 11313403   06/3142   5 4 3 2 1 0

Preface

This volume contains the proceedings of the 8th International Workshop on Software and Compilers for Embedded Systems (SCOPES 2004) held in Amsterdam, The Netherlands, on September 2 and 3, 2004. Initially, the workshop was referred to as the International Workshop on Code Generation for Embedded Systems. The first took place in 1994 in Schloß Dagstuhl, Germany. From its beginnings, the intention of the organizers has been to create an interactive atmosphere in which the participants can discuss and profit from the assembly of international experts in the field.

The name SCOPES has been used since the fourth edition in St. Goar, Germany, in 1999 when the scope of the workshop was extended to also cover general issues in embedded software design. Since then SCOPES has been held again in St. Goar in 2001; Berlin, Germany in 2002; Vienna, Austria in 2003; and now in Amsterdam, The Netherlands.

In response to the call for papers, almost 50 very strong papers were submitted from all over the world. All submitted papers were reviewed by at least three experts to ensure the quality of the workshop. In the end, the program committee selected 17 papers for presentation at the workshop. These papers are divided into the following categories: application-specific (co)design, system and application synthesis, data flow analysis, data partitioning, task scheduling and code generation.

In addition to the selected contributions, the keynote address was delivered by Mike Uhler from MIPS Technologies. An abstract of his talk is also included in this volume.

I want to thank all the authors for submitting their papers, and the program committee and the referees for carefully reviewing them. I thank Harry Hendrix and Jan van Nijnatten for supporting the review process and for compiling the proceedings. Finally, I thank Marianne Dalmolen for maintaining the web site and the local organization.

June 2004   Henk Schepers

Organization

SCOPES 2004 was organized by ACE Associated Compiler Experts and Philips Research in cooperation with EDAA.

Committee

General Chairs   Marco Roodzant, ACE (Associated Compiler Experts)
Henk Schepers, Philips Research

Local Organization   Marianne Dalmolen, ACE (Associated Compiler Experts)

Program Committee   Uwe Assmann, Linköpings Universitet
Lex Augusteijn, Silicon Hive
Shuvra Bhattacharyya, University of Maryland
Albert Cohen, INRIA
Alex Dean, North Carolina State University
Nikil Dutt, University of California at Irvine
Antonio González, Universitat Politècnica de Catalunya
    & Intel
David Gregg, Trinity College Dublin
Rajiv Gupta, University of Arizona
Seongsoo Hong, Seoul National University
Nigel Horspool, University of Victoria
Masaharu Imai, Osaka University
Daniel Kästner, AbsInt
Andreas Krall, Technische Universität Wien
Rainer Leupers, RWTH Aachen
Annie Liu, SUNY Stony Brook
Peter Marwedel, Universität Dortmund
Tatsuo Nakajima, Waseda University
Alex Nicolau, University of California at Irvine
Yunheung Paek, Seoul National University
Santosh Pande, Georgia Institute of Technology
Robert Pasko, IMEC
Sreeranga Rajan, Fujitsu
Miguel Santana, STMicroelectronics
Hans van Someren, ACE (Associated Compiler Experts)
Hiroyuki Tomiyama, Nagoya University
Bernard Wess, Technische Universität Wien
David Whalley, Florida State University

Referees

Christophe Alias
Cédric Bastoul
Marcel Beemster
Valerie Bertin
Doo-san Cho
Yulwon Cho
Junshik Choi
Jan van Dongen
Heiko Falk
Liam Fitzpatrick
Carlos Garcia
Laurent Gerard
Leszek Holenderski
Jan Hoogerbrugge
Martien de Jong
Saehwa Kim
Arvind Krishnaswamy
Fernando Latorre
Bengu Li
Klas Lindberg
Grigorios Magklis
Hyunok Oh
Bryan Olivier
Emre Ozer

Serge De Paoli
Jiyong Park
Sang-hyun Park
Greg Parsons
Zane Purvis
Robert Pyka
Frederic Riss
Ruben van Royen
Sergej Schwenk
Jaewon Seo
Aviral Shrivastava
Yoshinori Takeuchi
Sriraman Tallam
Hiroaki Tanaka
Thomas Thery
Osman Unsal
Xavier Vera
Manish Verma
Jens Wagner
Lars Wehmeyer
Sami Yehia
Thomas Zeitlhofer
Xiangyu Zhang
Xiaotong Zhuang

Table of Contents

Invited Talk

The New Economics of Embedded Systems 1
Michael Uhler

Application Specific (Co)Design

A Framework for Architectural Description of Embedded System 2
Daniela Cristina Cascini Peixoto and Diógenes Cecílio da Silva Júnior

Automatically Customising VLIW Architectures
with Coarse Grained Application-Specific Functional Units 17
Diviya Jain, Anshul Kumar, Laura Pozzi, and Paolo Ienne

ASIP Architecture Exploration for Efficient Ipsec Encryption:
A Case Study 33
Hanno Scharwaechter, David Kammler, Andreas Wieferink,
Manuel Hohenauer, Kingshuk Karuri, Jianjiang Ceng, Rainer Leupers,
Gerd Ascheid, and Heinrich Meyr

System and Application Synthesis

Compact Procedural Implementation in DSP Software Synthesis
Through Recursive Graph Decomposition 47
Ming-Yung Ko, Praveen K. Murthy, and Shuvra S. Bhattacharyya

An Integer Linear Programming Approach
to Classify the Communication in Process Networks 62
Alexandru Turjan, Bart Kienhuis, and Ed Deprettere

Predictable Embedded Multiprocessor System Design 77
Marco Bekooij, Orlando Moreira, Peter Poplavko, Bart Mesman,
Milan Pastrnak, and Jef van Meerbergen

Data Flow Analysis

Suppression of Redundant Operations in Reverse Compiled Code
Using Global Dataflow Analysis 92
Adrian Johnstone and Elizabeth Scott

Fast Points-to Analysis for Languages with Structured Types 107
Michael Jung and Sorin Alexander Huss

Data Partitioning

An Automated C++ Code and Data Partitioning Framework
for Data Management of Data-Intensive Applications 122
   *Athanasios Milidonis, Grigoris Dimitroulakos, Michalis D. Galanis,
   George Theodoridis, Costas Goutis, and Francky Catthoor*

Combined Data Partitioning and Loop Nest Splitting
for Energy Consumption Minimization............................... 137
   Heiko Falk and Manish Verma

On the Phase Coupling Problem Between Data Memory Layout
Generation and Address Pointer Assignment 152
   Bernhard Wess and Thomas Zeitlhofer

Task Scheduling

Dynamic Mapping and Ordering Tasks of Embedded Real-Time Systems
on Multiprocessor Platforms 167
   Peng Yang and Francky Catthoor

Integrated Intra- and Inter-task Cache Analysis
for Preemptive Multi-tasking Real-Time Systems..................... 182
   Yudong Tan and Vincent Mooney

A Fuzzy Adaptive Algorithm for Fine Grained Cache Paging 200
   Susmit Bagchi and Mads Nygaard

Code Generation

DSP Code Generation with Optimized Data Word-Length Selection 214
   Daniel Menard and Olivier Sentieys

Instruction Selection for Compilers that Target Architectures
with Echo Instructions... 229
   Philip Brisk, Ani Nahapetian, and Majid Sarrafzadeh

A Flexible Tradeoff Between Code Size and WCET
Using a Dual Instruction Set Processor 244
   Sheayun Lee, Jaejin Lee, Chang Yun Park, and Sang Lyul Min

Author Index 259

The New Economics of Embedded Systems

Michael Uhler

Chief Technology Officer
MIPS Technologies
uhler@mips.com

Abstract. There is a fundamental shift coming in the economic model used to build successful embedded systems. Below 100nm fabrication geometries, the cost of designing and creating masks for new semiconductor devices is projected to rocket up, making it uneconomical to create a new device for every system, or even to do another manufacturing pass to fix bugs.

So why is this an interesting topic at a workshop on software and compilers? Because the increased cost of hardware, and the increasing demand for new capability in embedded systems mean that programmable products will explode as the solution of choice to cost-effective embedded systems. However, the need to keep power dissipation under control means that both programmability and configurability will be critical in new system design. This puts an increased burden on compilers to generate code for configurable processors, and requires additional capability in software to manage the complexity.

This talk will briefly review the reasons for the economic change, but focus primarily on a vision for a new type of embedded system in which software and compilers play a critical role. In some sense, the original RISC concepts have returned in that software will assume an increasing role in the design of new embedded systems.

H. Schepers (Ed.): SCOPES 2004, LNCS 3199, p. 1, 2004.
© Springer-Verlag Berlin Heidelberg 2004

A Framework for Architectural Description of Embedded System

Daniela Cristina Cascini Peixoto[1] and Diógenes Cecílio da Silva Júnior[2]

[1] Computer Science Department
Universidade Federal de Minas Gerais, Brasil
cascini@dcc.ufmg.br
[2] Electrical Engineering Department
Universidade Federal de Minas Gerais, Brasil
diogenes@ufmg.br

Abstract. In this paper a new approach for describing embedded systems is presented. The approach is based on the composition of hardware and software components with the addition of an interface between them. Non-functional constraints for components and their interfaces can also be modeled and verified. As such, the component-based view presented here differs from traditional component-based views, where focus is laid on the functional part. The ideas discussed in this paper have been implemented in a tool. This tool enables the description of an embedded system through a specific language. It can also allow the behavioral simulation and the non-functional verification of the hardware and software components.

1 Introduction

As with all computer systems, the embedded computer is composed of hardware and software. In the early days of microprocessors much of the design time was spent on the hardware, in defining address decoding, memory map and so on. A comparatively simple program was developed, limited in size and complexity by memory size.

Current embedded system designs are complex and demand high development efforts. The design attention has shifted to software development and much of the hardware system is now contained on a single chip, in the form of a microcontroller [18].

The design of mixed hardware/software systems presents several challenges to the designer. Not the least of these is the fact that even though the hardware and the software are interdependent, they are typically described and designed using different formalisms, languages, and tools. These notations include a wide variety of hardware description languages, continuous modeling languages, protocol specification languages and dynamic synchronization languages.

Combining hardware and software designs tasks into a common methodology has several advantages. One is that accelerates the design process. Another is that addressing the design of hardware and software components simultaneously may enable hardware/software trade-offs to be made dynamically, as design progresses.

In this paper we propose a notation to describe embedded system architecture, exposing its gross organization as a collection of interacting hardware and software

H. Schepers (Ed.): SCOPES 2004, LNCS 3199, pp. 2–16, 2004.

components. A well-defined architecture allows an engineer to reason about system properties at a high level of abstraction. Typical properties of concern include protocols of interaction, bandwidths, memory size, and so on.

Our primary considerations here to support architectural abstractions, identify, classify and code the components and the ways they interact.

Another point is to verify the correctness of the design. It is needed that the final design has the same behavior as specified. It is also clear that some way is needed for the specification and verification of non-functional constraints. In our approach, domain modeling is used to ensure this.

Our framework provides a simulation environment to validate the functional specification of the components, as well as the interaction between them. This can be used to gain information about an embedded system before a prototype is actually built. Furthermore, this simulation allows designers to perform experiments that could be impractical in a prototyping environment. For example, designers can perform comparative studies of a single system using a variety of processors or other hardware components. This helps ensure completeness of the specification and avoids inconsistency and errors.

2 Related Works

There are four primary areas of related work that address similar problems. The first and most influential of these areas is software architecture description languages, tools and environments. The second area is environments for hardware-software codesign. This area includes environments for modeling, simulation and prototyping of heterogeneous systems. The third area is notations for specification of system-level design problems. Finally, the fourth area presents models for the design of embedded software.

2.1 Software Architecture Description Languages, Toolkits and Environments

Software architecture has been a very active research field in Software Engineering [9,16]. Its goal is to provide a formal way of describing and analyzing large software systems. Abstractly, software architectures involve the description of elements, patterns that guide the composition, and constraints on these patterns.

Numerous Architecture Description Languages (ADLs) have been created for describing the structure and behavior of software systems at the architectural level of abstraction. Most of these ADLs offer a set of tools that support the design and analysis of software system architectures specified with the ADL.

Examples of ADLs include Aesop [7], Rapide [10], Wright [3], UniCon [15], ACME [8] and Meta-H [5]. Although all of these languages are concerned with architectural design, each language provides certain distinctive capabilities: Aesop supports design using architectural styles; Rapide allows architectural designs to be simulated, and has tools for analyzing the results of those simulations; Wright supports the specification and analysis of interactions between architectural components; UniCon has a high-level compiler for architectural designs that supports a heterogeneous mixture of component and connector abstractions; ACME supports the interchange of architectural descriptions between a wide variety of different architecture design and analysis tools; Meta-H provides specific guidance for designers of real-time avionics control software.

However, none of these ADLs offers sufficient support to capture design properties of hardware components, such as organization or capacity.

Generically, the hardware architecture is described at the RTL (*Register Transfer Level*), what confuses its design with its final implementation. Widely used languages to support the description at this level are VHDL (*VHSIC Hardware Description Language*) and Verilog HDL. The hardware architecture can also specify an ISA (*Instruction Set Architecture*), which describes the computer architecture or a CPU (*Central Processor Unit*).

2.2 Hardware-Software Co-design Environments

Over the past several years there has been a great deal of interest in the design of mixed hardware-software systems, sometimes referred to as hardware-software co-design.

Approaches to hardware-software co-design can be characterized by the design activities for which hardware and software are integrated, which include: hardware-software co-simulation, hardware-software co-synthesis and hardware-software partitioning [1].

Numerous methodologies and languages have been created for each of these design activities. Examples include Ptolemy II [4], LYCOS [11] and POLIS [6].

Ptolemy II is an environment for simulation and prototyping of heterogeneous systems. Its focus is on embedded systems. Ptolemy II takes a component view of design, in that models are constructed as a set of interacting components. A model of computation governs the semantics of the interaction, and thus imposes a discipline on the interaction of the components.

LYCOS is a co-synthesis environment that can be used for hardware-software partitioning of an application onto a target architecture consisting of a single CPU and a single hardware component. LYCOS provides the choice between different partition models and partitioning algorithms, one of which is a novel algorithm, called PACE.

POLIS is a co-design system in which hardware-software partitioning is obtained by user interaction. In POLIS analysis and transformation are done on a uniform and formal internal hardware/software representation called Co-design Finite State Machines, CFSMs. Partitioning is done manually by assigning each CFSM to either hardware or software. POLIS will assist the designer providing estimation tool.

2.3 System Level Design Languages

A well-known solution in computer science for dealing with complexity is to move to a higher level of abstraction, in this case to system level. From this level, the design methodology works its way through several refinement steps down to the implementation.

Several languages were developed to deal with this question. Examples include SystemC [17] and Rosetta [2].

SystemC permits the specification and design of a hardware-software system at various levels of abstraction. It also creates executable specification of the design.

This language is a superset of C++. It provides the necessary constructs to model system architecture including hardware timing, concurrency, and reactive behavior that are missing in standard C++. However, SystemC does not provide any support for representing design aspects like timing, structural and physical constraints. For example, cycle time memory capacity or power consumption.

Rosetta is a non-executable language that addresses the problem of defining the constraints of the desired design and not its behavior. This language is mainly used to mathematically analyze the performance of a system. Rosetta provides modeling support for different design domains using multiple-domain semantics and syntaxes appropriate for each of them.

2.4 Embedded System Design Approaches

Architecture systems introduce the notion of components, ports and connector as first class representations. However, most of the approaches proposed in the literature do not take into account the specific properties of software systems for embedded devices.

Koala [12] introduces a component model that is used for embedded software in consumer electronic devices. Koala components may have several "provides" and "requires" interfaces. In order to generate efficient code from Koala specifications, partial evaluation techniques are employed. However, Koala does not take into account non-functional requirements such as timing and memory consumption. Koala lacks a formal execution model and automated scheduler generation is not supported.

PECOS (*Pervasive Component System*) [13] model provides a component-based technology for the development of embedded software systems. PECOS is divided into two sub-models: structural and execution. The structural model defines the entities (port, connector and components), its characteristics and properties. The execution model deals with execution semantics. It specifies the synchronization between components that live in different threads of control, cycle time and required deadlines that a component has to be executed. An automated scheduler is provided by the composite component for their children components.

These environments do not provide any mechanism for representation of the hardware components and the interaction between the hardware/software components.

3 LACCES Design Language

LACCES (*Language of Components and Connectors for Embedded Systems*) design language is used for capturing both embedded system architecture design expertise and the architectural constraints. The language provides constructs for capturing all requirements for design an embedded system with hardware and software components.

LACCES meet three fundamental requirements: it is capable of describing architectural structure, properties, and topology of individuals embedded system designs; it allows the behavioral and non-functional evaluation and analysis of the design; and the language supports incremental capture of architectural design expertise and incremental modifications of architectural descriptions.

This notation addresses several issues in novel ways:

- It permits the specification of hardware and software components and their interaction.
- It supports abstraction idioms commonly used by designers. These idioms are captured through a set of primitives. Different types of elements can be modeled.
- It provides a clear separation of concerns regarding important properties of a system, for example, computation and communication; behavior and structure; and functionality and timing.
- It has the ability to capture a broad range of system requirements, namely, functionality, timing, logical structure, and physical structure constraints.
- It defines a function to map the description to an executable specification that can be used to validate system functionality before implementation begins. It also helps to avoid inconsistency and errors of the functionality specification.

The first step towards the definition of the language was to survey several designs and compile a list of system primitives, which are constructs necessary to represent embedded systems. These primitives are broad enough to represent a large range of components and connectors and covers diverse aspects such as behavior, logical structure, timing and physical structure. These primitives form the basis of LACCES.

The set of primitives is also complete and consistent, so new structures can be represented without need to extend the language. It is also possible to combine these primitives to obtain more complex blocks, and to decompose a complex block or design into a collection of these primitives.

To accommodate the wide variety of auxiliary information LACCES supports annotation of architectural properties. Components and connectors can be annotated. These properties are described in terms of four different domains.

The motivating factor to use four orthogonal domains is the separation of concerns [14]. The first concern is the separation of time from functionality. This led to the use of two domains, *Behavioral* and the *Timing* domains.

A topological or logical organization is usually employed to facilitate the design capture. To represent this logical organization the *Structural* domain is used. It is a mapping of behavioral and timing representations onto a set of constraints such as capacity and organization.

The *Physical* domain is used to represent clients' and designers' physical requirements and constraints and actual implementation.

There is no direct relationship among objects in different domains. The domains can be partially or completely orthogonal to each other. Orthogonal domains mean that the domains are independent of each other and changes in one domain do not affect the other domain. For example, a single behavior, represented in the behavioral domain, can be mapped to several different implementations in the physical domain.

Each element may be represented in all four domains. Some elements may not have representation in some domains, especially in the physical domains if there are not specified physical constraints.

3.1 Components

Components are the core entity in this model. They are used to organize the computation and data into parts that have well-defined semantic and behavior.

A typical component contains:

- An *interface*, through which the module communicates with the environment;
- A *property description* that describes the functionality, structure, timing and physical characteristics of a component;
- Hierarchically, other components.

The interface is a "window" into a component that describes the sets of *ports*, *provides* and *requires* constituents of the component. Those interface constituents are visible to the parent architecture. Other components of the architecture can be wired to those ports and trigger the *provides* elements of the component. A component conforming to the interface must implement the operations specified in the *provides* constituents.

In LACCES the basic unit of functionality is called a process. Electronic systems are inherently parallel with many activities taking place concurrently. Processes provide the mechanism for simulating concurrent behavior.

A process is sensitive to events on the input ports of the component. When any of the events in the sensitive list occurs, the process begins its execution. The process may have its execution suspended and it will resume the execution from the point of suspension. The *provides* constituents are processes triggered by an event on the input ports of the component and the *requires* constituents are functions calls which are implemented into the connector.

Components may be either primitive or composite. Primitive component types and their primitives are currently defined by enumeration. Table 1 lists the component types currently supported and the primitives allowed for each type. The physical primitives for all hardware components are quite similar. They are: *chip name, package, manufacturer name, power consumption, dimension* and *cost*. For the *memory* and the *keypad* components *device type* and *number of keys* are added to their physical primitives, respectively. Composite components define components and connectors that constitute them.

Table 1. Primitives of Components.

Domains/ Type of Components	Behavioral	Timing	Structural
Memory	Read, Write, ReadSeq, WriteSeq, Erase, Reset, ReadWrite, Refresh, Lock	Access Time, Cycle Time	Organization, Capacity.
CPU	Reset, Interrupt	Instruction Cycle	Architecture Type, Word-Length
LCD_Module	Display	Display Delay	Capacity, Display Type
RTC	Interrupt, Alarm, Read, Write	Access Time	Resolution
ADC / DAC	AD/ DA Conversion, Interrupt	Conversion Time	Resolution, Accuracy, Architecture, Sampling Rate
Multiplier	Multiplication	Multiplication delay	Operand Length, Type
LCD_Driver	Pixel On/Off	Cycle Time	Matrix, Display Capacity
Timer	-	-	Prescaler, Clock Source
Event	Interrupt, Capture, Compare, Read, Write	Access Time	Resolution
PWM	Waveform Generation	Period, Duty-Cycle	Resolution
Timer/Counter	Interrupt, Read, Clear	Cycle Time	Resolution
Keypad	Interrupt	-	Number of Keys
Module	-	Execution Time	Data Length, Code Length

Primitive Components. The set of primitive components was selected opportunistically: we wanted to reflect components used in practice and to cover as wide a variety as possible.

Each of these is described below:

- Component type *Module* is a software component and corresponds to a compilation unit in a typical programming language. Designers define the behavioral primitives. Code may be represented as source or object.
- Component type *Memory* represents any device that can electronically store instruction and data. The memory component has the following operations: *read, write, readseq* (read sequential memory positions), *writeseq* (write into sequential memory positions), *reset, erase, readwrite* (read one position and write one data into it), *refresh* and *lock* (protect the memory against program writes or erases).
- Component type *CPU* represents the core of a microprocessor. The sequences of instructions executed by the *CPU* are represented in LACCES by software components. So, the behavior of this component consists of only the *reset* and *interrupt* operations.
- Components type *LCD Driver* and *LCD Module* are devices that provide the display capabilities.
- Component type *RTC* (*Real Time Clock*) provides a binary-code-decimal representation of the time and data to the system's main processor. Features of the *RTC* component may include *alarm* and *interrupt* operations.
- Components type *ADC* and *DAC* are data conversion devices. Their timing primitive is the *conversion time*. Important structural primitives are the following: *resolution, accuracy, sampling rate* and *architecture*.
- Component *Multiplier* is a peripheral and is not part of the CPU.
- Component *Timer* is constituted of *Timer/Counter*, *Event* and *PWM* components. The *Timer* module permits the microcontroller to perform the measurement of time. This component can be clocked by an internal or an external *clock source* and its *clock frequency* can be prescaled.
- Component type *Timer/Counter* carries out the counting of pulses, objects or events when used in conjunction with the right sort of sensor and interface. The *resolution* primitive determines the maximal number of bits that can be stored into the counter register.
- Component type *Event* corresponds to input capture and output compare modules of the *Timer* component. The input capture module can *capture* the *Timer/Counter* value at a given moment and the output compare module *compares* the values of two registers.
- Component type *PWM* provides some enhancements to the *Timer* structure. The *duty cycle* and the *period* of this component can be varied alternating the waveform appearance.
- Component type *MCU* represents an embedded system microcontroller. It is constituted of subcomponents that can be: Memory, CPU, RTC, ADC, DAC, Multiplier, LCD Driver, Timer (Event, PWM and Timer/Counter).
- Component type *Keypad* is a set of keys used to generate interrupts into the MCU. We can configure the *number of keys*.

Composite Components. LACCES supports the hierarchical decomposition of architectures. Specifically, component elements can be represented by one or more lower-level descriptions that provide additional detail. Each such description is termed a *representation*. A *representation* establishes and enforces an abstraction boundary between the structure, interfaces, and properties that a design component exposes to its environment and the details of the component's design and/or implementation. A *representation* consists of two parts: a *system* that describes the representation's structure, and a set of *bindings* that define a mapping between structure in the higher-level element encapsulating the *representation* and the lower-level elements defined in the *representation*'s system.

Adding a *representation* to the component allows the architecture to provide details about the lower-level design without compromising its higher-level abstraction as a single design element. When reasoning at an abstract level about the design it is appropriate to hide the complexity and simply think of it as a component that provides a specific service.

3.2 Connectors

Connectors mediate interactions among components. They establish the rules that govern component interaction and define how these rules are performed. We initiate communication through interfaces, but is the connector that carries out this communication. All the operations for communication needed by the components have to be implemented by connectors.

As a result of the separation of communication and computation, LACCES supports "plug-and-play". The communication protocol can be easily exchanged by use of another connector with compatible interfaces, whenever this is desirable in the design process. In the same manner, the components can also be exchanged with others, without affecting the communication protocol.

A typical connector contains:

- An *interface*, which identify the participants of the interaction;
- Like components, a *property description* that describes the functionality, structure, timing and physical characteristics of a connector.

Currently, only primitives connectors are supported.

Connector *interfaces* are defined as a set of roles. Each role of a connector defines a participant of the interaction represented by the connector. Examples of roles are the reading and writing of a FIFO, or the sender and receiver of a message passing connector.

In LACCES, connectors are instances of channels. Channels are templates – a typed, parameterized macro facility for specification of recurring patterns. These patterns are used by applying them to the appropriate types of parameters.

Templates define syntactic structures that can be expanded in place to produce new declarations. The behavior and the interface of channels can be incremented with new primitives. They are quite flexible, permitting the definition of new connectors.

A channel specifies which primitives are available for communication, defining the protocol. The protocol defines the allowable interactions between two components and provides guarantees about those interactions.

Table 2. Primitives of Channels.

Domains/ Connectors	Behavioral	Timing	Structural
Parallel	Send, Receive	Word Time	Data rate, Data Length
SPI	Send, Receive, Mode	Word Time	Data Rate, Data format(LSB or MSB)
I2C	Send, Receive, Ack	Word Time	Data Rate, Device address, Data Transfer
FIFO	Read, Write, Blocking	Cycle Time	Size, Data Types
UART	Send, Receive, Parity Check	Word Time	Baud rate, Data Length, Data Transfer
Analogue	Send, Receive	Word Time	Connection Type, Frequency
Semaphore	Wait, TryWait, Signal, GetValue	Access Time	Type (binary or integer)
IPC	Send, Receive	Word Time	Mensage Size

Channel Types. Channel types and their primitives are also defined by enumeration. Table 2 lists channels types currently supported and the primitives allowed for each. Like components, the physical primitives for channels are quite similar. However, channels define new primitives such as *number of wires*; *signal type* (*current* or *voltage*) for the analogue channel.

Different types of communication require different types of channels. For communication between hardware-hardware components, LACCES provides *SPI, I2C, UART, Analogue, Parallel* and *FIFO* channels. For communication between hardware-software components, LACCES provides *Parallel* and *FIFO* channels. The semantic of the hardware-software channels are context dependent. For communication between software-software components, LACCES provides *Parallel, FIFO, Semaphore* and *IPC* channels.

As for component types, we choose the cannel types opportunistically. Each of these is described below:

- Channel type *SPI* (*Serial Peripheral Interface*) is a synchronous serial data link that is standard across many Motorola microprocessors and other peripheral chips. The SPI is essentially a "three-wire plus n slave selects" serial bus.
- Channel type *I2C* (*Inter-Integrated Circuit*) is a bi-directional, two-wire, and synchronous channel. The two lines are a serial clock and a serial data link.
- Channel type *UART* (*Universal Asynchronous Receiver Transmitter*) is a serial and asynchronous standard communication.
- Channel type *FIFO* is a queue used to record the data transferred between components. The *FIFO* provides both block and nonblocking versions of access.
- Channel type *Analogue* is used to connect an input of an ADC or an output of a DAC to a hardware device. It is further characterized by the *type of the connection* that can be *single-ended* or *differential*.
- Channel type *Semaphore* is used to model critical sections for accessing shared resources. These resources are accessed only through two standard operations: *wait* and *signal*. The component can verify if the semaphore is blocked through the *TryWait* operation and the *GetValue* returns the value of the semaphore.
- Channel type *IPC* (*InterProcess Communication*) provides a mechanism to allow components to communicate and to synchronize their actions. IPC is provided by a

message system with two operations: *send* and *receive* a message. If two components want to communicate a communication link, called mailbox, must exist between them. Each mailbox supports a unique message.

- Channel type *Parallel* represents a register of a defined length. It permits the reading and writing of transmitting data by the components.

3.3   System

LACCES provides a system construct to represent configurations of components and connectors.

A system includes (among other things) a set of components, a set of connectors, and a set of attachments that describe the topology of the system. An *attachment* associates a port interface on a component with a role interface on a connector.

As an example, figure 1 shows an architectural drawing that illustrates a high level communication between software and hardware components. The software executes on an MSP430 microcontroller and the hardware component is an LCD module. For the designer's point of view, at a high level, the interaction occurs between the software and the LCD, although the actual interaction occurs between the hardware MCU and LCD module. The software component only generates information for displaying.

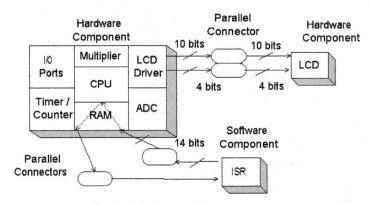

Fig. 1. A hardware-software system.

```
System Example1{
      Components{
            uses MSP430 as MyMCU; //Hw component
            uses LCD as MyLCD; //Hw component
            uses ISR as Random; //Sw component }
      Connectors{
            uses Parallel(14, 20 Mhz) as MyChannel,
            uses Parallel(1, 30 Mhz) as BridgeR;
            uses Parallel(14, 30 Mhz) as BridgeS; }
      Attachments {
            MyMCU.seg  to MyChannel.sender[0..9];
            MyMCU.com to MyChannel.sender[10..13];
            ...
            //Software connected with CPU
            MyMCU.MyCPU.inter to BridgeR.sender;
            BridgeR.Receiver to ISR.R1; ...} }
```

```
Component MSP430 : MCU{
      Interface{
                port in   i_o : bit[8];
                port out  seg: bit[29];
                port out  com: bit[4]; }
         Representation MSP430_Details{
           System MSP430_Details{
                Connector SFR: Parallel(14,20);//Special Function Register
                       ...
                Component My_CPU: CPU{
                         Interface{
                                port in inter : bit; //interrupt
                                port in res : bit; //reset
                                port out Datadisplay: bit[13];
                                ...
                                Provides{ Reset();
                                          Interrupt(); }}
                         Reset() sensitive res;
                         Interrupt() sensitive inter;
                         Architecture_type =Harvard;
                         Word_length = 16 bits; }
                Component MyADC: ADC{...}
                Component RAM: Memory{...}
                Component My_Timer: Timer{...}
                Component My_LCD: LCD_Driver{
                         Interface{
                                port in data : bit[13];
                                port out seg: bit[29], com: bit[3];
                                Provides{ Pixel_On_Off();}}
                         Pixel_On_Off() sensitive data;
                         Matrix = (8,3); // 8x3 dot matrix
                         Display_Capacity= (10,4); // 10 seg x 4 commons
                    }
             } // End System
             Attachments{ ... }
           } // Representation
           Chip_name= MSP430;
           Manufacturer_name = "Texas Instruments";
    } // End MCU
Component LCD : LCD_Module {
      Interface{
                Port in seg: bit[39], com: bit[15];
                Provides { Display(); }}
      Display() sensitive seg, com;
      Costs = $3,00; ...}
Component ISR: Module{
      Interface{
                port in R1:bit;
                port out Datadisplay : bit[13]; ...}
      ...
      DataGeneration()sensitive R1;
      Implementation{ // Source Code
                IN random.c;
                IMPLTYPE source;
      }
      Code_Length = 585 bytes;
      ...
      }
   }
```

Fig. 2. The description of the system.

Figure 2 illustrates the description of this system. The components and connectors are available from a library, and they have to be instantiated. LACCES provides some descriptions, but the users are encouraged to include more descriptions to ease the design of their system and to permit reuse of elements. A simplified description of the MSP430, with only the important constructs, are showed. The software component is an interrupt service routine (ISR) that generates a number to be displayed on the LCD Module.

4   LACCES Infrastructure

The LACCES design environment provides a set of basic tools for manipulating and evaluating LACCES designs and design expertise. The following five tools are:

- A **parser** that reads textual design, embedded system descriptions, expressed in the LACCES design language and converts them into an internal representation.
- A **type manager** that verifies designs are type-correct.
- An **analysis engine** that evaluates design analysis properties. It verifies if there is a logical correspondence among the domains. For example, one behavior primitive has one specific time to execute and structure and physical elements available.
- An **error reporting** system that alerts environment users of design problems.
- An **extraction behavior** system that provides a functional description of the architectural design for the external SystemC simulation tool.

The diagram in figure 3 depicts LACCES's basic architecture. This set of core tools supports the ability to capture and analyze both architectural specification and architectural design expertise expressed in the LACCES design language. It also provides the ability to evaluate individual designs to verify that they conform to their properties and functionality, and to report any anomalies discovered in evaluating the design.

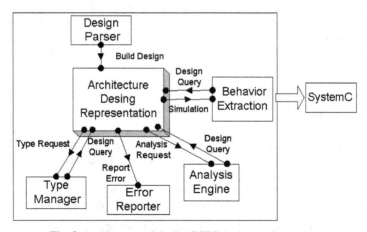

Fig. 3. Architecture of the LACCES design environment.

Up to now, we have built the LACCES compiler. The compiler consists of 10 C++ source codes modules, 1 Flex specification, 1 YACC specification, and 11 C++ include files. This yields a total of approximately 8.050 lines of source code. The behavior extraction and analysis engine are under construction.

4.1 Checking of Functional Requirements

LACCES provides to SystemC a behavioral description of the designed system. Each process defined in the behavioral structure is mapped into a SystemC process structure.

The designer has two options to specify an operation in the design: to use an operation already defined in LACCES or to provide a new definition. For software components, the designer has to provide all of the implementations of the operations specified in the behavior. For the other structures of the language, the user either uses the built-in behavioral primitives defined in the language or provides an implementation obeying the defined interfaces of the methods.

For connectors, the behavior and the interface can be expanded with new primitives. The user can specify new operations but they have to be implemented using the basic operations already defined in the language.

After the translation the system is simulated to validate the functional specification of the components and the connectors.

4.2 Checking of Non-functional Requirements

LACCES verifies if the properties can be mapped among the four domains. It compares if one function described into the behavioral domain and its timing constraints can be mapped into the structural and physical properties specified by the designer. This analysis is performed by the analysis engine system. For example, if an analogue channel is used with a bandwidth of 2 and a differential connection type, its number of wires described into the physical domain can not be less than 4.

This type of analysis is possible because the set of primitives are built-in elements in LACCES. This analysis helps ensure completeness of the specification and avoids inconsistency and errors.

After the functional and non-functional checking of the architecture of the embedded system, the prototype can be built.

5 Conclusions

LACCES improves support for abstraction that designers use in designing the architectures of embedded systems. We developed a notation and tools to implement this new model.

LACCES was developed taking into account the separation of concerns among the diverse system aspects. More precisely, separation of concerns between:

- Computation and communication, using the component and connector representation;
- Behavior and structure, using behavioral and structural orthogonal domains;

- Function and timing, using Behavioral and Timing orthogonal domains;
- Physic and structure, using Physical and Structural domains.

LACCES was developed from a list of primitive constructs able to capture a broad range of system.

We plan to extend our simulation environment that now is performed by SystemC, by allowing co-simulation of the software components, implemented in C or C++; and hardware components, implemented in SystemC.

Acknowledgments

We would like to thank the financial support of Lab. Engenharia de Computadores - LECOM/DCC/UFMG and CNPq under the grant CNPq-PNM.

References

1. Adams, J. K. and Thomas, D. E.: The Design of Mixed Hardware/Software Systems. *Design Automation Conference*, 1996.
2. Alexander, P., Kamath, R., Barton, D.: System Specification in Rosetta. *IEEE Engineering of Computer Base Systems Symposium*. Nashville, Edinburgh, UK, April 2000.
3. Allen, R., and Garlan, D.: Formalizing Architectural Connection. *In Proceedings of the 16th International Conference on Software Engineering*, pages 71-80, Sorrento, Italy, May 1994.
4. Bhattacharyya, Shuvra S., *et alli*. Heterogeneous Concurrent Modeling and Design in Java. *Memorandum UCB/ERL M03/27*, EECS, University of California, Berkeley, CA USA. 94720- July 16, 2003.
5. Binns, P. and Vestal, S.: Formal real-time architecture specification and analysis. *In Tenth IEEE Workshop on Real-Time Operation Systems and Software*, New York, NY, May 1993.
6. Chido, M., Engels, D., Hsieh , H., Giusto, P., Jurecska, A., Lavagno, L., Suzuki, K. and Sangiovanni- Vincentelli, A.: A case study in computer-aided co-design of embedded controllers. *Design Automation for Embedded Systems*, 1(1-2):51-67, January 1996.
7. Garlan, D., Allen, R., and Ockerbloom, J.: Exploiting Style in Architectural Design Environments. *In Proceedings of SIGSOFT'94: The Second ACM SIGSOFT Symposium on the Foundations of Software Engineering*, pages 179-185. ACM Press, December, 1994.
8. Garlan, D., Monroe, R., and Wile, D. Acme: An Architecture Description Interchange Language for Software Architecture. *Technical Report CMU-CS-95-219*, Carnegie Mellon University,1997 http://www.cs.cmu.edu/~acme.
9. Garlan, D., and Shaw, M.: An Introduction to Software Architecture. 1-39. *Advances in Software Engineering and Knowledge Engineering* Volume 2. New York, NY: World Scientific Press, 1993.
10. Luckhan, D. C., Augustin, L. M., Kenney, J. J., Vera, J., Bryan, D., and Mann, W.: Specification and Analysis of System Architecture using Rapide. *IEEE Transactions on Software Engineering, Special Issue on Software Architecture*, 21(4): 336-355, April, 1995.
11. Madsen, J., Grode, J., Knudsen, P. V., Petersen , M. E., and Haxthausen, A. E.: LYCOS: the lyngby co-synthesis system. *Journal for Design Automation of Embedded Systems*, 2(2):195–235, March 1997.
12. Ommering, R.V., Linden, F.V., Kramer, J., and Magee, J.: The Koala component model for consumer electronics software. *IEEE Computer*, 2000.

13. PecosProject. Composition environment.
    http://www.pecos-project.org/software.html. January, 2003.
14. Silva Jr, D. C. A Comprehensive Framework for the Specification of Hardware/Software
    Systems. PhD, University of Southern California, 2001.
15. Shaw, M., DeLine, R., Klein, D. V., Ross, T. L., Young, D. M.,and Zelesnik, G. Abstrac-
    tions for Software Architecture and Tools to Support Them. *IEEE Transactions on
    Software Engineering, Special Issue on Software Architecture*, 21(4):314-335, Abril,1995.
16. Shaw, M., and Garlan, D.: Software Architecture: Perspectives on an Emerging Discipline.
    Prentice Hall, 1996.
17. SystemC. http://www.systemc.org
18. Wilmshurst, T.: An Introduction to the Design of Small-Scale Embedded Systems. 2001,
    Palgrave.

Automatically Customising VLIW Architectures with Coarse Grained Application-Specific Functional Units

Diviya Jain[1], Anshul Kumar[1], Laura Pozzi[2], and Paolo Ienne[2]

[1] Department of Computer Science and Engineering
Indian Institute of Technology Delhi, India
{csa01022,anshul}@cse.iitd.ernet.in
[2] Processor Architecture Laboratory
Swiss Federal Institute of Technology Lausanne (EPFL), Switzerland
{laura.pozzi,paolo.ienne}@epfl.ch

Abstract. *Instruction Level Parallelism (ILP)* machines, such as *Very Long Instruction Word (VLIW)* architectures, and customised architectures are two para-digms that are used to increase the performance of processors. While a VLIW machine has multiple functional units, a customised processor is equipped with *Application-specific Functional Units (AFUs)*. Customisation has been proved beneficial on single issue machines, but its effect on multiple issue machines remains unanswered. Is a VLIW machine powerful enough to nullify the benefit of customisation? Or are the two benefits orthogonal and can be exploited together? In this paper, we answer positively to the latter question. We experimentally prove that insertion of automatically identified AFUs can improve performance of a VLIW architecture, and allow the designer of ILP processor to trade-off either issue-width or register file size. We have customised the Trimaran architecture and toolchain framework to model AFUs accurately and discuss the challenges of adding instruction-set extension support to a legacy toolchain.

1 Introduction

Two popular paradigms that have been employed in the past decades for the design of fast processors are ILP and customisation. The former allows issue and execution of multiple instructions in the same cycle, while the latter relies on customised functional units, designed specifically for an application to speed up execution. While the benefit of *Instruction Set (IS)* customisation has been studied and shown on simple RISC machines ([1], [2]), a detailed and comprehensive study of how customisation affects multiple issues machines, such as VLIWs, still needs to be done (see related work for simple exceptions). The obvious questions that arise are: Is a parametric VLIW processor already powerful enough so that the benefits of IS customisation are nullified? Or does automatic IS customisation provide an advantage that is not already exploited by parallel execution

H. Schepers (Ed.): SCOPES 2004, LNCS 3199, pp. 17–32, 2004.

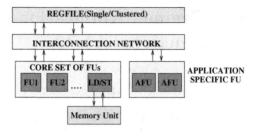

Fig. 1. VLIW architecture augmented with application-specific AFUs.

of standard instructions, as it happens in VLIWs? Furthermore, does the answer to the previous questions vary depending on the power of the unextended VLIW machine, in terms of number of registers, number of *Functional Units (FUs)*, issue width etc? These are the precise questions that this paper wants to answer. It does so by presenting a *completely automatic* framework comprising (1) the choice of IS customisation, i.e., of the *Application-specific Functional Units (AFUs)*, for each application studied and (2) extension of the standard Trimaran framework [17] for compiling and simulating the resulting IS-extended VLIW machine. The target architecture for this study is shown in Figure 1. A parametric VLIW is depicted, where the number of registers, the issue-width, and the number of Functional Units are variable. In addition, the VLIW is extended with AFUs, automatically selected within the framework. The rest of this paper is organised as follows: Section 2 compares the present study with previous contributions; Section 3 presents the overall methodology followed and the framework built. It also illustrates the various problems incurred in introducing efficient support for IS extensions in a legacy toolchain. Section 4 shows and discusses experimental results, and Section 5 will summarise our claims.

2   Related Work

This work presents a detailed study of IS extended VLIW machines, and as such it will be first compared with efforts that attempt such study to some extent.

An important attempt to study IS customisation for VLIW has been made in [7]. There, the authors investigate especially scalability, i.e., the varying of processor power such as number of registers and number of functional units, of a parameterized VLIW machine, and in part IS customisation. Only two simple and manual design examples are given for studying IS customisation, by adding special instructions in the same way as we add AFUs. However, the present paper gives a comprehensive study of the effect of IS customisation on VLIW, it shows benefits on a large set of benchmarks, and contains *combined* simulations of IS customisation *and* scalability. Finally, it uses automatically selected instructions, therefore showing benefits that do not require any manual intervention and detailed application study. All of the above differences also apply to two other previous studies [16, 18].

The second contribution of this paper is that of presenting a completely automatic framework, that spans from identification of IS customisation to extension of an architecture and toolchain for validation of results. Unlike the previous studies it enabled us to carry out the study of the effect of IS customisation on VLIW machines in a completely automatic way, without any designer intervention.

Most previous work in customised architectures is restricted to approaches which combine a complete instruction set definition or instruction selection process, architecture creation and instruction mapping onto a newly created architecture. These approaches [20, 11] primarily create from scratch a new instruction set and a new architecture which are tuned for a set of applications. Unfortunately, the design of complete ASIPs incurs the complexity and risks of a complete processor and tool set development. A similar approach outlined in [13] describes an automated system for designing architecture and microarchitecture of a customised VLIW processor and non-programmable, systolic array co-processors. Source code (in a subset of C) for a performance-critical loop nest is used as a behavioral specification of a coprocessor. However the system lacks the ability of analyzing and evaluating the application to map portions of it onto hardware, and requires user intervention. Another tool [5] generates an HDL netlist of a VLIW architecture for a customised algorithm and allows for some design space exploration. However the tool disregards the process of evaluating the application and automatic extraction of the performance critical sections of code. The philosophy undertaken instead in our approach is that of extending an available and proven processor design (possibly including its implementation as a hard-macro in a System-on-Chip design flow) and tool set after automatic extraction of subgraphs of application, so that design efforts must focus exclusively on the special instructions and the corresponding datapath. Many readily extensible processors exist today both in academia (e.g., [14, 3]) and industry (e.g., [10, 21, 6, 8, 7]), but very limited automatic methodologies to generate the extensions are generally available. Recent works [1, 19, 2] have made some steps toward an automatic methodology for the selection of custom instructions to augment the instruction set of an extensible processor and thus maximise its efficiency for a given application program. Yet, the results of these authors are limited by one or more of the following: they use unsophisticated speedup models [1], their results are only applicable to single-issue models, and/or their instruction selection methodology is too simple [19, 2].

The approach described in [4] is an attempt to automate the process of extraction of AFUs and the implementation of a complete system. The work describes a completely automatic methodology, and shows AFU benefits for a simple VLIW architecture. Our study, in addition, tries to answer further important questions like (1) Can clusters of only dataflow operations form potentially good AFUs? (2) Is a rich VLIW architecture already powerful enough to gain anything substantial from AFUs? (3) Are ILP and Instruction set customisation complimentary? Our work tries to prove that use of AFUs can outperform a very rich VLIW architecture at a very low cost by doing away with expensive high issue-width and large register files.

We use the algorithm depicted in [1] for our automatic IS extension, but in contrast with the original results of that work, we are here able to evaluate precise speedup measurements thanks to the presence of our automatically extended compilation and simulation framework.

3   Overview of the Methodology and of the Validation Framework

Our customised architecture synthesis methodology is composed of the following steps as shown in Figure 2: First, beneficial IS extensions are extracted from the application source code. The next step involves customisation of the processor architecture and synthesis of the new instruction set. Finally, code is generated and simulated for the extended architecture built, and statistics are collected in order to evaluate the performance gain achieved.

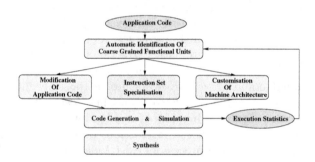

Fig. 2. Customised architecture synthesis methodology.

3.1   Automatic AFU Extraction

The complete process of automatic extraction of coarse grained AFUs is illustrated in Figure 3. Three separate phases can be distinguished: identification of potential AFUs, based on the algorithm published in [1] and applied to the application source code; evaluation of identified AFUs, based on profiling figures and on a speedup estimation model [12]; and selection of the final best promising AFUs. The identification algorithm extracts promising sections of code from the basic blocks of the embedded application under study, after an if-conversion pass has been applied in order to raise the identification potential and span beyond the basic block limit to some extent. The analysis starts from the *Directed Acyclic Graph (DAG)* representation of the enlarged basic blocks obtained after if-conversion. Nodes of the DAG are assembler-like instructions, while edges represent data dependency among instructions.

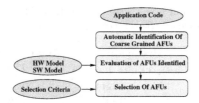

Fig. 3. Automatic AFU selection.

The algorithm extracts instructions satisfying user-given register-file input/ output constraints that result in maximal speedup using an approximate speedup metric. It analyses the dataflow graphs and considers all possible subgraphs. The input and output requirements of the subgraphs are calculated and only those satisfying all constraints are selected for further consideration. The number of subgraphs being exponential in the number of nodes of the graph, the algorithm has an exponential worst case complexity; yet, it exploits some graph characteristics which allow significant pruning of the search space and, in practice, it exhibits a subexponential complexity. Graphs with up to a couple of hundreds of nodes can be processed in a matter of minutes.

An approximate speedup estimation is then performed for the potential instructions extracted, in order to select the most promising candidates. The estimation consists in comparing the approximate subgraph execution time in software, as a sequence of instructions, with the accurate time the subgraph takes if implemented in hardware, as a single special instruction. The former number, software latency, is estimated using the baseline architecture opcode latencies, while for the hardware latencies, datapaths for all possible opcodes were synthesised and simulated in ASIC technology, and their area and delay were measured. Table 1 shows the measured hardware latency and area requirements for some operators. All delays have been expressed relatively to a multiply-accumulate, by considering that the baseline architecture can execute a multiply instruction in 3 cycles. Areas are also expressed relatively to the area of a multiply-accumulate. The total hardware latency for an AFU is calculated by summing the latency of all nodes in the critical path, and then the ceiling function is applied to it. This is also the number that is automatically passed to the machine description to define the latency of the newly introduced instructions.

Note that while the hardware latency model is rather accurate, the software model does not capture possible pipeline stalls, scheduling constraints etc. However, its simplicity is due to its use in the evaluation of millions of candidate AFUs. The software model is used for the choice of AFU candidates, and not for results evaluation. Section 4 provides speedup numbers which are the result of compilation and simulation and therefore are very accurate.

The last phase, selection of final AFUs, simply consists in choosing the best promising AFUs, according to the gain calculated in the previous phase (which is of course multiplied by frequency of execution, as obtained by profiling). These selected AFUs represent the IS extension of the VLIW machine, and they are passed on to the extended Trimaran framework, with their latency and area.

Table 1. Hardware delay and area of some operators. TSMC 0.18 um CMOS Technology and standard cells from Artisan were used.

Operator	Precision	Relative Delay	Relative Area
Multiply-Accumulator	32 bits x 32 bits + 64 bits	3.00	1.000
Adder	4 bits + 4 bits	0.33	0.001
Adder	8 bits + 8 bits	0.36	0.002
Adder	16 bits + 16 bits	0.60	0.003
Adder	24 bits + 24 bits	0.72	0.005
Adder	32 bits + 32 bits	0.75	0.007
Barrel shifter	8 bits	0.24	0.002
Barrel shifter	16 bits	0.33	0.004
Barrel shifter	32 bits	0.48	0.008
Barrel shifter (by constant amount)	any	0.00	0.000
Bitwise multiplexer	any	0.06	0.001

3.2   Validation Framework

The validation framework built is an extension of the Trimaran toolchain, which comprises a retargetable compiler and configurable simulator. The original framework provides for a parameterized VLIW architecture called HPL-PlayDoh. The HPL-PD opcode repertoire, at its core, is similar to that of a RISC-like load/store architecture, with standard integer, floating point (including fused multiply-add type of operations) and memory operations. Hence we consider the problem of extending the Trimaran infrastructure through the IS extension and the introduction of coarse-grain AFUs in the compiler infrastructure.

The Trimaran framework provides IMPACT (Illinois Microarchitecture Project utilizing Advanced Compiler Technology) which serves as a compiler front end for C. It is divided into three distinct sections each based upon a different IR. Elcor forms the compiler back-end, parameterized by a machine description, performing instruction scheduling, register allocation, and machine-dependent optimizations. A cycle-level simulator of the HPL-PD architecture which is configurable by a machine description in the HMDES (High level Machine Description) format, provides run-time information on execution time, branch frequencies, and resource utilization.

The first step involves defining a new machine operation and a new resource in the system. The operation will be performed by the resource which corresponds to a coarse-grain AFU in the architecture. The operation will be defined in terms of the operation format, the operation latency and the resource usage. After this, the compiler needs to be modified so that it is able to generate code for this new operation. To accomplish this, one requires a retargetable compiler parameterized with the machine description. The application code is modified so that the desired computation (to be carried out by the coarse-grain AFU) is replaced by an external function call. The *Intermediate Representation (IR)* of the compiler will consist of nodes corresponding to this function call.

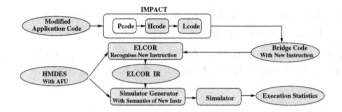

Fig. 4. Extension of the Trimaran infrastructure.

The IR is modified to replace these nodes by a new node corresponding to the operation. The compiler back-end will then treat this node as any other standard machine operation (e.g., ADD) but will generate code for it without trying to perform instruction selection. Finally, the operation semantics are defined inside the retargetable simulator so that various statistics can be generated.

The diagram in Figure 4 represents the modified Trimaran framework, to incorporate the identified AFUs. The shaded portions represent the components of the framework which were modified to extend the Trimaran infrastructure.

Modification of Application Code. The application program in C is modified, to replace the various operations intended to be performed by AFUs with an external function call. Depending on the type of AFU required, different approaches are taken.

Presently AFUs are identified as clusters of dataflow operations excluding loads and stores. Hence, the AFUs identified do not require access to memory, nor do they contain control flow operations. Note that the suitably modified application code is generated automatically.

Modelling of Single Output AFUs. In order to model the call to an AFU which provides a single computed value, a single function call is used; note that the overhead of a function call compared to that of a simple opcode execution is removed, as explained later. Consider the following piece of application code:

```
main() {
  int a = 2, b = 3, c = 4;
  while (a < 100) {
    a  = a * b + b * c;}}  // Identified AFU
```

To model the identified AFU the application code is instrumented and the identified AFU is replaced with a corresponding function call. The function representing the AFU is automatically defined in an external library to provide the correct semantics.

```
main() {                          int fun_AFU(int a, int b, int c) {
  int a = 2, b = 3, c = 4;            return  a * b + b * c; } // Model AFU
  while (a < 100) {
    a = fun_AFU(a, b, c); }}
```

Once the code is instrumented this way, it can be linked with the external library containing the definitions of the function calls for the AFUs identified. It can then be compiled and executed like the original application code, and verified to produce exactly the same output.

Modelling of Multiple Output AFUs. A different approach is required for modelling multiple output AFUs. Consider the following application code with the identified AFU:

```
main() {
    int a = 2, b = 3, c = 4, i, d = 1;
    for (i = 0; i < 5; i++) {
        a  = a * b + b * c;          //   Identified AFU with
        d  = d * c - c * b; }}       //   2 outputs (a and d)
```

The identified multiple output AFU is modelled as a combination of two single output ones; therefore, the instrumented code for the above example is:

```
main() {
                                int fun_AFU_one(int a, int b, int c)
    int a = 2, b = 3, c = 4, i;     { return a * b + b * c; }
    for (i = 0; i < 5; i++) {    int fun_AFU_two(int b, int c, int d)
        a = fun_AFU_one(a, b, c);    { return d * c - c * b; }
        d = fun_AFU_two(b, c, d); void fun_AFU(int a, int b, int c, int d)
        fun_AFU(a, b, c, d); }}      {}
```

The destination registers reserved for returning the computed values of `fun_AFU_one` and `fun_AFU_two` are used as the destination registers for the final computed values. An important point to note here is that the instructions introduced for the single output component are understood only by the Trimaran front-end compiler and used only to reserve destination registers. These are dummy instructions with no actual hardware defined to execute them; the only real instruction which is bound to an AFU is the instruction represented through a function call with an empty body; in the example, it is the function call `fun_AFU`.

Instruction Set Specialisation. Once the instrumented application code is ready, the next stage involves replacing the function call with the special machine instruction to invoke the customised AFU specially designed for it.

The instruction-set extension is done at the IMPACT the front-end stage of the Trimaran compiler. Among the many compilation phases of IMPACT, Hcode-level is best suited for the introduction of the new machine opcode, since function calls are easy to trap and replace, and no extra data-movement instructions (e.g., preparing the function arguments onto the stack) have been inserted till this phase. The new machine instruction introduced is recognised at the Hcode-level and at all the subsequent compilation phases of the Trimaran front-end. The interface between the Trimaran front-end compiler and the back-end compiler is modified, so that the back-end compiler can recognise the new machine instruction in the IR it receives and can schedule it accordingly. Note that the scheduler correctly accounts for the limited availability of read ports when using AFUs. The simulator too requires modifications to recognise the new machine instruction and to define the semantics of the coarse grained AFU.

Modelling Register File Ports. The register file design is one of the most critical design parts of a microarchitecture. The Trimaran infrastructure assumes that each functional unit has dedicated read and write ports and hence does not explicitly model them.

As we introduce AFUs in the machine architecture, we assume sharing by the AFU(s) of the otherwise dedicated ports of the FUs, and hence implicitly assume that the AFUs inputs have a crossbar or multiplexers to connect them to the register file. FUs reserve a random read or write port. AFUs get also a random read or write port, and in practice will have to use exactly those private ports that the FUs are not using at that very moment. The scheduler has to guarantee that the total number of used read ports or write ports at each cycle does not exceed some bound. Any scheduled operation will require, an issue slot of the resource corresponding to the appropriate FU (e.g., an ALU for an ADD), a number of read ports at issue cycle equal to the number of operands coming from the register file and a number of write ports at completion time (e.g., on the next cycle) equal to the number of values produced.

To model the above assumed architecture read ports and write ports are considered as resources in the HMDES machine description, and are required to be reserved for every operation.

Extending the Machine Architecture. The machine architecture is automatically modified to introduce the new FU using HMDES machine description language which involves defining its operation format, number and type of resources (FUs and AFUs), operation latency (calculated as shown in Section 3.1), resource usage and reservation table. Finally the semantics of the new operation are defined in the simulator which involves defining the value of the destination as a function of the values of the sources.

Challenges of Adding ISE Support to a Legacy Toolchain. Addition of Instruction Set Extensions to a compiler toolchain framework cannot be considered to be trivial. We present here some of the issues faced during the tool chain extension.

Representation of AFUs in the application code and its subsequent replacement with a machine operation forms an important part of the framework. In the present framework, if the function calls representing AFUs are allowed to propagate through various stages of compilation phases and replaced before the code scheduling, a large number of instructions are introduced to prepare the data for the function call (e.g, moving the various arguments to registers and/or stack). This forms an expensive overhead, and the simulation results fail to show any performance gain for the customised processor. However the replacement should be done after the profiling phase, as the intermediate representation is converted to code in high level language for profiling.

The extended tool chain should allow aggressive ILP optimizations like loop unrolling, predication, speculative execution, modulo scheduling, formation of hyperblocks etc to be applied to the extended opcode repertoire. Performance gain should be quoted after applying such optimizations during code generation for various architectures under consideration. There could be a loss of some of the optimizations due to introduction of new machine operations. This can be traced back to the stage at which AFU identification takes place. If the identification is performed before the various compiler optimizations are done, many operations which govern optimizations like common sub-expression elimination, loop invariant code motion, dead code elimination end up in an AFU, leading to generation of sub-optimal code. Hence it is important to ensure proper phase ordering among various stages of the framework.

Estimation techniques used during calculation of Speedup for the identified subgraphs, should be modified according to the base architecture. Calculation of hardware/software latencies using all the operations in the subgraph, which may be applicable to RISC cannot be applied to VLIW architecture, and may lead to poor selection of AFUs and a bad estimation of the expected speedup. The retargetable tool chain framework should accurately represent the machine architecture including the interconnection network between register files and AFUs, pipelining of customised functional units, etc. If these parameters are overlooked, the simulation results cannot be considered to be accurate. In the current framework, Trimaran was extended to support register ports to model the sharing of interconnection network between conventional FUs and AFUs.

4   Experimental Results

Our complete toolchain was applied to some of the standard benchmarks of the MediaBench [15] and EEMBC [9] suite.

The entire process consists of the following stages: (1) A first pass of compilation into the MachSUIF intermediate representation is applied, which parses the C-code into a *Data/Control Flow Graph (DFG/CFG)* representation. (2) Profiling is then performed and results annotated in the representation. (3) AFU identification and selection is performed by the algorithm described in Section 3.1. (4) The application code automatically annotated with the selected candidates forms an input to the next stage where the modified application code is automatically generated. (5) Finally, the automatically modified application code is fed to the extended Trimaran infrastructure for final compilation and cycle-exact simulation; the speedup obtained is thus calculated. The entire process of analyzing the application and preparing the Trimaran Infrastructure for it, is completely automatic and requires a few minutes to complete. However the time taken for cycle-exact simulation, depends on the application and its inputs and can vary between few seconds to about an hour.

Experiments were carried out on different baseline architectures, equipped with a varying number of FUs and register file ports. The various architectures considered are summed up in the Table 2. AFU identification was run for a limit of 7 inputs and 4 outputs in all cases. Some typical AFUs extracted from the benchmarks are depicted in Figure 5. The AFUs of type as shown in Figure 5(b) are extracted quite frequently and used to compute addresses for memory accesses.

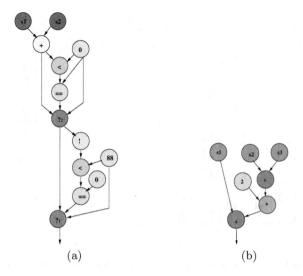

(a)   (b)

Fig. 5. (a)An AFU of HW latency 1 from adpcm, consisting of simple arithmetic & logic operations. (b)An AFU of HW latency 2 from autocor, computes address – e.g., Inputdata[i+lag].

4.1   Impact of AFUs on the Area

The benchmarks used and the number and total area of AFUs selected for each of them are described in Table 3. The area of an Integer ALU unit in HPL-PD architecture can be calculated to be 1, relative to the area of the MAC instruction. Hence it can be noted that the total area added for customisation (calculated as described in Section 3.1) is in most cases very limited.

Table 2. Different baseline architectures with varying number of FUs and register file ports.

Name	Integer FUs	Float FUs	Memory Units	Branch Units	Read ports	Write ports
2/1/1/1	2	1	1	1	7	4
4/2/2/1	4	2	2	1	14	8
i/i/2/i	infinite	infinite	2	infinite	infinite	infinite
4/2/i/1	4	2	infinite	1	infinite	infinite

Table 3. Number of AFUs per benchmark, and total area occupied relative to area of a MAC.

Benchmark	adpcmdecode	MD5	g721encode	autcor	fft	bezier
AFU count	5	3	15	3	8	6
Total AFU area	1.80	0.90	3.10	1.35	5.80	10.90

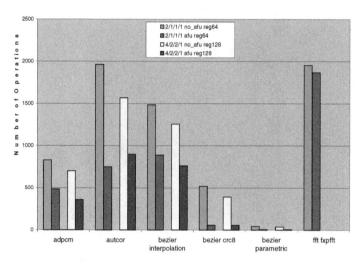

Fig. 6. Comparison of number of total operations for Non-AFU & AFU versions of 2/1/1/1 & 4/2/2/1 architectures.

It is worth noting that the use of AFUs reduces the length of the application program, since an AFU is a single instruction replacing a number of operations. Figure 6 quantifies the decrease in the size of the program (shown as number of total operations) when AFUs are employed, for two different baseline architectures. Note that some of the AFU area overhead might be compensated by the smaller footprint of the code and/or by smaller cache needs.

4.2   Impact of AFUs on Performance

Figure 7 shows the speedup of the various benchmarks processed, for a simple VLIW baseline architecture. With a modest area overhead, as shown in Table 3, a simple VLIW benefits from automatic instruction set specialisation. The typical causes for speedup are: 1) Quantization of each simple instruction in an integer number of cycles is avoided through chaining of operations; 2) Conventional FUs are freed up for other operations 3) Hardware parallelism is exploited in AFUs, sometimes to a larger extent than is possible in parallel software execution. 4) Register pressure is reduced in presence of AFUs, since some originally intermediate values need not be written to registers anymore. This in turn reduces register spills and allows the compiler to expose greater ILP e.g. through more loop unrolling.

In the following, we compare the effects of customising a VLIW, i.e., addition of AFUs, and scaling of its resources, i.e., adding FUs, increasing issue-width and register-file size. Figure 8 depicts the speedup achieved by various, increasingly powerful VLIW machines, with and without AFUs. These are the four architectures described in Table 2, with an increasing register file size, as shown in the caption. Values are normalised to the 2/1/1/1 architecture.

One can note that a 4/2/2/1 machine without AFUs performs similarly and generally much worse than a 2/1/1/1 machine with AFUs. This implies that

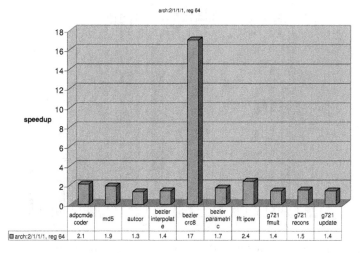

Fig. 7. Speedup of 2/1/1/1 architecture with AFUs over 2/1/1/1 without AFUs.

issue-width, register-file size and number of conventional FUs can be traded for the presence of much cheaper AFUs (with moderate area, recalling Table 3). Note that a saving in register ports is also involved. Hence addition of AFUs on top of a less powerful machine can be a better choice than increasing its issue width or number of registers. Secondly the graph reveals that even a rich VLIW architecture with its issue width pushed to an unrealistic maximum can still benefit significantly when augmented with simple automatically-extracted AFUs. This can be attributed to the fact that once maximum ILP has been extracted, carefully chosen AFUs can be beneficial, by simply reducing the execution time of the operations on the critical path. Thirdly, the graph provides us with an another important result: a few, small well chosen AFUs can empower a very simple VLIW machine like 2/1/1/1 to a level where it outperforms a very rich VLIW architecture with infinite resources but without AFUs (e.g., i/i/2/i and 4/2/i/1). Note that increasing the issue width, besides requiring the appropriate functional units, has a very significant cost on instruction memory bandwidth and on the number of register file ports required, whereas the microarchitectural cost of adding AFUs is much less important.

The experiments also reaffirm the premise that the advantage of AFUs does often go down with the increase in computational capabilities of the host architecture; and yet, in most cases, the advantage of specialisation remains significant also for very rich machines unlikely to be used in SoCs for several years to come.

In addition, we study the correlation of performance and register-file size. Registers are a limited resource in processors with the register file being somehow the non-scalable bottleneck of the architecture, especially for VLIW processors. In Figures 9 we show on a typical benchmark the dependence of cycle count on the number of registers available for the 2/1/1/1 architecture with and without AFUs. Naturally, the cycle count is decreasing monotonously and flattens for some high value: this is essentially the point when no spilling is required

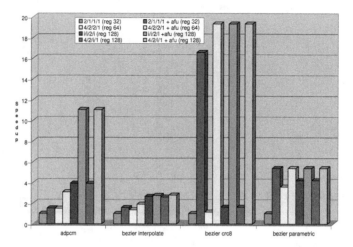

Fig. 8. Speedup of various architectures over the 2/1/1/1 architecture without AFUs.

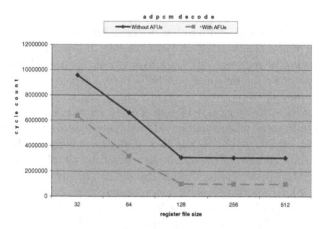

Fig. 9. Evaluation of adpcmdecode, with varying number of registers, without and with AFUs.

anymore. Note that, when using AFUs, a high performance is achieved with a much smaller number of register, when compared with the no-AFUs line suggesting that machines with smaller register files can be designed, when AFUs are employed.

5   Conclusions

The requirements of computing power in embedded applications are constantly growing and approaching the general-purpose computing requirements. This leads to two observable trends: On one side, architectures exploiting instruction level parallelism are making their way in embedded and system-on-chip applications, especially in the form of VLIW processors. On the other side, the customisation of processors for an application is another way of improving the performance for a moderate cost.

In this paper, we present a study on combining multiple-issue architectures and customisation techniques. We have done this by building an automated framework for experimentation and detailed architectural simulation; it is based on Trimaran which was extended to accommodate automatically inferred AFUs and hence to execute application specific complex instructions. We have discussed a number of issues to introduce such special instructions in the compiler framework without compromising the quality of the output. We show that the impact of instruction-set extensions on legacy toolchains is nontrivial. Finally, we have run benchmarks from the MediaBench and EEMBC suites through our framework to obtain precise simulation data. In particular, we show that the presence of AFUs can reduce tangibly the register file size and/or the issue-width of the baseline processor for the same performance.

In the future, we plan to adapt the existing instruction-set extension identification algorithms to exploit at best the specific potentials of VLIW machines.

References

1. K. Atasu, L. Pozzi, and P. Ienne. Automatic application-specific instruction-set extensions under microarchitectural constraints. In *Proceedings of the 40th Design Automation Conference*, pages 256–61, Anaheim, Calif., June 2003.
2. M. Baleani, F. Gennari, Y. Jiang, Y. Patel, R. K. Brayton, and A. Sangiovanni-Vincentelli. HW/SW partitioning and code generation of embedded control applications on a reconfigurable architecture platform. In *Proceedings of the 10th International Workshop on Hardware/Software Codesign*, pages 151–56, Estes Park, Colo., May 2002.
3. F. Campi, R. Canegallo, and R. Guerrieri. IP-reusable 32-bit VLIW Risc core. In *Proceedings of the European Solid State Circuits Conference*, pages 456–59, Villach, Austria, Sept. 2001.
4. N. Clark, H. Zhong, and S. Mahlke. Processor acceleration through automated instruction set customisation. In *Proceedings of the 36th Annual International Symposium on Microarchitecture*, San Diego, Calif., Dec. 2003.
5. F. Design. Art designer reference manual. April 2001.
6. J. Eyre and J. Bier. Infineon targets 3G with Carmel2000. *Microprocessor Report*, 17 July 2000.
7. P. Faraboschi, G. Brown, J. A. Fisher, G. Desoli, and F. Homewood. Lx: A technology platform for customizable VLIW embedded processing. In *Proceedings of the 27th Annual International Symposium on Computer Architecture*, pages 203–13, Vancouver, June 2000.
8. T. R. Halfhill. ARC Cores encourages "plug-ins". *Microprocessor Report*, 19 June 2000.
9. T. R. Halfhill. EEMBC releases first benchmarks. *Microprocessor Report*, 1 May 2000.
10. T. R. Halfhill. MIPS embraces configurable technology. *Microprocessor Report*, 3 Mar. 2003.

11. I.-J. Huang and A. M. Despain. Generating instruction sets and microarchitectures from applications. In *Proceedings of the International Conference on Computer Aided Design*, pages 391–96, San Jose, Calif., Nov. 1994.

12. P. Ienne, L. Pozzi, and M. Vuletic. On the limits of processor specialisation by mapping data ow sections on ad-hoc functional units. Technical Report CS Technical Report 01/376, LAP, EPFL, Lausanne, December 2001.

13. V. Kathail, S. Aditya, R. Schreiber, B. R. Rau, D. C. Cronquist, and M. Sivaraman. Pico: Automatically designing custom computers. *Computer*, 35(9):39–47, 2002.

14. A. La Rosa, L. Lavagno, and C. Passerone. A software development tool chain for a reconfigurable processor. In *Proceedings of the International Conference on Compilers, Architectures, and Synthesis for Embedded Systems*, pages 93–98, Atlanta, Ga., Nov. 2001.

15. C. Lee, M. Potkonjak, and W. H. Mangione-Smith. MediaBench: A tool for evaluating and synthesizing multimedia and communicatons systems. In *Proceedings of the 30th Annual International Symposium on Microarchitecture*, pages 330–35, Research Triangle Park, N.C., Dec. 1997.

16. B. Middha, V. Raj, A. Gangwar, A. Kumar, M. Balakrishnan, and P. Ienne. A Trimaran based framework for exploring the design space of VLIW ASIPs with coarse grain functional units. In *Proceedings of the 15th International Symposium on System Synthesis*, pages 2–7, Kyoto, Oct. 2002.

17. A. Nene, S. Talla, B. Goldberg, H. Kim, and R. M. Rabbah. *Trimaran—An Infrastructure for Compiler Research in Instruction Level Parallelism*. New York University, 1998.

18. K. V. Palem and S. Talla. Adaptive Explicitly Parallel Instruction Computing. In *Proceedings of the 4th Australasian Computer Architecture Conference*, Auckland, New Zealand, Jan. 1999.

19. F. Sun, S. Ravi, A. Raghunathan, and N. K. Jha. Synthesis of custom processors based on extensible platforms. In *Proceedings of the International Conference on Computer Aided Design*, pages 641–48, San Jose, Calif., Nov. 2002.

20. J. Van Praet, G. Goossens, D. Lanneer, and H. De Man. Instruction set definition and instruction selection for ASIPs. In *Proceedings of the 7th International Symposium on High-Level Synthesis*, pages 11–16, Niagara-on-the-Lake, Ont., Apr. 1994.

21. A. Wang, E. Killian, D. Maydan, and C. Rowen. Hardware/software instruction set configurability for system-on-chip processors. In *Proceedings of the 38th Design Automation Conference*, pages 184–88, Las Vegas, Nev., June 2001.

ASIP Architecture Exploration
for Efficient Ipsec Encryption: A Case Study

Hanno Scharwaechter, David Kammler, Andreas Wieferink, Manuel Hohenauer,
Kingshuk Karuri, Jianjiang Ceng, Rainer Leupers,
Gerd Ascheid, and Heinrich Meyr

Integrated Signal Processing Systems
Aachen University of Technology
Aachen, Germany
scharwaechter@iss.rwth-aachen.de

Abstract. *Application Specific Instruction Processors* (ASIPs) are increasingly becoming popular in the world of customized, application-
driven *System-on-Chip* (SoC) designs. Efficient ASIP design requires an
iterative architecture exploration loop-gradual refinement of processor
architecture starting from an initial template. To accomplish this task,
design automation tools are used to detect bottlenecks in embedded applications, to implement application-specific instructions and to automatically generate the required software tools (such as instruction set
simulator, C-compiler, assembler, profiler etc.) as well as to synthesize
the hardware. This paper describes an architecture exploration loop for
an ASIP coprocessor which implements common encryption functionality used in symmetric block cipher algorithms for *IPsec*. The coprocessor
is accessed via shared memory and as a consequence, our approach is easily adaptable to arbitrary processor architectures. In the case study, we
used Blowfish as encryption algorithm and a MIPS architecture as main
processor.

1   Introduction

The strong growth of internet usage during the past years and the resulting
packet traffic have put tight constraints on both protocol and hardware development. On the one hand, there is the demand for high packet throughput and
on the other hand, protocols have to meet the continuously changing traffic requirements like Quality-Of-Service, Differentiated Services, etc. Furthermore, the
increasing number of mobile devices with wireless internet access like laptops,
PDAs and mobile phones as well as *Virtual Private Networks* (VPNs) has made
security one of the most important features of today's networks. *IPsec* is probably the most transparent way to provide security to the internet traffic. In order
to achieve the security objectives, *IPsec* provides dedicated services at the *IP*
layer that enable a system to select security protocols, determine the algorithm
to use, and put in place any cryptographic keys required. This set of services
provides access control, connectionless integrity, data origin authentication, re-
jection of replayed packets (a form of partial sequence integrity), confidentiality

H. Schepers (Ed.): SCOPES 2004, LNCS 3199, pp. 33–46, 2004.

(encryption) and limited traffic flow confidentiality. Because these services are implemented at the *IP* layer, they can be used by any higher layer protocol, e.g. TCP, UDP, VPN etc.

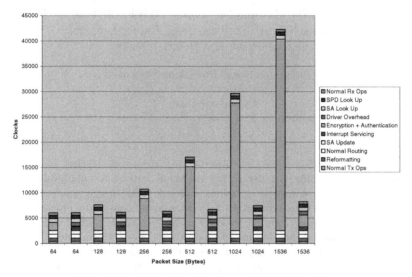

Fig. 1. Break-up of tasks in typical VPN traffic.

Integrating security warranties into the *IP* stack inevitably influences overall *IP* processing performance. Fig. 1 shows break-ups of tasks in implementations of VPN and their execution time related to the packet size. The columns alternately represent implementations of VPN in software and hardware, starting with a software implementation with an incoming packet size of 64 bytes. Since *data encryption* is the most computation intensive task in *IPsec*, it becomes one of the most promising candidates to increase overall packet processing performance. But encryption algorithms are an ever-changing area of computer science. Regularly they are cracked or replaced by newer ones. For example, currently the *Data Encryption Standard* (DES) is replaced by the *Advanced Encryption Standard* (AES). Implementing such algorithms completely in hardware (i.e as a separate *Application Specific Integrated Circuit* (ASIC)) is not feasible due to a lack of reuse opportunities. A good compromise between flexibility and efficiency are *Network Processing Units* (NPUs) which constitute a subclass of ASIPs. They offer highly optimized instruction sets tailored to specific network application domains (which in our case is encryption). Overall performance can be further enhanced by including specialized coprocessors to perform tasks like table lookup, checksum computation, etc. and by expanding the data path to support necessary packet modifications.

In order to design efficient NPUs like any other ASIPs, *design space exploration* (fig. 2) at the processor architecture level needs to be performed [7],[8]. Architecture exploration usually starts with an initial architectural prototype. The pure software implementation of the intended application is run and profiled on this prototype to determine probable performance bottlenecks. Based on the profiling results, the designer refines the basic architecture step by step (e.g. by adding custom instructions or fine-tuning the instruction pipeline) until it is optimally tailored towards the intended range of applications.

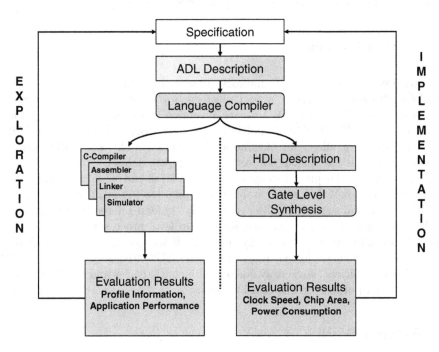

Fig. 2. Tool based processor architecture exploration loop.

This iterative exploration approach demands for very flexible *retargetable* software development tools (C-compiler for main processor, assembler, cosimu-lator/debugger etc.) that can be quickly adapted to varying target processor-coprocessor configurations as well as a methodology for efficient *Multiprocessor-SoC* exploration on system level. Retargetable tools permit to explore many alternative design points in the exploration space within short time, i.e. without the need of tedious complete tool re-design. Such development tools are usually driven by a processor model given in a dedicated specification language.

Although this approach is the basic reason for the success of *Architecture Description Languages* (ADLs), the link to the physical parameters such as chip area or clock speed gets lost. The necessity of combining the high level abstrac-tion and physical parameter evaluation in a single exploration is obvious.

In this paper we present an architecture exploration case study for a co-processor, supporting symmetric block cipher functionality using an ADL tool suite. Our main intention is to show the usage of the tools and their interaction. The remainder of this paper is organized as follows: In section 2 we give a short introduction to our tool suite that we used within this exploration followed by a discussion of the related work in section 3. The main body of the paper consists of the illustration of our target application with main focus on the encryption algorithm in section 4, followed by the detailed presentation of the successive refinement flow for the joint processor/coprocessor optimizations in section 5 as well as the obtained results. Section 6 concludes the paper.

2   System Overview

The architecture exploration framework presented in this paper builds on the *LISATek Processor Designer*, a tool platform for embedded processor design available from CoWare Inc. [4], an earlier version of which has been described in detail in [8]. The *LISATek* tool-suite revolves around the LISA 2.0 ADL. Amongst others, it allows for automatically generating efficient ASIP software development tools like instruction set simulator [12], debugger, profiler, assembler, and linker, and it provides capabilities for VHDL and Verilog generation for hardware synthesis [14]. A retargetable C-compiler [13][1] is seamlessly integrated into this tool chain and uses the same single "golden reference" LISA model to drive retargeting. A methodology for system level processor/communication co-exploration for multi-processor systems [21] is integrated into the LISA tool chain, too. We believe that such an integrated ADL-driven approach to ASIP design is most efficient, since it avoids model inconsistencies and the need to use various special-purpose description languages.

3   Related Work

The approaches that come closest to ours are Expression [7], ASIP Meister [17], and CHESS [9]. Similar to our approach with the LISA language, Expression uses a dedicated, unified processor ADL with applications beyond compiler retargeting (e.g. simulator generation). *Hardware Description Language* (HDL) generation from the Expression language is presented in [7]. The HDL generation is based on a functional abstraction and thus allows to generate the complete architecture.

Like our approach, ASIP Meister builds on the CoSy compiler platform [1]. However, it has no uniform ADL (i.e. target machine modeling is completely based on GUI entry) and the range of target processors is restricted due to a predefined processor component library. That is why the HDL generation of ASIP Meister is able to fulfill tight constraints regarding synthesis results, but sacrificing flexibility.

CHESS uses the nML ADL [6] for processor modeling and compiler retargeting. Unfortunately, only few details about retargeting CHESS have been published. Like LISA, nML is a hierarchical mixed structural/behavioral ADL that (besides capturing other machine features) annotates each instruction with a

---

[1] Based on CoSy compiler development system from ACE [1].

behavior description. While LISA permits arbitrary C code for behavior descriptions, such descriptions in nML are restricted to a predefined set of operators which probably limits the flexibility of CHESS. Build on nML, an HDL generator GO from Target Compiler Technologies [18] exists which results are unfortunately not publicly available. Furthermore, the project Sim-HS [20] produces synthesizable Verilog models from Sim-nML models. Here, non-pipelined architectures are generated and the base structure of the generated hardware is fixed. Additionally, to our knowledge none of the here mentioned frameworks provides support for retargetable MP-SoC integration at the system level, which was, due to our processor-coprocessor design, a major drawback.

There are several existing architectures for cryptographic coprocessors targeted towards embedded systems. Some general architectures are presented in [3], [11], [2], [10]. Chodowiec [3] and his group show that advanced architectural techniques can be used to improve performance for block cipher algorithms; they implement pipelines and loop-unrolling in an architecture based on a *Field Programmable Gate Array* (FPGA). Similar approaches are taken in [11] and [2] with regards to the *International Data Encryption Algorithm* (IDEA). They compare the differences in performance of serial and parallel implementations of IDEA using a Xilinx Virtex platform; power consumption is not considered. In [10], the authors explore a methodology for hardware-software partitioning between ASICs, *Digital Signal Processors* (DSPs) and FPGAs to optimize performance for customized encryptions units. The author of [10] also points out that since there are limited resources available to mobile communication devices, proper balance of performance and flexibility is important. He presents design choices associated with these factors in his FPGA-based implementation of IDEA.

4   Target Application

The *Internet Protocol* (IP) is designed for use in interconnected systems of *packet-switched* computer communication networks. It provides facilities to transmit blocks from sources to destinations which are identified by fixed length addresses. The protocol is specifically limited in scope to provide the functions necessary to deliver a datagram from source to destination, and there are no mechanisms for other services commonly found in host-to-host protocols.

Because of the need for an upgrade anyway, it was logical that the new version of the internet protocol – *IPv6* – should contain a native security system which would allow the users to communicate securely. At the same time, it must be realized that because the internet is a vast and complex network, the transition to the new version of the protocol will not be immediate. Hence the security implementation should be such that it would be compatible, and adaptable to *IPv4*.

IPsec focuses on the security that can be provided by the IP-layer of the network. It does not concern itself with application level security such as *Pretty Good Privacy* (PGP), for instance.

Security requirements can be divided into two distinct parts:

- Authentication & Integrity and
- Confidentiality.

These are independent of each other and can be used separately or together according to user requirements. The encryption and authentication algorithms used for *IPsec* are the heart of the system. They are directly responsible for the strength of the security the system can provide. *IPsec* generally claims for block cipher algorithms which support *Cipher Block Chaining* (CBC) mode [16]. Roughly spoken, this means that the encryption of a certain block of data is affected by the encryption of preceding blocks.

Our main application is the publicly available network stack implementation developed by Microsoft Research [5] known as *MSR IPv6*. To enhance *IPv6* performance, we identified and extracted the common path through this protocol including *IPsec* encryption. Based on this, we wrote an *IPv6* testbench. For the encryption we selected the Blowfish encryption algorithm.

Blowfish is a symmetric block cipher with 64-bit block size and variable length keys (up to 448 bits) designed by Bruce Schneier [16]. It has gained a wide acceptance in a number of applications. No attacks are known against it. This cipher was designed specifically for 32-bit machines and is significantly faster than DES. One of the proposed candidates for the AES called Twofish [15] is based on Blowfish. As most block cipher algorithms, Blowfish is a so called Feistel-Network which takes a block of size n, divides it in two halves of size $n/2$ and executes an iterative block cipher of the form

$$L_i = R_{i-1}$$
$$R_i = L_i \oplus F(R_{i-1}, K_i)$$

where K_i is a partial key of ith round,
L, R are the right and left halves, respectively, of size $n/2$, and
F an arbitrary round function.

Feistel-Networks guarantee reversibility of the encryption function. Since L_i is *xor*-ed with the output of f, the following holds true:

$$L_{i-1} \oplus F(R_{i-1}, K_i) \oplus F(R_{i-1}, K_i) = L_{i-1}$$

The same concepts can be found in DES, Twofish, etc. Blowfish supports all known encryption modes like CBC, ECB OFB64, etc. and is therefore a good candidate for *IPsec* encryption. Two main parts constitute the Blowfish encryption algorithm (fig. 3): *key expansion* and *data encryption*. The key expansion divides a given key into different 32-bit subkeys. The main key is 4168 bits wide and has to be generated in advance.

On the lowest level, the algorithm contains just the very basic encryption techniques *confusion* and *diffusion* [16]. *Confusion* masks relationships between plain and cipher text by substituting blocks of plain text with blocks of cipher text. Diffusion distributes redundancies of plain text over the cipher text by

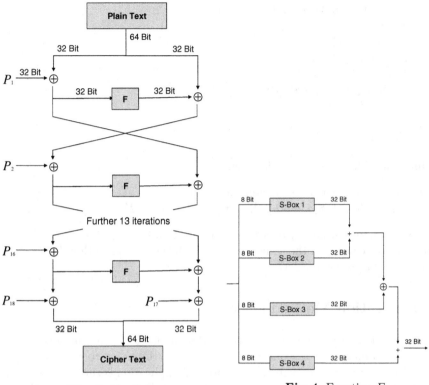

Fig. 3. Blowfish.   **Fig. 4.** Function F.

permuting blocks of cipher text. *Confusion* and *diffusion* depend strongly on the set of subkeys. 18 subkeys constitute a permutation array (P-array), denoted as

$$P_1, P_2, \ldots, P_{18}$$

for *confusion*. Four substitution arrays (S-Boxes) – each of 256 entries – denoted as

$$S_{1,0}, S_{1,1}, \ldots, S_{1,255}$$
$$S_{2,0}, S_{2,1}, \ldots, S_{2,255}$$
$$S_{3,0}, S_{3,1}, \ldots, S_{3,255}$$
$$S_{4,0}, S_{4,1}, \ldots, S_{4,255}$$

control diffusion.

The *data encryption* is basically a very simple function (fig. 4) which is executed 16 times. Each round is made of a key dependent permutation, as well as a key and data dependent substitution which constitute the very basic encryption techniques. The used operations are either additions or *xor*-connections and four memory accesses per round. The exact encryption procedure works as follows:

Divide x into two 32-bit halves x_L and x_R

For $i = 1$ to 16:

    $x_L = x_R \oplus P_i$

    $x_R = F(x_L) \oplus x_R$

    Exchange x_L and x_R

Exchange x_R and x_L (reverts first exchange)

$x_R = x_R \oplus P_{17}$

$x_L = x_L \oplus P_{18}$

Concatenate x_L and x_R

The function F looks like the following:

Divide x_L into four 8-bit-quarter a,b,c and d.

$$F(X_L) = ((S_{1,a} + S_{2,b} \bmod 2^{32}) \oplus S_{3,c}) + S_{4,d} \bmod 2^{32},$$

where $S_{i,j}$ designates index j of S-Box i for $i \in \{1 \ldots 4\}$ and $j \in \{0 \ldots 255\}$. Decryption works exactly in the same way, just with the difference that $P_1, P_2, \ldots,$ P_{18} are used in reversed order.

5   Exploration Methodology

The key functionality of the LISA processor design platform is its support for *architecture exploration*: In the phase of tailoring an architecture to an application domain LISA permits a refinement from profiled application kernel functionality to cycle accurate abstraction of a processor model. This process is usually an iterative one that is repeated until a best fit between selected architecture and target application is obtained. Every change to the architecture specification requires a complete new set of software development tools. Such changes, if carried out manually, will result in a long, tedious and extremely error-prone exploration process. The automatic tool generation mechanism of LISA enables the designer to speed-up this process considerably. The design methodology is composed of mainly three different phases: *application profiling, architecture exploration* and *architecture implementation phase*.

5.1   Application Profiling

The *application profiling phase* covers tasks to identify and select algorithm kernels which are candidates for hardware acceleration. Such kernels constitute the performance critical path of the target application and can be easily identified by instrumenting the application code in order to generate high-level language execution statistics by simulating the functional prototype.

For this purpose, we generated a C-compiler for a MIPS32 4K architecture by applying the LISA Compiler-Generator on the related LISA model, implemented our target application and profiled it with the LISA Profiler to obtain a general idea about bottlenecks and of possible hardware accelerations. The outcome was a pure functional specification of the instructions to be implemented.

As expected, it turned out that most of the execution time is spent in the encryption algorithm. More detailed, 80% of the computations are spent in the above mentioned F function according to its iterative execution.

5.2   Architecture Exploration

During the *architecture exploration phase* (fig. 2 in section 1), software development tools (i.e. C-compiler, assembler, linker, and cycle-accurate simulator) are required to profile and benchmark the target application on different architectural alternatives. Using the C-compiler, the software and architecture designers can study the application's performance requirements immediately after the algorithm designer has finished his work.

To support Blowfish encryption most efficiently, but without complete loss of flexibility to develop other symmetric *IPsec* encryption algorithms, we decided to implement an encryption specific instruction set processor. Furthermore, we wanted to provide a maximum amount of flexibility concerning hardware constraints, which led to a coprocessor design, that is accessed by its host processor via shared memory and provides special purpose encryption instructions. This implies that the coprocessor has to run at least with the same clock speed as the main processor, because otherwise the original implementation of the IP stack would be slowed down by the coprocessor.

In fig. 5, the resulting dual-processor platform is depicted. For both processors, a processor simulator automatically generated from a LISA model is applied. The processor models contain two bus instances, one for the program memory requests and one for the data accesses. For high simulation performance, the memory modules local to one processor are modeled inside the respective LISA model, e.g. the kernel segment ROM (kseg_rom) and the user segment ROM (useg_rom) of the MIPS32 main processor. Only the memory requests to the shared memory are directed to the SystemC world outside the LISA simulators.

The platform communication is modeled efficiently using the *Transaction Level Modeling* (TLM) paradigm [19] supported by SystemC 2.0. A LISA port translates the LISA memory API requests of the processors to the respective TLM requests for the abstract SystemC bus model. The bus model performs the bus arbitration and forwards the processor requests to the shared memory. This memory is used to communicate between the processors and thus exchange parameters as well as results of the encryption procedures implemented on the coprocessor and the original *IPv6* protocol stack implemented on the MIPS main processor. To access the coprocessor on C-code level, we extended the generated MIPS C-compiler by dedicated intrinsic functions, one for the encryption and the decryption procedure. These intrinsic functions have the same look and feel as the original functions of blowfish, but internally they push their parameters onto the shared memory block, poll a certain memory address, that indicates the end of the computation and pop the results from the shared memory block back to local memory for further processing on the MIPS. On the coprocessor side, the external memory is also polled for parameters. If now certain paramters are

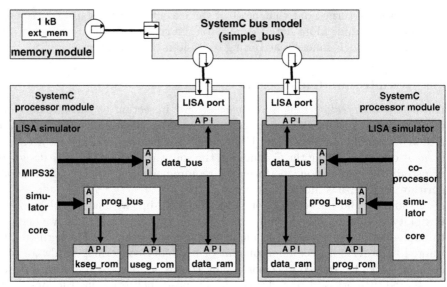

Fig. 5. Simulation setup.

found in the memory, the relevant computation is performed and the results are written back to the external memory.

Since F is iteratively executed within the encryption, the decryption and also in the key generation procedures of Blowfish, interleaved parallel execution of F in a dedicated pipeline is not possible, because results from iteration i are used as input in iteration $i + 1$. Another option was to develop instructions that cover partially behavior of F presented in fig. 4 and which can be executed in one cycle related to the MIPS cycle length. Therefore, our first design decision was to start from a RISC architecture including a 4-stage pipeline with fetch, decode, execution and writeback stage as in the initial LISA-model template. In the further discussed architecture co-exploration loops, the coprocessor core has been successively refined in order to reach a certain degree of efficiency. In the following, the required architecture co-exploration loops are discussed in detail.

Implementing the instructions, we started with a first educated guess and divided the function F (fig. 4) into four independent parts, each of which can be executed in one execution stage:

$$u = S_{1,a}$$
$$v = S_{2,b} + u$$
$$w = S_{3,c} \oplus v$$
$$x = S_{4,d} + x.$$

Each of these instructions takes an 8-bit quarter of the input of F, reads the according S-Box value (see section 4) from the memory and processes either an *xor* or an *add* instructions on this value. It has to be mentioned that each of the $S_{i,j}$-operators comprises an addition of an offset j to a base address S_i and reads the value of the computed address from memory. By calling these instructions in a sequence, we gained a first approach to support Blowfish by dedicated instructions. However, memory accesses and additions consume lots of computation time and therefore our instructions did not meet the cycle length constraint given by the MIPS architecture. Furthermore, the reusability of the instructions, with respect to other block cipher algorithms is also very limited.

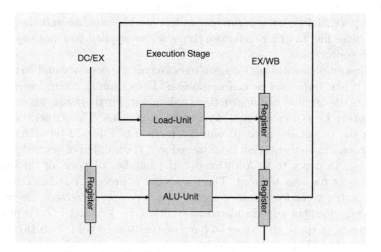

Fig. 6. Parallel S-Box access in the execution stage.

Refining our first approach, we decided to separate the core S-Box access from the remaining operations and to put it into a dedicated hardware unit. This unit was placed into the execution stage, such that it can be executed in parallel to other operations (fig. 6). As a consequence, the memory latencies related to S-Box accesses are completely hidden in the execution of the encryption instructions and do not affect system performance. We modified the encryption instruction putting focus on the number of additions in each of them. The result was that we developed four instructions, one for each S-Box, where each of them covers a S-Box access in the way that it calculates the address and pushes the result to the unit responsible for the pure S-Box memory access. Furthermore we developed an *add-xor* instruction and an *add-xor-xor* instruction to process the results from the S-Box accesses, so that we had now six instructions over all. This design made it possible to adapt our coprocessor speed to that of the MIPS architecture. In addition to this, the reusability for other block cipher algorithms is much better than in our first approach. For example, the *add-xor* instruction can be used as a pure *add* instruction just by setting one operand to zero.

5.3   Architecture Implementation

At the last stage of the design flow, the *architecture implementation phase* (fig. 2 in section 1), the ADL architecture description is used to generate an architecture description on *Register Transfer Level*(RTL). The *RTL-Processor-Synthesis* can be triggered to generate synthesizable HDL-code for the complete architecture. Numbers on hardware cost and performance parameters (e.g. design area, timing) can be derived by running the HDL processor model through the standard logic synthesis flow. On this high level of detail the designer can tweak the computational efficiency of the architecture by experimenting with different implementations of the data path.

First synthesis results from the architecture defined in exploration phase 3 showed the potential for area improvement in both the pipeline and the general purpose register file. In order to reduce chip size, we applied two more optimizations of the coprocessor.

In the first implementation loop, we removed all unnecessary and redundant functionality like *shift*, *mul* or *add* operations. For example, having an *add-xor* instruction made original *add* instructions redundant. Furthermore, we enhanced the architecture by *increment* and *decrement* operations. These operations can be used for the processing of loop counters, instead of using 32-bit *adders*.

In the second implementation loop, we reduced the number of general purpose registers from 15 down to 9. Additionally, the number of ports of the general purpose register file was reduced. The remaining coprocessor architecture just consists of instructions for memory access, register-copy, increment, decrement and xor. Along with these, 6 dedicated instructions for symmetric encryption as well as 9 general purpose and 3 special purpose registers to hold the S-Box values were implemented. This architecture is sufficient to comfortably implement an encryption, decryption and a key generation function for symmetric block cipher algorithms.

5.4   Experimental Results

The architecture parameters considered for our design decisions during exploration phase were code size and number of cycles. During the implementation phase, chip area and timing were taken into account. In tables 1 and 2, the processed iterations in *exploration phase* are numbered from *exploration 1* to *exploration 3* and from *synthesis 1* to *synthesis 3* in the *implementation phase*.

Table 1 shows that the employment of our coprocessor of *exploration 3* results in an overall speed-up of the Blowfish encryption algorithm by a factor of five.

Although the number of instructions of *exploration 2* is less than the corresponding number of *exploration 3* it turned out, that the timing constraint

Table 1. Simulation results in the architecture exploration phase.

	simulation results		
	exploration 1: (standalone simulation)	exploration 2: (first cop. approach)	exploration 3: (second cop. approach)
code size	531	235	267
number of cycles	917844	117546	176319

Table 2. Area Consumption in the architecture implementation phase.

	area consumption (kGates)		
architecture part	synthesis 1: (extended by encryption instructions)	synthesis 2: (eliminated redundant instructions)	synthesis 3: (with reduced register ports)
total	31.4	25.8	22.2
pipeline	21.1	15.0	14.9
register file	10.1	10.5	7.1

specified by the MIPS, cannot be met by the model *exploration 2*, whereas our final model of the *exploration phase* showed an equivalent timing to the MIPS processor.

Table 2 confirms our statements from section 5.3. The first synthesis resulted in a core which had an area consumption of 31.4 kGates. We were able to reduce this area size to 22.2 kGates. In the first implementation loop, the area consumption of the pipeline was reduced from 21.1 kGates down to 15.0 kGates. Furthermore, in the second implementation loop, we decreased the area of the register file by 3.4 kGates down to 7.1 kGates.

6   Conclusions

In this paper we illustrated the successive refinement flow of processor architectures within an architecture exploration procedure. In our case study we used an *IPv6* protocol stack implementation developed by Microsoft Research which we combined with the Blowfish block cipher algorithm as the *IPsec* encryption. We have designed a coprocessor for efficient implementation of symmetric block cipher algorithms by providing an application specific instruction set. To access the encryption procedures from the C-level, we inserted dedicated intrinsic functionality into the generated MIPS C-compiler. By using the whole LISA tool suite for our case study, we were able to show that overall IP processing can be very efficiently supported by a small set of hardware accelerations without loss of flexibility due to future developments in the area of symmetric encryption. Because of the very simple and common structure of the Blowfish encryption algorithm, we believe that our approach can be adapted to other block cipher algorithms as well.

References

1. ACE – Associated Computer Experts bv. *The COSY Compiler Development System* http://www.ace.nl.
2. O. Y. H. Cheung, K. H. Tsoi, P. H. W. Leong, and M. P. Leong. Tradeoffs in Parallel and Serial Implementations of the International Data Encryption Standard (IDEA). In *Lecture Notes in Computer Science, vol. 2162*, 2001.

3. P. Chodowiec, P. Khuon, and K.Gaj. Fast Implementations of Secret-Key Block Ciphers Using Mixed Inner- and Outer-Round Pipelining. In *FPGA*, 2001.
4. CoWare Inc. http://www.coware.com.
5. R. Draves, B. Zill, and A. Mankin. Implementing IPv6 for Windows NT. In *Windows NT Symposium Seattle*, Aug. 1998.
6. A. Fauth, J. Van Praet, and M. Freericks. Describing Instruction Set Processors Using nML. In *Proc. of the European Design and Test Conference (ED & TC)*, Mar. 1995.
7. A. Halambi, P. Grun, V. Ganesh, A. Khare, N. Dutt, and A. Nicolau. EXPRESSION: A Language for Architecture Exploration through Compiler/Simulator Retargetability. In *Proc. of the Conference on Design, Automation & Test in Europe (DATE)*, Mar. 1999.
8. A. Hoffmann, H. Meyr, and R. Leupers. *Architecture Exploration for Embedded Processors With Lisa*. Kluwer Academic Publishers, Jan.2003 ISBN 1-4020-7338-0.
9. D. Lanner, J. Van Praet, A. Kifli, K. Schoofs, W. Geurts, F. Thoen, and G. Goossens. Chess: Retargetable Code Generation for Embedded DSP Processors. In P. Marwedel and G. Goosens, editors, *Code Generation for Embedded Processors*. Kluwer Academic Publishers, 1995.
10. O. Mencer, M. Morf, and M. Flynn. Hardware Software Tridesign of Encryption for Mobile Communication Units. In *ASSP*, 1998.
11. M.Leong, O.Cheung, K. Tsoi, and P.Leong. A Bit-Serial Implementation of the International Data Encryption Algorithm (IDEA). In *IEEE Symposium on Field-Programmable Custom Computing Machhines*, 2000.
12. Achim Nohl, Gunnar Braun, Oliver Schliebusch, Rainer Leupers, and Heinrich Meyr. A Universal Technique for Fast and Flexible Instruction-Set Architecture Simulation. In *Proc. of the Design Automation Conference (DAC)*, Jun. 2002.
13. M. Hohenauer H. Scharwaechter, K. Karuri, O. Wahlen, T. Kogel, R. Leupers, G. Ascheid, and H. Meyr. A Methodology and Tool Suite for C Compiler Generation from ADL Models. In *Proc. of the Conference on Design, Automation & Test in Europe (DATE)*, Mar. 2004.
14. O. Schliebusch, M. Steinert, G. Braun, A. Nohl, R. Leupers, G. Ascheid, and H. Meyr. RTL Processor Synthesis for Architecture Exploration and Implementation. In *Proc. of the Conference on Design, Automation & Test in Europe (DATE)*, Mar. 2004.
15. B. Schneier, J. Kelsey, D. Whiting, D. Wagner, and C. Hall. Twofish: A 128-Bit Block Cipher. Jun. 1998.
16. B. Schneier. *Applied Cryptography*. Addison-Wesley Publishing Company, Boston, Jun. 1996. ISBN 0-471-11709-9.
17. S. Kobayashi, Y. Takeuchi, A. Kitajima, M. Imai. Compiler Generation in PEAS-III: an ASIP Development System. In *Workshop on Software and Compilers for Embedded Processors (SCOPES)*, 2001.
18. Target Compiler Technologies. CHESS/CHECKERS http://www.retarget.com.
19. T. Grötker, S. Liao, G. Martin, S. Swan. *System Design with SystemC*. Kluwer Academic Publishers, 2002.
20. V. Rajesh and R. Moona. Processor Modeling for Hardware Software Codesign. In *Int. Conf. on VLSI Design*, Jan. 1999.
21. A. Wieferink, T. Kogel, R. Leupers, G. Ascheid, and H. Meyr. A System Level Processor/Communication Co-Exploration Methodology for Multi-Processor System-on-Chip Platforms. In *Proc. of the Conference on Design, Automation & Test in Europe (DATE)*, Mar. 2004.

Compact Procedural Implementation in DSP Software Synthesis Through Recursive Graph Decomposition

Ming-Yung Ko[1], Praveen K. Murthy[2], and Shuvra S. Bhattacharyya[1]

[1] Department of Electrical and Computer Engineering, and
Institute for Advanced Computer Studies
University of Maryland at College Park, USA
{myko,ssb}@eng.umd.edu
[2] Fujitsu Laboratories of America
Sunnyvale, California, USA
pmurthy@fla.fujitsu.com

Abstract. Synthesis of digital signal processing (DSP) software from dataflow-based formal models is an effective approach for tackling the complexity of modern DSP applications. In this paper, an efficient method is proposed for applying subroutine call instantiation of module functionality when synthesizing embedded software from a dataflow specification. The technique is based on a novel recursive decomposition of subgraphs in a cluster hierarchy that is optimized for low buffer size. Applying this technique, one can achieve significantly lower buffer sizes than what is available for minimum code size inlined schedules, which have been the emphasis of prior software synthesis work. Furthermore, it is guaranteed that the number of procedure calls in the synthesized program is polynomially bounded in the size of the input dataflow graph, even though the number of module invocations may increase exponentially. This recursive decomposition approach provides an efficient means for integrating subroutine-based module instantiation into the design space of DSP software synthesis. The experimental results demonstrate a significant improvement in buffer cost, especially for more irregular multi-rate DSP applications, with moderate code and execution time overhead.

1   Introduction and Related Work

Due to the growing complexity of DSP applications, the use of dataflow-based, block diagram programming environments is becoming increasingly popular for DSP system design. The advantages of such environments include intuitive appeal; promotion of useful software engineering practices such as modularity and code reuse; and improved quality of synthesized code through automatic code generation. Examples of commercial DSP design tools that incorporate dataflow semantics include System Canvas from Angeles Design Systems [12], SPW from Cadence Design Systems, ADS from Agilent, Cocentric System Studio from Synopsys [2], GEDAE from Lockheed, and the Autocoding Toolset from Management, Communications, and Control, Inc. [15]. Research-oriented tools and languages related to dataflow-based DSP design include Ptolemy

H. Schepers (Ed.): SCOPES 2004, LNCS 3199, pp. 47–61, 2004.

from U. C. Berkeley [3], GRAPE from K. U. Leuven [8], Compaan from Leiden University [16], and StreamIt from MIT [5].

A significant body of theory and algorithms has been developed for synthesis of software from dataflow-based block diagram representations. Many of these techniques pertain to the *synchronous dataflow (SDF)* model [9], which can be viewed as an important common denominator across a wide variety of DSP design tools. The major advantage of SDF is the potential for static analysis and optimization. In [1], algorithms are developed to optimize buffer space while obeying the constraint of minimal code space. A multiple objective optimization is proposed in [18] to compute the full range of Pareto-optimal solutions in trading off code size, data space, and execution time. Vectorization can be incorporated into SDF graphs to reduce the rate of context switching and enhance execution performance [7, 14].

In this paper, an efficient method is proposed for applying subroutine call instantiation of module functionality to minimize buffering requirements when synthesizing embedded software from SDF specifications. The technique is based on a novel recursive decomposition of subgraphs in a cluster hierarchy that is optimized for low buffer size. Applying this technique, one can achieve significantly lower buffer sizes than what is available for minimum code size inlined schedules, which have been the emphasis of prior software synthesis work. Furthermore, it is guaranteed that the number of procedure calls in the synthesized program is polynomially bounded in the size of the input dataflow graph, thereby bounding the code size overhead. Having such a bound is particularly important because the number of module invocations may increase exponentially in an SDF graph. Our recursive decomposition approach provides an efficient means for integrating subroutine-based module instantiation into the design space of DSP software synthesis.

In [17], an alternative buffer minimization technique through transforming looped schedules is investigated. The transformation works on a certain schedule tree data structure, and the computational complexity of the transformation is shown to be polynomial in the number of leaf nodes in this schedule tree. However, since leaf nodes in the schedule tree correspond to actor appearances in the schedule, there is in general no polynomial bound in terms of the size of the SDF graph on the number of these leaf nodes. Therefore, no polynomial bound emerges on the complexity of the transformation technique in terms of SDF graph size. In contrast, our graph decomposition strategy extends and hierarchically applies a two-actor SDF graph scheduling theory that guarantees achieving minimal buffer requirements [1], and a number of theorems are developed in this paper to ensure that the complexity of our approach is polynomially bounded in the size of the SDF graph.

Buffer minimization and use of subroutine calls during code synthesis have also been explored in the *phased scheduling* technique [4]. This work is part of the StreamIt language [5] for developing streaming applications. Phased scheduling applies to a restricted subset of SDF graphs, in particular each basic computation unit (called a *filter* in StreamIt) allows only a single input and output. In contrast, the recursive graph decomposition approach applies to all SDF graphs that have *single appearance schedules* (this class includes all properly-constructed, acyclic SDF graphs), and furthermore, can be applied outside the tightly interdependent components of SDF graphs that do not have single appearance schedules. Tightly interdependent components are unique, maximal subgraphs that exhibit a certain form of data dependency [1]. Through extensive experiments with single appearance scheduling, it has been observed that tightly interdependent components arise only very infrequently in practice [1]. Integrating phased scheduling concepts with the decomposition approach presented in this paper is an interesting direction for further work.

Panda surveys data memory optimization techniques for compiling *high level languages (HLLs)*, such as C, including techniques such as code transformation, register allocation, and address generation [13]. Due to the instruction-level parallelism capability found in many DSP processors, the study of independent register transfers is also a useful subject. The work of [10] investigates an integer programming approach for code compaction that obeys exact timing constraints and saves code space as well. Since code for individual actors is often specified by HLLs, several such techniques are complementary to the techniques developed in this paper. In particular HLL compilation techniques can be used for performing intra-actor optimization in conjunction with the inter-actor, SDF-based optimizations developed in this paper.

2   Background and Notation

An SDF program specification is a directed graph where vertices represent functional blocks (*actors*) and edges represent data dependencies. Actors are activated when sufficient inputs are available, and FIFO queues (or *buffers*) are usually allocated to buffer data transferred between actors. In addition, for each edge e, the numbers of data values produced $prd(e)$ and consumed $cns(e)$ are fixed at compile time for each invocation of the source actor $src(e)$ and sink actor $snk(e)$, respectively.

A *schedule* is a sequence of actor executions (or *firings*). We compile an SDF graph by first constructing a *valid schedule*, a finite schedule that fires each actor at least once, and does not lead to unbounded buffer accumulation (if the schedule is repeated indefinitely) nor buffer underflow on any edge. To avoid buffer overflow and underflow problems, the total amount of data produced and consumed is required to be matched on all edges. In [9], efficient algorithms are presented to determine whether or not a valid schedule exists for an SDF graph, and to determine the minimum number of firings of each actor in a valid schedule. We denote the *repetitions* of an actor as this minimum number of firings and collect the repetitions for all actors in the *repetitions vector*. Therefore, given an edge e and repetitions vector q, the *balance equation* for e is written as $q(src(e))\,prd(e) = q(snk(e))\,cns(e)$.

To save code space, actor firings can be incorporated within loop constructs to form *looped schedules*. Looped schedules group sequential firings into schedule loops; each such loop is composed of a loop iteration count and one or more iterands. In addition to being firings, iterands also can be schedules, and therefore, it is possible to form nested looped schedules. The notation we use for a schedule loop L is $L = (nI_1I_2...I_m)$, where n denotes the iteration count and $I_1, I_2, ..., I_m$ denote the iterands of L. *Single appearance schedules (SAS)* refer to schedules where each actor appears only once. In inlined code implementation, an SAS contains a single copy of code for every actor and results in minimal code space requirements. For an acyclic SDF graph, an SAS can easily be derived from a topological sorting of the actors. However, such an SAS often requires relatively high buffer cost. A more memory-efficient method of SAS construction is to perform a certain form of dynamic programming optimization (called *DPPO* for *dynamic programming post optimization*) over a topological sort to generate a buffer-efficient, nested looped schedule [1]. In this paper, we employ the *acyclic pairwise grouping for adjacent nodes (APGAN)* algorithm [1] for the generation of topological sorts and the DPPO method described above for the optimization of these topological sorts into more buffer-efficient form.

3   Recursive Decomposition
of a Two-Actor SDF Graph

Given a two-actor SDF graph as shown on the left in Fig. 1, we can recursively generate a schedule that has a buffer memory requirement of the least amount possible. The scheduling technique works in the following way: given the edge AB, and $prd(AB) = n > cns(AB) = m$, we derive the new graph shown on the right in Fig. 1 where the actor set is $\{A_1, B_1\}$ and $prd(A_1B_1) = n \bmod m$. The actor A_1 is a hierarchical actor that represents the schedule $A (\lfloor n/m \rfloor B)$, and B_1 just represents B. Consider a minimum buffer schedule for the reduced graph, where we replace occurrences of A_1 a by $A (\lfloor n/m \rfloor B)$, and occurrences of B_1 are replaced by B. For example, suppose that $n = 3$ and $m = 2$. Then $3 \bmod 2 = 1$, the minimum buffer schedule for the reduced graph would be $A_1A_1B_1$, and this would result in the schedule $ABABB$ after the replacement. As can be verified, this later schedule is a valid schedule for the original graph, and is also a minimum buffer schedule for it, having a buffer memory requirement of $n + m - 1$ as expected.

However, the advantage of the reduced graph is depicted in Fig. 2: the schedule for the reduced graph can be implemented using procedure calls in a way that is more parsimonious than simply replacing each occurrence of A and B in $ABABB$ by procedure calls. This latter approach would require 5 procedure calls, whereas the hierarchical implementation depicted in Fig. 2 requires only 3 procedure calls. The topmost procedure implements the SAS $A_1A_1B_1 = (2A_1)B_1$, where A_1 is really a procedure call; this procedure call implements the SAS AB, which in turn call the actors A and B. Ofcourse, we could implement the schedule $ABABB$ more efficiently than simply using five procedure calls; for example, we could generate inline code for the schedule $(2AB)B$; this would have 3 blocks of code: two for B, and one for A. We would have to do a trade-off analysis to see whether the overhead of the 3 procedure calls would be less than the code-size increase of using 3 appearances (instead of 2).

We first state an important theorem from [1]:

(1)   (2)

Fig. 1.   A two-actor SDF graph and its reduced version.

Theorem 1: For the two-actor SDF graph depicted on the left in Fig. 1, the minimum buffer requirement over all schedules is given by $n + m - gcd(n, m)$.

Proof: See [1].

We denote $n + m - gcd(n, m)$ for a two-actor SDF graph depicted on the left in Fig. 1 as the *VBMLB (the buffer memory lower bound over all valid schedules)*. The definition of VBMLB also applies to an SDF edge. Similarly, for arbitrary SDF graphs, the VBMLB for a graph can be defined as the sum of VBMLBs over all edges.

Theorem 2 shows that the preservation of the minimum buffer schedule in the reduced graph in the above example is not a coincidence.

Theorem 2: The minimum buffer schedule for the reduced graph on the right in Fig. 1 yields a minimum buffer schedule for the graph on the left when the appropriate substitutions of the actors are made.

Proof: Let $gcd(n, m) = g$. The equation $gcd(n \bmod m, m) = g$ must hold since a fundamental property of the gcd is that $gcd(n, m) = gcd(n \bmod m, m)$. So the minimum buffer requirement for the reduced graph is given by $n \bmod m + m - g$ from Theorem 1. Now, when A_1 is replaced by $A(\lfloor n/m \rfloor B)$ to get a schedule for the original graph, we see that the maximum number of tokens is going to be reached after a firing of A since firings of B consume tokens. Since the maximum number of tokens reached in the reduced graph on edge $A_1 B_1$ is $n \bmod m + m - g$, the maximum number reached on AB when we replace A_1 by $A(\lfloor n/m \rfloor B)$ will be

$$n \bmod m + m - g + \left\lfloor \frac{n}{m} \right\rfloor m = n + m - g .$$

Hence, the theorem is proved. **QED.**

Theorem 3: An SAS for a two-actor graph satisfies the VBMLB if and only if either $n \mid m$ (n is dividable by m) or $m \mid n$. A 2-actor SDF graph where either $n \mid m$ or $m \mid n$ is called a *perfect SDF graph (PSG)* in this paper.

Proof: (Forward direction) Assume WLOG that $n > m$. Then the SAS is going to be $(m/(gcd(n, m)))A)((n/(gcd(n, m)))B)$. The buffering requirement of this schedule is $mn/gcd(n, m)$. Since this satisfies the VBMLB, we have

$$\frac{m}{gcd(n, m)} n = m + n - gcd(n, m) . \tag{1}$$

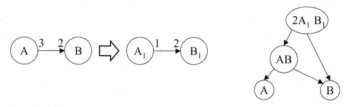

Fig. 2. A hierarchical procedural implementation of a minimum buffer schedule for the SDF graph on the left.

Since $n > m$, we have to show that (1) implies $m \mid n$. The contrapositive is that if $m \mid n$ does not hold then Equation 1 does not hold. Indeed, if $m \mid n$ does not hold, then $gcd(n, m) < m$, and $m/(gcd(n, m)) \geq 2$. In the R.H.S. of (1), we have $m - gcd(n, m) < m < n$, meaning that the R.H.S. is $< 2n$. This shows that (1) cannot hold.

The reverse direction follows easily since if $m \mid n$, then the L.H.S. is n, and the R.H.S. is $m + n - m = n$. **QED.**

Theorem 4: A minimum buffer schedule for a two-actor SDF graph can be generated in the recursive hierarchical manner by reducing the graph until either $n \mid m$ or $m \mid n$.

Proof: This follows by Theorems 2 and 3 since reduction until $n \mid m$ or $m \mid n$ is necessary for the terminal schedule to be an SAS by Theorem 3, and the back substitution process preserves the VBMLB by Theorem 2.

Theorem 5: The number of reductions needed to reduce a two-actor SDF graph to a PSG is polynomial in the size of the SDF graph and is bounded by $O(\log n + \log m)$.

Proof: This follows by Lame's theorem that the Euclidean GCD algorithm runs in polynomial time. A complete proof is given in [6].

Thus, we can implement the minimum buffer schedule in a recursive, hierarchical manner, where the number of subroutine calls is guaranteed to be polynomially bounded in the size of the original two-actor SDF graph.

4   Extension to Arbitrary SAS

Any SAS S can be represented as an *R-schedule*,

$$S = (i_L S_L)(i_R S_R) \ ,$$

where S_L is the schedule for a "left" portion of the graph and S_R is the schedule for the corresponding "right" portion [1]. The schedules S_L, S_R can be recursively decomposed this way until we obtain schedules for two-actor graphs. In fact, the decomposition above can be represented as a clustered graph where the top level graph has two hierarchical actors and one or more edges between them. Each hierarchical actor in turn contains two-actor graphs with hierarchical actors until we reach two-actor graphs with non-hierarchical actors. Fig. 3 shows an SDF graph, an SAS for it, and the resulting cluster hierarchy.

This suggests that the hierarchical implementation of the minimum buffer schedule can be applied naturally to an arbitrary SAS starting at the top-most level. In Fig. 3, the graph in (d) is a PSG and has the SAS $(2W_2)W_3$. We then decompose the actors W_2 and W_3. For W_3, the graph is also a PSG, and has the schedule $E \, (5D)$. Similarly, the graph for W_2 is also a PSG with the schedule $W_1(2C)$. Finally, the graph for W_1 is also a PSG, and has the schedule $(3A)B$. Hence, in this example, no reductions are needed at any stage in the hierarchy at all, and the overall buffering requirement is $20 + 2 = 22$ for the graph in (d), 10 for W_3, 8 for W_2, and 3 for W_1, for a total requirement of 43. The VBMLB for this graph is 29. The reason that even the hierarchical decomposition does not yield the VBMLB is that the clustering process amplifies the produced/consumed parameters on edges, and inflates the VBMLB costs on those edges.

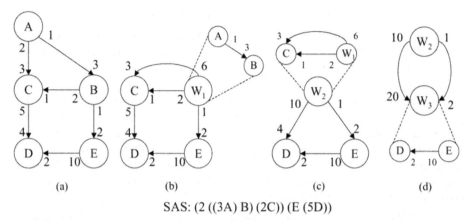

SAS: (2 ((3A) B) (2C)) (E (5D))

Fig. 3. An SAS showing how an SDF graph can be decomposed into a series of two-actor sub-graphs.

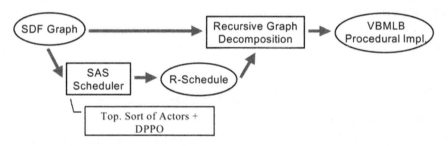

Fig. 4. An algorithm overview for arbitrary SDF graphs.

The extension to an arbitrary SDF graph, in other words, is to compute the VBMLB of the cluster hierarchy that underlies the given R-schedule. That is the goal the graph decomposition achieves and an algorithm overview is illustrated in Fig. 4. The VBMLB of the cluster hierarchy is calculated through summation over the VBMLB of all edges at each hierarchical level (e.g., W_1, W_2, W_3, and the top-most level comprising W_2 and W_3 in Fig. 3). We denote this cost as the *VBMLB for a graph cluster hierarchy* and for the example of Fig. 3, the cluster hierarchy VBMLB is 43 as computed in the previous paragraph.

To obtain an R-schedule, DPPO is a useful algorithm to start with. As discussed in Sect. 2, DPPO is a dynamic programming approach to generating an SAS with minimal buffering cost. Because the original DPPO algorithm pertains to direct implementation in SAS form, the cost function in the dynamic programming approach is based on a buffering requirement calculation that assumes such implementation as an SAS. If, however, the SAS is to be processed using the decomposition techniques developed in Sect. 4, the VBMLB value for an edge e,

$$prd(e) + cns(e) - gcd(prd(e), cns(e)) ,$$

is a more appropriate cost criterion for the dynamic programming formulation. This modified DPPO approach will evaluate a VBMLB-optimized R-schedule, which provides a hierarchical clustering suitable for our recursive graph decomposition.

Although we have shown that the number of decompositions required to reach a PSG is polynomial for a two-actor SDF graph, it is not obvious from this that the complexity of our recursive decomposition approach for arbitrary graphs is also polynomial. For arbitrary graphs, the clustering process expands the produced/consumed numbers; in fact, these numbers can increase multiplicatively. Because of the nature of the logarithm operator, however, the multiplicatively-increased rates still keep the decomposition process of polynomial complexity in the size of the input SDF graph. Full details on this complexity result can be found in [6].

Notice that we had to deal with multiple edges between actors in the above example. It is not immediately obvious whether there exists a schedule for a two-actor graph with multiple edges between the two actors that will simultaneously yield the VBMLB on each edge individually. We prove several results below that guarantee that there does exist such a schedule, and that a schedule that yields the VBMLB on any one edge yields the VBMLB on all edges simultaneously.

Consider the consistent two-actor graph shown in Fig. 5. The repetitions vector satisfies the following equations:

$$q(W_1)p_i = q(W_2)c_i \qquad \forall i = 1, ..., k . \qquad (2)$$

The fact that the graph is consistent means that (2) has a valid, non-zero solution.

Lemma 1: Suppose that $p_1 \leq ... \leq p_k$. Then $c_1 \leq ... \leq c_k$.

Proof: Suppose not. Suppose that for some i,j, we have $p_i \leq p_j$ but $c_i > c_j$. Equation (2) implies that $c_i/p_i = c_j/p_j$. But $p_i \leq p_j$ and $c_i > c_j$ implies $c_i/p_i > c_j/p_j$, contradicting (2). **QED**.

Now consider the two graphs shown in Fig. 6. Let these graphs have the same repetitions vector. Thus, we have

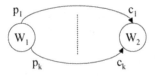

Fig. 5. A two-actor SDF multi-graph.

Fig. 6. Two two-actor graphs with the same repetitions vector.

$$q(A)p_1 = q(B)c_1 \text{ and } q(A)p_2 = q(B)c_2 . \tag{3}$$

Theorem 6: The two graphs in Fig. 6 (I) and (II) have the same set of valid schedules.

Proof: Suppose not. Suppose there is a schedule for (I) that is not valid for (II). Let σ be the firing sequence $X_1 X_2 ... X_{q(A)+q(B)}$, where $X_i \in \{A, B\}$. Since σ is not valid for (II), there is some point at which a negative state would be reached in this firing sequence in graph (II). By a negative state, we mean a state in which at least one buffer has had more tokens consumed from it than the number of tokens that have been produced into it. That is, after n_A, n_B firings of A and B respectively, we have $n_A p_2 - n_B c_2 < 0$ while $n_A p_1 - n_B c_1 \geq 0$. So,

$$0 \leq n_A p_1 - n_B c_1 < n_B \frac{c_2}{p_2} p_1 - n_B c_1 .$$

By (3), we have $c_1/p_1 = c_2/p_2$. Thus $n_B(c_2/p_2)p_1 - n_B c_1 = 0$, giving a contradiction. **QED**.

Theorem 7: The schedule that yields the VBMLB for (I) also yields the same VBMLB for (II).

Proof: Let σ be the firing sequence $X_1 X_2 ... X_{q(A)+q(B)}$, where $X_i \in \{A, B\}$, that yields the VBMLB for (I). By Theorem 6, σ is valid for (II) also. Since σ is the VBMLB schedule for (I), at some point, after n_A^*, n_B^* firings of A and B respectively, we have

$$n_A^* p_1 - n_B^* c_1 = p_1 + c_1 - gcd(p_1, c_1) \tag{4}$$

and for all other n_A and n_B in σ,

$$n_A p_1 - n_B c_1 \leq n_A^* p_1 - n_B^* c_1 . \tag{5}$$

We have that

$$n_A^* p_2 - n_B^* c_2 = n_A^* p_2 - n_B^* \frac{p_2}{p_1} c_1$$

$$= p_2 \left(n_A^* - \frac{c_1}{p_1} n_B^* \right)$$

$$= p_2 \left(n_A^* + \frac{p_1 + c_1 - gcd(p_1, c_1) - n_A^* p_1}{p_1} \right)$$

$$= p_2 \left(1 + \frac{c_1}{p_1} - \frac{gcd(p_1, c_1)}{p_1} \right)$$

$$= p_2 + c_2 - \frac{gcd(p_1, c_1)}{p_1} p_2$$

$$= p_2 + c_2 - gcd\left(p_1 \frac{p_2}{p_1}, \frac{c_1 p_2}{p_1}\right)$$

$$= p_2 + c_2 - gcd(p_2, c_2)$$

By (5), we have

$$n_A \le n_B \frac{c_1}{p_1} + 1 + \frac{c_1}{p_1} - \frac{gcd(p_1, c_1)}{p_1} \ .$$

Thus,

$$n_A p_2 - n_B c_2 \le \left(n_B \frac{c_1}{p_1} + 1 + \frac{c_1}{p_1} - \frac{gcd(p_1, c_1)}{p_1}\right) p_2 - n_B c_2 = p_2 + c_2 - gcd(p_2, c_2) \ .$$

Hence, this shows that σ yields the VBMLB for (II) also. **QED.**

Theorem 8: For the graph in Fig. 5, there is a schedule that yields the VBMLB on every edge simultaneously.

Proof: Follows from the above results.

5   CD-DAT Example

Given the CD-DAT example in Fig. 7, the DPPO algorithm returns the SAS $(7(7(3AB)(2C))(4D))(32E(5F))$. This schedule can be decomposed into two-actor clustered graphs as shown in Fig. 8. The complete procedure call sequence is shown in Fig. 9, where each vertex represents a subroutine, and the edges represent caller-callee relationships. The generated C style code is shown as well in Fig. 10. The total buffer memory requirement is:

$$(32 + 7 - 1) + (4 + 7 - 1) + (2 + 3 - 1) + 5 + 1 = 58$$

This is a 72% improvement over the best requirement of 205 obtained for a strictly inlined implementation of a SAS. The requirement of 205 is obtained by using a buffer merging technique [11].

6   Experimental Results

Our optimization algorithm is particularly beneficial to a certain class of applications. The statement of Theorem 3 tells us that no reduction is needed for edges with production and consumption rates that are multiples of one another. We call such edges *uni-*

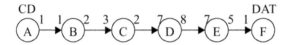

Fig. 7. A CD-DAT sample rate converter example.

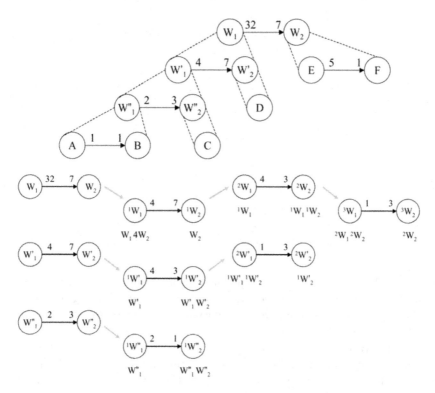

Fig. 8. The recursive decomposition of the CD-DAT graph.

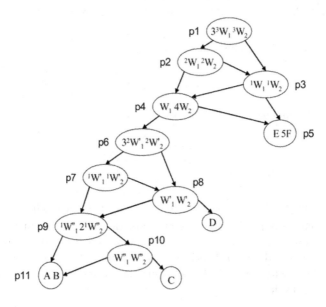

Fig. 9. Procedure call sequence for the CD-DAT example.

```
p1() {
    for (int i=0; i<3; i++) {
        p2();
    }
    p3();
}

p2() {
    p4();
    p3();
}

p3() {
    p4();
    p5();
}

p4() {
    p6();
    for (int i=0; i<4; i++) {
        p5();
    }
}
```

```
p5() {
    inline of actor E;
    for (int i=0; i<5; i++) {
        inline of actor F;
    }
}

p6() {
    for (int i=0; i<3; i++) {
        p7();
    }
    p8();
}

p7() {
    p9();
    p8();
}

p8() {
    p9();
    inline of actor D;
}
```

```
p9() {
    p11();
    for (int i=0; i<2; i++) {
        p10();
    }
}

p10() {
    p11();
    inline of actor C;
}

p11() {
    inline of actor A;
    inline of actor B;
}
```

Fig. 10. Generated C code for the CD-DAT example.

form edges. Precisely, if an edge e has production and consumption rates m and n, respectively, then e is uniform if either $m|n$ or $n|m$. Our proposed strategy can improve buffering cost for *non-uniform* edges and generate the same buffering cost as existing SAS techniques for uniform edges.

We define two metrics for measuring this form of uniformity for a given SDF graph $G = (V, E)$ and an associated R-schedule S. For this purpose, we denote E_c as the set of edges in the cluster hierarchy associated with S. Thus, $|E_c| = |E|$ since every $e \in E$ has a corresponding edge in one of the clustered two-actor subgraphs associated with S. The set E_c can be partitioned into two sets: the uniform edge set E_u, which consists of the uniform edges, and the non-uniform edge set E_{nu}, which consists of the remaining edges.

Metric 1: Uniformity based on edge count:

$$U_1(G, S) = \frac{|E_u|}{|E|}.$$

Metric 2: Uniformity based on buffer cost:

$$U_2(G, S) = \frac{\sum_{e \in E_u} b(e)}{\sum_{e \in E} b(e)},$$

where $b(e)$ is the buffer cost on edge e for the given graph and schedule.

Our procedural implementation technique produces no improvement in buffering cost when uniformity is 100% (note that 100% uniformity for Metric 1 is equivalent to 100% uniformity for Metric 2). This is because if uniformity is 100%, then the two-actor graphs in the cluster hierarchy do not require any decomposition to achieve their associated VBMLB values.

Table 1: Experimental results for real applications.

	actor count	edge count	U_1 (%)	U_2 (%)	buffer cost ratio (%)
aqmf235_2d	20	22	90	88	88
aqmf235_3d	44	50	76	70	76
aqmf23_2d	20	22	90	86	93
aqmf23_3d	44	50	80	70	87
nqmf23	32	35	82	84	86
cd2dat	8	7	42	4	9
cd2dat2	6	5	40	10	21
dat2cd	5	4	50	17	14
filtBankNu	26	28	82	83	90
cdma2k_rev	143	157	96	77	90

We examined several SDF applications that exhibit uniformity values below 100%, and the results are listed in Table 1. The first three columns give the benchmark names and graph sizes. Uniformity is measured by the proposed metrics and is listed in the fourth and fifth columns. The R-schedule in the uniformity computation is generated by the combination of APGAN and DPPO [1]. The last column is the *buffer cost ratio* of our procedural implementation over an R-schedule calculated by the combination of APGAN and DPPO. A lower ratio means that our procedural implementation consumes less buffer cost. The first five *qmf* benchmarks are multirate filter bank systems with different depths and low-pass and high-pass components. Following those are three sample rate converters: *cd2dat*, *cd2dat2*, and *dat2cd*. The function of *cd2dat2* is equivalent to *cd2dat* except for an alternative breakdown into multiple stages. A two-channel non-uniform filter bank with depth of two is given in *filtBankNu*. The last benchmark *cdma2k_rev* is a CDMA example of a reverse link using HPSK modulation and demodulation under SR3.

Uniformity and buffer cost ratio are roughly in a linear relationship in Table 1. To further explore this relationship between buffer cost ratio and uniformity, we experimented with a large set of randomly-generated SDF graphs, and the results are illustrated in Fig. 11. Both charts in the figure exhibit an approximately proportional relationship between uniformity and buffer cost ratio. The lower the uniformity, the lower the buffer cost ratio.

To better understand the overheads of execution time and code size for procedural over inlined implementation, we examined the cd2dat and dat2cd examples in more detail. In the experiment for *cd2dat*, we obtained 0.75% and 10.85% execution time and code size overheads, respectively, compared to inlined implementations of the schedules returned by APGAN and GDPPO. In the experiment for *dat2cd*, the overheads observed were 1.26% and 9.45% respectively. In these experiments, we used the Code Composer Studio by Texas Instruments for the *TMS320C67x* series processors. In gen-

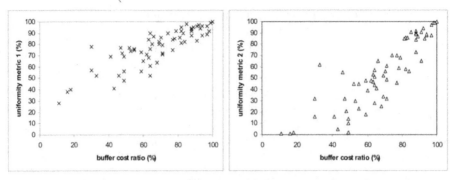

Fig. 11. Relationship between uniformity and buffer cost ratio for random graphs.

eral the overheads depend heavily on the granularity of the actors. In the applications of Table 1, the actors are mostly of coarse granularity. However, in the presence of many fine-grained (low complexity) actors, the relative overheads are likely to increase; and for such applications, the procedural implementation approach proposed in this paper is less favorable, unless buffer memory constraints are especially severe.

7   Conclusion

In this paper, an efficient method is developed for applying subroutine call instantiation of module functionality when synthesizing embedded software from an SDF specification. This approach provides for significantly lower buffer sizes, with polynomially bounded procedure call overhead, than what is available for minimum code size, inlined schedules. This recursive decomposition approach thus provides an efficient means for integrating subroutine-based module instantiation into the design space of DSP software synthesis. We develop metrics for characterizing a certain form of uniformity in SDF schedules, and show that the benefits of the proposed techniques increase with decreasing uniformity. Directions for future work include integrating the procedural implementation approach in this paper with existing techniques for inlined implementation. For example, different subgraphs in an SDF specification may be best handled using different techniques, depending on application constraints and subgraph characteristics (e.g., based on uniformity, as defined in this paper, and actor granularity). Integration with other strategies for buffer optimization such as phased scheduling [4] and buffer merging [11] are also useful directions for further investigation.

Acknowledgement

This research was supported in part by the Semiconductor Research Corporation (2001-HJ-905).

References

[1]   S. S. Bhattacharyya, P. K. Murthy, and E. A. Lee. *Software Synthesis from Dataflow Graphs*. Kluwer Academic Publishers. 1996.

[2]   J. Buck and R. Vaidyanathan. Heterogeneous modeling and simulation of embedded systems in El Greco. In *Proceedings of the International Workshop on Hardware/Software Co-Design*, May 2000.

[3]   J. Eker et al. Taming heterogeneity — the Ptolemy approach. *Proceedings of the IEEE*, January 2003.

[4]   M. Karczmarek, W. Thies, and S. Amarasinghe. Phased scheduling of stream programs. *Proceedings of Languages, Compilers, and Tools for Embedded Systems (LCTES'03)*, pages 103-112, San Diego, California, June 2003.

[5]   M. Karczmarek, W. Thies, and S. Amarasinghe. StreamIt: A Language for Streaming Applications. *Proceedings of the International Conference on Compiler Construction*, Grenoble, France, April 2002.

[6]   M. Ko, P. K. Murthy, and S. S. Bhattacharyya. Compact procedural synthesis of DSP software through recursive graph decomposition. Technical Report UMIACS-TR-2004-41, Institute for Advanced Computer Studies, University of Maryland at College Park, 2004.

[7]   K. N. Lalgudi, M. C. Papaefthymiou, and M. Potkonjak. Optimizing computations for effective block-processing. *ACM Transactions on Design Automation of Electronic Systems*, 5(3):604-630, July 2000.

[8]   R. Lauwereins, M. Engels, M. Ade, and J. A. Peperstraete. Grape-II: A system-level prototyping environment for DSP applications. *IEEE Computer Magazine*, 28(2):35-43, February 1995.

[9]   E. A. Lee and D. G. Messerschmitt. Synchronous dataflow. *Proceedings of IEEE*, vol. 75, pp. 1235–1245, September 1987.

[10] R. Leupers and P. Marwedel. Time-constrained code compaction for DSP's. *IEEE Transactions on Very Large Scale Integration (VLSI) Systems*, 5(1):112-122, March 1997.

[11] P. K. Murthy and S. S. Bhattacharyya. Buffer merging : a powerful technique for reducing memory requirements of synchronous dataflow specifications. *ACM Transactions on Design Automation of Electronic Systems*, 9(2):212-237, April 2004.

[12] P. K. Murthy, E. G. Cohen, and S. Rowland. System Canvas: A new design environment for embedded DSP and telecommunication systems. In *Proceedings of the International Workshop on Hardware/Software Co-Design*, April 2001.

[13] P. R. Panda, F. Catthoor, N. D. Dutt, et. al. Data and Memory Optimization Techniques for Embedded Systems. *ACM Transactions on Design Automation for Electronic Systems*, 6(2):149-206, April 2001.

[14] S. Ritz, M. Pankert, V. Zivojnovic, and H. Meyer. Optimum vectorization of scalable synchronous dataflow graphs. *Proceedings of the International Conference on Application Specific Array Processors*, pp. 285-296, October 1993.

[15] C. B. Robbins. *Autocoding Toolset software tools for automatic generation of parallel application software*. Technical report, Management, Communications & Control, Inc., 2002.

[16] T. Stefanov, C. Zissulescu, A. Turjan, B. Kienhuis, and E. Deprettere. System design using Kahn process networks: the Compaan/Laura approach. In *Proceedings of the Design, Automation and Test in Europe Conference*, February 2004.

[17] W. Sung and S. Ha. Memory Efficient Software Synthesis using Mixed Coding Style from Dataflow Graph. *IEEE Transactions on VLSI Systems*, Vol. 8, pp 522-526, October 2000.

[18] E. Zitzler, J. Teich, and S. S. Bhattacharyya. Multidimensional exploration of software implementations for DSP algorithms. *Journal of VLSI Signal Processing Systems for Signal, Image, and Video Technology*, pp. 83-98, February 2000.

An Integer Linear Programming Approach
to Classify the Communication in Process Networks

Alexandru Turjan, Bart Kienhuis, and Ed Deprettere

Leiden Institute of Advanced Computer Science (LIACS)
Leiden, The Netherlands
aturjan@liacs.nl

Abstract. New embedded signal processing architectures are emerging that are composed of loosely coupled heterogeneous components like CPUs or DSPs, specialized IP cores, reconfigurable units, or memories. We believe that these architectures should be programmed using the Process Network model of computation. To ease the mapping of applications, we are developing the *Compaan* compiler that automatically derives a Process Network (PN) description from an application written in input Matlab. In this paper, we investigate a particular problem in nested loop programs, which is about classifying the interprocess communication in the PN representation of the nested loop program. The global memory arrays present in the Matlab code have to be replaced by a distributed communication structure used for sending data to the network processes. We will show that four types of communication exists, each exhibiting different requirements when realizing them in hardware of software. We present two compile time tests that decide the type of the communication corresponding to a particular static array. These tests are based on Integer Linear Programming and have become an important part of our Compaan compiler.

1 Introduction

Applications that are envisioned for the next decade in the area of multi-media, imaging, bioinformatics, and classical signal processing have a ferocious appetite for compute power. To satisfy this appetite, new embedded signal processing architectures are emerging. These are typically composed of loosely coupled heterogeneous components that exchange data using programmable interconnections such as a switch matrix or a network on chip (NoC). The components can be CPUs or DSPs, specialized IP cores, reconfigurable units, or memories. Also, a central control microprocessor is present for the configuration of the components at run-time using a low-bandwidth bus. An impression of such architecture is shown in Figure 1. Aside from the use of specialized heterogeneous components and instruction level parallelism on the CPUs, these architectures will employ more and more *task level parallelism* to deliver the required performance.

From a technology standpoint, companies and research institutions are already able to build instances of the presented architecture. Three examples are, for example, the *Picochip* from PicoChip, the *Virtex Pro* from Xilinx, and although still in research, the *SpaceCAKE* architecture from Philips. The PicoChip combines 430 simple RISC architectures on a single die [10]. Xilinx combines FPGA technology with four embedded

H. Schepers (Ed.): SCOPES 2004, LNCS 3199, pp. 62–76, 2004.

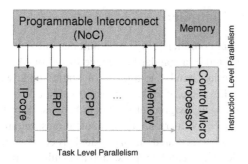

Fig. 1. Embedded Signal Processing Architecture consisting of loosely coupled heterogeneous components like CPUs, DSPs, Specialized IP cores, Reconfigurable Components, and Memories.

PowerPCs on their Virtex-Pro chips [22]. Philips is researching the SpaceCAKE architecture which consists of a heterogeneous mix of memories, CPUs like the MIPS or the ARM and DSPs [15]. We observe that the problem with these heterogeneous architectures is not building them, but *programming* them, i.e., writing programs that take advantage of the offered heterogeneity and task-level parallelism. Writing a program for such an architecture means partitioning the application over the various components of the architecture and generating embedded software for each component. In case of a CPU or DSP, this means writing a piece of C code and in case of an IP core or reconfigurable unit, it means writing a VHDL or Verilog program. This partitioning and compilations are very time consuming and error prone, which makes the deployment of the heterogeneous architectures difficult.

We believe that the PN model of computation is suitable to cope with the heterogeneity of the new embedded architectures. Still, writing application in a PN format is a time consuming process. Therefore, we are developing the *Compaan* compiler [7, 14], which automatically derives a Process Network (PN) description from an application written in Matlab. Using Compaan, we can quickly derive PNs from existing applications and then map them on heterogeneous embedded architectures.

In this paper, we investigate a particular problem in the Compaan compiler regarding the ability to classify the interprocess communication in a PN. Within Compaan, we distribute the memory arrays present in the input program over a number of communication structures used for transmitting data between network's processes. We will show that four types of communication exist, each exhibiting different requirements when a hardware or software implementation is generated. Each communication structure in a process networks is classified to one of the four types, using two tests that are described in this paper. These tests can be performed at compile time and have become an important part of our Compaan compiler.

This paper is organized as follows. In Section 2, we explain our Compaan compiler project. The four kinds of communication in a process network are presented in Section 3. In Section 4 we presented related work. In Section 5 and Section 6, we present the two tests used for a compile time classification of the communication structures in a process network. In Section 7 we present some results and we conclude this paper in Section 8.

2   The Compaan Compiler

The aim of the *Compaan* compiler [7, 14] is to automatically derive a PN description
from an application written in a standard language like C or Matlab as shown in Figure 2. It presents on the left-hand side a piece of Matlab code with four assignment
statements (F1 .. F4). This piece of code is transformed in a PN, as given in the right-
hand side. In Compaan, each assignment statement becomes a process and each static
array (r1 and r2) is replaced by distributed communication structures; in this case FIFO
buffers. Once the PN has been created, the individual processes can either be described
as Java [3] or C++ code [5], or can be represented as synthesizable VHDL suitable for
mapping onto a hardware platform [23]. As an example, we can map process F1 and F4
onto a CPU and processes F2 and F3 onto dedicated IP cores or reconfigurable block.
The FIFOs are mapped either onto the communication structure or directly implemented
as FIFOs.

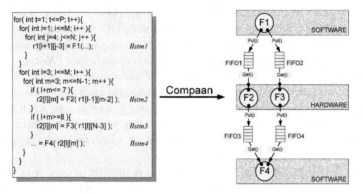

Fig. 2. From a sequential application to functionally equivalent Process Network.

An application written as a Process Network exhibits *distributed memory* and *distributed control* [14]. The distributed memory and control are essential when programming a distributed architecture as given in Figure 1, as the model of computation of a PN
matches the way the architecture operates. Distributed memory means that not all components read and write to the same memory block, which usually leads to memory bottlenecks. Instead, components exchange data over separated communication channels,
each channel being addressed by only two components acting in a Producer/Consumer
manner. Distributed control means that each component can make progress on its own;
it is not under the control of some global controller, which fits the loosely coupled
components.

The Compaan compiler itself consists of three tools. The first tool, called *Mat-
Parser*, uses exact data dependence analysis to transforms the initial Matlab code into
single assignment code (SAC). The second tool, called *DgParser*, converts the SAC into
a Polyhedral Reduced Dependence Graph (PRDG) data structure, which is a compact
mathematical representation of the DG in terms of polyhedra. The third tool, called
Panda, converts the PRDG into a Process Network, associating a process with each
node of the PRDG.

3   Problem Description

In the single assignment code obtained after running MatParser, data is being communicating between assignment statements by sharing global single assignment arrays. In order to derive a PN, the single assignment code is broken into processes. Since we now have multiple processes accessing the global arrays, we need to replace them with distributed communication structures. We do not want to map the static array onto some shared memory, which is the typical approach. Shared memory contradicts with the desirable notion of distributed memory. Instead, we want to map the static array onto a truly distributed communication structure. This procedure represents an essential step in Panda that we call *Linearization* [12].

In Figure 3, we show two functions F1 and F2 which are respectively the producer of data in array $a(x)$ and the consumer of data in array $a(i)$. In Panda, these two functions F1 and F2 are split into separate processes to form a process network. Due to the splitting, we need to replace the static array a by a new communication structure. This would typically be an unbounded FIFO buffer that is accessed using a *blocking-read* primitive. However, the question is whether we can always do this replacement, as indicated by the question mark in Figure 3. To answer this question, we investigate the characteristics of accessing static arrays. As we will show, four different types of communicating data are possible.

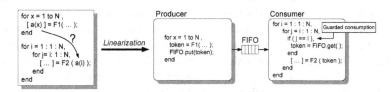

Fig. 3. Linearization of static array a.

3.1   Producer/Consumer Model

The tool DgParser translates the single assignment program to a polyhedral reduced dependence graph (PRDG). This PRDG is accepted by Panda, which transforms the PRDG in such a way that each edge of the graph represents a point-to-point communication. In this process, the original static arrays have been partitioned over a number of edges. For example, in Figure 2, the static array r1 and r2 are both replaced by two FIFO buffers. This means that the content of the arrays is distributed over four FIFO buffers. This step is beyond the scope of this article but is an essential step in Panda. Once the point-to-point communication is established, each edge representing the point-to-point communication needs to be linearized between a producer and a consumer node. Each edge can be abstracted to a simple Producer/Consumer (P/C) pair, as shown in Figure 3. The Producer and the Consumer have parameterized polyhedral iteration domains that are related through an affine transformation. Depending on this transformation, described by the mapping matrix M and the structure of the for-loops in

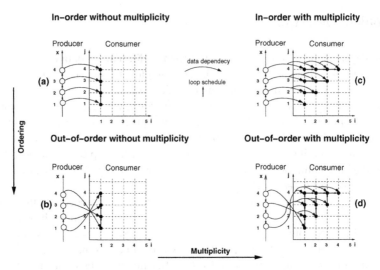

Fig. 4. The four types of communication of a static array in a Producer/Consumer pairs.

the original Matlab program, we have found that four different kinds of communicating data can be distinguished in process networks.

These four types of communication are given in Figure 4. They result from the *ordering* of the iterations at the Producer and the Consumer processes and the existence of *multiplicity* for a given token, which means that a token that is sent by the Producer is read more than once at the Consumer side. In Figure 4, we represent the iterations with small circles. These iterations are ordered as indicated by the small arrows representing the loop schedule of the for-loops in the original Matlab program. We also show the relationship between the production of data at an iteration and the consumption of that data at one or more iterations, using a data-dependency function.

In Figure 4(a), we see that the schedule of both the producer and consumer are the same. The producer iterates from 1 to 4 using an iterator x. The consumer iterates in the same order from 1 to 4 using an an iterator j. We can see that data produced at one iteration is consumed at the consumer side in the same order, and by only one iteration. For example, the data produced at iteration x = 3 is consumed at iteration j = 3. In Figure 4(b), we see that although the schedule of both the Producer and Consumer is the same, the Consumer consumes data in the opposite order due to the dependency. We can see that data produced at one iteration is consumed at the consumer side in the opposite order by only a single iteration. For example, the data produced at iteration x = 3 is consumed at iteration j = 2. In Figure 4(c), we see that the schedule of the Consumer is two-dimensional (i,j). We see that for some iterations a token from the Producer is consumed more than once. This consumption takes place in the same order as it is produced. For example, we see that the token created at $x = 3$ is consumed multiple times at iterations $(i, j) = (1, 3), (2, 3), (3, 3)$. Finally, In Figure 4(d), we see again that the schedule of the Consumer is still two-dimensional and that at some iterations a produced token is consumed more than once. However, in this case, the tokens are consumed in a different order from the one in which they are produced, due to the dependency function. For example, we see that the token produced at $x = 3$ is consumed out-of-order multiple times at iterations $(i, j) = (1, 2), (2, 2)$. We have named the four communication types as shown in Table 1.

Table 1. The four types of communication.

Name	Type	Figure
IOM-	In Order without Multiplicity	4(a)
OOM-	Out Of Order without Multiplicity	4(b)
IOM+	In Order with Multiplicity	4(c)
OOM+	Out Of Order with Multiplicity	4(d)

Looking at the example code given in Figure 3, we observe that the communication of a is of type IOM+. Now, by making small changes to the program, we will show how the other three types can be obtained. If we remove the j for-loop, we obtain a the linearization of a of type IOM-. If we take again the original example, but let iterator x run from 4 to 1, we get that the linearization of a is of type OOM+. If we remove again iterator j, we observe that the linearization of a is of type OOM-.

So we know that four types of linearization exist in any nested loop program when we want to replace the static array by a distributed communication structure. We need to investigate in which linearization case we can simply replace the static array with a FIFO buffer accessed by a put/get primitive. Only in the case of type IOM-, we can simply replace the variable by a FIFO. However, in the example given in Figure 3 where multiplicity takes place we can still rely on a simple FIFO linearization by adding a guard if-statement to take care of the life-time of a token read from the FIFO [18].

In the case of the two remaining communication types, two additional elements may be needed. If re-ordering is an issue, a controller is needed that re-orders a stream of tokens using some private memory to temporarily store tokens for reordering. If multiplicity is involved, a controller is needed that indicates when the life-time of a token comes to an end and the token can be released. The controller for reordering, the life-time controller, and the reordering memory define what we call the *Extended Linearization Model* (ELM), which has been introduced in [17, 18]. In these papers we also explain how to derive at compile time the re-ordering and the life-time controller. In the ELM we place the reordering memory and the controllers at the Consumer process, but between processes we still model the use of FIFO buffers, thereby adhering to the PN model of computation.

Depending on the type of communication, a static array is replaced in the following way:

- **IOM-** An in-order P/C pair is linearized using only a FIFO buffer.
- **IOM+** An in-order with multiplicity P/C pair is linearized using a FIFO buffer and controller to determine the life-time of a token.
- **OOM-** An out-of-order P/C pair is linearized using a FIFO buffer, reordering memory, and a controller to perform the reordering. Since multiplicity is not involved,

each time the controller accesses the reordering memory for reading data, the corresponding memory location can be immediately released.
- **OOM+** An out-of-order with multiplicity P/C pair is linearized using a FIFO buffer, reordering memory, and a controller to perform reordering and to determine the life-time of a token.

Notice that the implementations of the linearization models described above increase in their complexity (both hardware and software), from IOM- to OOM+. Therefore, it is very important to select the correct linearization type. The implementation of IOM- and IOM+ are closely related, except that in IOM- a controller is needed to know when to release data from the FIFO. The implementation of OOM- and OOM+ requires additional reordering memory and at least one reorder controller. Of the four models identified, OOM+ is the most expensive linearization to be realized. It is also the generic linearization since it subsumes all other possible linearization.

3.2   Definition of Multiplicity and Re-ordering

We now give a formal definition of a P/C pair, multiplicity and reordering.

Definition 1 *A P/C pair is a tuple* $< \mathcal{C}(p), f, P(p), \prec >$, *where* $\mathcal{C}(p) \subset R^n$ *is a parameterized polytope,* $f : R^n \to R^m$ *is an affine function,* $P(p) = f(\mathcal{C}(p) \cap Z^n)$, *and* $\prec$ *is the lexicographical order.*

The set of integer points inside the parameterized polytope $\mathcal{C}(p)$ is called the *Consumer domain*, or the *Consumer iteration space*. The affine function f specifies the data dependencies and is represented by an $(m \times n)$ integral matrix M, and an m-dimensional offset vector O, i.e., $f(x) = Mx + O$. There are no additional constraints imposed to the mapping matrix M. As a consequence, the *Producer domain (iteration space)* is represented by a *linearly bounded lattice* (LBL) [16] given by the integer polyhedral image:

$$P(p) = f(\mathcal{C}(p) \cap Z^n) = \{i \in Z^m \mid i = Mk + O \land k \in (\mathcal{C}(p) \cap Z^n)\}. \quad (1)$$

If $x \in \mathcal{C}(p)$ and $y \in P(p)$ are two elements (or *iteration points (IPs)*) such that $y = f(x)$, we say that the IP x consumes data produced by the IP y. Although $P(p)$ is by definition an LBL, in [18], we have shown that the Producer iteration space can be represented as union of polytopes. Therefore, without loss of generality, in the remainder of this paper we assume that the Producer is a polytope. We also assume that $O = 0$, such that f is represented only the matrix M.

Depending on the mapping matrix M, and on the schedule of producing and consuming data as given by the lexicographical order, four different kinds of P/C pairs can be distinguished (see Figure 4) based on the following two definitions:

Definition 2 *A P/C pair is **in-order** iff the mapping preserves the order, i.e. every two Consumer iteration points* $x_1 \prec x_2$ *are mapped onto two Producer iteration points* $(y_1 = Mx_1)$ *and* $(y_2 = Mx_2)$ *such that* $y_1 \preceq y_2$. *If the P/C pair is not in order it is called **out-of-order**.*

Definition 3 *A P/C pair is* **without multiplicity** *iff the mapping* $M : (C \cap Z^n) \to P$ *(i.e., the mapping M restricted to the Consumer domain) is injective. Otherwise we say that the P/C pair is* **with multiplicity**.

According to the previous definitions, an arbitrary P/C pair belongs to one of the four types as given in Table 1. The implementation cost of the linearization types increases from IOM- to OOM+. Therefore, to come to an optimal replacement of the static arrays, we need to be able to know at compile time to which type of communication an arbitrary P/C pair belongs.

4 Related Work

By replacing the shared arrays with FIFO buffers we get a flexible communication structure which allows to find a good balance between memory reuse and inter-process parallelism [9, 1]. There are several papers that are dealing with compile-time analysis of memory reuse in static nested loop programs. In [19] an approach is presented for a fixed linearization of the memory array. In [20, 11] a constructive approach is given in context of the single assignment language ALPHA, based on which the maximum life-time of an array can be derived for an optimal memory projection. In [8], in the process of parallelizing a static algorithm by removing output dependences, the authors propose a method of partial array expansion. In [4] an approach is presented to compute the bounding box for the elements that are simultaneously in use. The size of the original array is reduced to the bounding box and the array is accessed using modulo operations, improving in this way the memory usage. All the techniques presented so far rely on polytope manipulations and integer linear programming.

We have already presented a solution to determine the type of communication in [17]. In that paper, we presented a technique based on the Ehrhart theory [2] to determine the ordering and multiplicity. By comparing pseudo polynomial expressions, we could determine whether the schedule at the Consumer and Producer are the same. We could also determine if the pseudo polynomial was larger than one, indicating that multiplicity was involved. Although the presented procedure gives a definitive answer for the type of communication, the complexity of the pseudo polynomial calculations, the comparison of the pseudo polynomials, and the fact that the software implementation of Ehrhart cannot always derive a pseudo polynomial, made the approach unsuitable for our compiler.

5 Solution Approach

To classify a P/C pair to one of the four types, we need to be able to identify if data is reused more than once, and whether the ordering of producing data at the Producer side is the same as the order of consuming it at the Consumer. In this section, we present the techniques which allow us to determine the type of an arbitrary P/C pair. In Section 5.1, we provide a test that determines if a P/C pair is with or without multiplicity. In Section 5.2, we describe a test which determines whether a P/C pair is in-order or out-of-order. Using these two tests, we can determine at compile time to which of the four categories (IOM-, IOM+, OOM-, OOM+) an arbitrary P/C pair belongs.

5.1   The Multiplicity Test (MT)

The *Multiplicity Test* is used to check whether two Consumer iterations consume one and the same token. Consider an arbitrary P/C pair $< \mathcal{C}(p), M, P(p), \prec >$. According to *Definition 3*, this pair has multiplicity if there exist two different Consumer points x and y such that they are consuming the same token from the Producer as specified by the mapping M. These conditions can be captured in the following system that forms by definition the *Multiplicity Problem* (MP):

$$\text{MP}: \quad \begin{cases} x \in (\mathcal{C}(p) \cap Z^n), \\ y \in (\mathcal{C}(p) \cap Z^n), \\ x \neq y, \\ Mx = My. \end{cases} \tag{2}$$

In the first two equations, we take a point x and y from the Consumer that according to the third equation, are not the same. However, if we can find more than one point that map x and y via M to the same producer point, we have found that data is reused and thus multiplicity is involved. Therefore, the problem of deciding whether a P/C pair has multiplicity is reduced to testing the existence of a solution for the MP.

5.2   The Reordering Test (RT)

The *Reordering Test* is used to determine whether the order of producing tokens at the Producer side is the same as the order in which they are consumed at the Consumer side. According to *Definition 2* a P/C pair $< \mathcal{C}(p), M, P(p), \prec >$ is out-of-order if two different Consumer points $y \prec x$ exist such that $Mx \prec My$. These conditions can be captured in the following system that forms by definition the *Reordering Problem* (RP):

$$\text{RP}: \quad \begin{cases} x \in (\mathcal{C}(p) \cap Z^n), \\ y \in (\mathcal{C}(p) \cap Z^n), \\ x \prec y, \\ My \prec Mx. \end{cases} \tag{3}$$

In the first two equations, we take a point x and y from the Consumer, where x is lexicographically smaller than y according to Equation 3. However, If we can find more than one point that map x and y via M in such a way that x is still lexicographically smaller than y at the producer side, we have found that data is consumer in-order. Therefore, the problem of deciding whether reordering takes place in a P/C pair is reduced to testing the existence of a solution for the RP.

6   Realization of the Solution

In the previous section we introduced two tests. In this section we will show how they can be used in practice. In solving the systems, we exploit the fact that we can represent a Matlab program in terms of a PRDG. In such a PRDG, the iteration domains are represented by means of polytopes, allowing us to employ integer linear programming to find solutions to the MP and RP problems in an efficient way. Consequently, we can implement these tests and solve them to find the proper communication structure at compile time.

6.1 Empty Domain Test

Both the Multiplicity Test and the Reordering Test are so called *Existence tests* as we only need to determine whether a given system of constraints contains a solution. We are not interested in what the solution is, and therefore, do not need to compute this. A system of constraints has a solution if and only if it contains at least a single integer point. The procedure to determine if a polytope contains at least a single integer point is what we call the *Empty Domain Test* (ET). In both the RP and MP case, we build up a polytope and if such polytope contains at least a single integer point, a solution exists for the RP or MP.

To perform the Empty Domain Test, we can make use of integer linear programming (ILP) tools like *Pip* [6] or *Omega* [21]. These tools only work on systems of linear constraints, while the Multiplicity Problem and the Reordering Problem contain non-linear constraints. In case of the RP, the lexicographical order operator $\prec$ allows the following decomposition:

$$x \prec y \Leftrightarrow (x \prec_1 y) \vee (x \prec_2 y) \vee \dots \vee (x \prec_n y), \tag{4}$$

where, $x \prec_i y$ means that $x_1 = y_1, x_2 = y_2, \dots, x_{i-1} = y_{i-1}, x_i < y_i$. Suppose x and y are defined on a two-dimensional domain. Then the lexicographical expansions is represented by two polytope domains $\mathcal{D}_1 = \{(x_1, x_2) \in D \mid x_1 < y_1\}$ and $\mathcal{D}_2 = \{(x_1, x_2) \in D \mid x_1 = y_1 \wedge x_2 < y_2\}$.

In case of the MP, the negation is the non-linear operator. This negation can be rewritten to two inequalities, as follows:

$$x \neq y \Leftrightarrow y \prec x \vee x \prec y, \tag{5}$$

where we use again Equation 4 to convert the lexicographical operators to linear constraints.

Given the Empty Domain test and how to rewrite the appearance of the non-linear operation in the MP and RP, we now solve the MP and RP systems.

6.2 Solving the Multiplicity Test

By rewriting the negation in the Multiplicity problem given in Equation 2, using the substitution from Equation 5, the Multiplicity Problem is decomposed into two sub-problems: the *Primal Multiplicity Problem* and the *Dual Multiplicity Problem*:

$$\text{PMP}: \begin{cases} x \in (\mathcal{C}(p) \cap Z^n), & (1) \\ y \in (\mathcal{C}(p) \cap Z^n), & (2) \\ x \prec y, & (3') \\ Mx = My. & (4) \end{cases} \qquad \text{DMP}: \begin{cases} x \in (\mathcal{C}(p) \cap Z^n), & (1) \\ y \in (\mathcal{C}(p) \cap Z^n), & (2) \\ x \succ y, & (3'') \\ Mx = My. & (4) \end{cases}$$

The two sub-problems have the property that if (x, y) is a solution for one of them, it is also a solution for the MP. As a consequence:

$$\text{ET(MP)} = \text{ET(PMP)} \vee \text{ET(DMP)}. \tag{6}$$

On the other hand, if (x, y) is a solution for PMP then (y, x) is also a solution for DMP. In this way the MT is reduced to solving the empty test only of the PMP or the DMP. Therefore, in the remainder of this section, we will describe the solution for just the PMP problem. Given the lexicographical decomposition procedure expressed in Equation 4, the PMP is further decomposed into a series of n disjoint subproblems PMP_i, where $i = \overline{1, n}$:

$$\text{PMP}_i : \begin{cases} x = (x_1, x_2, ..., x_n)^T \in (\mathcal{C}(p) \cap Z^n), \\ y = (y_1, y_2, ..., y_n)^T \in (\mathcal{C}(p) \cap Z^n), \\ \begin{cases} (y_1, ..., y_{i-1}) = (x_1, ..., x_{i-1}), \\ x_i < y_i, \end{cases} \\ Mx = My \end{cases} \tag{4}$$

such that:

$$\text{ET(PMP)} = \bigvee_{i=1}^{n} \text{ET(PMP}_i). $$

If we find the existence of a solution for any of these systems, we thus find a solution for the MT. This signifies that multiplicity is involved in the linearization on the P/C pair under investigation. Hence, as soon as we have found the existence of a solution, we can stop.

Optimization. A substantial reduction of Empty Domain test can be achieved by using the Hermite Normal Form of the mapping matrix M [13]. The *Hermite Normal Form* (HNF) can be used to decompose an integral matrix M, using an unimodular matrix C, into an unique lower triangle matrix H such that:

$$M = [H0] \, C. \tag{7}$$

The unimodular matrix C does not affect the multiplicity as it always has an inverse. Hence, the multiplicity information is still contained in H. Therefore, by taking the HNF of the mapping matrix M, we obtain H that still captures the multiplicity characteristics of M. Suppose we obtain t zero columns when taking the HNF of M. Thus, the size of H is $n - t$, which is less or equal than the size of M. Consequently, we need to test less MP systems for empty domains.

6.3   Solving the Reordering Test

By rewriting the negation in the Reordering Problem given in Equation 3, using the substitution from Equation 4, the Reordering test is decomposed in a number of systems that need to be tested using the Empty Domain test. Suppose the Consumer domain is contained into a n-dimensional iteration space such that $x = (x_1, x_2, ..., x_n)^T$ and $y = (y_1, y_2, ..., y_n)^T$ are two different points in the same Consumer domain. Suppose that the matrix M has k rows : $M = \begin{bmatrix} M_1 \\ \vdots \\ M_k \end{bmatrix}$. Using the lexicographical decomposition procedure, the RP is decomposed into $n \times k$ disjoint subproblems given as RP_{ij}, where $i = \overline{1, n}$ and $j = \overline{1, k}$:

$$\text{RP}_{ij} : \begin{cases} x = (x_1, x_2, ..., x_n)^T \in (C \cap Z^n), \\ y = (y_1, y_2, ..., y_n)^T \in (C \cap Z^n), \\ \begin{cases} (y_1, ..., y_{i-1}) = (x_1, ..., x_{i-1}), \\ x_i < y_i, \\ (M_1 x, ... M_{j-1} x) = (M_1 y, ..., M_{j-1} y), \\ M_j y > M_j x, \end{cases} \end{cases}$$

such that:

$$\text{ET(RP)} = \bigvee_{i=1}^{n} \text{ET(RP}_{ij}).$$

This means that if we find the existence of a solution for any of these systems, we thus find a solution for the RP. This signifies that re-ordering is involved in the linearization on the P/C pair under investigation. Hence, as soon as we have found the existence of a solution, we can again stop.

Although the number of the subproblems is large, it can be reduced by choosing the order in which we test the systems in a smart way. In this way, we exploit the fact that we do not have to test the remaining systems, as soon as a solution is found. We have found that starting the empty domain tests in the following sequence of problems $\text{RP}_{1,1}...\text{RP}_{1,k}...\text{RP}_{n,1}...\text{RP}_{n,k}$ is a good strategy for minimizing the number of evaluations. This is due to the fact that the probability of finding a solution decreases with the polyhedron volume in which the search is being performed.

7 Experimental Results

In Table 2, we present the results for eight real applications written in Matlab for the domain of imaging and signal processing. The first column in the table shows the number of P/C pairs that appear in a particular algorithm. This is followed by the number of Empty Domain tests needed for the Reorder Test and the Multiplicity Test to classify these P/C pairs. The numbers for the MT are obtained without using the proposed optimization procedure. The last four columns give the four different communication types and how many of the P/C pairs belong to that type. Using functional simulation, we verified for each algorithm that the classification is indeed done correctly.

Table 2 clearly shows that the most occurring type is IOM- (80%) and the least occurring type is OOM+ (1%). This is good, as the IOM- requires only a simple FIFO buffer. The OOM+ requires also re-ordering memory and a controller, but hardly appears in networks. The second most occurring type is IOM+ (10%) which is also nice, as only a FIFO buffer is needed with some simple additional control to keep track of

Table 2. Experimental results: classification of the edges in real-life examples to one of the four communication types using the Reordering Test and the Multiplicity Test.

Algorithm	P/C pairs	RT	MT	IOM-	IOM+	OOM-	OOM+
QR-Decomp	12	73	30	12	0	0	0
SVD	118	1283	565	84	4	30	0
Faddeev	28	205	78	24	3	1	0
Gauss-Elimin	11	17	6	7	0	1	3
DigBeamFormer	98	408	196	88	4	6	0
Motion Estim	98	882	294	98	0	0	0
M-JPEG	50	178	93	33	17	0	0
Stereo Vision	173	1470	518	172	0	1	0

the life time of a token. Together with type IOM-, we can say that in 90% of the cases, a FIFO buffer can indeed be used to linearize a static array in a Matlab program.

The number of Empty Domain tests performed to classify the P/C pairs of a network is quite large. Given the complexity of the Pip and Omega algorithms (integer linear programming is NP complete), the RT and MT tests are time and memory consuming procedures. We have presented already a possible optimization for the MT procedure. We are investigating a similar procedure for RT. Further optimizations to reduce the number of tests are currently subject to further research.

8   Conclusion

In this paper, we presented the problem of classifying a static array appearing in a Matlab program to one of four communication types. The linearization for these types is needed when we break down a Matlab program into processes, as the static array is now accessed by multiple processes. The array is replaced by a distributed communication structure such as a FIFO buffer to avoid the use of shared memory access. Shared memory contradicts the desired characteristics of distributed memory in a PN. Using the distributed communication structure, a static array is explicitly specified by communication between processes, thus really decoupling the processes.

To classify a P/C pair to one of the four types, we presented two tests. The Reorder test determines if re-order takes place on the communication between an arbitrary P/C pair. The Multiplicity test determines if reuse of data takes place on the communication between an arbitrary P/C pair. Both tests have been formulated as integer linear programming problems. This makes the solution suitable for implementation in a compiler.

The presented tests are not specific to the Compaan compiler. They work for any nested loop program in which static arrays need to be replaced by distributed communication structures. We have tested and classified eight real-life examples to validate our approach. We have shown that, on average, in 90% of the cases the static array can be replaced by a FIFO buffer. In 10% of the cases additional control logic and additional memory is needed at the Consumer process, besides a FIFO buffer, to make the linearization work. Although a FIFO buffer is placed between processes in this case, in practice the FIFO and reordering memory are combined in a single memory structure.

References

1. T. Basten and J. Hoogerbrugge. Efficient execution of process networks. In *Communicating Process Architectures - 2001, Proceedings*, pages 1–14, Bristol, UK, September 2001.
2. P. Clauss. Counting solutions to linear and nonlinear constraints through ehrhart polynomials: Applications to analyse and transform scientific programs. In *10th International Conference on Supercomputing, Philadelphia*, May 1996.
3. J. Davis II, C. Hylands, B. Kienhuis, E. A. Lee, J. Liu, X. Liu, L. Muliadi, S. Neuendorffer, J. Tsay, B. Vogel, and Y. Xiong. Heterogeneous concurrent modeling and design in java. Technical Report Memorandum UCB/ERL M01/12, University of California, Dept EECS, Berkeley, CA USA 94720, Mar. 2001.
4. E. De Greef, F. Catthoor, and H. De Man. Memory size reduction through storage order optimization for embedded parallel multimedia applications. In *Parallel Processing and Multimedia*, Geneva, Switzerland, July 1977.
5. E. de Kock, G. Essink, W. Smits, P. van der Wolf, J.-Y. Brunel, W. Kruijtzer, P. Lieverse, and K. Vissers. YAPI: Application modeling for signal processing systems. In *Proc. 37th Design Automation Conference (DAC'2000)*, pages 402–405, Los Angeles, CA, June 5-9 2000.
6. P. Feautrier. Parametric Integer Programming. In *RAIRO Recherche Opérationnelle, 22(3): 243-268*, 1988.
7. B. Kienhuis, E. Rypkema, and E. Deprettere. Compaan: Deriving process networks from matlab for embedded signal processing architectures. In *Proceedings of the 8th International Workshop on Hardware/Software Codesign (CODES)*, San Diego, USA, May 2000.
8. V. Lefebvre and P. Feautrier. Automatic storage management in paralel programs. volume 24, pages 649 – 671. Parallel Computing, nov 1998.
9. T. Parks. Bounded scheduling of process networks. T. M. Parks, Bounded Scheduling of Process Networks, Technical Report UCB/ERL-95-105. PhD Dissertation. EECS Department, University of California, Berkeley CA 94720, December 1995.
10. http://www.picochip.com.
11. F. Quillere and S. Rajopadhye. Optimizing memory usage in the polyhedral model. In *ACM Transactions on Programming Languages and Systems*, volume 22, pages 773–815, September 2000.
12. E. Rijpkema. *From Piecewise Regular Algorithms to Dataflow Architectures*. PhD thesis, Delft University of Technology, 2001.
13. A. Schrijver. *Theory of Linear and Integer Programming*. John Wiley & Sons Ltd., 1986.
14. T. Stefanov, C. Zissulescu, A. Turjan, B. Kienhuis, and E. Deprettere. System design using kahn process networks: The compaan/laura approach. In *Proceedings of DATE2004*, Paris, France, Feb 16 – 20 2004.
15. P. Stravers and J. Hoogerbrugge. Homogeneous multiprocessoring and the future of silicon design paradigms. In *Proceedings of the Int. Symposium on VLSI Technology, Systems, and Applications*, Apr. 2001.
16. J. Teich and L. Thiele. Partitioning of processor arrays: A piecewise regular approach. *Integration, the VLSI journal*, 14:297–332, February 1993.
17. A. Turjan, B. Kienhuis, and E. Deprettere. A compile time based approach for solving out-of-order communication in kahn process networks. In *Proceedings of the IEEE 13th Int. Conf. on Application-specific Systems, Architectures and Processors (ASAP'02)*, San Jose, California, July 2002.
18. A. Turjan and B. Kienhuis. Storage management in process networks using the lexicographically maximal preimage. In *Proceedings of the IEEE 14th Int. Conf. on Application-specific Systems, Architectures and Processors (ASAP'03)*, The Hague, The Netherlands, June 24-26 2003.

19. V. Vanhoof, I. Bolsens, and H. De Man. Compiling multi-dimensional data streams into distributed dsp asic memory. In *In Proc. IEEE Int. Conf. Comp. Aided Design*, Santa Clara, CA, August 1989.

20. D. Wilde and S. Rajopadhye. Memory reuse in the polyhedral model. In *In Proc. Euro-Par96*, Lyon, France, August 2002.

21. P. William. The Omega Test: A Fast and Practical Integer Programming Algorithm for Dependence Analysis. *Communications of the ACM*, 35(8):102–114, 1992.

22. http://www.xilinx.com.

23. C. Zissulescu, T. Stefanov, B. Kienhuis, and E. Deprettere. LAURA: Leiden Architecture Research and Exploration Tool. In *Proc. 13th Int. Conference on Field Programmable Logic and Applications (FPL'03)*, 2003.

Predictable Embedded Multiprocessor System Design

Marco Bekooij[1], Orlando Moreira[1], Peter Poplavko[1,2], Bart Mesman[1,2], Milan Pastrnak[1,2], and Jef van Meerbergen[1,2]

[1] Philips Research Laboratories, NL-5656 AA Eindhoven, Netherlands
[2] Eindhoven University of Technology, NL-5600 MB Eindhoven, Netherlands

Abstract. Consumers have high expectations about the video and audio quality delivered by media processing devices like TV-sets, DVD-players and digital radios. Predictable heterogenous application domain specific multiprocessor systems, which are designed around a networks-on-chip, can meet demanding performance, flexibility and power-efficiency requirements as well as stringent timing requirements. The timing requirements can be guaranteed by making use of resource management techniques and the analytical techniques that are described in this paper.

1 Introduction

Multimedia signal processing and channel decoding in consumer systems is, for performance and power-efficiency reasons, typically performed by more than one processor. The processing in these embedded systems has often stringent throughput and latency requirements. In order to meet these requirements the system must behave in a predictable manner such that it is possible to reason about its timing behavior. The use of analytical methods is desirable because simulation can only be used to demonstrate that the system meets its timing requirements given a particular set of input stimuli. During the design of a multiprocessor system these analytical methods are needed for the derivation of the minimal hardware such that the timing requirements can be met. Given an instance of the multiprocessor system, these methods are needed to program the system in such a way that the timing requirements are met.

A traditional implementation of a predictable multiprocessor system for channel decoding and video processing is a pipe of tightly coupled dedicated hardware blocks with some glue logic for the communication between the blocks. However, there are many reasons to consider this design style as becoming less viable.

First of all, we are currently witnessing the convergence of previously unrelated application domains. For example, ordinary TV-sets are gradually evolving from straightforward terminals to interactive multimedia terminals. Digital auto radios are being combined with navigation systems, and wireless telephone functionality which provides a low bandwidth uplink. DVD players are evolving into DVD writers with complex graphics pipelines that allow to include special effects in our home-brew videos. This convergence leads to heterogeneity and

H. Schepers (Ed.): SCOPES 2004, LNCS 3199, pp. 77–91, 2004.
© Springer-Verlag Berlin Heidelberg 2004

many options, which all must be supported in a robust and efficient way by the
multiprocessor system. The flexibility that is needed in these systems is often
more than can be provided with dedicated hardware blocks. The reason is that
these blocks are typically designed for one particular function. Also the order of
the hardware blocks is fixed in a dedicated hardware pipe while the same blocks
could be reused in different applications if the order could be adapted.

Another important reason why a pipe of tightly coupled dedicated hardware
blocks becomes a less viable solution, is that the applications become more dynamic as new algorithms seek to take advantage of the disparity between average
and worst-case processing. Also the increased interaction with the environment
makes systems more dynamic. Often tasks and complex data types are created
and deleted at run-time based on non-deterministic events like pressing of a remote control button. This results in many irregularities in the control flow of
the application which can be handled effectively by sequential processors but
not with dedicated hardware. This dynamism requires more scheduling freedom
than can be provided by tightly coupled and synchronized hardware blocks.

The so-called "design productivity gap" states that the increase in our ability
to design embedded systems does not match with the exponential growth over
time of the number of transistors that can be integrated in an IC as described by
Moore's law. To close the gap, system design methods must harness exponential
hardware resource growth. This requires a modular, scalable design style, which
is definitely not the case for a pipe of dedicated hardware blocks. The design
style must also be composable, which is the case if the correctness (including the
timing) of a complete system can be established by using only the (independently
proven) features of its components.

The rapid increase of the masks' cost makes it necessary to design a single
System-on-Chip (SoC) for a complete product family. The required flexibility
of these SoCs make programmable multiprocessor systems an attractive option.
A tradeoff between flexibility and performance must be made due to the power
dissipation limit of approximately one 1W of cheap plastic IC-packages and of
approximately 100 mW for battery powered devices. So, for power-efficiency
reasons these systems will typically contain a mix of dedicted hardware blocks,
application domain specific processors, and general purpose microprocessors.
It is therefore necessary that the timing analysis techniques are applicable for
systems in which application domain specific processors and dedicated hardware
blocks are applied that do not support preemption.

A Network-on-Chip (NoC), like the network proposed by the Æthereal project [1], seems a promising option to connect processors with each other. A connection in such a network describes the communication between a master and a
slave and such a network can offer differentiated services for these connections.
Connections with a guaranteed througput service which have a guaranteed minimum bandwidth, a maximum latency, a FIFO transaction ordering and end-to-
end flow-control are essential for the design of predicatable systems as will be
explained in the next sections.

The outline of this paper is as follows. In Section 2, the characteristics of the target application domain are described, and our model that captures the behavior of the application is introduced. The resource management techniques which are described in Section 3, bound the sources of uncertainty in the system such that reasoning about the timing behavior of the system becomes possible. A multiprocessor system architecture which allows resource budgets allocation and enforcement is described in Section 4. The timing analysis and scheduling techniques are described in more detail in respectively Section 5 and Section 6. Finally, in Section 7 we state conclusions and indicate future work.

2   Application Domain Model

Applications like high quality multi-window television with pixel processing enhancement, graphics and MPEG-video decoders require a computational performance in the order of 10-100 giga operations per second. Such a performance can not be provided by a single processor and requires a multiprocessor system.

In such an application the user can start and stop *jobs* that process video streams which are displayed after scaling in a separate windows. A job consists of tasks which are created (deleted) as the job starts (stops). Figure 1 shows an application that consist of an MPEG2 video-decoder job, an MPEG1 video-decoder job, a mixer job, a contrast correction job and an audio decoder job. The MPEG2 job consists for example of an IDCT, a VLD, and some other tasks. The tasks communicate via FIFO channels. The tasks within a job are activated on data availability. In some cases, it is necessary to activate tasks in a job by an event like a clock signal, instead of the presence of new input data. For example, assume that the mixer job in Figure 1 must produce a video frame every 20 ms. In this case the mixer should redisplay the previous frame after a clock pulse of a 50 Hz clock in the case that the decoding of an MPEG2 frame takes more than 20 ms.

The MPEG1 and MPEG2 decoder jobs have a soft real-time requirement, i.e. it is desirable that these jobs produce a new video frame every 20 ms. The mixer and contrast correction job in Figure 1 have hard real-time requirements, i.e. these jobs must produce a new video frame every 20 ms as is required by the display. Also the audio decoder has hard-real time requirements because an uninterrupted audio stream must be produced which is synchronized with the video stream.

The jobs are described as Synchronous Data Flow (SDF) graphs [2] [3], such that the throughput and latency of the jobs can be derived with analytical techniques. Tradionally these SDF graphs are used because they make compile time scheduling possible which eliminates the run-time scheduling overhead. However, also run-time scheduling of SDF graphs can be an attractive option, as will be discussed in Section 5 of paper.

An example of an SDF is shown in Figure 2. The nodes in an SDF are called actors. Actors are tasks with a well defined input/output behavior and a execution time which is less than equal to a specified worst-case execution time.

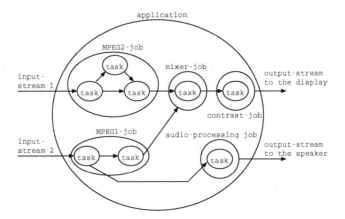

Fig. 1. An application which consist of jobs. Jobs are started and stopped by the user. Jobs consist of tasks which communicated via FIFO channels.

The black dot in Figure 2 is a token. A token is a container in which a fixed amount of data can be stored. The edges in the SDF are called data edges and denote data dependencies. The number at the head of a data edge denotes the number of tokens that an actor consumes when it is fired. The number at the tail of an edge denotes the number of tokens an actor produces when it is fired. An actor is fired as soon as on every incomming edge of the actor at least the number of tokens are available as is specified at the head of the data edge. These tokens are consumed from the input edges of the actor before the execution of an actor finishes. The number of tokens specified at the tail of every output edge of the actor is produced before the execution of the actor finishes. Tasks with internal state are modeled in an SDF with a self edge, like the self edge of actor A3 in Figure 2. This self edge is given one initial token such that the next execution can not start before the previous execution is finished.

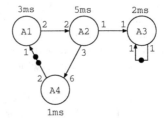

Fig. 2. An SDF graph.

Tokens are, in the SDF model, consumed in the same order as they are produced. Therefore, FIFOs can be used as buffers in the communication channels. The maximal number of tokens that can be stored in a FIFO is called the FIFO capacity. FIFOs with a fixed capacity can be modelled in an SDF graph with

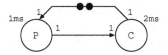

Fig. 3. SDF model of a FIFO with a capacity of 2 tokens between a producing and consuming actor.

an additional data edge from a consumer (C) to the producer (P) as is shown in Figure 3. The number of initial tokens should be equal to the FIFO capacity.

To be able to design a fully predictable system that can meet the timing requirements, it is necessary to bound the uncertainty that can be introduced by the user, the application and the hardware. The uncertainty is bounded by the resource management techniques that are described in the next section. Given that the uncertainty is bounded, a guaranteed minimal throughput and maximal latency can be derived for each job, with the analysis techniques that are described in Section 5.

3   Resource Management

The uncertainty introduced by the application, the hardware and the environment can make reasoning about the timing behavior of jobs difficult or even impossible. The resource management techniques described in this section bound the uncertainty such that the timing behavior of jobs can be derived.

We distinguish the uncertainty in the resource supply from the uncertainty in the resource demand. The uncertainty in the resource supply is due to resource arbitration in the hardware of the multiprocessor system. Resource arbitration of busses and the replacement policy of cache lines, are examples. The uncertainty in the resource demand is due to the data value dependent processing (e.g., conditional branches in the program code) and external events. External events are for example generated by the user to start and stop jobs.

The uncertainty in resource supply is bounded by making use of predictable hardware arbitration schemes. An arbitration scheme is predictable in the case it is known how long it maximally takes before a resource becomes available. The minimal time that the resource stays available must also be known. An example of a predictable arbitration scheme for a bus is Time Division Multiple Access (TDMA). In this scheme, it is guaranteed that the bus can be obtained after a fixed amount of time and that during a fixed amount of time the data can be transfered via the bus.

The uncertainty in the resource demand is bounded by making use of admission control and hardware resource budget enforcement. Admission control takes care that sufficient hardware resources are available when a job is started. If there are insufficient resources available in the system then the user is notified that the job is rejected. Resource budgeting guarantees that an actor of a job gets a certain amount of memory, bandwidth and processor cycles. By enforcing budgets it becomes impossible for an actor to claim more resources than its budget. Due to these enforced budgets the interference of actors of different jobs is bounded. With enforced resource budgets, it looks for a job as if it runs on its own private hardware. In other words, resource budget enforcement creates for each job its own virtual platform with private hardware resources.

Resource budgets are determined by the resource manager at the start-up of a job. Hard real-time, soft real-time and best effort jobs are treated differently. For hard real-time jobs it is unacceptable that a single deadline is missed, and per definition these jobs do not support graceful degradation. Therefore, the worst-case amount of resources that could be needed during the execution of a hard real-time job must be allocated by the resource manager. For soft real-time jobs, less than the worst-case amount of resources can be allocated because missing of a deadline results in some diminished value for the end user. The allocated resource budgets are based on a prediction of the behavior of the job. If more resources are needed during the execution than are allocated, then the job will miss a deadline or the job can reduce the required amount of resources by reducing the quality of its end result. In case the quality must be reduced for a longer period of time, then the job can ask the resource manager for an increase of its budget. For best-effort jobs there are no timing constraints defined. A faster average execution time of a best-effort job is appreciated by the end user. These jobs can make use of the resources which are either not allocated to hard real-time and soft real-time jobs or are not used by the real-time jobs during their execution.

The architecture template of the proposed predictable multiprocessor system is described in the next section. In such a system resource budgets can be enforced and predictable arbitration mechanisms are applied.

4   Multiprocessor Template

The architecture template of the proposed multiprocessor system is shown in Figure 4. The processors in this template are, together with their local data memory, connected to the Network Interface (NI) of a NoC. The transfer of data between a local memory and a network interface is performed by a Communication Assist (CA). A processor together with its local instruction and data memory, communication assist and network interfaces is grouped into a leaf. The leafs are connected to the routers of our network. Network links connect the routers in the desired network topology.

A processor in a leaf has a separate Instruction Memory (I-mem) and Data Memory (D-mem) such that instruction fetches and data load and store operation do not cause contention on the same memory port. A wide range of memory access time variation due to contention on a memory port is intolerable because this would result in an unpredictable execution time of the instructions of the processor. A processor can only access its local data memory. Given a 1 cycle access time of a local memory there is no reason to make it cacheable.

Every processor in this template has its own private memory which improves the scalability of the system. Such a multiprocessor system is intended for mes-

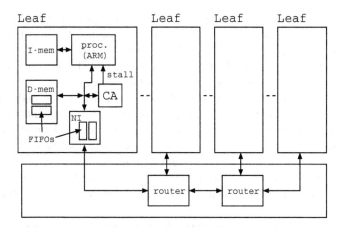

Fig. 4. Multiprocessor template.

sage passing which is a suitable programming paradigm for most signal processing applications. Because message passing is used instead of the shared address
space communication model there is no memory bottleneck to a central shared
memory. Coherency can't be a problem in a system which makes use of message
passing in the case that there is only one producer and one consumer for every
data item that is communicated between processors.

Communication between actors on different processors takes place via a virtual point to point connection of the NoC. The result of the producing actor is
written in a logical FIFO in the local memory of the processor. Such a logical
FIFO can be implemented with the C-HEAP [4] communication protocol, without use of semaphores. A communication assist polls at regular intervals whether
there is data in this FIFO. As soon as the CA detects that there is data available
it copies the data into a FIFO of the NI. There is one private FIFO per connection in the NI. Then the data is transported over the network to the NI of the
receiving processor. As soon as the data arrives in this NI, it is copied by the CA
into a logical FIFO in the memory of the processor that executes the consuming
actor. The data is read from this FIFO after the consuming actor has detected
that there is sufficient data in the FIFO. Flow control between the producing
and consuming actor is achieved by making sure that data is not written into a
FIFO before it is checked that there is space available in this FIFO.

Data is stored in the local memory of the processor before it is transfered
accross the network. This done for a number of reasons. First of all, the bandwidth of a connection is set by configuring tables in the network for a longer
period of time. The bandwidth reserved for a connection will typically be less
than the peak data rate generated by the producing actor. Therefore a buffer is
needed between the processor and the network to average out the data rate such
that the bandwidth provided by the network is well utillized. The size of this
buffer is significant given the assumption that the actors produce large chunks
of data at large intervals. On the other hand the network will transfer very small
chunks of data (3 words of 32 bits) at very small intervals (2 ns). Given that

large memories are inherently slow it is desirable to split the large logical FIFO between the processor and the network, in a small (32 word) dedicated FIFO per connection in the network interface and a large logical FIFO in the local memory of the processor. The task of the CA is then copying of the data between FIFOs in the NI and FIFOs in local memory of the processor.

Another important reason to store data in a local memory and not via the network in a remote memory is that the latency of the load and store operations that are executed on the processor should not depend on the latency of the network. A longer latency of load and store operations whould result in a longer worst-case execution time of the actors and would effectively decrease the performance of the processor. By making use of a FIFO in the local memory, the computation performed by the processor can be overlapped by the communication that is performed by the CA.

Finally, there is no need to send addresses over the network because the remote memories are not accessed via the network by a processor nor by a communication assist. This will save network bandwidth and will improve the power efficiency of the multiprocessor system. Only data can be sent over the network because the configuration of the network and the communication assists determine between which FIFOs data is transported.

The CA is also responsible for the arbitration of the data memory bus. The applied arbitration scheme [5] is such that a low worst-case latency of memory store and load operations is obtained and that a minimal throughput and maximal latency per connection is guaranteed. In this scheme the time is divided in intervals P of p cycles. Each interval P is subdivided in intervals Q of q cycles. During each interval Q it is guaranteed that the processor can access the memory at least once. This guarantees that a load/store operation of the processor takes at most q cycles. If the processor does not access the memory during an interval Q, then this access can take place in a successive interval Q that belongs to the same interval P. This way the processor can access the memory at most p/q cycles per interval P. The processor is stalled by the CA till the next period P if it issues more than p/q load and store operations per interval P. Therefore there are at least $p - p/q$ cycles per interval P for the communication assist to copy data between the NI and the local memory. A predefined portion r of the $p - p/q$ cycles is allocated per connection for copying of data between the CA and the NI. The minimal throughput and maximal latency for a connection is guaranteed because data can be copied between the local memory and the CA for at least r cycles per p cycles.

In the proposed architecture the communication between actors that run on different processors has a guaranteed minimal throughput and a maximal latency. Given these characteristics, the communication can be modeled as if it takes place through completely independent virtual point-to-point connections. These connections are modeled together with the actors of a job in one SDF graph. Given this SDF graph, the guaranteed minimal throughput of the job can be determined with the analysis techniques that are described in the next section.

5   Analysis Techniques

It is assumed that initially a sequential C-description of a job is provided, which is the input of our analysis and simulation flow (see Figure 5). This sequential C description is manually rewritten into another C-description in which the task level parallelism in the job is made explicit. In a successive rewriting step care is taken that all tasks have actor semantics, i.e. they do not start before there are tokens on all inputs, have a bounded execution time and consume tokens of a fixed size. Also the WCET of the actors is determined by analysis of the program flow [6]. The SDF graph that is obtained represents a job.

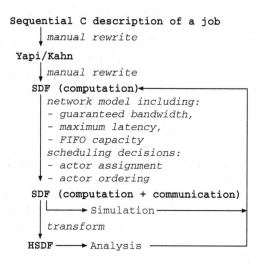

Fig. 5. Analysis and simulation flow.

The actors in the SDF are assigned to processors and ordered by a scheduler (see Section 6). The actor assignment and order is modeled with additional edges and actors in the same SDF graph. In the case that actors communicate via the network then a model of a connection in the network replaces edges in the SDF graph. This network connection model consist of SDF actors and edges. This model includes the FIFOs between the processor, the CA and the network. A description of such a network connection model is out of the scope of this paper.

The SDF graph in which the job, the network as well as the actor assignment and actor order is modeled is transformed into a Homogeneous Synchronous Data Flow (HSDF) graph on which the timing analysis is performed. An algorithm which can transform any SDF graph into a HSDF graph is described in [3]. An HSDF graph is a special kind of an SDF graph in which the execution of an actor results in the consumption of one token from every incoming data edge of the actor and the production of one token on every outgoing data edge of the actor.

An HSDF graph can be executed in a self-timed fashion, which is defined as a sequence of firings of HSDF actors in which the actors start immediately when there are tokens on all their inputs. If the HSDF graph is a strongly connected graph and a FIFO ordering is maintained for the tokens, then the self-timed execution of the HSDF graph has some important properties. A FIFO ordering is maintained if the completion events of firings of the same actor occur in the same order as the corresponding start-events. This is the case if an actor in the HSDF graph belongs to a cycle with only one token otherwise the actor must have a constant execution time. In [7] the properties of the self-timed execution of an HSDF graph are derived with max-plus algebra.

The most important property of the self-timed execution of an HSDF graph is, that it is deadlock-free if there is on every cycle in the HSDF graph at least one initial token. Secondly, the execution of the HSDF graph is monotonic, i.e. decreasing actor execution times result in non-increasing actor start times. Third, an HSDF graph $G(V, E)$ will always enter a periodic regime. More precisely, there exist a $K \in \mathbb{N}$, an $N \in \mathbb{N}$ and a $\lambda \in \mathbb{R}$, such that for all $v \in V$, $k > K$ the start time $s(v, k + N)$ of actor v in iteration $k + N$ is described by:

$$s(v, k + N) = s(v, k) + \lambda \cdot N \tag{1}$$

Equation 1 states that the execution enters a periodic regime after K executions of an actor in the HSDF graph. The time one period spans is $\lambda \cdot N$. So, λ is equal to the inverse of the average throughput. The number of iterations in one period is denoted by N.

The Maximum Cycle Mean (MCM) of the HSDF, which is equal to λ, is given by equation 2. In this equation is CM the Cycle Mean of a simple cycle $c \in G$ (see equation 3). In this equation denotes $tokens(c)$ the number of tokens on the edges in a cycle c. The Worst Case Execution Time (WCET) of actor v is denoted by WCET(v).

$$\mathrm{MCM}(G) = \max_{c \in G} \mathrm{CM}(c) \tag{2}$$

$$\mathrm{CM}(c) = \sum_{v \ on \ c} \mathrm{WCET}(v)/tokens(c) \tag{3}$$

The number of iterations in one period is denoted by N. The value of N can be derived with the following procedure. First, all critical circuits are derived which are cycles $c \in G$ with a cycle mean equal to the MCM. Then, a critical graph $G^c(V^c, E^c)$ is derived which consists of all nodes and edges in G which belong to critical circuits. For each maximal strongly connected subgraph G^s in G^c the number of tokens t_s^p on every simple path p in the subgraph is derived. Then a value $d_s = gcd(t_s^{p1}, t_s^{p2}, ..., t_s^{pn})$ is derived for each subgraph G^s, in which gcd denotes the greatest common divisor. The number of iterations N in one period is equal to $lcm(d_{s1}, d_{s2}, ..., d_{sm})$ in which lcm denotes the least common multiple.

The value K can be derived by simulating the HSDF graph in a self-timed fashion given that all actors have an execution time equal to their worst-case execution time. The value K is the first iteration in which the start-times of the actors correspond to equation 1.

The worst-case start-times of the actors during the transient state as well as the steady state can be derived by simulation. During this simulation, all actors must have an execution time equal to their worst-case excecution time. Due to the monotonicity of the HSDF are the start-times observed during this simulation are worst-case start times. Given equation 1 there is no need to simulate beyond the first period of the periodic regime.

So far it was assumed that jobs run independently, i.e., they do not interact with each other and the external world, or, if they do, that interaction does not violate the timing contraints of the job. However, in many signal processing system the input data is provided by an external source which provides a new input sample every clock period. An example of such a source is an A/D converter. A similar situation occurs often at the output of the system where an external sink consumes an output sample every clock period. An example of such a sink is a D/A converter. Given such an external source and/or sink it should be guaranteed that the samples produced by the source can always be stored in the FIFO between the source and the system. It should also be guaranteed that there are always sufficient samples in the FIFO between the system and the sink.

The source and sink are modeled as actors in the HSDF graph as is shown in Figure 6 in order to verify whether the FIFOs at the input and output of the system do not overflow or underflow. The source and sink actors are given a WCET of $1/f_{clock}$, which is the length of 1 clock period. The self edge with one initial token garantees that the next execution of the source and sink actor can not start before the previous execution is finished. Thus, the self-edge in combination with the WCET of the source and sink actors enforce a maximal execution frequency of these actors during the self-timed execution of the HSDF graph in the simulator. During simulation it should be verified that the time between succesive executions of the source as well as the sink actor is exactly one clock period. If this is the case, then it is guaranteed that in an implementation of the system, FIFO1 between source and the rest system never overflows and FIFO2 between the system and the sink never underflows. The reason is that actors can not start later than they start during a simulation run in which all actors have an execution time equal to their worst-case execution time. If the actors are started earlier then a token in FIFO1 can never be consumed later than during the simulation run, which results in the same or less tokens in FIFO1. If the actors starts earlier, then a token is never produced later in FIFO2 than during the simulation run, which results in a greater or equal number of tokens in FIFO2 in the implementation.

It depends on the applied scheduling strategy whether the actor assignment as well as actor ordering decisions are made during the execution of a job, or before a job is started. In the case that a decision is taken after the job is started, then the decision, out of all possible decisions, which would lead to as late as possible actor start-times is modeled in the SDF. The pros and cons of the different scheduling strategies are the topic of the next section.

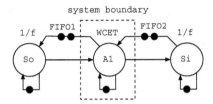

Fig. 6. HSDF graph which is used to prove that, given a strict periodic source and sink, the FIFOs at the input and at the output of the system have sufficient capacity.

Table 1. Comparison of scheduling strategies.

Scheduling strategy	Assignment	Ordering	Invocation time
Fully-static	compile-time	compile-time	compile-time
Static order	compile-time	compile-time	run-time
Static assignment	compile-time	run-time	run-time
Fully dynamic	run-time	run-time	run-time

6   Scheduling Strategies

Scheduling decisions can be taken before a job is started or during the execution of the job. Taking scheduling decisions during the execution of the jobs (at run-time) implies some run-time overhead. This run-time overhead can be reduced if these schedule decisions are made before the job is started (at compile-time). Schedule decisions that are taken at compile-time imply that some freedom in the schedule is removed in order to reduce the run-time overhead. Therefore, the scheduling strategy that should be selected depends on the knowledge that is available at compile-time of the job and the amount of run-time scheduling overhead that is introduced when scheduling decisions are taken at run-time. A comparison of the scheduling strategies is given in Table 1. These scheduling strategies differ in whether the actor to processor assignment, the execution order of the actors on a processor and the start-times of the actors are determined at compile or at run-time. For all these scheduling strategies techniques exist to guarantee the timing. In the next paragraphs the characteristics of these scheduling strategies are described in more detail.

In the fully-static scheduling strategy, the assignment of actors to processors as well as the order in which the actors are executed and the start-times of the actors, are determined by a scheduler before the job is started. This scheduling strategy requires that the processors have the same global time reference such that at run-time the actors can be started at the right moment in time. A disadvantage of this scheduling strategy is that a global notation of time is difficult to realize due to deep sub-micron effects in a large system with many processors. Another disadvantage of the fully static scheduling strategy is that the length of the schedule is fixed and does not decrease if the execution times of the actors decrease. Decreasing execution times of actors result in more idle processor cycles. The main advantage of the fully static scheduling strategy is that explicit synchronization between actors is not required because actors are started after it is guaranteed that their input data is available and that there is space to store their results.

In the static order scheduling strategy the assignment of actors to processors as well as the order in which the actors are executed are determined by a scheduler before the job is started. An actor is started as soon as its input tokens are available and it is the next actor to be executed on a processor according to the predefined cyclic execution order. Checking whether there is input data implies run-time overhead. A decrease in the execution time of the actors results in a shorter schedule. The remaining processor cycles can be used by another job. An important property of the static order scheduling strategy is that only the throughput of the system is decreased if the execution time of an actor is larger than the execution time assumed by the scheduler. It can not result in a deadlock of the system. This opens the possibility to determine the assignment and order of actors of soft real-time jobs by the scheduler based on a predicted execution time of the actors instead of on the worst-case execution time of the actors.

In the static assignment scheduling strategy the assignment of actors is determined before the SDF graph is started. After the SDF graph is started the activation of an actor occurs as soon as its input tokens become available and it is the next actor to be executed on the processor according to the predefined cyclic activation order. The difference with the static order scheduling strategy is that an actor in the cyclic list of actors that are executed on the same processor returns immediately if there are insufficient input tokens for this actor. After an actor is skipped then the next actor in the cyclic list checks whether there are sufficient input tokens. This arbitration scheme is predictable because for a token in front of a FIFO a worst-case waiting time (W) can be defined before it is consumed by actor A1. A token is in front of a FIFO if it is the first token to be consumed from the FIFO. The worst-case waiting time (W) equals the sum of the WCET of all actors, except actor A, in the cyclic execution list. The arbitration on a processor can be modeled implicitly in the implementation aware SDF graph by increasing the WCET of actor A1 with the worst-case waiting time (W). It can be proven with that tokens during self-timed execution of the implementation aware SDF graph do not arrive earlier than in the implementation. This proof is omitted due to lack of space. That arbitration can be modeled implicitly in an SDF model is plausible because actors should produce their results within their worst-case execution time and it is irrelevant whether the production of a result takes time due to computation performed on the input data or due to waiting because other actors have to finished first their execution on the same processor.

An important advantage of the static assignment scheduling strategy is that the assignment of the actors to processors does not require a compile-time ordering step. The actor assignment problem is basically a bin packing problem where the total load on a processor may not exceed 100%. Currently we investigate whether the assignment of actors can be performed by an on-line algorithm just before the SDF graph is started. An advantage of the static assignment scheduling strategy is that the pipeline is automatically filled when the SDF graph of a job is started while an explicit encoded pre- and post-amble is needed in the static order scheduling strategy. The main disadvantage of the static assignment scheduling strategy is that the minimal required FIFO capacity will typically be larger than is needed for a static order schedule with the same throughput.

In the fully dynamic scheduling strategy the assignment of actors to processors as well as the execution order and start-times of the actors are determined at run-time. The actor to processor assignment is adapted at run-time such that the computational load of the processors is kept balanced. Load balancing can result in a shorter execution time of the jobs. Moving an actor at run-time from one processor to another implies, in our architecture, that data must be copied from one memory into another memory. We expect that for the multi-media signal processing domain, the gain in processor cycles obtained by balancing the processor load does typically not outweigh the cost of moving data. The reason is that, for this application domain, the difference between the worst-case and the average-case execution time of the actors in the jobs is often not large enough.

7   Conclusion and Future Work

The processing in many consumer systems is performed by embedded multiprocessor systems for performance and power-efficiency reasons. The processing in these systems has usually stringent throughput and latency requirements. This paper presents a multiprocessor architecture and an SDF-model of the jobs in an application which enables reasoning about the timing behavior of the system. A scalable multiprocessor system is obtained by making use of a network on chip for the communication between processors. The network provides virtual point-to-point connections with a guaranteed throughput and maximal latency such that the timing of the system can be derived with the presented analysis techniques.

Without significant hurdles a digital channel decoder, a simple graphics pipeline and some audio post processing functions were described in an SDF model. Currently, an SDF model of an arbitrarily shaped object video decoder is under development. For this video decoder it is challenge to find a way to allow switching between an SDF graph for I-frame decoding and another SDF graph P-frame decoding.

References

1. E. Rijpkema, K.G.W. Goossens, A. Rădulescu, J. Dielissen, J. van Meerbergen, P. Wielage, and E. Waterlander, "Trade offs in the design of a router with both guaranteed and best-effort services for networks on chip," Design, Automation and Test in Europe Conference (DATE), 2003, pp. 350–355.

2. E.A. Lee and D.G. Messerschmitt, "Synchronous data flow," Proceedings of the IEEE, 1987.

3. S. Sriram and S.S. Bhattacharyya, *Embedded Multiprocessors: Scheduling and Synchronization*, Marcel Dekker, Inc, 2000.

4. O.P. Gangwal, A. Nieuwland, and P. Lippens, "A scalable and flexible data synchronization scheme for embedded hw-sw shared-memory systems," International Symposium on System Synthesis, 2001, pp. 1–6, ACM.

5. S. Hosseini-Khayat and A.D. Bovopouplos, "A simple and efficient bus management scheme that supports continous streams," ACM Transactions on Computer Systems, 1995, vol. 13, pp. 122–140.

6. Y-T. S. Li and S. Malik, *Performance analysis of real-time embedded software*, ISBN 0-7923-8382-6, Kluwer academic publishers, 1999.

7. F. Bacelli, G. Cohen, G.J. Olsder, and J-P. Quadrat, *Synchronization and Linearity*, John Wiley & Sons, Inc., 1992.

Suppression of Redundant Operations in Reverse Compiled Code Using Global Dataflow Analysis

Adrian Johnstone and Elizabeth Scott

Royal Holloway, University of London
{A.Johnstone,E.Scott}@rhul.ac.uk

Abstract. We describe an unusual application of dataflow analysis to reverse compilation from assembler source to ANSI-C. Most real architectures support (or more usually, mandate) the use of register-based operands in computations and provide *status* bits which are set as an implicit side-effect of arithmetic instructions. Naïve translation of these semantics into C yields programs which are dominated by references to registers and the calculation of status results. The target processor for our reverse compiler is particularly prone to these effects since the functional units are surrounded by pipeline registers which must be loaded and unloaded around each computation, but the problem is common to all reverse compilers: how to render the computational core of a low-level algorithm in high level code that is comfortable for a human to read and which maintains the low level semantics. We apply a brute-force dataflow analysis to provide exact use-define information at all program points and then follow the use-define relationships to back-substitute expressions in an effort to remove register references. We also suppress dead status code calculations and perform limited alias analysis for some special purpose registers which can be accessed *via* more than one name. We show that use of these techniques can significantly reduce the degree to which the underlying architecture 'shows through' into the resulting C translation and that the computation times required are manageable for one-off translations.

1   Introduction

This paper describes an unusual application of dataflow analysis in the design of a reverse compiler from hand-written assembler source to ANSI-C. Our translator (`asm21toc`) starts from assembler source for the ADSP-21xx fixed point DSP, and produces equivalent high level language source that is suitable for input to scheduling compilers for modern VLIW and superscalar processors. The translator was developed for commercial use, specifically the porting of legacy embdedded DSP code to VLIW embedded processors in mobile telecommunications applications, allowing a considerable investment in cellular protocols to be preserved. We shall show that significant reductions in the size of reverse compiled programs may be achieved through register expression substitution and dead expression elimination, but that exhaustive global dataflow analysis is required to maintain program semantics.

H. Schepers (Ed.): SCOPES 2004, LNCS 3199, pp. 92–106, 2004.

Very few programs for contemporary processors are written in assembly level languages. One reason for abandoning low level languages is well known: programmer productivity is widely held to be roughly constant in lines of code *per* week of effort independent of the language used, and so it is natural for programmers to work using high level languages. More significantly, it is increasingly difficult to hand write *correct* assembler code for superscalar and VLIW processors that do not provide hardware interlocks to ensure that the sequential semantics of the assembler operations are maintained in the event of a hazard.

One class of processors for which many applications are still programmed at machine level comprises the Digital Signal Processors (DSPs) which are specialist microprocessors with architectures optimised for the execution of digital signal processing algorithms, particularly the Fast Fourier Transform. DSPs are usually used in low cost, low power systems, and this requirement coupled with the unusual architectural features has led to the development of several families of processors with highly constrained register-to-function-unit pathways and small virtual address spaces. The resulting devices are difficult compiler targets, and some manufacturer supplied C compilers for these architectures produce code that is a factor 20 larger than that produced by an expert human programmer. Given that typical systems only have a few kilo-instructions worth of program memory, hand written assembler applications are far more common than compiled executables.

The DSP application area has recently seen the introduction of data-parallel architectures based on both Single Instruction Multiple Data (SIMD) and Very Long Instruction Word (VLIW) styles of processing. SIMD processors such as the ADSP 2116x combine several data paths on a single chip with instructions broadcast from a single instruction stream. The multiple data paths operate in lockstep, with multiple data elements having the same operation applied to them in any given instruction cycle. VLIW processors similarly feature multiple data paths which are synchronised together, but in this case the instruction word is wide enough to allow operations in each of the data paths to be separately specified. One such family of processors, the TMS320C6x, allows eight data paths to be controlled in this way. In addition, on some processors the data paths themselves are pipelined and therefore display the usual data hazards associated with pipelined operation.

Exploiting the parallelism available in such devices requires independent computations to be scheduled for execution in the same instruction slot. Typically there is no hardware interlock, that is no mechanism for specifying and ensuring at runtime that dependent computations are correctly sequenced. Debugging applications which contain sequencing errors is notoriously hard: we know of one very experienced DSP programmer whose output fell to around one line *per* day whilst attempting to manually resolve resource contention and data dependency issues in a small assembler programmed application for the TMS320C6x. It is clear that these architectures can only reasonably be programmed using high level languages that incorporate safe schedulers into their code generator phases.

Thus arises a cultural and practical problem. Users of such devices are traditionally low-level language programmers who take great pride in their ability to exploit machine-level programming and deprecate high level programming as inefficient. Historically, this has been justified since high-level language compilers for these architectures generate poor code.

The new architectures, on the other hand, mandate the use of high level language compilers. A new generation of high-level DSP programmers is often faced with a body of legacy assembly code for processors with complex internal structures featuring pipeline registers and irregular computational units. Our goal is to ease the porting of large applications from traditional DSP architectures to the new scheduled processors by providing reverse compilations that both preserve the semantics of the assembler level program and provide an ANSI-C rendering that is comfortable for humans to read. To that end, we expend considerable effort on preserving comments and on minimising the extent to which code is reordered. Our twin goals are to (i) allow companies to preseve their intellectual property by automatically porting arduously hand-wrought assembler code to scheduled compiled code for the new processors and (ii) to support program comprehension by high level language programmers that do not have low level DSP experience. Our industrial partners have successfully deployed asm21toc in both these contexts.

2   Translation Modes

A naïve translation from assembler source may be achieved by declaring a set of C variables corresponding to internal machine registers and representing each machine instruction as a small C expression. Unfortunately the resulting C program will display many references to these special variables, and on some architectures the operation of the underlying algorithm is likely to be obscured by redundant loading of registers.

A related problem with naïve translation is that of status calculations: most real architectures implement conditional branches through the testing of status registers which are written to as a side effect of computations[1]. On such architectures, a simple add instruction will typically cause four bits to be set in a status register indicating: the sign of the result; whether a signed arithmetic overflow occurred; whether the result was zero and whether there was a carry out from the most significant bit of the result. A simplistic translation of the machine level add opcode therefore requires five C statements: one for the addition and four bit manipulation operations to set up the status bits.

In our reverse compiler we found that these two problems significantly reduced the quality of the translated C code and made it almost useless for the purposes of program comprehension. We therefore added a global dataflow analyser that generated exact use-define information at all program points and then

---

[1] A significant exception is the MIPS architecture in which conditional branches are calculated on the basis of a general purpose register.

back-substituted references to machine registers where possible. After substitution, a large number of dead expressions remain and these can then be eliminated from the final output.

The `asm21toc` translator provides the following three levels of translation.

1. 'Literal' translation in which, as far as possible, the output C program matches the input assembler program line for line. Jumps and branches in the original code are translated using `goto` statements and labels. The functional structure of the program is elucidated by examining call instructions in the original source, and any portions of code that are shared between functions (or, equivalently, functions with more than one entry point) are disambiguated by making copies of the shared code.
2. Control flow directed translation in which high-level control flow structures are recovered by applying Sharir-style [Sha80] reductions to the control flow graph.
3. Data flow directed translation in which register usages are back substituted where possible, and any dead register definitions arising from this back substitution are deleted.

A level 1 translation displays aspects of the underlying architecture. Levels 2 and 3 may be combined to give a translated program in which such machine specific details are largely suppressed.

A primary requirement of our translator is to warn users reliably when the limits of the tool have been reached. Some aspects of hand-written code are not statically visible. In particular, self-modifying code, global processor mode changes and indirect jumps may all render the detailed runtime semantics statically invisible. When such a condition is detected, we apply one of two strategies:

1. instantiate code into the translated output which simulates the processor feature in question, or
2. issue an error message and continue to output code that *may* be incorrect.

The users of our tool prefer machine details to be suppressed, so except in very common cases such as the aliasing of `do` loop counter registers (which form a stack on the ADSP-21xx) we adopt strategy 2 and provide advice to the user on how to rework the translated C.

We note in passing that, in contrast to conventional architectures, on the ADSP-21xx self-modifying code is easily detected because in normal operation the program is held in a separate memory space to the variables. In a set of programs totaling 122,979 instructions we found only 16 writes to program memory of which about half were genuine examples of self-modifying code.

In general, applications translated by our tool are unlikely to be recompiled as-is because they are usually embedded systems which access specific hardware registers and features outside of the processor. In addition, some processor details such as arithmetic precision and rounding modes may need to be carefully handled during a port. The expected application is to generate C code that will then be manually modified and so the emphasis is on human readability, although not, of course, at the expense of incorrect translation.

In what follows we describe the intermediate form for our translator and the dataflow analysis algorithm used to generate the use-define and substitution information which controls the substitution and dead code elimination phases. We give statistical results showing the number of expressions removed from the translated code as a result of these transformations.

3   Related Work

In the literature, *decompilation* is the term most commonly applied to translators which go from low to high level. We prefer to use the term 'decompilation' to denote systems that attempt to uncompile code which has been produced by a compiler, and the term 'reverse compilation' to cover the more general problem of rewriting hand-written code as high level source. Hand-written code is more general (and thus harder to translate) because human programmers can use aspects of the processor for which no straightforward C equivalent exists, such as multiple entry functions, inter-functional jumps and self-modifying code.

We also distinguish between tools that start from a binary executable and those that work from the assembler source. We are impressed by working binary decompilers but remain unconvinced as to the usefulness of such tools when porting programs since so much of the readability of programs derives from the use of meaningful variable names and comments. Of course, these arguments do not apply to binary-binary translators which have been used successfully in porting applications between the MIPS and Alpha architectures [Sit92]. Probst et al. [PKSdf] describe techniques for dynamic liveness analysis which could be used to resolve some of the non-statically determinable properties of our processor as described above: in particular the manipulation of global processor modes, although in practice, we believe that such modes are usually initialised at program startup and not usually changed during execution in our kinds of applications.

Reverse compilers, by their very nature, are tools that are not required routinely. As a result, many reverse compilers are constructed on an *ad hoc* basis and used briefly before being discarded. Other systems are developed for commercial use by companies specialising in re-engineering and are not documented in the research literature. A rare comparison of industry practice and a research decompiler may be found in [FC99]. Possibly the best developed and most widely applicable reverse compiler is Cifuentes' decompiler of PC binaries [CG95]. Another x86 decompiler was reported by Fuan and Zongtang [FZL93] and Cifuentes comments on this and several other projects, mostly of only historical interest, in her thesis [Cif94]. More formal approaches to reverse compilation were adopted in the ReDo project [BB94] and more recently Alan Mycroft has described applications of type inference algorithms to register-transfer level program descriptions [Myc99]. The FermaT workbench[War01] is a mature tool with strong formal methods underpinnings that specifically targets assembler level code, providing a set of program transformations that allow abstraction to a high level description. There is a much broader literature on source-to-source re-engineering where the input and output languages are either dialects of the same language, or at least both are high level languages. The ASF+SDF toolkit, for instance, has been used for automatic conversion of legacy COBOL source [vdBHKO02].

In earlier papers we have discussed the front end of our translator; the difficulty of translating some constructs (including self-modifying code and dynamic jumps); and the frequency of those constructs in real programs [JSW99,JSW00a]. We have also given results concerning the frequency of non-reducible control flow in real programs [JSW00b] and here use substantially the same sets of industry generated source code to show that large scale dataflow analysis can lead to the suppression of large proportions of the machine-level code in the resulting high level programs.

4   Dataflow Analysis

Optimising compilers must perform fast dataflow analysis because the edit-compile-run cycle must execute within a few minutes at most for compilers which are being used for routine development. The literature is well stocked with papers that argue against the usefulness of interprocedural optimisation [RG89] given that only rather small improvements in run-time efficiency have been observed which must be set against order-of-magnitude increases in compilation time. These analyses in any case usually produce only approximate results in terms of may-use and may-define sets.

We require exact dataflow analysis, that is the evaluation of dataflow functions over every possible execution path in the program. On the other hand, translation time is far less of a concern when performing reverse compilation since our users intend to work with the translated C, not to modify the original assembler source. As a result, translation is essentially one-off. In practice translation times are usually at most a few minutes on current desktop machines. The AP application shown in our results section, for instance required less than one minute on a 1GHz Pentium-M.

5   Dataflow Controlled Translation

asm21toc is built using our rdp translator generator [JS98] which comprises an LL(1) parser generator with integrated facilities for symbol table handling, graph management and set manipulation. The source language for rdp is an extended Backus-Naur Form that accepts annotations controlling the production of a *Reduced Derivation Tree* (RDT). In asm21toc, the RDT forms the expression part of a composite control flow and call graph that is constructed semi-automatically during the parse.

Figure 1 shows a source file containing ADSP assembly code. The syntax of the language is rather unusual for an assembler being based around algebraic style statements, so that at first glance it might be mistaken for a high-level language. The essential characteristic of an assembler is preserved, though: there is a

```
.module test;
.entry main;
.var/dm v1,v2,v3,v4;
.const x=5;

main: ax0 = dm(v1);
      ay0 = dm(v2);

      af = ax0 + ay0;
      ar = pass af;

      dm(v3) = ar;

      if ne af = ax0 + ay0;

      call sub;
      dm(v3) = ar;
      rts;

sub:  ar = af - ax0;
      rts;

.endmod;
```

Fig. 1. Assembler source example.

one-to-one correspondence between ADSP-21xx assembler executable statements and machine code instructions. On the ADSP-21xx, data memory is accessed *via* a globally defined array called dm. Variables are declared in line 3 as

```
.var/dm v1,v2,v3,v4;
```

which reserves addresses in data memory and creates symbolic names for them. Variables may be accessed with statements such as ax0 = dm(v1) which assigns the value of variable v1 (the contents of dfata memory location v1) to register ax0. The control flow graph derived from the example assembler code is shown in Figure 2.

There are some subtleties to trap the unwary: the statements mr = 0 and mr = 1 assemble into instructions with different opcodes. The first assembles to a clear instruction which also clears the overflow status bit. The second assembles to a data transfer instruction which does not modify the status registers. This detail, and all of the other use and define semantics for both status bits and data registers is specified in the BNF file that is input to rdp. The translator can be set to display the full results of the dataflow analysis within the control flow graph, as illustrated in Figure 3.

The solid arrows in Figure 3 represent control flow edges. The dotted edges represent opportunities for register variable substitution. (The layout here has been automatically generated with the VCG tool which is supplied with asm21toc as the main means of visualisation.)

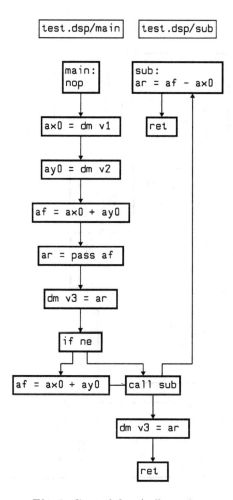

Fig. 2. Control flow/call graph.

Within each node, the corresponding expression is shown along with any labels that are defined for that line of source and up to four sets of registers. Node 415, for instance, corresponds to line 21 of the test file and is labeled **sub:**. Its expression is **ar = af - ax0**. The d (define) set shows that data register **AR** is defined along with status bits **AZ, AN, AV** and **AC**. Of these, only **AR** is live as it forms an output parameter for function **sub**. The expression uses data registers **AX0** and **AF** of which only **AX0** is substitutable. The dotted substitution arrow indicates that the corresponding definition of **AX0** is at node 388. Register **AF** is not substitutable because the definitions of **AF** at lines 423 and 403 reach this usage, and which applies depends on the conditional at line 403.

The code output by the translator for this graph is shown in Figure 4. The global variables representing processor registers (such as **A21TOC_status** are declared in **a2c_main.h**. For illustrative purposes, we have only commented out

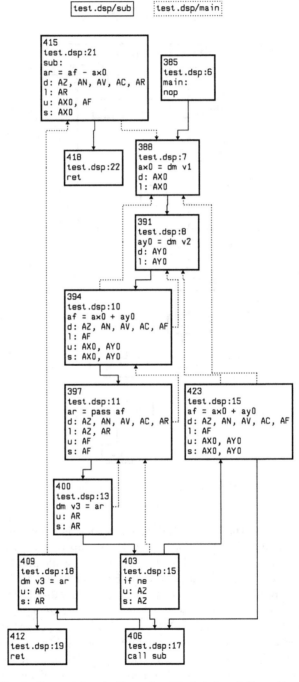

Fig. 3. Control flow/call graph with dataflow information.

```c
#include "a2c_main.h"

/* Define manifest constants */
#define x 5

/* Declare variables local to this module */
 long int v1;
 long int v2;
 long int v3;

/* Function prototypes */
void main(void);
static void sub(void);

/* Function bodies */
void main(void)
{
  /* ax0 = v1; all uses substituted  */
  /* ay0 = v2; all uses substituted  */
  af = (v1) + (v2);
  A21TOC_status = ar = ((v1) + (v2));
  /* all uses substituted, status live */
  A21TOC_AZ = A21TOC_status == 0;
  v3 = (((v1) + (v2)));
  if (!A21TOC_AZ)
    af = (v1) + (v2);
  sub();
  v3 = (af - (v1));
  return;
}

static void sub(void)
{
  /* ar = af - (v1); all uses substituted  */
  return;
}
```

Fig. 4. Translated code with substitutions.

dead expressions rather than deleting them from the code. The dm(vn) expressions in the ADSP source have been converted to variables and substituted across register names where possible. Most register expressions are killed as a result of this substitution, although care must be taken when the status side-effect is required downstream in a conditional. We should also note here that the dataflow analysis can also be used to back substitute intermediate variables allowing more complex expressions to be built up in the output.

6   Propagation of Dataflow Information

asm21toc performs global dataflow analysis based on define-use analysis. Our algorithm calls and returns from all sub-prodcedures, exercising exhaustively all execution paths through the application until stability is achieved. This is practical only because

1. our applications are small: the code space for ADSP21xx family processors is opnly 16K words long, and
2. we can allow very long reverse compilation times relative to dataflow analyses used in conventional compilers because reverse compilation is essentially a one-off process and not part o fth enormal code development loop.

The exhaustive traversal requires worst case exponential time, and it is certainly possible to construct artificial examples that will not terminate in reasonable time, but we have not yet encountered real applications that display such deeply nested and widely branching characteristics.

The d and u (define and use) sets are filled in for each node by the parser. We use an exhaustive slot-wise data flow propagation algorithm to construct the l and s (live and substitutable) sets. The algorithm provides substantial opportunities for optimisation, but is fast enough even in this crude form for our purposes. We assume the reader is familiar with slot-wise data-flow algorithms as described in standard texts. We give here a sketch of the exhaustive traversal part of our algorithm.

We iterate over each node in the control flow graph and then, for each usage at each node perform a recursive propagation back up through the control flow graph. The back propagator returns TRUE if the path is still live after propagation, that is, if a matching define was not found. During this back propagation, we perform the following at each node.

1. If this node is not in a function, then return killed path. This handles so-called 'orphaned code' which might be debugging code, an unlabeled basic block (which is a programmer error) or an interrupt service routine.
2. If this node has already been visited for this use, return killed path.
3. If node has a matching definition, insert in live set and return killed path.
4. If node is a call node then scan up the called function from each of its exits (return instructions) and then return logical OR of all such paths.
5. If we have come back to the node at which we started then return killed path.
6. If there are no in-edges, then we are at the top of the main-line function, so return live path.
7. Else recurse through each control flow in-edge.

As a side effect of this process, we keep track of how many unique definitions have been encountered for a given usage. If there are none, then an error message is output since this corresponds to the use of a register before it has been initialised. If there is exactly one, then the register usage may be substituted. The register is added to the **s** set and a dotted arrow is added to the corresponding definition. For each definition, we also calculate the number of non-substitutable usages. If there are none, then the expression has been killed and may be deleted from the translated output.

7   Results

To illustrate the effect of this dataflow analysis three sets of code were prepared and tested at the interprocedural (but not inter-modular) level. Most applications are split into a large number of separate modules which are separately compiled and linked together. Our translator performs this linking step internally, but due to the way in which source files were supplied to us by our industrial partners we were not always able to construct complete systems, and hence the lack of inter-modular testing. The three data sets are essentially those used in our earlier paper on control flow patterns in assembler programs [JSW00b], with some small modifications to remove modules that contain only declarations.

1. IP is a set of image processing functions written for a multiprocessor ADSP-21xx system. This set contains trick code and examples of highly optimised functions written for maximum speed and code density.
2. TC comprises functions for the implementation of mobile telecommunications protocols. The host system had relatively abundant memory and this code is less tightly optimised than IP.
3. ME is drawn from Analog Devices' own examples for the ADSP-21xx. These functions are designed to be comprehensible and are the least tightly optimised.

One large complete application was tested at intermodular level: this corresponds to the set AP in the tables.

The impact of the transformations is best illustrated by the compaction of AP: of the 1,899 data register definitions 845 were deleted after substitution and of the 2,521 status bit definitions only 327 were instantiated in the translated code.

Table 1 shows the results in more detail. For each set, we show the total number of instructions, the number of status bit definitions and the number of data register definitions. The ADSP-21xx instructions set between zero and five status bits for each operation, so the instruction mix affects the ratio of status bit definitions to instruction counts. We then show the number of these

Table 1. The impact of compression.

Source set	Instructions	Status defines	Data defines	Status live	Data live	Data substitutions	Data deletions	% status suppressed	% data suppressed
AP	2,784	2,521	1,899	327	1,503	1,926	845	78.03	44.49
IP	41,246	32,642	32,245	416	3,124	11,640	1,595	98.73	4.89
TC	2,901	2,688	2,078	316	1,537	2,112	911	88.24	43.84
ME	3,789	2,310	2,914	183	1,370	3,256	1,031	92.10	35.38

definitions that are live in each case. Dead data expressions may arise either from instructions whose goal is to set the status bits for a later conditional branch, or because the lack of inter-modular translation for sets AP, IP and TC leaves dangling output parameter values which are in reality used following a call from another module. The number of substitutions is the total number of substitutions performed. In the case of a register that is substituted into an expression that is itself then substituted all instances count. The number of deletions is the number of data register expressions that are killed as a result of substitution and may therefore be suppressed. The final two columns show the proportion of status and data register expressions that are suppressed in the final output.

The figures for set AP are exact in the sense that all dataflow paths in the application have been explored. The figures for the other three sets represent only a lower bound for the number of data register expressions suppressed and give an exaggerated view of the number of status definitions suppressed. This is because control paths that leave the modules are not followed. In general this will exaggerate the number of dead status calculations (because, for instance, some status values may be return values from functions) and depress the number of data register expressions that are suppressed for the cases where input and output parameters are carried in registers. This effect is seen most markedly in the IP set, where many of the functions are placed in their own module. We have included these rather anomalous figures here mainly for comparability with our earlier paper, although they do show *inter alia* the necessity to perform full global dataflow analysis in reverse compilation since the suppression mechanisms are essentially disabled if only global analysis is attempted.

Anecdotally, we expected between one third and one half of all data register expressions to be suppressed and around three quarters of all status operations. These rules of thumb are largely borne out by the results here subject to the caveats above. Experiments based on complete large applications would be desirable.

8   Conclusions, Further Work and Acknowledgements

We have shown that significant reductions in the size of reverse compiled programs may be achieved through register expression substitution and dead expression elimination. Of course, any good optimising compiler would perform these transformations whilst compiling the translated program onto the new architecture, so we do not claim that these reductions improve run time efficiency. The purpose of performing the compression is to render the code comfortable for humans to read, allowing the high level programmer to see the algorithm-level control and data flow without being exposed to the large number of memory-register moves and status calculations present in a naïve translation.

Our reverse compiler has been used by one of our industrial partners to port two large applications from the ADSP-21xx processor to scheduled code for the TMS320C6x processor. An ongoing area of interest is the extension of our dataflow analysis to allow function signatures and type information to be extracted. We are also examining *expression-related variable* sets; that is partitions of the global set of variables into subsets that are related by virtue of appearing together in expressions. By this means we hope to improve the code visualisation aspects of the reverse compiler to further assist program comprehension.

An obvious experiment might be to take some C source, forward compile it with the manufacturer supplied GNU-C compiler and then reverse compile, comparing efficiencies. Sadly, the GNU-C implementation for the ADSP-21xx is so poorly implemented that it is not a serious contender for production use, and in any case our goal is to *cross-*reverse compile, so our efforts have concentrated on optimising with respect to the idiosyncracies of the TMS320C6x compiler. We shall report elsewhere on the results of a study (provisionally entitled *Up, down and sideways* in which we compare two back ends for our tool, one generating ANSI-C as described here and one generating so-called sequential assembler for the TMS320C6x. Sequential assembler may be used as input to the scheduler. As one might expect, programme comprehension is best served *via* the ANSI-C translation (the *up and down* route) but some performance gains can be achieved with assembler-to-assembler *sideways* translation.

We would like to thank the directors of Image Industries Ltd for access to their source code; Georg Sander who wrote the VCG tool which produced Figures 2 and 3 and the very helpful comments from the anonymous referees.

References

[BB94]   Peter T. Breuer and Jonathan P. Bowen. Decompilation: the enumeration of types and grammars. *Transactions on Programming Languages and Systems*, 16(5):1613–1648, September 1994.

[CG95]   C. Cifuentes and K. J. Gough. Decompilation of binary programs. *Software — Practice and Experience*, 25(7):811–829, July 1995.

[Cif94]   Cristina Cifuentes. *Reverse compilation techniques*. PhD thesis, Queensland University of Technology, July 1994.

[FC99]   L. Freeman and C Cifuentes. An industry perspective on decompilation. In *Proc Internat. Conference on Software Maintenance*. IEEE, 1999.

[FZL93]   C Fuan, L. Zongtian, and L. Li. Design and implementation techniques of the 8086 C decompiling system. *Mini-micro systems*, 14(4):10–18, 1993.

[JS98]   Adrian Johnstone and Elizabeth Scott. rdp – an iterator based recursive descent parser generator with tree promotion operators. *SIGPLAN notices*, 33(9), September 1998.

[JSW99]   Adrian Johnstone, Elizabeth Scott, and Tim Womack. Reverse compilation of Digital Signal Processor assembler source to ANSI-C. In *Proc Internat. Conference on Software Maintenance*. IEEE, 1999.

[JSW00a]   Adrian Johnstone, Elizabeth Scott, and Tim Womack. Reverse compilation for Digital Signal Processors: a working example. In *Proc 33. Hawaii Intnl. Conf. Sys. Sci*. IEEE, 2000.

[JSW00b]   Adrian Johnstone, Elizabeth Scott, and Tim Womack. What assembly language programmers get up to: control flow challenges in reverse compilation. In *Proc. 4th Eur. Conf. Soft. Maint. & Reengineering*. IEEE, 2000.

[Myc99]   Alan Mycroft. Type-based decompilation. In S Doaitse Swierstra, edi-
            tor, *Proc. 8th European Symposium on programming (ESOP'99), Lecture
            notes in Computer Science 1383*, pages 208–223, Berlin, 1999. Springer.

[PKSdf]   Mark Probst, Andreas Krall, and Bernhard Scholz. Register liveness
            analysis for optimizing binary translation. In *Working Conference on
            Reverse Engineering*, pages 228–235. IEEE computer society, October
            2002 (also at http://www.complang.tuwien.ac.at/cd/wcre_02.pdf).

[RG89]   Stephen E. Richardson and Mahadevan Ganapathi. Interprocedural
            optimization: experimental results. *Software Practice and Experience*,
            19(2):149–169, February 1989.

[Sha80]   Micha Sharir. Structural analysis: a new approach to flow analysis in
            optimising compilers. *Computer Languages*, 5(3/4):141–153, 1980.

[Sit92]   Richard L Sites. Binary translation. *Digital Technical Journal*, 4(4):137–
            152, 1992.

[vdBHKO02] M.G.J. van den Brand, J. Heering, P. Klint, and P.A. Olivier. Compiling
            language definitions: the ASF+SDF compiler. *ACM Transactions on
            Programming Languages and Systems*, 24(4):334–368, 2002.

[War01]   M. Ward. The fermat assembler re-engineering workbench. In *Inter-
            national Conference on Software Maintenance*. IEEE computer society,
            November 2001.

Fast Points-to Analysis
for Languages with Structured Types

Michael Jung and Sorin Alexander Huss

Integrated Circuits and Systems Lab.
Department of Computer Science
Technische Universität Darmstadt, Germany
{mjung,huss}@iss.tu-darmstadt.de

Abstract. The C programming language is still ubiquitous in embedded software development. For many tools that operate on programs written in pointer languages like C, it is essential to have a good approximation of the information about where the pointer variables possibly may point to at runtime. We present a points-to analysis, which is based on Steensgaard's approach to points-to analysis [12], but achieves a higher level of precision.

1 Introduction

Due to high production volumes in the embedded systems field, resources assigned to software development cause only a small fraction of the overall costs. Keeping the expenses for hardware per device low is thus more important. This situation causes some reluctance in adopting programming languages like Java, which trade low requirements on runtime resources for efficient software development methods. Not surprisingly, Lanfear and Balacco arrive in their market study at the conclusion that "C remains the language of choice for embedded developers" (see [8]).

We believe that code transformation approaches such as, e.g., *Partial Evaluation* (see [7]) have an enormous, but not yet exploited potential to raise the productivity of software development especially for embedded systems. With such approaches, generic code can automatically be tailored to specific applications, thus achieving specialized and therefore less resource demanding versions of the code. However, advanced optimizations or code transformations on programs written in pointer languages such as C do not yield good results if they cannot apply as precise as possible information on where the program's variables possibly may point to at runtime. In general, it is not possible to compute points-to information with absolute precision (see [10]). However, various analysis algorithms have been developed, which compute conservative approximations at different levels of result precision and computational complexity (see [5], [9]). The one that is described in [13] was quite influential, since it produces results

H. Schepers (Ed.): SCOPES 2004, LNCS 3199, pp. 107–121, 2004.

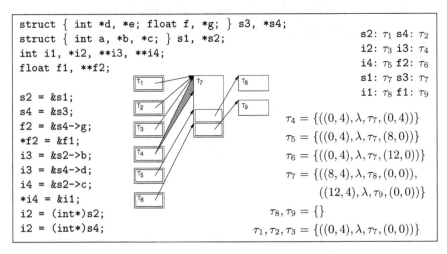

Fig. 1. Sample C code and analysis result.

which are significantly more precise than those of trivial analyses[1] (see [4]), while it has an almost linear time complexity.

This paper reports on a fast points-to analysis that is quite similar to the methods described in [13] and [12], but with an increased level of precision. The proposed approach is flow-insensitive, which means that the order of program statement execution is irrelevant. In general, the algorithm needs the complete source code of the program to be analyzed. This is usually called "whole-program analysis". The analysis process is inter-procedural, but context-insensitive, which means that the results which stem from function calls are unified over all function call sites. Components of structured variables are considered. All heap allocations from a single call site are mapped to a single abstract location.

Points-to information can be represented adequately by means of storage shape graphs (see [2]). We call the nodes of such a graph "abstract locations". They represent a set of actual memory locations, which cannot be distinguished by the analysis. An abstract location can point to other abstract locations, but in order to restrict the size of the graph, each node is limited to point to a single node only. This means that all abstract locations pointed to by a single node have to be merged. Figure 1 shows a short C code fragment taken from [12] and the storage shape graph produced by the proposed analysis. For now, please ignore the equations in the lower right part of the figure – their meaning will be explained later. With exception of s1 and s3 all storage locations of variables are represented by distinct abstract locations. The abstract locations for s1 and s3 had to be merged, since pointers to s1 as well as to s3 are assigned to the variable i2.

---

[1] The address-taken analysis, e.g., which assumes that each variable can possibly point to each variable whose address is taken anywhere in the program.

The remainder of this paper is organized as follows. In section 2 we discuss related work. Section 3 defines a C language subset, which will be instrumental for compact presentation. The data structures used to describe the storage shape graphs are introduced in section 4. In section 5 we introduce a set of rules, one for each kind of language statements, which establish constraints on the storage shape graph. A storage shape graph, which satisfies all constrains, gives a safe points-to approximation. Section 6 describes an algorithm, which produces such graphs. Some experimental results are summarized in section 7.

2   Related Work

The points-to analysis proposed in the sequel may be considered as an extension to the method described by Bjarne Steensgaard [12], which, in turn, is a modification to his own work reported on in [13]. Inescapably the form of presentation used in this paper is influenced by the mentioned articles. The first rough-cut idea, which initiated the work that let to this paper, was actually brought up by Steensgaard in a short discussion by email with one of the authors.

The main enhancements compared to [12] are the following: First, our analysis produces more precise results. Points-to analysis is applied to answer questions like "Which memory locations (both function variables and heap allocated memory) may be accessed by the expression *s2->c (often called *access path*) at runtime?". The lower the number of locations, the more precise is the analysis result. The source code fragment shown in Fig. 1 is virtually the same as the one Steensgaard uses as an example in his article. His analysis, however, would have to join τ_8 and τ_9 to become a single abstract location, which means that access paths to variables i1 and f1, respectively, would be aliased.

The improved precision compared to [12] is due to the following facts. In order to guarantee for a linear relation between the size of storage shape graphs and of analyzed programs, the information on where a pointer in a field points to has to be of constant size. This is why two abstract locations are joined whenever a pointer may point to both of them, instead of storing a set of references. Steensgaard's analysis does roughly the same for pointer offsets: If a pointer may point to two different offsets in the same abstract location, then it is assumed that nothing is known about the offset. This means that all fields of the abstract location have to be joined into a single embracing field. In contrast to that, our analysis incorporates ranges of pointer offsets, which are represented by a pair of numbers that represent offset and width of the range (depicted by the gray area in Fig. 1). The proposed analysis has therefore to join the fields only, which are located in this range. Some figures of merit in terms of precision are given in the results section of this article.

Furthermore, we consider our analysis to be conceptually simpler and therefore easier to implement. Steensgaard distinguishes four kinds of abstract locations. The proposed analysis, in contrast, applies a single kind of representation. This leads to a more compact algorithm, which we consider to be more concise.

Manuvir Das describes in a recent paper [3] another improvement to Steensgaard's analysis. His studies of real world C programs revealed that the prevalent use of pointers is in passing the addresses of struct type objects or updateable values (like, e.g., in calls of the scanf function). The analysis takes advantage of this fact by avoiding joins at the top level of pointer chains whenever possible. Although the algorithm is part of a higher complexity class, which is due to the fact that it is less conservative, in practice it is almost as fast as Steensgaard's analysis and nearly as precise as other algorithms that scale worse. Although Manuvir Das' approach is orthogonal to and may also be combined with our analysis, we did not yet pursue this idea.

3   Source Language Definition

For the sake of a compact illustration we present our points-to analysis for programs written in a language (see Fig. 2), which we borrowed from [12] being essentially a subset of the C programming language (see [6]). Extending the analysis to support the complete C language specification is relatively straightforward. f, p, r, x and y range over all possible variable names and constants, n over all possible field names. We do not have to consider control statements since the outlined analysis is flow-insensitive.

$$
\begin{aligned}
S ::= \ & x =_\square y \\
| \ & x =_\square \&y \\
| \ & x =_\square *y \\
| \ & x =_\square \text{allocate}(y) \\
| \ & *x =_\square y \\
| \ & x =_\square \text{op}(y_\square \ldots y_\square) \\
| \ & x =_\square \&y \rightarrow n \hspace{3em} \text{(a)} \\
| \ & x =_\square \text{fun}(f_\square \ldots f_\square) \rightarrow r \ \{S^*\} \ \text{(b)} \\
| \ & x =_\square p(y_\square \ldots y_\square) \hspace{2em} \text{(c)}
\end{aligned}
$$

Fig. 2. Syntax of the considered source language.

Some pecularities of the compiler implementation, which are intentionally not specified in [6], have to be provided. Namely, these are the sizes of the different basic types and the sizes and offsets of components of structured types[2]. This information is being used to attribute each assignment statement by the size of the assigned value and to compute offsets into structured memory locations (see Fig. 2(a)). Aside from that, types are irrelevant: The analysis gracefully handles component accesses to basic type variables as well as assignments of basic type values to variables with structured types and vice versa – which is supported in C due to unsafe type casts.

---

[2] Note that the analysis presented in [12] applies symbolic offsets and is therefore somewhat less implementation dependent.

The allocate(y) function dynamically allocates y bytes of memory. Arithmetic and other primitive operations are described by op($y_{\blacksquare}\ldots y_{\blacksquare}$) expressions. Figure 2(b) shows the syntax for function definitions: The $f_{\blacksquare}$ to $f_{\blacksquare}$ variables are function parameters and the r variable (which is hidden in C programs) holds the function's return value. Function calls (Fig. 2(c)) have call-by-value semantics.

4   Data Structures

We define a set of data structures, which are exploited in the points-to analysis in order to denote the storage shape graph. Fig. 1 details some examples.

$$\tau = \{f_1, \ldots, f_n\} \tag{1}$$
$$f = (q, \lambda, \tau, p) \tag{2}$$
$$q = (o, s) \tag{3}$$
$$p = (l, u) \tag{4}$$
$$o, l \in \mathbb{N}_0^+ \cup \{\bot\} \tag{5}$$
$$s, u \in \mathbb{N}_0^+ \cup \{\top\} \tag{6}$$
$$\lambda = \mathsf{lam}(\tau_1, \ldots, \tau_n)(\tau) \tag{7}$$

A storage shape graph G is a set of abstract locations τ, each representing a set of storage locations of the program being analyzed. These can be named locations like variables or function parameters, as well as anonymous ones like memory blocks allocated on the heap. To be able to represent structured objects, an abstract location consists of a set of non-overlapping fields f. An object, which is always accessed as a whole (typically a variable of basic type), carries one field only (or none, if the analysis detects that it never points anywhere; after all, we are interested in pointers only). Objects with sub-components being accessed in the analyzed program are represented by an abstract location with possibly more than one field. There is not necessarily a one-to-one mapping between the components of a storage location with structured type and the fields of an abstract location. On the one hand, a single field can represent a set of adjacent components of a memory location. Since an abstract location may represent a set of actual memory locations, a single field can also represent components from distinct memory locations. A field has a certain extent (o, s) in its abstract location with offset o and size s. It can hold a pointer to an abstract location τ and/or to an abstract function $\lambda = \mathsf{lam}(\tau_1, \ldots, \tau_n)(\tau)$, which in turn represents a set of functions, whose parameters and return variables are described by abstract locations $\tau_1, \ldots, \tau_n$, and τ, respectively. Fields contain a second tuple (l, u) which, whenever the field holds a pointer to an abstract location τ, describes the range of possible offsets $[l, l + u)$ into the memory locations represented by τ. An offset range $(0, \top)$ means that the pointer can point anywhere into the object. For a field extent this value means that the field spans the complete abstract location. $(\bot, 0)$ as an offset range or field extent descriptor means that the value is not yet constrained in any way. This descriptor value is transient and will not be present in the final storage shape graph, unless the program being analyzed dereferences uninitialized pointers. Two fields or two abstract functions are equal when they are structurally equal, but abstract locations (τ), field extents (q) and offset ranges (p) have an identity (possibly implemented by the use of tags), and equality is defined by identity.

We define a sub-interval-like (Eqn. 8) and an intervals-overlap-like relation (Eqn. 9) on field extents and offset ranges, which will be helpful in being concise later on:

$$(o_1, s_1) \trianglelefteq (o_2, s_2) \Leftrightarrow o_2 \leq o_1 \wedge o_2 + s_2 \geq o_1 + s_1 \tag{8}$$

$$(o_1, s_1) \bowtie (o_2, s_2) \Leftrightarrow o_1 + s_1 > o_2 \wedge o_2 + s_2 > o_1 \tag{9}$$

The aforementioned restriction, that the fields of abstract locations may never overlap, can now be denoted as

$$\forall \tau \in G : \forall ((o_i, s_i), \lambda_i, \tau_i, p_i), ((o_j, s_j), \lambda_j, \tau_j, p_j) \in \tau :$$
$$i \neq j \Leftrightarrow (o_j, s_j) \not\bowtie (o_i, s_i) \tag{10}$$

5   Constraint Deduction

This section defines a rule for each kind of statement of the language defined in section 3, which establishes constraints on the storage shape graph. A storage shape graph that conforms to all constraints implied by these rules and all the statements of a given program, is valid with respect to this program. The order of statement consideration is irrelevant.

To keep the rules compact we define two more relations on fields and abstract locations. The first is an inclusion-like relation:

$$((o_1, s_1), \lambda, \tau, (l_1, u_1)) \trianglelefteq \tau_2 \Leftrightarrow$$
$$\exists ((o_2, s_2), \lambda, \tau, (l_2, u_2)) \in \tau_2 :$$
$$(o_1, s_1) \trianglelefteq (o_2, s_2) \wedge (l_1, u_1) \trianglelefteq (l_2, u_2) \tag{11}$$

Intuitively, it states that an abstract location contains a certain field. Consider, however, that field extents and offset ranges do not have to be equal; field extent and offset range of the abstract location's field only have to be at least as 'wide' as those of the field given at the relation's left hand side (e.g., $((0, 4), \lambda, \tau, (4, 4)) \trianglelefteq \{ \dots, ((0, 8), \lambda, \tau, (0, 8)), \dots \}$).

The second relation is defined as:

$$\tau_1 \, {}_{(l_1, u_1)}\trianglelefteq^s_{(l_2, u_2)} \, \tau_2 \Leftrightarrow$$
$$\forall ((o, s), \lambda, \tau, q) \in \tau_1 : (o, s) \bowtie (l_1, u_1 + s) \Rightarrow$$
$$((l_2, u_2 + s), \lambda, \tau, q) \trianglelefteq \tau_2 \tag{12}$$

This relation is being used to establish constraints on the storage shape graph due to variable assignments. Thinking operationally, it is the analog of copying

$$\frac{A \vdash x : \tau_1 \quad A \vdash y : \tau_2 \quad \tau_2 \; {}_{(0,0)}\trianglelefteq^s_{(0,0)} \tau_1}{A \vdash satisfied(x =_s y)}$$

$$\frac{A \vdash x : \tau_1 \quad A \vdash y : \tau_2 \quad \exists\lambda : ((0,s), \lambda, \tau_2, (0,0)) \trianglelefteq \tau_1}{A \vdash satisfied(x =_s \&y)}$$

$$\frac{A \vdash x : \tau \quad \exists\tau', \lambda' : ((0,s), \lambda', \tau', (0,0)) \trianglelefteq \tau}{A \vdash satisfied(x =_s allocate(y))}$$

$$\frac{A \vdash x : \tau_1 \quad A \vdash y : \tau_2 \quad \exists\tau_3, l, u, \lambda, s' : ((0,s'), \lambda, \tau_3, (l,u)) \in \tau_2 \quad s' \geq sizeof(void*) \quad \tau_3 \; {}_{(l,u)}\trianglelefteq^s_{(0,0)} \tau_1}{A \vdash satisfied(x =_s *y)}$$

$$\frac{A \vdash x : \tau_1 \quad A \vdash y : \tau_2 \quad \exists\tau_3, l, u, \lambda, s' : ((0,s'), \lambda, \tau_3, (l,u)) \in \tau_1 \quad s' \geq sizeof(void*) \quad \tau_2 \; {}_{(0,0)}\trianglelefteq^s_{(l,u)} \tau_3}{A \vdash satisfied(*x =_s y)}$$

$$\frac{A \vdash x : \tau \quad A \vdash y_i : \tau_i \quad \exists\tau' : \forall i \in [1 \ldots n] : \tau_i \; {}_{(0,0)}\trianglelefteq^{sizeof(y_i)}_{(0,0)} \tau' \quad \tau' \; {}_{(0,0)}\trianglelefteq^s_{(0,0)} \tau \quad \exists\tau^*, \lambda : ((0,s), \lambda, \tau^*, (0, T)) \trianglelefteq \tau}{A \vdash satisfied(x =_s op(y_1 \ldots y_n))}$$

$$\frac{A \vdash x : \tau_1 \quad A \vdash y : \tau_2 \quad \exists\tau_3, l, u, \lambda_3, s' : ((0,s'), \lambda_3, \tau_3, (l,u)) \in \tau_2 \quad s' \geq sizeof(void*) \quad ((0,s), \lambda_3, \tau_3, (l + offset(n), u)) \trianglelefteq \tau_1}{A \vdash satisfied(x =_s \&y \to n)}$$

$$\frac{A \vdash x : \tau \quad A \vdash r : \tau'_r \quad \forall i \in [1, \ldots, n] : A \vdash f_i : \tau'_i \quad \exists\tau', l, u, s', \lambda : ((0,s'), \lambda, \tau', (l,u)) \in \tau \quad s' \geq s \quad \forall i \in [1, \ldots, n] : s_i = sizeof(f_i) \quad s_r = sizeof(r) \quad \lambda = lam(\tau_1, \ldots, \tau_n)(\tau_r) \quad \forall i \in [1 \ldots n] : \tau_i \; {}_{(0,0)}\trianglelefteq^{s_i}_{(0,0)} \tau'_i \quad \tau'_r \; {}_{(0,0)}\trianglelefteq^{s_r}_{(0,0)} \tau_r \quad \forall x \in S^* : A \vdash satisfied(x)}{A \vdash satisfied(x =_s fun(f_1, \ldots, f_n) \to r \{S^*\})}$$

$$\frac{A \vdash x : \tau \quad A \vdash p : \tau'_p \quad \forall i \in [1, \ldots, n] : A \vdash y_i : \tau'_i \quad \exists\tau', l, u, s', \lambda : ((0,s'), \lambda, \tau', (l,u)) \in \tau'_p \quad s' \geq sizeof(void*) \quad \forall i \in [1, \ldots, n] : s_i = sizeof(y_i) \quad \lambda = lam(\tau_1, \ldots, \tau_n)(\tau_r) \quad \forall i \in [1, \ldots, n] : \tau'_i \; {}_{(0,0)}\trianglelefteq^{s_i}_{(0,0)} \tau_i \quad \tau_r \; {}_{(0,0)}\trianglelefteq^s_{(0,0)} \tau}{A \vdash satisfied(x =_s p(y_1, \ldots, y_n))}$$

Fig. 3. Constraint deduction from program statements.

a block of data of size s from location τ_1 at an offset which is in the interval $[l_1, u_1)$ into location τ_2 at an offset of the interval $[l_2, u_2)$.

Figure 3 defines for each kind of statement a set of relations on components of the storage shape graph, which have to hold in order that the graph is valid for the program considered. A defines the mapping of the program's variable identifiers to abstract locations in the storage shape graph. The rule for the *address-of* (&) operation for example is

$$\frac{A \vdash x : \tau_1 \quad A \vdash y : \tau_2 \quad \exists\lambda : ((0,s), \lambda, \tau_2, (0,0)) \trianglelefteq \tau_1}{A \vdash satisfied(x =_s \&y)}$$

It states that if the program being analyzed contains a statement of the form x=&y and if variables x and y are mapped to abstract locations τ_1 and τ_2, respectively, then τ_1 has to contain a field, which

1. is located right at the beginning of τ_1,
2. is *at least* as wide as a pointer value,
3. may or may not point to a function, and
4. points to the abstract location, which represents variable y (possibly among others) at
5. an offset known to be in a range which includes 0,

in order that the storage shape graph is valid with respect to the statement.

These requirements are derived from the C language semantics, but they are relaxed in order to allow for a fast analysis that computes a conservative approximation. Statements 1 and 2 are due to the extent $(0, s)$ of the field required to be part of τ_1. s is the size of a pointer value, since a pointer value is the data being assigned and because the parser provides information on the width of assigned values (indicated by the indexed s at the $=$ operator). Note that the $\trianglelefteq$ relation does not require τ_1 to have a field with an extent of exactly $(0, s)$, but rather a field, whose extent comprises $(0, s)$ (see Eqn. 11). This is why line 2 states that the field has to be *at least* as wide as a pointer value. Statement 3 basically denotes that λ may be **lam**()(), which does not represent a function. However, it may as well point to some real function, if x is assigned a pointer to a function in another program statement. In statement 4 τ_2 is required to be the abstract location, which represents y. Since y may be aliased with other variables, τ_2 may also represent these. The offset range $(0, 0)$ captures the offset 0 exactly. As defined by the C language semantics, this is the offset into y to which x will point after statement x = &y is executed. However, due to another statement, x may also point to some other offset. That is why it is not required for the field in τ_1 to point exactly to offset 0, but rather to any offset in a range, which includes 0. Once again, this is due to the definition of the $\trianglelefteq$ relation.

Because of space constraints we cannot give an explanation for each and every rule. Instead, we highlight some subtleties: The rule for allocate statements is similar to the *address-of* rule, but the abstract location pointed to is anonymous. Consider how the rules for pointer indirections apply the offset ranges. The rule for &y $\rightarrow$ n is a combination of *pointer indirection* and *address-of* rule with an extra offset addition. Regarding the rule for primitive operations: If a pointer value is used in an arithmetic expression, then it might be possible to reclaim it from the computed value, which therefore can possibly point to all abstract locations to which one of the operands may point. Beyond that all information on the offset range is lost (consider ptr++ expressions), which is why it is forced to $(0, \top)$. The rules for *function definition* and *function call* basically enforce the flow of pointers from actual parameters to formal parameters by means of function pointer variables.

6   Constraint Solving

A set of constraints can be deduced for a given program, by means of the rules given in section 5. A storage shape graph which satisfies these constraints is

$\mathbf{cjoin}(s, p_1, \tau_1, p_2, \tau_2)$:
  if (not replaying)
    $\mathbf{pending}(p_1) = \mathbf{pending}(p_1) \cup$
      $\{<\mathbf{cjoin}, s, p_1, \tau_1, p_2, \tau_2>\}$
    $\mathbf{pending}(\tau_1) = \mathbf{pending}(\tau_1) \cup$
      $\{<\mathbf{cjoin}, s, p_1, \tau_1, p_2, \tau_2>\}$
    $\mathbf{pending}(p_2) = \mathbf{pending}(p_2) \cup$
      $\{<\mathbf{cjoin}, s, p_1, \tau_1, p_2, \tau_2>\}$
  let $(l_1, u_1) = p_1, (l_2, u_2) = p_2$ **in**
  if $(l_1 \neq \perp \wedge l_2 \neq \perp)$
    forall $(p', \lambda', \tau', q') \in \tau_1$ **do**
      if $(p' \bowtie (l_1, u_1 + s))$
        $\mathbf{join}(\{((l_2, u_2 + s), \lambda', \tau', q')\}, \tau_2)$

$\mathbf{join}(\tau_1, \tau_2)$:
  let $\tau = \mathbf{ecr\text{-}unite}(\tau_1, \tau_2)$ **in**
  $\tau = \tau_1 \cup \tau_2$
  forall $f_3 = (p_3, \lambda_3, \tau_3, q_3) \in \tau$
  forall $f_4 = (p_4, \lambda_4, \tau_4, q_4) \in \tau$
    if $(f_3 \neq f_4 \wedge p_3 \bowtie p_4)$
      $\mathbf{join}(p_3, p_4)$ $\mathbf{join}(\lambda_3, \lambda_4)$
      $\mathbf{join}(\tau_3, \tau_4)$ $\mathbf{join}(q_3, q_4)$
      $\tau = \tau \setminus \{f_4\}$
  $\mathbf{pending}(\tau) = \mathbf{pending}(\tau_1) \cup$
    $\mathbf{pending}(\tau_2)$
  if $(\tau_1 \neq \tau)$ **execute-pending**(τ_1)
  if $(\tau_2 \neq \tau)$ **execute-pending**(τ_2)

$\mathbf{join}(p_1, p_2)$:
  let $(l_1, u_1) = p_1, (l_2, u_2) = p_2$ **in**
  let $l = min(l_1, l_2)$ **in**
  let $u = max(l_1 + u_1, l_2 + u_2) - l$ **in**
  let $p = \mathbf{ecr\text{-}unite}(p_1, p_2)$ **in**
  $p = (l, u)$
  $\mathbf{pending}(p) =$
    $\mathbf{pending}(p_1) \cup \mathbf{pending}(p_2)$
  if $(p_1 \neq p)$ **execute-pending**(p_1)
  if $(p_2 \neq p)$ **execute-pending**(p_2)

$\mathbf{join}(\lambda_1, \lambda_2)$:
  let $\mathbf{lam}(\tau_1, \ldots, \tau_n)(\tau) = \lambda_1$ **in**
  let $\mathbf{lam}(\tau'_1, \ldots, \tau'_m)(\tau') = \lambda_2$ **in**
    forall $i \in [1, \ldots, min(n, m)]$ **do**
      $\mathbf{join}(\tau_i, \tau'_i)$
    $\mathbf{join}(\tau, \tau')$
    $\lambda_1 = \lambda_2 = \mathbf{lam}(\tau'_1, \ldots, \tau'_{max(n,m)})(\tau')$

$\mathbf{add\text{-}offset}(p_1, o, p_2)$:
  if (not replaying)
    $\mathbf{pending}(p_1) = \mathbf{pending}(p_1) \cup$
      $\{<\mathbf{add\text{-}offset}, p_1, o, p_2>\}$
  let $(l_1, u_1) = p_1$ **in**
  if $(l_1 \neq \perp)$ **let** $p' = (l_1 + o, u_1)$ **in**
    $\mathbf{join}(p', p_2)$

Fig. 4. Constraint enforcing functions.

valid with respect to the program. This section describes an algorithm for the construction of such graphs.

In an initialization step all named program variables are mapped to distinct abstract locations with an initially empty set of fields. Thereafter, the algorithm iterates over all statements of the program being analyzed, and invokes functions, which modify the storage shape graph such that the constraints corresponding to the current statement are satisfied. We first describe these constraint enforcing functions, which are outlined in Fig. 4.

There are three **join** functions for abstract locations, abstract functions and ranges (i.e. both field extents and offset ranges), respectively. The operands of a join function call are merged. We exploit disjoint-set forests with path compression (see [14]) to achieve fast union operations. The abstract location or range which results from the join operation are represented by an equivalence class representative (ecr) of the class of merged objects. Overlapping fields of joined abstract locations are then combined. Two joined ranges are represented by a range, which is as small as possible and still covers the original ranges.

The $\mathbf{cjoin}(s, p_1, \tau_1, p_2, \tau_2)$ function enforces a constraint of the form $\tau_1 \underset{p_1}{\overset{s}{\trianglelefteq}}_{p_2} \tau_2$. However, it is unknown if τ_1, p_1 and p_2, which all affect τ_2, already are determined completely at the time the cjoin function is being called. Program statements not considered yet may result in constraints which affect τ_1, p_1 and p_2, when the algorithm progresses. To handle this problem, the concept of *pending actions* is introduced. A pending cjoin action is attached to p_1, τ_1 and p_2, which is executed as soon as on of their values changes. However, the pending action is only attached, if the cjoin is not executed as a pending action too.

Calling **add-offset**$((l, u), o, p)$ ensures that $(l + o, u) \unlhd p$ holds at the point in time when the analysis runs to completion. This function applies the concept of pending actions too.

```
x =ₛ y:
    let τ₁ = ecr(x), τ₂ = ecr(y) in
    cjoin(s, (0, 0), τ₂, (0, 0), τ₁)


x =ₛ &y:
    let τ₁ = ecr(x), τ₂ = ecr(y) in
    let τ₃ = {((0, s), lam()(), τ₂, (0, 0))} in
    join(τ₃, τ₁)


x =ₛ op(y₁, . . . , yₙ):
    let τ = ecr(x), τ' = {} in
    ∀i ∈ [1, . . . , n] do
        let τᵢ = ecr(yᵢ) in
            let s' = sizeof(yᵢ) in
                cjoin(s', (0, 0), τᵢ, (0, 0), τ')
    cjoin(s, (0, 0), τ', (0, 0), τ)


x =ₛ allocate(y):
    let τ₁ = ecr(x) in
    let τ₂ = {((0, s), lam()(), {}, (0, 0))} in
    join(τ₂, τ₁)


x =ₛ *y:
    let τ₁ = ecr(x), τ₂ = ecr(y), τ₃ = {} in
    let p = (⊥, 0), s' = sizeof(void*) in
    let τ₄ = {((0, s'), lam()(), τ₃, p)} in
    join(τ₄, τ₂)
    cjoin(s, p, τ₃, (0, 0), τ₁)
```

```
*x =ₛ y:
    let τ₁ = ecr(x), τ₂ = ecr(y), τ₃ = {}, p = (⊥, 0) in
    let τ₄ = {((0, sizeof(void*)), lam()(), τ₃, p)} in
    join(τ₄, τ₁)
    cjoin(s, (0, 0), τ₂, p, τ₃)


x =ₛ &y → n:
    let τ₁ = ecr(x), τ₂ = ecr(y), τ₃ = {}, λ₃ = lam()()
    let p = (⊥, 0), p' = (⊥, 0) in
    let τ₄ = {((0, sizeof(void*)), λ₃, τ₃, p)} in
    join(τ₄, τ₂)
    add-offset(p, offset(n), p')
    let τ₅ = {((0, s), λ₃, τ₃, p')} in
    join(τ₅, τ₁)


x =ₛ fun(f₁, . . . , fₙ) → r:
    let τ = ecr(x), τ'ᵣ = ecr(r) in
    let ∀i ∈ [1, . . . , n] : τ'ᵢ = ecr(fᵢ) in
    let λ = lam(τ₁ = {}, . . . , τₙ = {})(τᵣ = {}) in
    join({((0, s), λ, {}, (⊥, 0))}, τ)
    cjoin(sizeof(r), (0, 0), τ'ᵣ, (0, 0), τᵣ)
    ∀i ∈ [1, . . . , n] do
        cjoin(sizeof(fᵢ), (0, 0), τᵢ, (0, 0), τ'ᵢ)


x =ₛ p(y₁, . . . , yₙ):
    let τ = ecr(x), τ'ₚ = ecr(p) in
    let ∀i ∈ [1, . . . , n] : τ'ᵢ = ecr(yᵢ) in
    let λ = lam(τ₁ = {}, . . . , τₙ = {})(τᵣ = {}) in
    join({((0, sizeof(void*)), λ, {}, (⊥, 0))}, τ'ₚ)
    cjoin(s, (0, 0), τᵣ, (0, 0), τ)
    ∀i ∈ [1, . . . , n] do
        cjoin(sizeof(yᵢ), (0, 0), τ'ᵢ, (0, 0), τᵢ)
```

Fig. 5. Construction of the storage shape graph.

Figure 5 gives a short program fragment for each possible kind of statement, which applies the functions defined in the last three paragraphs for the construction of a valid storage shape graph. The program fragments are derived directly from the rules given in Fig. 3. The ecr function maps a variable to its abstract location, which is represented by an equivalence class representative of the set of already merged abstract locations. We give a short step-by-step example in Fig. 6, which illustrates the process of building the storage shape graph. Figure 6(a) shows the graph right after the initialization step. Each one of the program's variables is represented by a single abstract location. Since the order in which program statements are considered is irrelevant for the end result, we start the

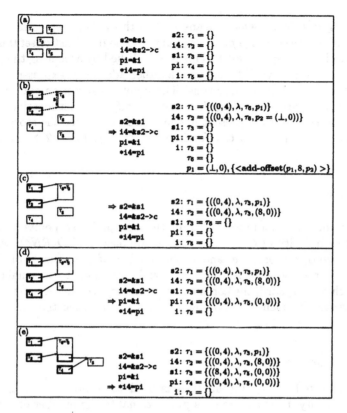

Fig. 6. Illustration of storage shape graph construction.

analysis with the second statement (i4=&s2->c) as shown in Fig. 6(b). If the statement would actually be executed, i4 would point to the same object as s2 would, but at an offset, which is greater than that of s2 by offset(c). This is reflected in the rule for statements of the kind $x =_s \&y \rightarrow n$ in Fig. 5 (second rule in the right column). The first **join** operation of this rule enforces that τ_3 represents the abstract location which variable y points to, and p represents the corresponding offset. The **add-offset** call ensures that offset range p' includes $p + 8$ and the second **join** coerces variable x's abstract location to point to τ_3 at an offset in the range p'. However, since the analysis did not yet consider the first statement of our example, s2 does not point anywhere. That is why a new abstract location τ_6 is introduced as a placeholder for the abstract location s2 will point to eventually. We know that τ_1 and τ_2 both point into τ_6 at offset p_1 and p_2, respectively. We know nothing yet, however, about the ranges p_1 and p_2 other than 'p_2 is $p_1 + 8$'. That is why an **add-offset** pending action is attached to p_1, which is executed as soon as more information on p_1 becomes available. This happens in Fig. 6(c), which depicts what happens when statement s2=&s1 gets analyzed. The rule for this kind of statements is the second one in the left column of Fig. 5. One of the results is that the abstract location of variable s1

(τ_3) gets merged with τ_6, which means that both of them represent the same abstract location. Offset range p_1 is now known to hold at least offset 0 meaning that p_2 has to hold at least offset 8. This is established by executing the pending **add-offset** action. Figure 6(d) analyzes another address-of expression, but no pending actions are triggered this time. The pointer indirection statements, as shown in Fig. 6(e), are interesting since they modify abstract locations of variables not being syntactically present in the expression. Once the storage shape graph is constructed, it is easy to infer facts like "expression *s2->c may access variable i".

7   Evaluation

While we do not present a proof, we argue that the proposed points-to analysis has a space complexity of $O(N)$ and a time complexity of $O(RN^2)$, where N denotes the size of the program and R the number of components of the program's largest struct type, respectively. Although, according to personal communications with Steensgaard, the complexity measures given in his article are not consistent, we are confident that our algorithm is as efficient as the one described in [12].

7.1   Space Complexity

The space allocated during the analysis is used to record the storage shape graph. The memory demands are thus proportional to the number of locations, functions, fields, field extends, pointer offsets, and pending actions, which the graph is composed of. During the first stage of the analysis an abstract location is created for each named variable and for each function parameter in the source code. An abstract function, as well as an abstract location that contains a field which points to the function, is created for each function definition. As can be seen, after the initialization step, the size of the storage shape graph is linearly dependent on the program size N. It remains to be argued that the second analysis stage adds a number of storage graph components, which is at most linear to N.

For each statement of the program being analyzed, one of the functions given in Fig. 5 is executed once. Each one of these functions introduces at most a small number of new graph components. The function for statements of the kind x $=_s$ &y creates a field in the abstract location of x, which points to the abstract location of y. Both a field and an abstract location are created in the function for x $=_s$ allocate(y) and a pointer offset for x $=_s$ &y $\rightarrow$ n like statements[3]. The number of calls of a constraint enforcing function from Fig. 4 is linear to the textual

---

[3] Some statements in the algorithms shown in Fig. 4 and Fig. 5 introduce new storage shape components just to be able to be more concise. An efficient implementation would not create new components here. The pointer offset p' for example, which is introduced in the **add-offset** function in Fig. 4, is used only to ensure that $(l_1 + o, u_1) \trianglelefteq p_2$, without having to handle pending actions.

length of the statement currently considered. For $x =_s op(y_1, \ldots, y_n)$ like statements, e.g., the number of **cjoin** calls is linear to the number of operands. This means that the accumulated number of calls of constraint enforcing functions from the functions given in Fig. 5 is $O(n)$.

The constraint enforcing functions given in Fig. 4 join components, but they do not create new ones. One exception is the **cjoin** function, which introduces at most a single new field into the abstract location τ_2 for each external call from one of the functions in Fig. 5.

A constant number of new pending actions are attached to graph components only in the **cjoin** and the **add-offset** functions and only if they are directly called by one of the functions given in Fig. 5. The number of pending-actions attached to storage graph components is thus linear to the program size as well.

The overall size of the storage shape graph is therefore $O(N)$, with N denoting the size of the analyzed program.

7.2   Time Complexity

According to our arguments in section 7.1 the number of graph components is $O(N)$. Since a **join** operation removes a graph component logically, the total number of **join** invocations is restricted to $O(N)$ as well.

The most expensive **join** function is the one that merges abstract locations (**join**(τ_1, τ_2) in Fig. 4). The **ecr-unite** function is of $O(\alpha(N, N))$, where α is the inverse Ackerman's function [14], which is almost constant. For compact presentation, the combination of the fields of both abstract locations is done in a nested loop. However, if the fields are sorted by position, this can be easily achieved in $O(R)$, where R is the number of components of the program's largest struct type. The **joins** in the loop body are already accounted for by the argument in the previous paragraph. The number of pending actions attached to the abstract locations is $O(N)$ too. Since $O(R) \subseteq O(N)$ and $O(\alpha(N, N)) \subseteq O(N)$ hold, the complexity of the **join** function is $O(N)$ times the complexity class of executing a pending action.

A pending action is either a pending **cjoin** or an **add-offset** operation. Both functions do not execute other pending actions. With complexity class $O(R)$, the **cjoin** function is the most costly one. This is due to the loop, which iterates over the fields of τ_1. The **join** operation, which is a short hand for joining λ', τ' and q' with the corresponding components of τ_2, is already accounted for.

The overall complexity for performing the proposed analysis on a program of size N is thus $O(RN^2)$, whereas R denotes the number of components of the largest struct type of the program.

7.3   Experimental Results

The proposed analysis algorithm was implemented as part of our PEAC tool, which eventually will evolve into a *Partial Evaluator for Ansi C*. The tool is implemented in C++, it was compiled with the GNU Compiler Collection ver-

Table 1. Results.

bench-mark	time [ms]	LOC	AST nodes	# of vars. 1	2	3	4	5	6	7	16	20	22	34	270	# of vars. ([13]) 1	2	3	4	5	6	7	8	14	15	16	18	22	24	26	30	32	44	74	78	113	285	624
anagram	62	590	3,271	3	1											3			1	1																			
bc	1,244	6,098	28,003	5	1								1			5	2							2		2								1					
ft	170	1,207	7,359	2												2																							
ks	94	733	4,941	1	2											1	2	1																					
yacr2	342	3,072	13,424	2		3	1									1		3	1																			
compress	103	804	4,412	1	2											4	1																					
eqntott	400	2,450	13,162	8	5											8	2			1	1	1															
espresso	16,760	11,691	94,100	17	10			1	1	1		1				19	12	2	2	1	2	1		1	1		1				1	1	1					
li	3,050	7,355	40,049	3			1	1	1	2					1	4	1	2	1	2						1												1
sc	3,906	7,129	42,997	4		2	1	2						1		10		5	4	2			1	1	1						1					1	1	
alvinn	46	261	1,607	10												9																							
ear	453	2,443	13,195	4	1										1	23	3	2		1							1											

sion 3.3.2. The following benchmarks were carried out on a Pentium MMX 233MHz running the Sarge version of Debian GNU/Linux.

Tab. 1 summarizes characteristic results from applying our analysis method to the freely available programs of Todd Austin's pointer intensive benchmark suite [1] as well as to some of the programs of the SPEC'92 benchmark suite [11]. These programs are typical benchmarks for points-to analyses and often applied in other publications. The stated CPU times were derived from performing points-to analysis on top of the abstract syntax tree representation. Parsing and variable name resolution do not contribute to these figures.

The remainder of the table presents the number of abstract locations in the computed storage shape graph, which represent a given number of aliased variables in the program. There is just one couple of variables in the *anagram* source code, e.g., which our analysis can not differentiate. This means that, based on our analysis, each pointer referencing one of the two variables may as well point to the other. For *yacr2* there exists one group of three non distinguishable variables and three pairs of two such variables. Abstract locations that represent only a single variable are only accounted for if they are pointed to from another location. The remainder are variables whose addresses are never taken, which makes their number non meaningfull.

These results are given for our own analysis as well as for the one described in [13] [4]. The proposed analysis achieves at least the same precision as Steensgaard's initial work and is more precise in most of the cases.

8 Conclusion

This paper presents a new fast points-to analysis for languages with structured types. The proposed analysis computes alias information with a higher level of precision than the one described in [12]. In addition, we are confidend that both have the same complexity in time and space while the proposed analysis is conceptually simpler.

---

[4] Unfortunately this kind of results is not reported on in [12], which is closer to our analysis.

Acknowledgments

Bjarne Steensgaard kindly and extensively answered questions regarding his articles. Thanks to Todd Austin for making his benchmarks available. This research was funded by Fiat-GM-Powertrain.

References

1. T. M. Austin, S. E. Breach, and G. S. Sohi. Efficient detection of all pointer and array access errors. In *SIGPLAN Conference on Programming Language Design and Implementation*, pages 290–301, 1994.
2. D. R. Chase, M. Wegman, and F. K. Zadeck. Analysis of pointers and structures. In *1990 ACM SIGPLAN Conference on Programming Lanuage Design and Implementation*, pages 296–310.
3. M. Das. Unification-based pointer analysis with directional assignments. *ACM SIGPLAN Notices*, 35(5):35–46, 2000.
4. M. Hind and A. Pioli. Which pointer analysis should i use? In *International Symposium on Software Testing and Analysis*, pages 113–123, 2000.
5. M. Hind. Pointer analysis: Haven't we solved this problem yet? In *2001 ACM SIGPLAN-SIGSOFT Workshop on Program Analysis for Software Tools and Engineering (PASTE'01)*, Snowbird, UT, 2001.
6. International Organization for Standardization. *ISO/IEC 9899 – 1999, Programming Languages – C*, 1999.
7. N. Jones, C. Gomard, and P. Sestoft. *Partial Evaluation and Automatic Program Generation*. Prentice Hall, 1993.
8. C. Lanfear and S. Balacco. The embedded software strategic market intelligence program 2001/2002, volume iv, February 2002. Venture Development Corp.
9. D. Liang and M. J. Harrold. Efficient points-to analysis for whole-program analysis. In *7th European Engineering Conference*, pages 199–215, 1999.
10. G. Ramalingam. The undecidability of aliasing. *ACM Transactions on Programming Lanuages and Systems (TOPLAS)*, 16(5):1467–1471, September 1994.
11. SPEC. Standard performance evaluation corp.: Cpu92. http://www.spec.org.
12. B. Steensgaard. Points-to analysis by type inference of programs with structures and unions. In *Computational Complexity*, pages 136–150, 1996.
13. B. Steensgaard. Points-to analysis in almost linear time. In *Symposium on Principles of Programming Languages*, pages 32–41, 1996.
14. R. E. Tarjan. Efficiency of a good but not linear set union algorithm. *Journal of the ACM*, 22(2):215–225, 1975.

An Automated C++ Code and Data Partitioning Framework for Data Management of Data-Intensive Applications[*]

Athanasios Milidonis[1], Grigoris Dimitroulakos[1], Michalis D. Galanis[1], George Theodoridis[2], Costas Goutis[1], and Francky Catthoor[3]

[1] VLSI Design Lab., Dept. of Elect. and Comp. Eng., University of Patras,
Rio 26110, Greece
milidon@vlsi.ee.upatras.gr
[2] Section of Electr. & Computers, Dept. of Physics, Aristotle Univ. of Thessaloniki,
54124, Greece
[3] IMEC, Kapeldreef 75 B-3001 Leuven, Belgium

Abstract. An automated framework for code and data partitioning for the needs of data management is presented. The goal is to identify the main data types from the data management perspective and to separate them from the many smaller data in the code. First, static and dynamic analysis is performed on the initial C++ specification code. Based on the analysis results the data types of the application are characterized as crucial or non-crucial. Afterwards, the code is automatically rewritten in such a way that the crucial data types and the code portions that manipulate them are separated from the rest of the code. Thus, the complexity is reduced allowing the designer to easily focus on the important parts of the code to perform further refinements and optimizations. Experiments on well-known multimedia and telecom applications prove the correctness of the performed automated analysis and code rewriting as well as the applicability of the introduced framework in terms of execution time and memory requirements. Comparisons with Rational's Quantify[TM] suite demonstrate the failure of Quantify to analyze correctly the initial code for the needs of data management.

1 Introduction

Current and future multimedia applications and other with similar behavior (e.g. protocol network applications) are characterized by high complexity, diverse functionality, huge amount of data transfers, and large data storage requirements [1]. They are usually described by large specification codes using high-level OO-based description languages such as C++ or SystemC. The conventional design procedure for such kind of applications starts by studying and analyzing the initial code to identify its crucial parts in terms of different design factors such as performance, data transfers and storage needs, and power consumption. Next, these crucial parts are refined, optimized, and mapped to predefined or custom-developed platforms [2].

---

[*] This work was partially funded by the Iracleitos project.

H. Schepers (Ed.): SCOPES 2004, LNCS 3199, pp. 122–136, 2004.
© Springer-Verlag Berlin Heidelberg 2004

In the majority of the cases only a small amount of the code – that is distributed sparsely over small sets of code lines – is important in terms of the considered design and quality factors [3], [4]. Given that the modern applications are described by hundreds of thousands code lines, there is a strong need to automatically identify the crucial parts of the initial specification code and separate them from the rest of the code. In this way the complexity of the application is reduced, the exploration freedom is increased, and the designer can easily focus on the important parts of the application to perform code refinements and optimizations [1].

For the data processing itself, the identification of the crucial kernels (usually inner loops) has been treated quite well in the past. But since modern applications are data dominated, a distinct step called background data management (or memory management) should be presented in the stage of mapping the application's data types to the background memory. This step aims at reducing the (complex) data transfers and storage requirements of the application and mapping the data structures efficiently on the hierarchical memory organization of the underlying platform [1], [5], [15]. The foreground memory management focuses on the register files and the registers' existence in the data-path. In contrast, the background memory consists of larger on- or off-chip memories that require a separate (set of) access cycle(s).

To reduce design complexity and to increase exploration freedom, the first sub-step of (background) memory management is to categorize the application's data types in crucial and non-crucial from the data management perspective. As crucial data types are considered the ones whose refinement has a large impact on important design factors such as the total memory's power consumption, performance, and total memory size. After the identification of the crucial data types, code transformations and optimizations should be applied only on the these data types to reduce the data transfers and storage requirements, while the code associating with the less important data types should not be considered. Figure 1 shows the amount of the design time that required for an MPEG-4-based video application during a project elaborated in the year 2001 by a well-known design house [1]. At the left side it is shown the exact time that MPEG-4 was designed with a two months penalty for distinguishing the background memory's data types manually. At the right side it is shown by estimation that the design time without the above distinction would be two times larger.

Considering the complexity and the large sizes of initial specification codes of the modern applications, the development of an automated flow for partitioning the code in crucial and non-crucial parts is necessary for the needs of data management. The automatic partitioning in crucial and non-crucial data has not been tackled earlier in literature. To the best our knowledge at this point there is no academic or commercial framework that performs the above partitioning automatically and efficiently.

In this paper an automated framework for deriving the crucial code's parts from the data management perspective and automatically isolating them from the rest of the code is presented. First, static and dynamic analysis is performed on the initial C++ code. Based on the analysis results, the data types are characterized as crucial or non-crucial. Afterwards, the code is automatically rewritten in such a way that the data to be stored in foreground memory and the associated code portions that manipulate them are placed inside new generated functions and are abstracted from the code portions related to background memory's data. A set of experiments on well-known applications proves on one hand the correctness of the performed analysis and automated rewriting and on the other hand the efficiency of the proposed framework in terms of execution time and memory requirements. Moreover, comparisons with Rational's Quantify™ suite demonstrate the failure of existing analysis frameworks like Quantify to perform correctly the required analysis while the rewriting step is totally missing.

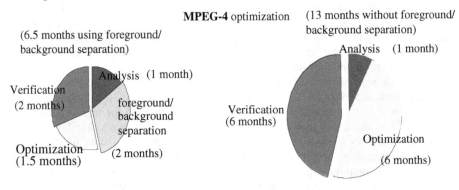

Fig. 1. Foreground/background separation shortens the exploration time

The paper is organized as follows: In section 2, previous work on data management and existing code partitioning tools are discussed. In section 3 the proposed framework is introduced and its implementation is discussed in details in section 4. The experimental results on well-known multimedia applications and comparisons with similar commercial frameworks are given in section 5. Finally, the conclusions are listed in section 6.

2   Data Management and Code Partitioning

One of the major bottlenecks of the modern applications is the huge amount of data transfers and storage requirements. This results in high power dissipation and performance degradation [1], [5], [15]. Experiments have shown that the energy consumption of the memory and related busses of the initial unoptimized code exceeds by far the consumption of the data paths and control logic. Also, the data transfers between the data paths and memory bound the system's performance, while the memory hierarchy dominates the silicon area. Thus, a lot of data management techniques, also called memory management techniques, have been proposed in recent years [1], [5]-[8]. Good overviews can be found in [15] and [16].

The basic concept of all the data management techniques is to apply code refinement and optimisations in specific code portions, which are responsible for high memory energy, to reduce the data transfers or to derive a memory architecture where the frequent memory accesses are performed on small memories. It must be noticed that in the majority of cases the data management code transformations are applied before the conventional compiler transformations [1].

In [1] and [5] the Data Transfer and Storage Exploration (DTSE) methodology has been proposed by IMEC. It starts by analyzing the initial specification code, identifying its crucial parts and manually separating them from the rest of the code. Next, platform-independent control- and data-flow transformations are applied to the code's crucial parts to increase the locality and regularity of memory accesses, remove redundant data transfers, and exploit data reuse opportunities. Afterwards, platform-dependent transformations are taken place to increase the data bandwidth and derive the memory organization. In the Bologna-Torino cluster also a focus on memory partitioning has been initiated. E.g. in [6], after performing profiling on the initial code and identifying the memory accesses patterns, the use of a special scratch-pad memory called Application Specific Memory (ASM) or the memory partitioning according to the application memory access patterns have been proposed. Thus, frequently memory accesses are performed on small on/off chip memories resulting in reduced energy dissipation. At Irivine, the main focus has been on memory-aware compilation. E.g. in [7] the use of an on-chip scratch-pad memory is proposed to reduce the energy due to memory access. Also, the application of code transformations for minimizing the power consumption of the on chip and the off-chip (DRAM) memory has been presented. At Penn State the main focus has been on transformations. E.g. in [8] special memory management techniques for improving the energy consumption of the cache memory have been presented. It must be stressed that none of the above approaches has a direct automated way to partition the code in background and foreground memory portions (crucial and non-crucial data types). Also, several other groups have started working on such issues recently.

Considering the complexity and the large sizes of the initial code descriptions of modern applications, some tools to identify the important parts of the code for data management needs have been presented. But it will be shown that these lack important features for our context since none of the them characterize correctly the data types as crucial or non crucial from the memory management perspective and they do not automatically separate the code's crucial parts from the non-crucial ones.

Rational's Quantify [9] focuses on function calls and its output is a dynamic function flow graph without giving any information about which parts of the code contain the largest amount of memory accesses and which were the most frequently accessed data types. IMEC's ATOMIUM [14] is another software suite that deals with the desired profiling for memory management. ATOMIUM offers a complete code analysis but with respect to memory management it still lacks two issues. First, it works only for C codes, while a growing portion of the modern multimedia applications are described in C++. Although the EDG compiler [11] offers a C++ to C conversion it turns out to be not very sufficient for further manipulation of the re- writing code. That occurs because all data type and function names change during the conversion and intermediately, new data types are introduced. For that reason, the original C++ code should be used for dynamic analysis since EDG introduces some data accesses overhead. Moreover, the produced C code can not always be executed since the compiler in its current version has problems converting to C dynamic C++ instructions (e.g. new, delete). So, the partitioning of the crucial data types and the associated code that manipulates them should be achieved on the original C++ code. Certainly, that step would have to be performed manually in the pre-processing step since ATOMIUM doesn't perform it automatically.

3 General Description of the Introduced Framework

The proposed framework has two goals. The first goal is to reduce the design complexity by focusing on the important parts of the code, while the second one is to hide some undesired constructs that should/can not be handled by the background data management stage.

To achieve these goals the initial code should be separated in at least two distinct hierarchical layers [1]. The first layer should contain the crucial data types (usually arrays) as far as memory energy consumption, access bandwidth or size is concerned and the corresponding code portions (nested loops and manifest conditions) that manipulate them, as well. The second layer, which is called with functions from the first layer, contains the rest of the code. Among the two above layers only the first one is considered for exploration during the background data management step. The second layer that can still contain small non-crucial arrays should be handled by the foreground memory management (register oriented) steps, which are tightly integrated in more conventional instruction-level compilers.

To perform such code partitioning, profile information needs to be extracted by analysing the initial code. Then, the application's data types are characterized as crucial or non-crucial in terms of background memory management. Next, the code is rewritten automatically so that the crucial data types and the associated code portions, which manipulate them, are separated from the rest of the code resulting in the construction of the two layers. If several "dynamically created tasks" are present, then the above approach is performed per "dynamically created task". We then also foresee another "top-layer" that contains these tasks (usually implemented by means of a thread library). Hence, in total we have 3 layers, of which the data management related one is the middle layer 2.

In C++, a data type may be defined as an array of a class instance. Our approach focuses on arrays as class states or local arrays inside function bodies since these are the ones that are considered as unique structures from memory management perspective. The code portions that manipulate them should be considered for moving from layer 2 (data management layer) to 3 (register management layer) and vice versa. For this consideration we take into account whether the objects (instances of each class that contains crucial arrays) contribute significantly to the memory's total power consumption. An array is characterized as crucial if during the execution of the code it is accessed very frequently and/or it requires large memory amount for storage. For that reason the code portions that manipulate it are moved in layer 2. On the contrary, the code portions that don't manipulate any crucial array are moved in layer 3.

The proposed code separation does not prevent any conventional complier to apply the required code transformations. As it has been mentioned, the data management precedes the conventional instruction-level compiler optimizations. Thus, after the application of the code transformations related to memory management, which are applied to the code of layer 2, the whole code is recombined and is fed to the transformation level compiler. Also, as it is explained in the code rewriting step further on, no problems related to linker arise. Finally, as it has been mentioned, the proposed approach does not perform the actual code transformations for the data management needs but only identifies and separates automatically the initial code in crucial and non-crucial from the data management perspective.

To automatically implement the above some existing software frameworks have been used. The EDG compiler [11] is used to convert the initial C++ source code to C code. This transformation has been adopted since good public domain software tools are available that extract important profile information on C source codes in an efficient way. The SUIF2 compiler [10] is such a tool and it is used to obtain static analysis information. Since it takes as an input only C code, the information that is extracted should be correlated with the original C++ source code. It must be noticed that the produced C code is not used for further manipulation (code refinement and transformations) but only for performing static analysis and gathering profiling information. Finally, the lexical analyzer LEX [13] is used for adding to the original C++ code special structures (e.g. counters, cost functions etc.) that are used for storing dynamic analysis information. Figure 2 shows the proposed flow.

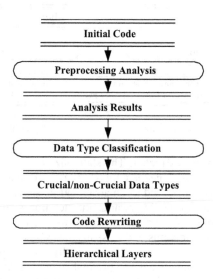

Fig. 2. General Flow

Initially in the Preprocessing/Analysis step, the C++ source code is converted to C and useful profiling information is extracted by performing static and dynamic analysis using properly developed SUIF2 scripts. Continuing in the Data Type classification step all data types are assigned with a weight produced by a (access and size) cost function determining how crucial they are from memory management perspective. Finally, after determining which of the data types are the crucial ones the initial C++ source code is rewritten by separating them in layers 2 and 3, in the rewriting step. Following, all the sub-steps of the above flow are described in details.

4 Detailed Description

4.1 Pre-processing Analysis

Profile information needs to be extracted always before memory management exploration on the given application. The motivation of the analysis is to have a good knowledge on which of the application's data types are most frequently accessed and which require a lot of memory space to be stored.

In this step, two kinds of analysis are performed namely the static and dynamic ones. Figure 3 (i) shows the exact flow that is followed for static analysis. First, the EDG compiler generates C source code from the initial C++ code of the application. Continuing, using the developed scripts the SUIF2 compiler operates on the C code and information about the Function Flow Graph (FFG), the structure definitions as

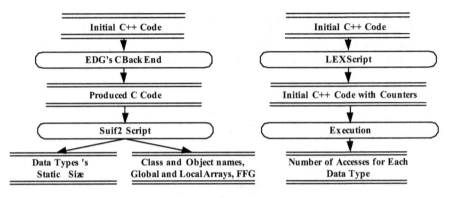

Fig. 3. (i) Static Analysis Flow   (ii) Dynamic Analysis Flow

well as their static sizes are extracted. The static size of a structure is considered as the total memory space that is needed for storing an instance of that structure. As mentioned, a structure is considered as an array and its static size is the sum of all its elements' memory storing space. Afterwards, the step traces all the structural declarations, and then the names of their instances. However, the EDG compiler slightly changes the names of the functions and class instances when converting from C++ to C source code. For that reason the flow automatically uses properly developed scripts to reverse these changes and reveal the original names of the initial C++ code. In figure 4 is shown as an example a part of one of the previously mentioned SUIF2 scripts that we generated for the proposed flow. By that script all the data types of the input code are identified and for each of them the information about their static size is gained. For this implementation a SUIF2 technique for searching for special structures inside the code is used called *iterator* and specific functions from the SUIF2 library are called for giving to the output the needed information.

Dynamic analysis needs to be performed in order to find out which of the data types are most frequently accessed. Figure 3 (ii) explains the way that this task is accomplished. From the previous analysis, all class, object and array names are well known. Also, all the functions of each class have been scanned. The proposed flow automatically produces scripts properly developed by us, which are used by LEX and which operate on the initial C++ source code. The main idea is to place an increment instruction of a variable underneath each instruction of the initial code of an array access. For each array a unique variable is declared for counting its accesses. Another function is also placed inside the code, which has the mission of printing the number of accesses for each array before the execution ending. The above are accomplished using developed by us C scripts that generate LEX scripts which identify the end of the main function of the initial C++ code. Then, they write before it, printing instructions of the memory accesses of each of the code's array. Additionally, properly developed scripts are used to create some extra header files for storing the new data types for counting the arrays' accesses and memory sizes as well as the function for printing the results of dynamic analysis. Next, the code is executed and all information about the accesses of each array is extracted.

```
void do_file_set_block(FileSetBlock* file_set_block){
Iter<StructType> it = object_iterator<StructType>(file_set_block);
for (; it.is_valid(); it.next()){ StructType& st= it.current();
int bit_sz;
IInteger ii= st.get_bit_size();
if(ii.is_c_int()){
bit_sz=ii.c_int();
printf("%s%d",st.get_name().c_str(),bit_sz);}}}
```

Fig. 4. SUIF2 script for extracting the memory size of all the input code's data types

4.2 Data Type Partitioning

All the above critical information is going to be used for deciding which data types are the crucial ones from the background data management perspective. For that reason a cost function must be employed which will use the extracted information from static and dynamic analysis and will assign to each data type a weight. In that way, a measure of how crucial each data type is, is obtained. Figure 5 describes the assignment of weights.

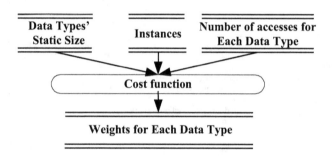

Fig. 5. Weight Assignment Procedure

For each data type instance its static size and the number of accesses during the execution time is taken into account. The proposed automated flow uses a simple cost function, which is described in Eq. (1). However depending on the designer's intentions the weights in this cost function may change since a new one can be given as an input. Also, for the reason that each data type doesn't use its entire memory space at each instance when it is processed, the designer should also be able to give as an input the exact required memory space of each data type that is usually processed instead of the total declared size that is usually overestimated.

$$\text{Weight} = \text{number of accesses} * \text{static size} \tag{1}$$

After the weight assignment to each instance of the initial code's data types, the designer should determine the threshold beyond which each instance is considered as crucial. This shall be given to the automated flow as an input.

4.3 Code Rewriting

Next, using special LEX scripts, the corresponding code portions that manipulate the non-crucial arrays are rewritten automatically in new generated functions and their body is placed in layer 3 and are not considered for memory management optimizations. Layer 2 contains the rest of the code which includes the manipulation of crucial arrays and the calls of new generated functions of layer 3. The main functionality of those scripts is the identification of class function bodies and the basic blocks inside them. As basic block is considered a group of instructions which doesn't contain a jump instruction except for the function call instructions. Only the last instruction of a basic block must be a jump instruction. A basic block that doesn't access crucial arrays will be used as the body of a newly generated function and its function call replaces this basic block at the initial code flow. In order to implement this efficiently all variables and arrays accesses by the considered basic block need to be scanned. All the arrays and references of the local variables must pass as inputs through the function's parameter list while all the global arrays and variables should remain unchanged in the new function body. The function prototype declaration of each newly created function is declared inside the corresponding class declaration. Figure 6 shows an example of the automated rewriting. Beside every newly generated function is automatically printed a comment which declares that these function contents belong to layer 3.

```
class classA{
public:
int b;
void functionA(void);
};
void classA::functionA(void){
int a,c,d;
a=2;
b=3;
c=a+2;
d=b+1;
if(c)
d=c+1;
}
```

```
class classA{
public:
int b;
void f1(int &a,int &c,int&d);
void functionA(void);
};
void classA::functionA(void){
int a,c,d;
f1(a,c,d);
if(c)
d=c+1;
}
```

```
void classA::f1(int &a,int &c,int &d){//Layer3
a=2;
b=3;
c=a+2;
d=b+1;
}
```

Fig. 6. (i) initial code   (ii) separation of a basic block to layer 3

By rewriting the initial C++ code as described above no compilation problems occur and the functionality of the program is identical compared to the initial one. It must be noticed that the code rewriting's output code is as readable and as understandable as the original code. In this way the designer that will use the produced code as input for a memory management optimization step will not meet any extra difficulties for understanding and transforming the code. For the same reason, neither the optimizing compiler is perturbed.

By separating the crucial code from the non-crucial one the previously discussed hierarchical layers are formed. Figure 7 shows the automated rewriting procedure. At this point, the designer has clear advantages concerning the task of background memory management exploration. He has a very good knowledge of which are the code's data types, their memory size, the names of their instances, and the number of times they are accessed during the execution time. He also knows the crucial data types that are stored in background memory and any design effort from background memory

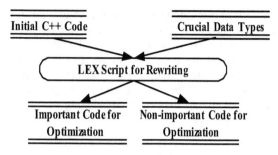

Fig. 7. Code Rewriting Procedure

management refinement should be focused only on them. Also the lines of source code that now are to be examined are drastically reduced. Moreover, because the code of layer 3 is fully separated in different functions it can be kept in a separate file that is protected so that no errors can be introduced. By this way, the manual application of the transformations that follow can only be present in Layer 2 code. This clearly limits the verification and debugging effort as shown also in Figure 1. All the above information combined with the automated way of extracting, leads to a seriously reduced design time for the given application.

4.4 Rewriting Example

In this paragraph an example on a small but realistic application code is given to better understand the proposed contribution. Figure 8 (i) shows the initial C++ code of the multimedia full search algorithm. It contains a motion estimation procedure in which the data types (arrays) cur, prev, vec_x, and vec_y are processed. The main target is to distinguish which of the above arrays could be stored in foreground and which in background memory and finally to separate in layer 3 the corresponding code portions that process only the foreground memory's data types by implementing the code rewriting step.

After automatically applying the proposed pre-processing analysis step, static and dynamic analysis information is extracted for each array. Table 1 shows the number of accesses for each array during execution time and the number of bits required for their memory storage.

Continuing, during the data type assignment step a weight is assigned to each array according to a weight function. The results are shown in Table 1.

Table 1. Analysis results for full search algorithm code

Data types	# of Accesses	Storage size (bits)	Weight
cur	5702400	811008	4624692019200
prev	5436736	811008	4409236389888
vec_x	2509	3168	7948512
vec_y	2509	3168	7948512

As can be seen, the weights of cur and prev arrays are a million times larger than those of vec_x and vec_y. For that reason, the first two data types are considered crucial and can be stored in background memory while the last two should be stored in foreground memory. In this simple code this is also obvious for the designer of the code but for complex codes with dozens arrays and fews of thousands lines of high level source code this is not trivial at all. Automated analysis is then essential. Next, the automated flow scans all the input code's basic blocks and identifies those which don't access any data types from the background memory. It rewrites these basic blocks as bodies of new layer 3 functions as shown in figure 8 (ii). By this way, not only the foreground-background data types are distinguished but the corresponding code portions are also separated.

```
class full_s{
public :
int curr[144][176] ;
int prev[144][176] ;
int vec_x[9][11];
void fs_motion_estimation(int
cur[N][M],int prev[N][M],
int vec_x[N/B][M/B],int
vec_y[N/B][M/B]) ;
};
void full_s ::fs_motion_estimation(int
cur[N][M],int prev[N][M],
int vec_x[N/B][M/B],int
vec_y[N/B][M/B]){
int x,y,i,j,k,l,p1,p2,min,dist;
for(x=0;x<N/B;x++)
for(y=0;y<M/B;y++){
   min=65280;
  for(i=-p;i<p+1;i++)
for(j=-p;j<p+1;j++){
   dist=0;
   for(k=0;k<B;k++)
for(l=0;l<B;l++){
     p1=cur[B*x+k][B*y+l];
     if((B*x+i+k)<0 ||
(B*x+i+k)>(N-1) ||
   (B*y+j+l)<0 ||
(B*y+j+l)>(M-1))
     p2=0;
   else
      p2=prev[B*x+i+k][B*y+j+l];
      dist+=abs(p1-p2);}
   if(dist<min){
   min=dist;
   vec_x[x][y]=i;
   vec_y[x][y]=j;}}}}
```

```
class full_s{
public :
int curr[144][176] ;
int prev[144][176] ;
int vec_x[9][11];
void fs_motion_estimation(int
cur[N][M],int prev[N][M],
int vec_x[N/B][M/B],int
vec_y[N/B][M/B]) ;
void
f1(&dist,&min,vec_x,vec_y,&i,&j,&x,&y)
};
void full_s ::fs_motion_estimation(int
cur[N][M],int prev[N][M],
int vec_x[N/B][M/B],int
vec_y[N/B][M/B]){
 int x,y,i,j,k,l,p1,p2,min,dist;
 for(x=0;x<N/B;x++)
for(y=0;y<M/B;y++){
   min=65280;
   for(i=-p;i<p+1;i++)
for(j=-p;j<p+1;j++){
   dist=0;
   for(k=0;k<B;k++)
for(l=0;l<B;l++){
     p1=cur[B*x+k][B*y+l];
     if((B*x+i+k)<0 ||
(B*x+i+k)>(N-1) ||
      (B*y+j+l)<0 || (B*y+j+l)>(M-1))
     p2=0;
   else
     p2=prev[B*x+i+k][B*y+j+l];
     dist+=abs(p1-p2);}
   f1(dist,min,vec_x,vec_y,i,j,x,y)
}}}
```

```
//Layer 3:
void
f1(&dist,&min,vec_x,

vec_y,&i,&j,&x,&y)
{

if(dist<min){
min=dist;
vec_x[x][y]=i;
vec_y[x][y]=j;
}
}
```

Fig. 8. (i)initial motion estimation   (ii)basic block separation to layer 3

Comparing all the above described steps of the proposed flow with Rational's Quantify suite it can be said that the only information given by Quantify is the number of times the fs_motion_estimation procedure was executed which is '1'. However, this is not sufficient information for deciding which data types should be placed in foreground and background memory. Also, no code rewriting is performed by Quantify for separating the foreground-background code portions. The last difference is also valid for the ATOMIUM tool suite at IMEC and the Xtel at EPFL, which handle C code which is not sufficient as explained in section 2. For these reasons it is proved the uniqueness of the automated flow's operations.

5   Experimental Results

To verify the effectiveness and validity of the introduced framework, experiments on five well-known codes have been performed. The tested codes are parts of multimedia and telecommunication algorithms.

More specifically, the OFDM baseband transmitter is based on the physical layer of the IEEE 802.11a specification. JPEG is an international standard for the compression of multilevel still images. Cavity Detection is a medical image-processing algorithm and ADPCM is a voice codec. Finally, the last benchmark tested is VIC [12] which contains a group of applications. The one among them that the proposed flow's experiments focused on is a video application implementing the H.261 standard.

Table 2 shows the measurements taken by the proposed flow for all applications. It must be noticed that in order to verify the correctness of those measurements special modifications on the code of the experimented applications have been performed since no tool exists to perform measurements similar to what the introduced flow

Table 2. Tool's analysis results vs counters placed by hand for arrays memory accesses

Data types	Accesses (Tool)	Accesses (counters by hand)	Static size (Bytes)	Weight
JPEG				
Dct	786508	786508	525504	4,13313E+11
Quantize	65664	65664	527552	34641174528
Zigzag	131200	131200	528576	69349171200
Entropy	13104	13104	549824	7204893696
OFDM				
Scrambler	69127	69127	1784	123322568
Fec	99876	99876	4080	407494080
Interleaver	15360	15360	2304	35389440
Cp	94176	94176	4608	433963008
CAVITY DETECTION				
g_image	4572708	4572708	8192000	3.74596E+13
GaussBlur	1271696	1271696	8192000	1.04177E+13
DetectRoot	1271696	1271696	8192000	1.04177E+13
c_image	1021930	1021930	8192000	8.37165E+12
ADPCM				
Encoder	4761	4761	3648	17368128
Decoder	11105	11105	3648	40511040
VIC				
Decoder	140	140	1536	215040
P64Decoder	13565	13565	198208	2,689E+09
Matcher	104	104	96	9984
TclObject	757	757	128	96896

does. For that reason, concerning each class state accesses, counters have been placed by hand inside the function bodies under each static appearance of a class state and their results after execution have been compared with the proposed flow's measures. It is obvious that the proposed flow's results are correct since they are the same with the ones of the counters placed by hand.

Table 3 shows the measurements taken by Quantify ™. For the VIC application there are no measurements since it operates on Linux and no Quantify suit is available. It is clear that it doesn't give the appropriate profiling information for defining how crucial each data type is. In particular, Quantify ™ measures only the number of times an object's function is called. Thus, Quantify ™ measures the number of all function calls, which are made dynamically. No information is produced about the accesses of each state of an object and none for the total static size of an object. This lack of profiling information using Quantify ™ may lead to totally useless results concerning the declaration of data types as crucial or non-crucial.

Table 3. Object function calls of Quantify

CAVITY DETECTION		OFDM	
Data types	Function Calls (Quantify)	Data types	Function Calls (Quantify)
G_image	4572708	Scrambler	40
Gaussblur	1271696	Fec	40
Detectroot	1271696	Interleaver	40
C_image	1021930	Cp	40
JPEG		ADPCM	
Data types	Function Calls (Quantify)	Data types	Function Calls (Quantify)
Dct	1024	Encoder	10
Quantize	1024	Decoder	26
Zigzag	1024		
Entropy	1024		

As can be seen, Tables 2 and 3 give different results on how crucial a data type is. As an example of how misleading the results of Quantify are, it could be assumed, looking at Table 3, that for JPEG, Entropy is one of the most crucial data types. However, since Entropy's total memory accesses are eventually the least of all, as reported in Table 2, Entropy should actually be characterized as the least crucial data type of JPEG.

Table 4 shows the crucial data types of each benchmark, the memory that is required for processing each application by the proposed flow, and the execution time needed to conclude the flow. By focusing only on the most crucial data types of each application, the target code is significantly reduced. In these experiments, the crucial data types are selected as those whose sum of weights exceeds 80% of the total application weight.

Table 4. Tool's Memory, Time requirements and applications' code size total decrement

Apps.	Total Lines	Crucial Lines	Crucial Data Types	Memory Requirements (bytes)	Exec. Time (sec)
JPEG	935	140	Dct	22684	21
OFDM	1050	406	Fec,Cp,Scrambler	5204	3
Cavity Detect	576	303	g_image,Gauss_blur / Detect_roots	2352	3
ADPCM	417	417	Encoder,Decoder	4124	2
VIC	9208	1417	P64Decoder	5972	5

6 Conclusions

The automated flow presented in this document implements the code data memory partitioning from a background memory management perspective. It is a prototype tool flow, which separates the useful code, for background memory management optimization purposes, from the rest of the C++ code. This is a task that no other existing system level design tool performs. The benefit of using this tool is a serious reduction on the design time of a given application. The exact part of the code that would have to be explored from an optimization point of view is revealed. This is usually a small part comparing to the total size of the application code. The rest of the code can be temporarily ignored for exploration purposes. Moreover, a large gain in verification time is obtained by this separation process.

References

1. F. Catthoor, S. Wuytack, E. De Greef, F. Balasa, L.Nachtergaele, A. Vandecappelle.: CUSTOM MEMORY MANAGEMENT METHODOLOGY – Exploration of Memory management Organization for Embedded Multimedia System Design. Kluwer Academic Publishers (1998)
2. D. Gajksi, F. Vahid, S. Narayan, and J. Gong.: Specification and Design of Embedded Systems. Prentice Hall (1994)
3. R. Luepers.: Code Optimization for Embedded Processors. Kluwer Academic Publishers (2002)
4. S. Edwards, L. Lavagno, E. Lee, and A. Sangiovanni-Vincentelli.: Design of Embedded Systems: Formal Models. Validation, and Synthesis. Proc. of IEEE, pp. 366-390 (1997)
5. F. Catthoor, K. Danckaert, C. Kulkarni, E. Brockmeyer, P. Kjeldsberg, T. Achteren, and T. Omnes.: Data Accesses and Storage Management for Embedded Programmable Processors. Kluwer Academic Publishers (2002)
6. A. Macci, L. Benini, and M. Poncino.: Memory Design Techniques for low Energy Embedded Systems. Kluwer Academic Publishers (2002)
7. P. Panda and N. Dutt.: Memory Issues in Embedded Systems-on-Chip Optimization and Exploration. Kluwer Academic Publishers (1999)
8. M. Kandemir, J. Ramanujam, and A. Choudhary.: Improving cache locality by combination of loop and data transformations. IEEE Trans. on Computers, pp.159-167 (1999)

9. "Rational Quantify for Windows v2001A", Rational Software Corporation.
10. G. Aigner, A. Diwan, D. L. Heine, M. S. Lam, D. L. Moore, B. R. Murphy, and C. Sapunt-zakis.:An overview of the SUIF2 compiler infrastructure. Technical report, Stanford University (2000)
11. C++ Front End. Propiertary Information of Edison Design Group, www.edg.com
12. VideoConferencingTool,,www-nrg.ee.lbl.gov/vic
13. J. R. Levine, T. Mason, D. Brown.:Lex & Yacc. O'REILLY & Associates Inc.
14. http://www.imec.be/atomium
15. L. Benini, G. De Micheli.:System-level power optimization techniques and tools. ACM TODAES, Vol.5, No.2, pp.115-192, (2000)
16. P. Panda, F.Catthoor, N.Dutt, K.Danckaert, E.Brockmeyer, C.Kulkarni, A.Vandecappelle, P.G. Kjeldsberg.: Data and Memory Optimizations for Embedded Systems. ACM TODAES, Vol.6, No.2, pp.142-206, (2001)

Combined Data Partitioning and Loop Nest Splitting for Energy Consumption Minimization

Heiko Falk and Manish Verma

University of Dortmund, Computer Science 12, D-44221 Dortmund, Germany

Abstract. For mobile embedded systems, the energy consumption is a limiting factor because of today's battery capacities. Besides the processor, memory accesses consume a high amount of energy. The use of additional less power hungry memories like caches or scratchpads is thus common. This paper presents a combined approach for energy consumption minimization consisting of two complementary and phase-coupled optimizations, viz. data partitioning and loop nest splitting. In a first step, data partitioning partitions large arrays found in typical embedded software into smaller ones which are placed onto an on-chip scratchpad memory. Although being effective w. r. t. energy dissipation, this optimization adds overhead to the code since the correct part of a partitioned array has to be selected at runtime. Therefore, the control flow is optimized as a second step in our framework. In this phase, loop nests containing *if*-statements are split using genetic algorithms leading to minimized *if*-statement executions. However, loop nest splitting leads to an increase in code size and can potentially annul the program layout achieved by the first step. Consequently, the proposed approach iteratively applies these optimizations till a local optimum is found.

The proposed framework of combined memory and control flow optimization leads to considerable energy savings for a representative set of typical embedded software routines. Using an accurate energy model for the ARM7 processor, energy savings between 20.3% and 43.3% were measured.

1 Introduction

The emergence of portable or mobile computing and communication devices such as cellular phones, pagers, handheld video games etc. is probably the most important factor driving the need for low power design. Current battery technologies such as Li-Io have capacities of 90 Watt-hours$/kg$ [1], meaning that 10 hours of operation for a device consuming 20 W of operating power would require a battery weight of around $2.2\,kg$. Thus, the cost and weight of the batteries become bottlenecks that prevent the reduction of system cost and weight unless efficient low power design techniques are adopted.

Since it has been shown that 50%–75% of the power consumption in embedded multimedia systems is caused by memory accesses [2, 3], the efficient utilization of memories is of major interest for the construction of low power devices. Main memory is the slowest and the most energy consuming memory type. On one hand, the high amount of main memory accesses is a reason for its high energy dissipation. On the other hand, the high latency during main memory accesses causes several wait states to a processor. To avoid these problems, a very effective way of energy reduction is to build up a memory hierarchy.

H. Schepers (Ed.): SCOPES 2004, LNCS 3199, pp. 137–151, 2004.

Additional memories are able to reduce the number of main memory accesses for frequently used instructions or variables. *Caches* are well known and included in many processor designs. Besides the data memory itself, they consist of an additional tag memory and of logic components enabling the fast comparison of addresses with the contents of the tag memory. The advantage of caches is their easy integration into a system since the detection of cache hits is done automatically by the hardware. For embedded systems, caches are often not well suited due to their inherently high energy consumption during tag memory access and comparison. Additionally, the accurate determination of worst case execution times often is difficult in a cache-based environment which is a critical issue for embedded real-time systems [4].

Recently, the utilization of *scratchpad memories* has become an important alternative to caches [5, 6]. A scratchpad is a small memory mapped into the processor's address space requiring only simple address decoders. The absence of logic components checking the validity of data is the reason for their low energy consumption. However, this property requires a careful mapping of instructions or data to the memory which has to be done by the programmer or the compiler.

This paper presents a novel combination of automated compiler optimizations for achieving an energy efficient utilization of scratchpad memories. For a given ARM7 based system architecture, a *data partitioning* step is performed first [7]. In this step, parts of a program and of its data are assigned optimally (i. e. least energy consuming) to the scratchpad. In particular, large arrays frequently found in data-dominated embedded software are split into several pieces. Data partitioning enables the storage of fragments of the original array in the scratchpad which was impossible before.

Since the software must take care of accessing the correct part of a split array, *if*-statements dynamically selecting the appropriate sub-array have to be inserted into the program's code. Although being beneficial w. r. t. energy consumption, data partitioning adds overhead to the software. The execution of the additional *if*-statements requires several CPU cycles and can lead to degraded pipeline performance due to pipeline stalls. To avoid this overhead, we apply a significantly improved loop splitting technique for control flow optimization (originating from [8, 9]) as the second step after data partitioning. This optimization minimizes *if*-statement executions so that the negative side-effects of data partitioning are largely eliminated. The improved control flow is achieved at the cost of increased code size. The size of the program and data objects placed on the scratchpad is bounded by the scratchpad size. Any increase in code size could potentially invalidate the program and data layout achieved in the previous step. Nevertheless, the size of frequently executed program objects is increased by a small amount and a hill-climbing approach can be utilized to obtain a locally optimal solution.

The main contribution of this paper is the successful exploration of the synergy effects of these two individual optimizations. The results clearly show that our control flow optimization is able to eliminate overheads caused by data partitioning. However, data partitioning enables loop nest splitting in our framework since loop nest splitting without data partitioning would be impossible. These two optimizations are related to each other in a phase-coupled sense and complement each other such that, when combined, they lead to considerable energy savings. Our proposed combined approach ensures that the finally generated code contains a minimum of control flow overhead but a maximum of data stored in low energy scratchpads. Additionally, the recently presented algorithms for loop nest splitting are extended substantially. Using the techniques described in this paper, we are able to relax restrictions imposed by the original analysis algorithms [8, 9] so that more general classes of applications can be optimized.

A survey of work related to memory hierarchy exploitation and low power code generation is given in section 2. The phase-coupled algorithm for combined data partitioning and loop nest splitting is presented in section 3. Section 4 presents the techniques used for data partitioning, whereas loop nest splitting and its new extensions are described in section 5. Section 6 contains a detailed description of the measured experimental results, and section 7 summarizes and concludes this paper.

2   Related Work

Code optimizations for caches include well-known techniques like *loop tiling*, *loop interchange* or *loop fusion* [10, 11]. Since applications spend most of their runtime in innermost loops, these optimizations concentrate on loop nests. The iteration space of loop nests is reordered in such a way that a higher locality of data accesses is achieved. The higher the spatial and temporal locality of data accesses, the fewer cache misses occur during program execution resulting in a more efficient cache utilization. Even nowadays, locality optimization is an area of ongoing research. In [12], loops are aligned so that the time between two successive accesses to the same memory location (*temporal locality*) is minimized. A graph based optimization strategy is used in [13] to cluster array references in loops with spatial or temporal reuse. This technique leads to average reductions of cache misses by 13.8%.

Array padding [10] is a good example of a data layout transformation. Here, unused data locations are inserted between columns of an array so as to reduce cache set conflicts and cache miss jamming. An approach for simultaneous generation of optimized data layouts and temporal locality improvement is presented in [14]. In this article, geometric models and algorithms are used to minimize TLB misses.

Panda et al. [15] presented an efficient use of a memory hierarchy by placing the most commonly used variables onto the scratchpad. The dynamic copying of array parts was studied in [5]. However, the preconditions imposed by this algorithm are very restrictive so that only a limited class of applications can be analyzed. An approach for statically placing both data and program parts onto a scratchpad memory basing on the analysis of instruction execution and variable accesses is presented in [16]. In that paper, only whole variables are considered at a time. Consequently, a large non-scalar variable (i. e. an array) could either be placed onto the scratchpad as a whole or not at all, potentially leading to a sub-optimal memory utilization.

A methodology of source code transformations for data access and storage management (*DTSE*) is presented in [17]. The described techniques can be applied to complex memory hierarchies consisting of multi-level caches and on-chip memories. However, the authors only focus on the optimization of data flow and neglect that the control flow gets very irregular since many additional *if*-statements are inserted. This impaired control flow has not yet been targeted by the authors. The results given in our paper clearly show the importance of combining data and control flow optimizations for the design of low power embedded systems. In the following section, we present the combined approach for phase-coupled data partitioning and loop nest splitting.

3   Algorithm for Phase-Coupled Energy Minimization

As will be described in section 4, data partitioning improves scratchpad utilization but impairs the control flow due to the addition of *if*-statements. Loop nest splitting improves the control flow but increases the code size and can potentially annul the allocation of the scratchpad. Hence, it is obvious that both optimizations influence each other. As a consequence, data partitioning and loop nest splitting need to be applied in a phase coupled manner which is described in this section.

```
1 Algorithm(ΔSPLIT) {
2    Energy = INFINITY;
3    SPLIT = DataPartitioning();
4    do {
5       LoopNestSplitting(SPLIT);
6       OldEnergy = Energy;
7       if (SP-Objects <= ScratchpadSize)
8          Energy = ComputeEnergy(SPLIT);
9       else
10         Energy = INFINITY;
11      SPLIT -= ΔSPLIT;
12      ΔEnergy = OldEnergy - Energy;
13   } while(ΔEnergy ≥ 0);
14   return(OldEnergy); }
```

Fig. 1. Algorithm for energy minimization

The proposed algorithm (cf. fig. 1) implements a hill-climbing approach. It starts with an initial scratchpad allocation obtained after data partitioning (line 3) followed by loop nest splitting (line 5). Since data partitioning defines which basic blocks and array fragments are placed on the scratchpad, code size increases of individual basic blocks after loop nest splitting may lead to an invalid solution exceeding the scratchpad's capacity. This situation is checked after loop nest splitting (lines 7–10). For a valid allocation, the energy consumption is computed (line 8) and the change in energy dissipation caused by loop nest splitting is calculated (line 12). Since ΔEnergy is positive in this case, the algorithm's loop steps into a second iteration. There, the algorithm must necessarily stop since no better valid solution can be obtained due to the optimality of the integer linear programming based approach of data partitioning.

However, if the initial allocation is invalid, the algorithm iteratively tries to obtain a valid solution. For this purpose, the splitting point SPLIT originally stemming from data partitioning is adjusted by a user defined offset ΔSPLIT, and loop nest splitting is re-applied again. The algorithm stops when it has ascertained a locally optimal solution. Since neither data partitioning nor loop nest splitting modify existing data dependencies between array elements, the algorithm of figure 1 does not need to do data dependence analysis.

4   Data Partitioning

Considering aggregate array variables as the candidates for placement onto the small on-chip memory is not the ideal decision, as this may lead to the under-utilization of the on-chip memory and to a high energy consumption by the application. The proposed data partitioning approach rectifies the aforesaid problem by partitioning an array present in the application into smaller array variables. The energy consumption of the application is then reduced by placing one of the smaller array variables onto the on-chip memory, which is not large enough to contain the whole array variable. The data partitioning approach works in the following stepwise manner:

1. Whenever beneficial, the scratchpad is maximally filled with arrays entirely fitting into this memory [16].
2. Among all remaining arrays, one candidate array A is chosen for partitioning.
3. For A, a splitting point SPLIT is computed leading to the maximum reduction of energy consumption. If no splitting point exists leading to a reduction of energy dissipation, A is not split. It is proceeded to step 2 where another array is chosen.
4. Given the array A and the splitting point, the original application is transformed.

The array having the highest valence (i. e. energy consumption per element) which could not be placed on the scratchpad memory in its entirety by the algorithm presented in [16] is chosen in step 2. Step 3 is solved in a phase coupled manner using *integer linear programming (ILP)* (cf. section 4.1). The step of application transformation is described in section 4.2.

4.1   Integer Linear Program

The formulation of the integer linear program for data partitioning is based on the observation that the splitting of an array implicitly leads to changes of an application's code due to the selection of the correct fragment of a split array during runtime. If an array A is to be split, only those basic blocks of an application need to be modified which access A. These modified basic blocks which access a split array A are termed as *referencing basic blocks* in the following.

   For a program containing m basic blocks referencing an array A of length n, the integer linear program used for data partitioning is basically formulated using a set $V := V_{BB} \cup V_{RBB} \cup DD \cup V_A$ of binary decision variables. V_{BB} and V_{RBB} each consist of m decision variables. A variable v^i_{BB} equal to 1 ($1 \leq i \leq m$) (v^i_{RBB} resp.) denotes the case where basic block i (referencing basic block i, resp.) is placed on the scratchpad. DD is a single binary variable which is equal to 1 only if array A is partitioned. A variable $v^j_A \in V_A$ equal to 1 ($1 \leq j \leq n$) models the splitting of array A at position j.

   Using these decision variables, data partitioning is formulated as a knapsack problem. To each basic block, referencing basic block and split parts of array A, their corresponding sizes are attached. The integer linear program contains constraints in order to ensure that the size of all objects placed on the scratchpad does not exceed the scratchpad's capacity. Additional constraints are included guaranteeing the consistency of an actual assignment of values to the decision variables (e. g. if a referencing basic block RBB_i is placed on the scratchpad, its original counterpart BB_i must not be considered).

   The objective function to be maximized during data partitioning models the energy savings achieved by an assignment of values to the decision variables, compared to the energy consumption of an unpartitioned application totally stored in background main memory. The objective function considers all energy related aspects of data partitioning: access frequencies of basic blocks and array elements, the savings due to the placement of objects on the scratchpad and the overhead due to the more complex code of the referencing basic blocks in order to access the correct part of a split array at runtime. For more details, the interested reader is referred to the original publication [7].

```
#define SIZE 100




int A[SIZE];
for (i=0; i<SIZE/2; i++)
  for (j=0; j<i; j++) {
    data = A[i+j];
    ... }
```

→

```
#define SIZE 100
#define SPLIT 70
#define READ_ACCESS(value,index)
  if (index < SPLIT) value = Aleft[index];
  else value = Aright[index-SPLIT];
int Aleft[SPLIT],Aright[SIZE-SPLIT];
for (i=0; i<SIZE/2; i++)
  for (j=0; j<i; j++) {
    READ_ACCESS(data,i+j);
    ... }
```

Fig. 2. A typical code fragment before and after data partitioning

4.2 Application Transformation

The application transformation step takes an application code, a chosen array A and a splitting point SPLIT as inputs and outputs a transformed application. Specifically, A is replaced by two smaller arrays Aleft and Aright (cf. figure 2) which are generated according to SPLIT. The application code is modified in such a way that all accesses to the array A are replaced by an *access macro*. The access macro determines which of the two smaller arrays are being referenced on the basis of the index expression and the splitting point SPLIT. Figure 2 displays a typical example of the original and the modified application codes. The access macro in the figure 2 represents a read access to the array A. A similar access macro can also be constructed for the write accesses as well, though it is omitted for the sake of simplicity of the code examples.

As can be seen from figure 2, the proposed way of data partitioning leads to a bi-partitioning of arrays. Generally, the integer linear program can easily be rewritten so that n-way partitions are supported. In the context of the ARM7 based system studied in section 6, it turned out that the generation of partitions larger than 2 is disadvantageous since the resulting complex if-then-else structures over-compensate any savings. Similarly, an e. g. trapezoidal array partitioning is not beneficial due to the increased control flow overhead.

5 Loop Nest Splitting for Control Flow Optimization

As described in the previous section, preprocessor macros containing *if*-statements are inserted in a program's code for selecting the correct partition of a split array during runtime. Given that array references typically occur in the innermost loops of embedded software, these *if*-statements constitute an overhead w. r. t. runtime and energy consumption which should not be neglected. We propose to apply a substantially improved variant of *loop nest splitting* [8] for the optimization of these *if*-statements.

The transformation presented in our paper determines ranges of loop iterations where all *if*-statements in the loop nest are provably satisfied. Using this information, the loop nest is rewritten so that no *if*-statement is executed for these iteration ranges. In figure 3, the example code shown in figure 2 is depicted before and after loop nest splitting (note that the access macro shown in figure 2 is expanded now). Loop nest splitting detects that the outer i loop iterates from 0 to 49, while the inner j loop steps from 0 to the actual value of i. Considering the condition i+j<70 inserted by data partitioning, it is recognized that this condition must necessarily be true for i ≤ 35. Using

```
                                    for (i=0; i<50; i++)
                                      if (i<=35)
                                        for (; i<=35; i++)
                                          for (j=0; j<i; j++) {
                                            data = Aleft[i+j];
                                            ... }
for (i=0; i<50; i++)
  for (j=0; j<i; j++) {              else
    if (i+j<70)                        for (j=0; j<i; j++) {
      data = Aleft[i+j];       →         if(i+j<70)
    else                                   data = Aleft[i+j];
      data = Aright[i+j-70];             else
    ... }                                  data = Aright[i+j-70];
                                          ... }
```

Fig. 3. A typical code fragment before and after loop nest splitting

this information, a new *if*-statement (the *splitting-if*) is inserted in the loop nest exactly checking this condition. Since i<=35 implies that i+j<70 is true, the *then*-part of the splitting-if consists of the body of the i loop without any *if*-statements. To minimize executions of the splitting-if, a second i loop is inserted in the *then*-part counting to the corresponding bound of the iteration ranges (i. e. this loop ensures that all iterations of the i loop up to i <= 35 are executed without any further evaluation of the splitting-if). The *else*-part of the splitting-if is an exact copy of the original loop body. Using this code transformation, a reduction of *if*-statement executions from 1,125 down to 610 can be achieved for the codes depicted in figure 3.

The techniques for loop splitting presented previously [8] are limited such that only restricted classes of loops can be analyzed. Since all loop bounds are required to be constant, a loop nest as depicted in figure 3 could not be optimized. Section 5.1 briefly reflects the basic concepts of loop nest splitting. In section 5.2, the techniques of [8] are significantly extended enabling the optimization of more general classes of applications.

5.1   Analysis Techniques for Loop Nest Splitting

This section gives a brief summary of the recently published concepts for splitting loop nests [8]. For a given loop nest $\Lambda = \{L_1, \ldots, L_N\}$ of depth N, L_l denotes a single loop l with its index variable i_l and the lower and upper bounds, lb_l and ub_l, respectively. Every loop L_l can contain one or more *if*-statement whose conditions depend on the index variables of Λ. Such conditions are said to be loop-dependent. The *if*-statements must have the format if $(C_1 \oplus C_2 \oplus \ldots)$ where C_x are loop-dependent conditions that are combined using logical operators $\oplus \in \{\wedge, \vee\}$. Every single loop-dependent condition C of an *if*-statement has to be an affine expression of the index variables i_l and can thus be represented as $C = \sum_{l=1}^{N} (c_l * i_l) + c \geq 0$ for constants $c_l, c \in \mathbb{Z}$.

The analysis for loop nest splitting consists of three different stages. In the first step called **Condition Optimization**, all loop-dependent conditions C are analyzed separately using a genetic algorithm (*GA*). GAs are employed since ILP is not suitable due to the non-linear objective function. For every condition C and every loop L_l, two values $lb'_{C,l}$ and $ub'_{C,l}$ are determined during this step. These values represent ranges of iterations of the loop nest where condition C is satisfied for all index variables i_l with $lb'_{C,l} \leq i_l \leq ub'_{C,l}$. These values are chosen in such a way that a loop nest splitting using

$lb'_{C,l}$ and $ub'_{C,l}$ minimizes the total execution of *if*-statements. For this purpose, the fitness function of the GA computes the total number of executed *if*-statements after loop nest splitting for a given set of $lb'_{C,l}$ and $ub'_{C,l}$ values. These computations are done very efficiently in linear time using a set of numerical formulas. The fewer the number of executed *if*-statements, the higher is the fitness of an individual.

Since this GA gives optimized results only for a single condition of an *if*-statement, these partial results need to be combined which is done during **Global Search Space Construction**. Here, for every condition C and its associated values $lb'_{C,l}$ and $ub'_{C,l}$, a polyhedron [18] P_C is generated. In general, a polyhedron P is a set of points in an N-dimensional geometric space which is defined by linear inequalities: $P = \{x \in \mathbb{Z}^N \mid Ax \geq b\}$ for an integer matrix A and a constant vector b. For the construction of P_C, constraints of the format $i_l \geq lb'_{C,l}$ and $ub'_{C,l} \geq i_l$ are used. Furthermore, appropriate constraints for all lower and upper loop bounds are needed: $i_l \geq lb_l$ and $ub_l \geq i_l$. If two conditions C_x and C_y are connected using the `&&` operator in an *if*-statement, the corresponding polyhedra P_x and P_y are intersected. For the `||` operator, the union of polyhedra is used. This way, polyhedra can be built representing those iterations of the loop nest where a single *if*-statement is satisfied. Since all *if*-statements in a loop nest need to be fulfilled for loop nest splitting, all these polyhedra representing a single *if*-statement need to be combined using the intersection. The resulting polyhedron G called the *global search space* represents those loop nest iterations where all *if*-statements are satisfied.

Due to the nature of the union operator, G is a finite union of polyhedra: $G = R_1 \cup R_2 \cup \ldots \cup R_M$. Each polyhedron R_r of G defines a region where all *if*-statements in a loop nest are satisfied. But it should be avoided to use all such regions of G for loop nest splitting since this would lead to an increased number of executions of *if*-statements. Therefore, a second GA is applied to G for a **Global Search Space Exploration**. The goal of this second GA is to select only those regions R_r of G leading to a total minimization of *if*-statement executions. After the termination of the GA, only the constraints of the selected regions R_r are considered for generating the conditions of the splitting if-statement.

5.2   Modeling and Analysis of Loops with Non-constant Bounds

Although the techniques summarized in the previous section already lead to large improvements [8], they are not applicable in the area of efficient memory hierarchy exploitation. As previously mentioned, all loop bounds lb_l and ub_l are explicitly required to be constant. This section presents extensions and improvements of [8] which eliminate this restriction and allow loop nest splitting to be applied to more general classes of embedded software, including popular sorting algorithms and DSP filter routines.

The only advantage of constant loop bounds as required in [8] is the simplicity of the GA for condition optimization. For values $lb'_{C,l}$ and $ub'_{C,l}$ generated by the GA, the fitness function only evaluates some formulas consisting of sum-of-products of the constant loop bounds and $lb'_{C,l}$ resp. $ub'_{C,l}$. This way, the exact number of *if*-statement executions can be computed and minimized. The restriction to constant loop bounds is not used elsewhere during loop nest splitting. In general, the basic structure of loop nest splitting as previously summarized is able to treat non-constant loop bounds, since the employed polyhedral models support complex iteration spaces.

Hence, we decided to maintain the basic structure of the analysis algorithms for loop nest splitting consisting of condition optimization, global search space construction and search space exploration. The problem formulation for loop nest splitting is given by:

Definition 1 (Loop Nest Splitting). *Let* $\Lambda = \{L_1, \ldots, L_N\}$ *be a loop nest of depth N. For every loop* $L_l \in \Lambda$, *a pair* (lb'_l, ub'_l) *is computed defining an interval of the index variable* i_l. *For* $lb'_l \leq i_l \leq ub'_l$, *all loop-variant* if*-statements in* Λ *are satisfied.* (lb'_l, ub'_l) *is chosen such that a minimization of* if*-statement executions is achieved.*

Since this is similar to the satisfiability of constraints with simultaneous minimization of an objective function, definition 1 describes an NP complete problem. The use of GAs here is motivated by their ability to find high-quality solutions especially for such complex optimization problems [19]. Furthermore, other well-known optimization strategies (e. g. ILP) can not be used due to the non-linearity of the objective function.

As already mentioned, polyhedral models are an integral part of the analysis. Since they base on linear inequalities, we allow loop bounds to be affine expressions:

Definition 2 (Affine Loop Bounds). *Let* $\Lambda = \{L_1, \ldots, L_N\}$ *be a loop nest of depth N.*
1. *For the outermost loop* L_1, *the bounds* lb_1 *and* ub_1 *are constant values.*
2. *For any other loop* $L_l \in \{L_2, \ldots, L_N\}$, *the loop bounds are affine expressions of the surrounding variables* $i_1, \ldots, i_{l-1}$. *Hence, the index variable* i_l *iterates between*

$$lb_l = \sum_{j=1}^{l-1} (c'_j * i_j) + c' \leq i_l \leq \sum_{j=1}^{l-1} (c''_j * i_j) + c'' = ub_l \qquad (c'_j, c', c''_j, c'' \in \mathbb{Z} \; const.)$$

The constant outermost loop bounds ensure that Λ is still fully analyzable at compile time due to the absence of data dependencies. The variable inner bounds imply that the number of *if*-statement executions subject to condition optimization not only depends on the values $(lb'_{C,l}, ub'_{C,l})$ generated by the GA. Now, implicit dependencies on a variable i_j exist if the bounds of an inner loop L_l depend on i_j. Hence, the formerly used formulas computing the *if*-statement executions are invalid. Instead, the GA's fitness function is restructured such that it models Λ after splitting using a set of $(lb'_{C,l}, ub'_{C,l})$ values. For this purpose, the following chromosomal encoding is employed:

Definition 3 (Chromosomal Encoding). *Let* $\Lambda = \{L_1, \ldots, L_N\}$ *be a loop nest.*
1. *A chromosome* C *is an array of integer values of length* $2 * N + 1$.
2. *For* $l \in \{1, \ldots, N\}$, *gene* $C[2 * l - 1]$ $(C[2 * l]$ *resp.) denotes* $lb'_{C,l}$ $(ub'_{C,l}$ *resp.). This way, the GA defines the regions of iterations with satisfied condition* C.
3. *Gene* $C[2 * N + 1]$ *stores the innermost loop* λ *for loop nest splitting. This gene states that loop nest* Λ *is split at loop* L_λ, *i. e. the splitting-*if *is placed in loop* L_λ.

The pseudo-code of the fitness function for optimizing a condition C is depicted in figure 4. The main goal of this function is to update two counters accurately. The first one (if_count) stores the number of *if*-statement executions for a given chromosome C. penalty counts how many times condition C is not satisfied when it is supposed by C that it should be satisfied. Using penalty, illegal individuals generated by the GA are detected.

Principally, this fitness function contains the entire loop nest Λ as can be seen from lines 3 and 17 of figure 4 (dots denote the omitted loops $L_2, \ldots, L_{N-1}$). For every loop, code is required to model Λ after a potential splitting (lines 4–15 resp. 18–25). When entering a loop L_l, it is first checked whether L_l contains the splitting-if (cf. lines 4 and 18). If this is not the case, the algorithm proceeds to loop L_{l+1} (line 15).

Otherwise, L_l contains the splitting-if (lines 6 and 20) whose execution requires to increment if_count (lines 5 and 19). The splitting-if for loop L_l checks genes $C[1], \ldots, C[2*l]$ and verifies that the index variables $i_1, \ldots, i_l$ actually are within the ranges specified by these genes. If the splitting-if is true, the duplicated loop L_l (cf. the second i loop in figure 3) counting to the new upper bound $ub'_{C,l}$ is executed next (lines 7 and 21). Within this loop, the remaining loop nest $L_{l+1}, \ldots, L_N$ can be found (lines 8–9). Since the splitting-if is true when executing this code, it is assumed that condition C is also true so that counter if_count is not altered in lines 7–10 resp. 21–22. But since the GA can generate illegal individuals for which condition C is false, care has to be taken to detect these situations. Lines 10 and 22 check whether the condition C is true or not. If it is false, an

```
1  double fitness(lb'_{C,1}, ub'_{C,1}, ..., lb'_{C,N}, ub'_{C,N}, λ) {
2    int if_count=0, penalty=0;
3    for (lb_1 ≤ i_1 ≤ ub_1) {
4      if (λ==1) {
5        if_count++;
6        if (i_1 ≥ lb'_{C,1} && i_1 ≤ ub'_{C,1}) {
7          for (i_1 ≤ ub'_{C,1})
8            ...
9            for (lb_N ≤ i_N ≤ ub_N)
10             if (!satisfied(C)) penalty++;
11        } else
12          ...
13          for (lb_N ≤ i_N ≤ ub_N)
14            if_count++;
15      } else
16        ...
17        for (lb_N ≤ i_N ≤ ub_N) {
18          if (λ==N) {
19            if_count++;
20            if (i_1 ≥ lb'_{C,1} && i_1 ≤ ub'_{C,1} && ... &&
                    i_N ≥ lb'_{C,N} && i_N ≤ ub'_{C,N}) {
21              for (i_N ≤ ub'_{C,N})
22                if (!satisfied(C)) penalty++;
23            } else
24              if_count++;
25          } ... }
26    if (penalty==0)
27      return((double) (1/if_count));
28    else
29      return((double) (1/(penalty+ERR))); }
```

Fig. 4. Fitness function for condition optimization

illegal individual is detected and counter penalty is incremented.

Finally, some code is required for a false splitting-if in loop L_l. In analogy to figure 3, the remaining loop nest $L_{l+1}, \ldots, L_N$ is copied into the *else*-part of the splitting-if (see lines 11–13). In loop L_N, the counter if_count is incremented (lines 14 and 24) since an *if*-statement checking condition C would be executed.

The fitness function terminates by returning the fitness of an individual based on the counters if_count and penalty. If an individual is valid, counter penalty is zero (line 26) and the inverse of if_count is returned to the GA. This way, individuals implying few *if*-statement executions have a high fitness. For an invalid individual (line 29), a large constant ERR is added to penalty, and the inverse of this sum is passed to the GA. This way, illegal individuals can never have a better fitness than legal ones.

As can be seen from figure 4, this fitness function has exponential complexity. Its runtime now depends on the depth N of a loop nest and the actual loop bounds. Affine loop bounds (cf. definition 2) ensure that the following analysis steps of global search space construction and search space exploration do not need to be modified since the affine bounds can directly be modeled by corresponding polyhedral constraints.

Table 1. CPU cycles for memories

Memory Type	#Cycles
Scratchpad	1 Cyc
Main mem. (16 bit)	1 Cyc + 1 wait state
Main mem. (32 bit)	1 Cyc + 3 wait states

Table 2. Energy consumption of memories

Memory Type	Size	Energy [nJ]	Memory Type	Size	Energy [nJ]
Scratchpad	128 B	0.53	Scratchpad	256 B	0.61
Scratchpad	512 B	0.69	Scratchpad	1 kB	0.82
Scratchpad	2 kB	1.07	Scratchpad	4 kB	1.21
Scratchpad	8 kB	2.07	Main (16 bit)	512 kB	24.0
Main (32 bit)	512 kB	49.3			

6   Benchmarking Results

The data partitioning and loop nest splitting techniques presented in this paper are fully implemented. To demonstrate the efficacy of our combined approach, typical embedded system benchmarks were passed through the algorithm described in section 3. The unchanged original source codes and the finally generated codes of the benchmarks (i. e. the code after data partitioning and loop nest splitting) were fed into an energy-aware research compiler [20] for the ARM7 architecture. During compilation, all optimizations were enabled to explore the maximum optimization potential. The generated assembly outputs of the compiler were finally processed by a simulator and an energy profiler. Both the compiler and the energy profiler make use of an instruction-level energy model [21] for the ARM7 having a very high accuracy of 98.3%. This way, the energy consumption and runtimes of our benchmarks can be computed reliably. The key characteristics of this energy model are briefly summarized in tables 1 and 2. Since data partitioning and loop nest splitting are performed at the level of C source codes as also illustrated by the code examples given in sections 4 and 5, our framework can easily be ported to other processors by simply providing an appropriate energy model.

For the experiments, benchmarks from different domains were selected. First, we used a 40 order *FIR* filter as a typical embedded DSP algorithm. Second, the sorting algorithms *insertion sort (INS)* and *selection sort (SELS)* were analyzed. Finally, a complete MPEG4 motion estimation routine *(ME)* was studied. The relevance of the extensions for loop nest splitting presented this paper is clearly demonstrated by the fact that a splitting of the FIR, INS and SELS benchmarks is impossible using the restricted techniques originally presented in [8]. The runtimes of our implemented tools are very low, not more than 39.8 CPU seconds are required to execute the algorithms described in sections 4 and 5 on a Sun Blade 1000 running at 750 MHz. The maximum contribution of loop nest splitting to these runtimes only amounts to 5.18 CPU seconds. Experiments were conducted by varying the scratchpad sizes. The following figures 5 and 6 show the impact of our optimization methodology for scratchpad sizes which are individually tuned for every benchmark, but kept fixed during all measurements. In these cases, a memory size of 1.8 kB was used for FIR, and 1.3 kB were used for INS and SELS. The ME routine with its large video frames was analyzed using a memory size of 119 kB. In order to demonstrate the stability of the proposed optimization methodology, detailed results for a large variety of scratchpad sizes are given in figure 7 using the SELS benchmark.

Figure 5 shows the effects of the combination of data partitioning and loop nest splitting on the energy consumption of the benchmarks. All results are shown as a percentage of the original unoptimized benchmark codes denoted as 100%. For both data

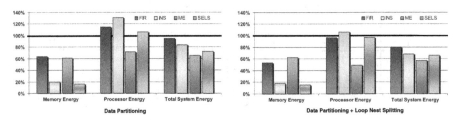

Fig. 5. Relative energy consumption after data partitioning and loop nest splitting

partitioning and loop nest splitting, the relative energy consumed by the memory system (i. e. background main memory and on-chip scratchpad), by the ARM7 processor and by the total system (i. e. processor plus memories) is depicted.

The left diagram of figure 5 clearly shows that data partitioning is a highly effective optimization w. r. t. the memory system. From column Memory Energy, it can be seen that the partitioning of arrays and the placement of parts of arrays onto a scratchpad leads to energy savings between 36.7% (FIR) and 84.2% (SELS). Due to the impaired control flow after data partitioning, the energy consumed by the ARM7 processor generally increases when compared to the original code version. Column Processor Energy shows additional energy consumptions between 6% (SELS) and 30.8% (INS). In the case of the ME benchmark, an energy reduction of 28.6% was measured. This is due to the fact that ME is very data-intensive and needs to access memory very frequently. Since the ARM7 CPU accesses an on-chip memory much faster than the main memory, the processor does not execute as much energy consuming wait states as before data partitioning. For the entire system (column System Energy), the techniques described in section 4 lead to total energy savings between 5.7% (FIR) and 34.7% (ME) with an average improvement of 21.3%.

The right diagram of figure 5 illustrates the relative energy consumption of the benchmarks after combined data partitioning and loop nest splitting. As can be seen by comparing the columns Memory Energy of both charts of figure 5, loop nest splitting conserves the energy savings for the memory system achieved by data partitioning. In the case of the FIR benchmark, additional savings of memory energy by 9.9% were measured. The notably less *if*-statement executions for this benchmark imply less instruction fetches from the memories leading to this result. Column Processor Energy of figure 5 clearly shows that the techniques presented in chapter 5 are able to eliminate the penalties introduced by data partitioning completely. After loop nest splitting, the energy consumption of the ARM7 for the FIR and SELS benchmarks is better than the original unoptimized code. In the case of the INS benchmark, the ARM7 consumes only 5.8% more energy than before any optimization. But also in this case, loop nest splitting has proven to be highly effective, since it reduces the energy dissipation by 25%. For the ME benchmark, loop nest splitting leads to an energy reduction for the ARM7 processor of 22.3% compared to the measurements immediately after data partitioning. Column System Energy illustrates the total savings achieved by the methodology proposed in this paper. It can be seen that the combined energy dissipation of the ARM7 and its memories drops between 20.3% (FIR) and 43.3% (ME) with an average saving of 32.3% compared to the unoptimized benchmarks.

With respect to the runtimes of the benchmarks, the combination of data partitioning and loop nest splitting also is quite beneficial. Figure 6 illustrates the relative runtimes of the benchmarks after each optimization step. Again, the 100% base line denotes the runtime of the original benchmark versions before any optimization. Due to the fact that *if*-statements are inserted in the code of the benchmarks during data partitioning (compare section 4), the execution times of almost all benchmarks increase by 8.7% (SELS) up to 36.7% (INS). Only in the case of the data-intensive ME benchmark, a speed-up of 28.2% was measured which is due to the reduction of wait states as explained above. Loop nest splitting is able to eliminate the negative effects of data partitioning nearly totally. Compared to the runtimes after data partitioning, speed-ups between 9.3% (SELS) and 31.1% (ME) were measured. In total, we are able to improve the runtimes of two benchmarks slightly

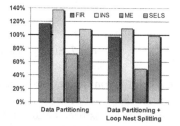

Fig. 6. Relative runtimes after data partitioning and loop nest splitting

(FIR: 2.5%, SELS: 1.5%) after the application of both optimizations while simultaneously achieving high gains w. r. t. energy dissipation. For the INS benchmark, a moderate total runtime degradation of 9.7% was still measured after loop nest splitting, whereas the ME benchmark was accelerated by 50.6%.

Finally, the influence of varying scratchpad sizes on energy consumption and runtimes is depicted in figure 7. The left diagram of this figure illustrates the total energy consumption of all code versions of the SELS benchmark for eleven different scratchpad sizes. It is not surprising that the original unoptimized benchmark consumes the same high amount of energy for all scratchpad sizes. This is due to the fact that no data can be placed onto the scratchpad memory at all due to the large size of the occurring arrays. In contrast, data partitioning is effective in energy consumption minimization already for very small memory sizes. In the case of a 256 bytes memory, only negligible improvements were measured which are not visible due to the resolution of figure 7. But already for 512 bytes, visible improvements were observed. With larger scratchpad sizes, data partitioning achieves higher gains due to the fact that less costly accesses to the main memory are performed. This way, a monotonically decreasing curve has been obtained. The same holds for loop nest splitting applied after data partitioning. Here, loop nest splitting is able to reduce the energy consumption considerably for scratchpads larger than 600 bytes. Again, a monotonic regression can be observed clearly demonstrating the stability of our combined optimization methodology.

With respect to the runtimes of the SELS benchmark (cf. right diagram of figure 7), a similar behavior of combined data partitioning and loop nest splitting for various scratchpad sizes has been measured. Again, the unoptimized benchmark requires constant execution times for all scratchpad sizes. Starting from considerably increased runtimes for small scratchpads, the overhead of data partitioning gets smaller the larger the on-chip memory becomes. This behavior is due to the high latencies imposed by main memory accesses which are minimized most effectively by data partitioning for larger scratchpads. In contrast, the benefits of loop nest splitting are already visible for scratchpad sizes starting from 512 bytes. From this point on, the impact of loop

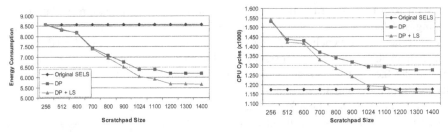

Fig. 7. Energy and performance comparison (Selection Sort)

nest splitting on the performance of the benchmark becomes larger as the speed-ups increase. For a scratchpad size of 1,024 bytes, a runtime nearly equal to the one of the original code has been obtained. For 1,200 bytes, the code generated by the proposed optimization methodology is faster than the original code so that loop nest splitting is able to over-compensate the overheads of data partitioning.

7   Conclusions

This paper presents a new approach for energy dissipation minimization of embedded software forming a homogeneous framework for low power code generation. In a first step, a data layout optimization is performed by partitioning large arrays into smaller pieces which can be put on low-energy scratchpad memories. Motivated by the introduction of a severe control flow overhead during this step, we propose to apply a control flow optimization step afterwards. Loop nest splitting has proven to be highly effective in generating a very regular control flow in the hot-spots of applications making it suitable to eliminate the negative effects of array partitioning.

Besides this entirely new combination of optimizations, the second major contribution of this paper is a significant extension of the analysis algorithms for loop nest splitting. Using these extended techniques, tight restrictions of the original algorithms can be relaxed so that more general classes of applications are transformed. Without these extensions, the optimization of three benchmarks analyzed in this work would have been impossible justifying the efforts spent on the loop nest splitting algorithms.

The results presented in this paper demonstrate that our combined optimization methodology is highly beneficial. The partitioning of arrays and placement of data onto a scratchpad leads to average reductions of energy dissipation of 21.3% for an actual ARM7 based system. In contrast, the runtimes of the benchmarks increase in almost all cases due to the control flow overhead. Loop nest splitting removes this overhead leading to improved runtimes for all benchmarks. Furthermore, loop nest splitting achieves an additional reduction of energy consumption. In total, the successive application of data partitioning and loop nest splitting as proposed in this paper leads to energy savings of up to 43.3% with an average gain of 32.3%.

Since all techniques presented in this paper are implemented such that the optimizations are performed at the level of C source codes before any assembly code generation for the ARM7 processor, our framework is inherently portable to other embedded processors. For this purpose, basically only an accurate energy model needs to be provided.

References

1. Wahlström, J.: Energy Storage Technology for Electric and Hybrid Vehicles – Matching Technology to Design Requirements. KFB Kommunikationsforskningsberedningen, Stockholm, Sweden (1999)
2. Stan, M.R., Burleson, W.P.: Bus-invert coding for low-power i/o. IEEE Transactions on VLSI Systems **3** (1995)
3. Wuytack, S., Catthoor, F., Nachtergaele, L., et al.: Power exploration for data dominated video applications. In: Proc. of ISLPED, Monterey (1996)
4. Marwedel, P., Wehmeyer, L., Verma, M., Steinke, S., Helmig, U.: Fast, predictable and low energy memory references through architecture-aware compilation. In: Proc. of ASP-DAC, Yokohama (2004)
5. Kandemir, M., Ramanujam, J., Irwin, M.J., Vijaykrishnan, N., Kadayif, I., Parikh, A.: Dynamic management of scratch-pad memory space. In: Proc. of DAC, Las Vegas (2001)
6. Banakar, R., Steinke, S., Lee, B.S., Balakrishnan, M., Marwedel, P.: Scratchpad memory: A design alternative for cache on-chip memory in embedded systems. In: Proc. of CODES, Estes Park (2002)
7. Verma, M., Steinke, S., Marwedel, P.: Data partitioning for maximal scratchpad usage. In: Proc. of ASP-DAC, Kitakyushu (2003)
8. Falk, H., Marwedel, P.: Control flow driven splitting of loop nests at the source code level. In: Proc. of DATE, Munich (2003)
9. Falk, H., Marwedel, P., Catthoor, F.: Chapter 17. In: Control Flow driven Splitting of Loop Nests at the Source Code Level. Volume Embedded Software for SOC. Kluwer Academic Publishers, Boston (2003) 215–229
10. Bacon, D.F., Graham, S.L., Sharp, O.J.: Compiler transformations for high-performance computing. ACM Computing Surveys **26** (1994)
11. Muchnick, S.S.: Advanced Compiler Design and Implementation. Morgan Kaufmann, San Francisco (1997)
12. Fraboulet, A., Huard, G., Mignotte, A.: Loop alignment for memory accesses optimization. In: Proc. of ISSS, San Jose (1999)
13. Kandemir, M.: A compiler-based approach for improving intra-iteration data reuse. In: Proc. of DATE, Paris (2002)
14. Loechner, V., Meister, B., Clauss, P.: Precise data locality optimization of nested loops. The Journal of Supercomputing **21** (2002) 37–76
15. Panda, P.R., Dutt, N., Nicolau, A.: Memory Issues in Embedded Systems-On-Chip. Kluwer Academic Publishers, Massachusetts (1999)
16. Steinke, S., Wehmeyer, L., Lee, B.S., Marwedel, P.: Assigning program and data objects to scratchpad for energy reduction. In: Proc. of DATE, Paris (2002)
17. Catthoor, F., Danckaert, K., Kulkarni, C., Brockmeyer, E., Kjeldsberg, P.G., van Achteren, T., Omnes, T.: Data Access and Storage Management for Embedded Programmable Processors. Kluwer Academic Publishers, Massachusetts (2002)
18. Wilde, D.K.: A library for doing polyhedral operations. Technical Report 785, IRISA Rennes, France (1993)
19. Bäck, T.: Evolutionary Algorithms in Theory and Practice. Oxford University Press (1996)
20. Steinke, S., Wehmeyer, L., et al.: The *encc* energy aware c compiler homepage. http://ls12-www.cs.uni-dortmund.de/research/encc/ (2002)
21. Steinke, S., Knauer, M., Wehmeyer, L., Marwedel, P.: An accurate and fine grain instruction-level energy model supporting software optimizations. In: Proc. of PATMOS, Yverdon-Les-Bains (2001)

On the Phase Coupling Problem
Between Data Memory Layout Generation
and Address Pointer Assignment

Bernhard Wess and Thomas Zeitlhofer

Institute of Communications and Radio-Frequency Engineering
Vienna University of Technology
{bernhard.wess,thomas.zeitlhofer}@nt.tuwien.ac.at

Abstract. Digital signal processors provide dedicated address generation units that support zero-cost address pointer modifications within
a limited offset range. In order to fully exploit these features, program
variables must be carefully placed in memory. However, the problem of
generating optimum data memory layouts is NP-hard. Efficient heuristics are available for offset ranges ± 1 and ± 2. For an arbitrary set of
zero-cost address offsets, optimum memory layout generation can be
represented as a quadratic assignment problem (QAP) and solved by
a heuristic technique such as simulated annealing (SA). A total number
of $N!$ layouts exist where N is the number of different program variables. The solution space becomes even larger in case of multiple address
pointers. For each coloring of the access sequence, which corresponds to
a specific address pointer assignment, an optimum memory layout has to
be found by solving a separate QAP. So far no efficient heuristics exist for
combining memory layout generation with address pointer assignment.
We show that for a fixed layout optimum address pointer assignments
can produced for a given maximum number of K address pointers. The
complexity of this algorithm is of $O(N^K)$. It has been applied to the OffsetStone benchmark suite. As can be demonstrated by some examples,
memory layout generation and address pointer assignment are strongly
interdependent problems. We introduce a new algorithm that iterates
over several optimized layout generation and optimum pointer assignments steps. Experimental results indicate that compared to SA this
new technique produces results of equal quality in less time.

1   Introduction

Digital signal processors (DSPs) have dedicated address generation units (AGUs)
that support address computation in parallel to data-path operations. AGUs allow indirect addressing with address pointer updates by some fixed values without adversely affecting performance. Typical offset values for these zero-cost
increment/decrement operations are ± 1. Some AGU architectures provide dedicated offset registers. Once such a register is initialized by a value m, address
pointers can be updated by offset m. Operations of this type do not employ datapath resources and thus can be executed in parallel to other machine operations

H. Schepers (Ed.): SCOPES 2004, LNCS 3199, pp. 152–166, 2004.
© Springer-Verlag Berlin Heidelberg 2004

at no extra cost. In contrast, explicit address register and modify register load operations introduce both code size and speed overhead. Minimizing addressing overhead requires to carefully place program variables in data memory and to look for optimized address pointer assignments. Unfortunately, these problems are NP-hard.

The rest of the paper is organized as follows. Sec. 2 defines the offset assignment problem and its relation to the bandwidth minimization problem. The case of multiple address pointers is discussed in Sec. 3 where a new iterative optimization procedure is introduced. Sec. 4 presents experimental results for this technique. Conclusions and directions for future work are given in Sec. 5.

2 Offset Assignment

Let V be a set of program variables. Each variable $v_i \in V$ is identified by index $i \in \{1, 2, \ldots, N\}$ with $N = |V|$.

A variable access stream $S = [v_{s(1)}, v_{s(2)}, \ldots, v_{s(M)}]$ is defined by a function

$$s : \{1, 2, \ldots, M\} \to \{1, 2, \ldots, N\} \tag{1}$$

where M denotes the stream length and $N \leq M$. The image $s(\ell)$ of any $\ell \in \{1, 2, \ldots, M\}$ defines the program variable $v_{s(\ell)}$ on position ℓ in the access stream S.

A memory layout is a permutation

$$\pi : \{1, 2, \ldots, N\} \to \{1, 2, \ldots, N\} \tag{2}$$

that assigns addresses to all program variables which appear in the access stream S. Equivalently, a layout can be regarded as a string φ of nodes with each node of V appearing exactly once. The correspondence between these two definitions is simply that $\pi(i) = k$ with $v_i \in V$ if and only if v_i is the kth element of φ.

Let us assume that an address register points to v_i and it should be used for accessing v_j. To this end, the address pointer has to be modified by address offset $\pi(j) - \pi(i)$. AGUs of DSPs support zero-cost address pointer updates for a limited set of offset values. Obviously, costs can be minimized by memory layout optimization. This problem is denoted as offset assignment (OA). Let c_{ij} with $i, j \in \{1, 2, \ldots, N\}$ be a cost value for redirecting an address pointer from address i to the new address j. Additionally, let t_{ij}^S specify how often address j is accessed right after address i in S. For a single address pointer, the address computation costs can be expressed by

$$C_1 = \sum_{i=1}^{N} \sum_{j=1}^{N} c_{ij} t_{\pi(i)\pi(j)}^S. \tag{3}$$

Modifying π such that C_1 becomes a minimum in Equ. 3 is a quadratic assignment problem (QAP) [1]. Since it is NP-hard, optimum solutions can be found just for small values of N.

Let us assume that the AGU supports zero-cost address updates for a symmetric range $\pm r$ where r is any positive integer. With

$$c_{ij} = \begin{cases} 0 \text{ for } |j - i| \le r, \\ 1 \text{ otherwise,} \end{cases} \tag{4}$$

Equ. 3 gives the required number of address pointer reload operations.

We define an undirected graph $G = (V, E)$ to represent the access transitions between program variables in S and call G the access graph of S. Each node in the graph corresponds to a unique program variable. For the rest of the paper, we use the notation $v \in V$ both for program variables of S and nodes of G. There is an undirected edge $e = (v_i, v_j) \in E$ in G with weight $w(e)$ if the program variables v_i and v_j are adjacent $w(e)$ times in S. Note that G is always a connected graph.

As an example, consider the program variable set $V = \{a, b, c, d, e, f, g, h\}$ which is accessed in the sequence

$$S = \{f, a, b, g, e, d, f, h, c, d, h, f, d, e, g, a, f, h, d\}. \tag{5}$$

Fig. 1a shows the corresponding access graph G. Fig. 1b defines a memory layout that corresponds to π in Fig. 1c and which can also be represented by the string

$$\varphi = bgaefdhc. \tag{6}$$

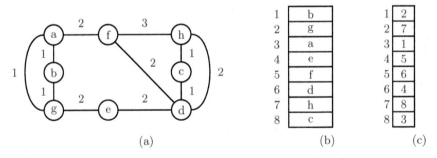

(a)   (b)   (c)

Fig. 1. Variable access stream $S = \{f, a, b, g, e, d, f, h, c, d, h, f, d, e, g, a, f, h, d\}$: (a) access graph, (b) memory layout, (c) permutation π.

Given a layout π, C_1 can be derived from G by summing up the weights of all edges that connect nodes whose absolute address offsets are larger than r,

$$C_1 = \sum_n w(e_n) \text{ with } e_n = (v_i, v_j) \in E, |\pi(i) - \pi(j)| > r. \tag{7}$$

OA for a single address pointer with zero-cost update range ± 1 is called simple offset assignment (SOA). An efficient SOA heuristic has been proposed in [2] that looks for a minimum-weighted path in the access graph defined by the access stream S. Meanwhile several improvements have been proposed. As shown in [3], SOA combined with variable coalescing allows to produce best results compared to currently existing SOA techniques.

OA is related to the bandwidth minimization problem (BMP) of graphs. The bandwidth bw of π is defined as the maximum distance between the images under π of any two nodes that are connected by an edge,

$$bw(\pi) = \max\{|\pi(i) - \pi(j)| \mid (v_i, v_j) \in E\}. \tag{8}$$

Fig. 1b shows a bandwidth 2 layout. The bandwidth BW of G is defined as the least possible bandwidth for any layout of G,

$$BW(G) = \min\{bw(\pi) \mid \pi \text{ is a layout of } G\}. \tag{9}$$

As an example, $BW(G) = 2$ for our access graph in Fig. 1a.

In contrast to the BMP, the objective of OA is not to find $BW(G)$ but to produce a layout π for a given modify range $\pm r$ such that the layout cost C_1 becomes a minimum. We say π is an offset r layout if it is optimized for modify range $\pm r$. All layouts π with $bw(\pi) \leq r$ are offset r layouts. Obviously, if $BW(G) \leq r$ then all layouts π with $BW(G) \leq bw(\pi) \leq r$ lead to $C_1 = 0$.

The general BMP of graphs is NP-hard [4]. However, Saxe [5] showed that the problem $BW(G) \overset{?}{\leq} k$ for some fixed constant k can be solved in polynomial time. Particularly, a linear-time algorithm exists for the problem $BW(G) \overset{?}{\leq} 2$ [6].

As mentioned above, generating optimum memory layouts is NP-hard even for the specific case $r = 1$. An efficient OA algorithm that produces offset 2 layouts is discussed in [7]. This algorithm finds optimum memory layouts if $BW(G) \leq 2$ otherwise a heuristic is applied that minimizes C_1.

3   General Offset Assignment

General offset assignment (GOA) is the problem of optimizing the memory layout for multiple address pointers. In case of GOA, both memory layout and address pointer assignment are optimized. Assigning address pointers can be regarded as K-coloring the access stream S. For K homogeneous address pointers, an optimum solution has to be found out of K^{M-1} different colorings by simple exhaustive search. A coloring of S is a partition that decomposes $\{1, 2, \ldots, M\}$ into K disjoint subsets. Each subset defines an access stream

$$S_k = [v_{s_k(1)}, v_{s_k(2)}, \ldots, v_{s_k(M_k)}] \tag{10}$$

with

$$s_k : \{1, 2, \ldots, M_k\} \to \{1, 2, \ldots, M\} \text{ and } \sum_{k=1}^{K} M_k = M. \tag{11}$$

For each S_k, all elements appear in the same relative order as in S.

We calculate the overall address computation costs by

$$C_K = \sum_{k=1}^{K} \sum_{i=1}^{N} \sum_{j=1}^{N} c_{ij} t^{S_k}_{\pi(i)\pi(j)}. \tag{12}$$

The goal is to minimize C_K by optimizing the memory layout π and the partitioning of S. This optimization problem consists of K interdependent QAPs with a solution space size of $N!K^{M-1}$ which is far too big to be practicable even for small numbers of K, N, and M. In [8], simulated annealing (SA) is applied for solution space exploration. Heuristically reducing GOA to K SOA problems by decomposing variable set V into disjoint subsets are proposed in [2, 9]. These techniques are restricted to the offset cost function C_1 and $r = 1$ in Equ. 4. Considering only disjoint subsets is not necessarily a good strategy and may lead to suboptimal solutions as shown in Sec. 3.2.

In case of multiple address pointers the access graph G is defined by the union of the access graphs $G_k(V_k, E_k)$ that correspond to access streams S_k

$$G(V, E) = G\left(\bigcup_{k=1}^{K} V_k, \bigcup_{k=1}^{K} E_k \right). \tag{13}$$

Assuming a symmetric range as defined in Equ. 4 we introduce the *maximum bandwith-r graph*

$$\hat{G}(V, \hat{E}, r) \text{ where } |\hat{E}| = \max\{|(v_i, v_j)| \in V \times V \mid BW(\hat{G}) = r\}. \tag{14}$$

This graph defines *all* zero-cost transitions for a given range r and layout π. Fig. 2 shows the structure of $\hat{G}$ for $r = 2$. Note that $\hat{G}(V, \hat{E}, r)$ is an *interval*

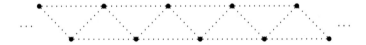

Fig. 2. Topology of a *maximum bandwith-2 graph*.

$graph^1$ and assuming $|V| > 2r + 1$ we find $BW(\hat{G}) = r$, maximum clique size $\omega(\hat{G}) = r + 1$, and maximum degree $\Delta = 2r$.

Minimizing Equ. 12 for symmetric update ranges may also be interpreted as mapping the access graph G onto the maximum bandwith-r graph $\hat{G}$ subject to the cost function

$$C_K = \sum_{e \in \tilde{E}} w(e) \text{ with } \tilde{E} = \{(v_i, v_j) \in E \mid (v_i, v_j) \notin \hat{E}\}. \tag{15}$$

---

[1] For a detailed discussion of interval graphs see [10].

An optimized mapping may be generated by

1. permutation of vertices, which corresponds to memory layout (π) modifications and/or
2. adding/removing edges to/from the access graph G, which corresponds to pointer assignment (s_k) modifications.

3.1   Offset 2 Layout Generation Algorithm

The offset 2 layout generation algorithm in [7] is based on Garey's algorithm [6] for the problem $BW(G) \overset{?}{\leq} 2$. It starts with an initial layout consisting of a single program variable (node of the access graph). The algorithm recursively constructs a complete layout by adding program variables to the current partial layout.

A partial layout π' is defined on a subset of the nodes $V' \subset V$. If π'_1 is a partial layout defined on V'_1 and π'_2 is a partial layout on $V'_2 \supseteq V'_1$, we say that π'_2 is an extension of π'_1 if $\pi'_2(v_i) = \pi'_1(v_i)$ for all $v_i \in V'_1$. Garey's algorithm constructs a complete layout if there is one containing the initial layout. It terminates as soon as it detects that the current partial layout cannot be extended to a complete layout.

We say $v_i \in V'$ is an active node of the partial layout π' if $(v_i, v_j) \in E$ with $v_j \in V \setminus V'$. The set of successors of an active node v_i is defined by

$$Q(v_i) = \{v_j | (v_i, v_j) \in E \text{ with } v_j \in V \setminus V'\}. \tag{16}$$

For the number of successors of an active node v_i, we use the notation $n(v_i) = |Q(v_i)|$. Let X be the set of active nodes, then all successors are given by set $Y = \bigcup_i Q(v_i)$ for all $v_i \in X$.

Garey's algorithm is based on an exhaustive list of actions for the different circumstances which can arise in the process of extending partial layouts. There are three types of partial layouts defined by a string φ:

- Type A: $\varphi = \alpha a b$ where at most a and b are active.
- Type B: $\varphi = \alpha \langle a_m b_m \rangle \ldots \langle a_1 b_1 \rangle$ for some $m \geq 1$ where at most a_1 and b_1 are active.
- Type C: $\varphi = \alpha\_a_m\_\ldots\_a_1$ for some $m \geq 1$ where at most a_1 is active.

α represents blanks (_) and inactive nodes which have already been permanently placed. Type B defines two strings $\alpha a_m b_m \ldots a_1 b_1$ and $\alpha b_m a_m \ldots b_1 a_1$.

Let φ_n represent a partial layout of one of the three types. By looking at how the active nodes interact with their successors, it may be obvious that φ_n cannot be completed with bandwidth 2. Otherwise the algorithm will find a sufficiently general extension φ_{n+1} which can be completed with bandwidth 2 whenever φ_n can be. φ_{n+1} is again of one of the three basic types. If any suitable extension is found, the string φ_n is replaced by φ_{n+1}. This process continues until either reaching an impasse or a complete layout. Fig. 3 shows for an example access graph how the algorithm iteratively constructs a layout starting with the initial layout $\varphi_0 = \_b$.

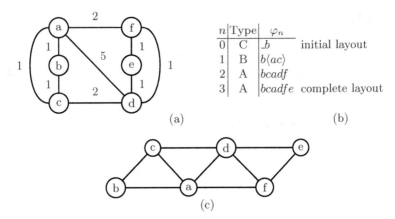

(a)

(b)

(c)

Fig. 3. Variable access stream $S = \{a, b, c, d, e, f, a, d, a, d, a, c, d, f, a, d\}$: (a) access graph G, (b) offset 2 layout generation with the initial layout $\varphi_0 = {\_b}$, (c) $BW(G) = 2$ and therefore G can be mapped onto $\hat{G}$, especially we find $G = \hat{G}$.

Garey's algorithm determines in $O(N)$ steps with $N = |V|$ whether or not the access graph $G = (V, E)$ has a bandwidth 2 layout beginning with the initial layout ${\_v}$ where $v \in V$. By investigating all possible initial layouts, we have an $O(N^2)$ algorithm for deciding whether or not $BW(G) \leq 2$.

It is obvious that a partial layout π represented by some string φ cannot be extended to a complete bandwidth 2 layout in the following cases:

- φ is of type A with $n(a) > 1$ or $n(b) > 2$.
- φ is of type B with $|Q(a) \cup Q(b)| > 2$ or $n(a) = n(b) = 2$.
- φ is of type C with $n(a) > 3$.

Additionally, there are more subtle cases where partial layouts of type C with $n(a) = 3$ or $n(a) = 2$ cannot be completed. We refer to [6] for a detailed discussion.

For generating optimized offset 2 layouts, we make a heuristic extension step each time Garey's algorithm would terminate. We extend a partial layout φ_n to φ_{n+1} by adding a node set $Z \subseteq Y$ to φ_n such that $\sum_k w(e_k)$ becomes a maximum where $e_k = (v_i, v_j)$ with $|\pi_{n+1}(i) - \pi_{n+1}(j)| \leq 2$, $v_i \in X \cup Z$, and $v_j \in Z$. Here X denotes the active nodes of φ_n, Y the set of all successors, and $\pi_{n+1}(i)$ gives the address of v_i in layout φ_{n+1}.

In each heuristic extension step $\varphi_n \to \varphi_{n+1}$, at most two nodes are added at the right end of φ_n. These nodes are new active nodes in φ_{n+1}. All nodes of φ_n that are still active in φ_{n+1} contribute to the layout cost. If φ_n represents a layout of type C, then additional nodes may fill some blanks.

For the access graph in Fig. 4a, there is no bandwidth 2 layout since node a has degree 5. As shown in Fig. 4b, beginning with initial layout ${\_b}$, the layout generation algorithm would produce the offset 2 layout $\varphi = bcadfe$ with $C_1 = 1$ in $n = 3$ steps. φ_1 represents a partial layout of type B which is heuristically extended to φ_2 of type A. In this step, the set of active nodes is $X = \{a,c\}$ and the successor set is $Y = \{d,e,f\}$. d and f become new active nodes in φ_2. a remains active because its successor node e has not been placed. Since node e cannot be placed within the modify range ±2 of a, the partial layout cost is increased by the weight of edge (a,e).

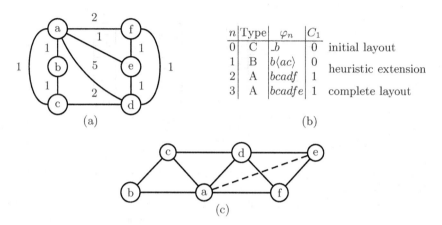

n	Type	φ_n	C_1	
0	C	_b	0	initial layout
1	B	$b\langle ac\rangle$	0	heuristic extension
2	A	bcadf	1	
3	A	bcadfe	1	complete layout

(a)   (b)

(c)

Fig. 4. (a) Access graph G with $BW(G) > 2$, (b) offset 2 layout generation with heuristic extension of partial layout $\varphi_1 = b\langle ac\rangle$ to $\varphi_2 = bcadf$, (c) optimized mapping (Equ. 15) of G onto $\hat{G}$ – dashed lines indicate $e \notin \hat{E}$.

3.2   Optimum Address Pointer Assignment

GOA consists of OA in conjunction with address pointer assignment (APA). In [11], an optimum algorithm for APA is introduced for a fixed memory layout π. It is assumed that π has been optimized in a previous step. This algorithm generates an optimum APA that minimizes the cost function

$$C = I + (K+1)\,C_K. \tag{17}$$

K is the number of available address pointers, I the number of pointer initializations, and C_K represents the number of address pointer reloads. The definition of C in Equ. 17 ensures that APAs with a minimum number of address pointers and a minimum number of reloads are generated. This optimum APA algorithm takes as input the variable access stream, a fixed memory layout, and produces an optimum APA. It builds an assignment tree where all nodes at the same level correspond to different address pointer settings at some point in the access stream. Each path in the tree from the root to a leaf is a mapping of memory accesses to address pointers.

Fig. 5 shows the first three levels of the assignment tree for the variable access stream $S = [d,c,c,d,b,e,a,f]$ with $K = 2$ pointers and memory layout π that is shown in Fig. 6a. A zero-cost offset range ±1 is assumed. The pointer assignment

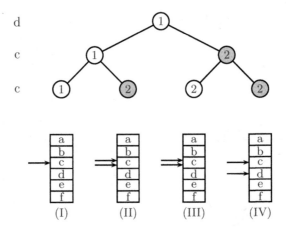

Fig. 5. Assignment tree pruning.

is indicated by the node color and the numbers inside the nodes are the costs C defined by Equ. 17 with $K = 2$. For first element in the access stream (here d) we can assign a pointer arbitrarily. The initialization cost for this pointer is 1 as shown in the root node of Fig. 5. For homogeneous address registers, the pointer settings (II) and (III) in Fig. 5 are equivalent. Within a group of equivalent nodes, only one lowest-cost node needs to be kept when continuing with the assignment tree construction. Ties are broken arbitrarily. The complete assignment tree for access stream $S = [d, c, c, d, b, e, a, f]$ with $K = 2$ pointers and memory layout π in Fig. 6a is shown in Fig. 6c.

The coloring of the nodes on the path from the root to the lowest cost node yields the optimum address pointer assignment with

$$C_K = \lfloor C/(K+1) \rfloor \tag{18}$$

pointer reloads and

$$I = C \bmod (K+1) \tag{19}$$

pointer initializations. For our example in Fig. 6, $C_2 = 0$ and $I = 2$. The variable access stream S is partitioned into the sub-streams

$$S_1 = [d, c, c, b, a] \text{ and } S_2 = [d, e, f]. \tag{20}$$

Note that in contrast to S, all address offsets in layout π are in the zero-cost range ± 1 both for S_1 and S_2.

The maximum width $W_{\max}$ of the assignment tree is bounded by

$$W_{\max} \leq \binom{N+K}{K} - 1 < N^K. \tag{21}$$

Consider all nodes of one tree level, that is, at a given $\tilde{\ell}$ in the access stream. Each node corresponds to a specific address pointer setting where an address

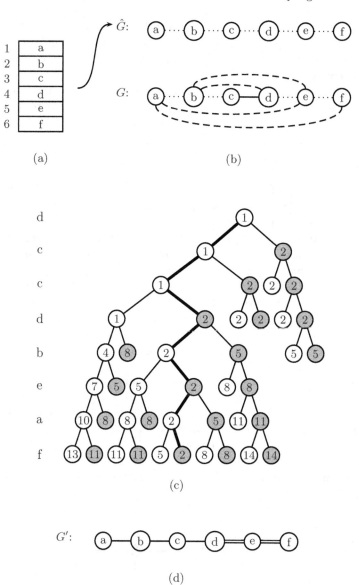

Fig. 6. APA for variable access stream $S = [d, c, c, d, b, e, a, f]$: a) Memory layout, b) maximum bandwith-1 graph $\hat{G}$ and access graph G – dashed lines indicate $e \notin \hat{E}$, c) optimum APA for $K = 2$ indicated by a minimum weighted path, d) optimum APA produces a modified access graph $G' = \hat{G}$ – double lines indicate transitions of address pointer 2.

pointer is either directed to a program variable or is uninitialized ($N + 1$ possible assignments). The costs for succeeding accesses $\ell > \tilde{\ell}$ just depend on the contents of the address pointers at access $\tilde{\ell}$. Since a homogeneous address pointer file is assumed, any two tree nodes are equivalent if their corresponding address pointer settings are equal except for permutations. So for K address pointers, the number of nodes that have to be distinguished is given by the number of K-combinations of $N + 1$ elements.

This optimum APA algorithm has been applied to all access streams included in the OffsetStone benchmark suite [12]. Experimental results are discussed in [11].

3.3   Iterative GOA

In Sec. 3.2 and Sec. 3.1 the two optimization mechanisms for GOA have been discussed independently. Generating highly optimized results requires to consider both, memory layout and address pointer assignment. However, these two phases are highly interdependent. While often optimum APAs may be generated for a fixed memory layout (compare Sec. 3.2) by modifications of the access graph, algorithms for memory layout optimization operate on given access graphs.

Lets consider the GOA optimization problem with respect to the maximum bandwith-r graph $\hat{G}$. According to Equ. 15 the goal is to modify the access graph G such that it becomes a subgraph of $\hat{G}$ (zero-cost solution) or to minimize the (weighted) number of edges from G that are not edges in $\hat{G}$.

Given an access sequence and considering a single address pointer we can define an initial access graph G. Applying memory layout optimization we map the vertices of G onto vertices of $\hat{G}$ thereby minimizing the costs (Equ. 15). To further decrease the costs we can perform APA which generates the modified access graph G' where $C'_K \leq C_K$. As G' is better adapted to $\hat{G}$ it seems reasonable to permutate the layout and search for a better mapping of vertices from G' to $\hat{G}$. That is, memory layout optimization is now performed for the modified access graph G'. Using the same arguments as before this process may be iterated up to some stop criterion. This is the motivation for our new GOA optimization algorithm as shown in Fig. 7.

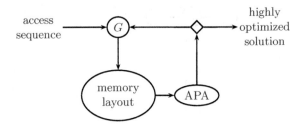

Fig. 7. Iterative GOA optimization algorithm.

Lets consider the access sequence S=[0, 1, 2, 3, 1, 4, 2, 5, 3, 6, 7, 1, 8, 2, 9, 3, 4] as a demonstrative example. In the following figures dashed lines indicate $e \in E\backslash\hat{E}$, dotted lines indicate $e \in \hat{E}\backslash E$, and double lines indicate transitions

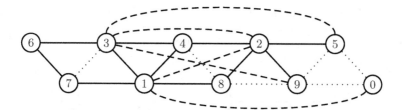

Fig. 8. Initial access graph G and memory layout π.

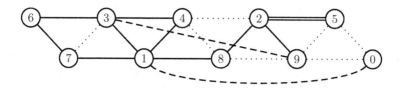

Fig. 9. Initial memory layout and modified (APA) access graph G'.

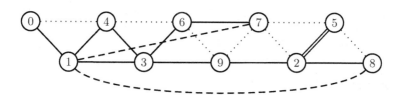

Fig. 10. Memory layout π' and access graph G'.

of address pointer 2. We assume a symmetric update range $r = 2$ and two address registers. Using the algorithm discussed in Sec. 3.1 we find the initial memory layout show in Fig. 8. Optimum APA (Sec. 3.2) for the memory layout in Fig. 8 generates the modified access graph in Fig. 9. Note that APA has removed 5 edges from the access graph and only two non zero-cost transitions are remaining. The modified access graph G' is then used to generate the memory layout π' in Fig. 10 Applying APA again reduces the costs further as shown in Fig. 11. In last iteration the generated memory layout achieves $G'' \subset \hat{G}$ hence we have found a zero-cost solution. Note that in this case the address pointer

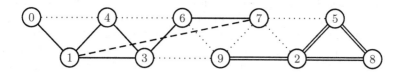

Fig. 11. Memory layout π' and access graph G''.

assignment groups the program variables into two disjoint subsets. Comparing to Fig. 6d we see that this is not necessarily the case. In Fig. 6d program variable *d has to be accessed* by both address pointers in order to achieve an optimum solution.

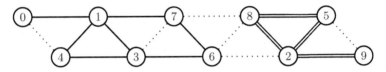

Fig. 12. Memory layout π'' and access graph G''.

In general, the proposed algorithm does not correspond to a strict search path iterating from one solution to the next but corresponds to a search tree. The optimum APA algorithm may produce more than one optimum pointer assignment and therefore several access graphs may contribute to new memory layouts. The width of this search tree may increase in each iteration so we introduce an upper limit W_I and investigate only the W_I best solutions. The iterations may be stopped when no new memory layouts or pointer assignments are produced. Additionally, we limit the maximum number of iteration to a range of 10^2 up to 10^3.

4   Experimental Results

The algorithm proposed in Sec. 3.3 has been applied to several artificial generated access sequences for a symmetric update range with $r = 2$ and two address pointers. In Tab. 1 the performance is compared to the simulated annealing approach [8]. The table shows the number of required address pointer reloads (Equ. 18) for the proposed algorithm and simulated annealing. For iterative GOA the solution also depends on the initial memory layout. To demonstrate this effect Tab. 1 shows the results for an optimized initial memory layout (IG_0) and an unoptimized initial memory layout which corresponds to the first appearance of program variables (IG_1). Iterative GOA generates solutions comparable to simulated annealing but typically in less time. The runtime of SA for larges sequences (75/50) is about 15 minutes while iterative GOA produces results in about 1 minute.

We have also applied iterative GOA to a set of 179 sequences from the Offset-Stone benchmarks [12] where the length of these access sequences is up to 100. For 34 of these examples an optimum solution is already found for a single address pointer. Again we assume $r = 2$ and two available address pointers. Fig. 13 shows a histogram of achieved cost reduction compared to the initial layout. In these examples up to 1000 iterations are performed and the initial memory layout is unoptimized and corresponds to the first appearance of program variables.

Table 1. Performance comparison of iterative GOA – shown is the number of required address pointer reloads (Equ. 18 for $K = 2$), M access sequence length, N number of program variables, IG_0 iterative GOA with optimized initial memory layout, IG_1 iterative GOA with first appearance initial memory layout, SA simulated annealing.

M	N	IG_0	IG_1	SA
75	50	11	10	11
75	50	12	9	10
75	50	8	9	10
60	40	8	10	6
60	40	6	5	5
60	40	6	7	8
45	30	4	7	3
45	30	6	8	7
45	30	2	6	1

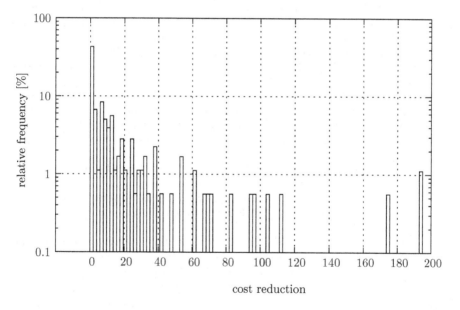

Fig. 13. Histogram of cost value reduction for iterative GOA.

5   Conclusions

Address pointer assignment (APA) and memory layout generation are highly interdependent phases in general offset assignment problems. We have shown that optimized solutions can be generated by iteratively applying efficient algorithms for APA and memory layout generation. The proposed algorithm has been demonstrated on artificial and real world examples. Compared to simulated annealing approaches we generate equivalent solutions typically in less time. An efficient exploration of the combined search space is subject to ongoing research.

References

1. B. Wess and M. Gotschlich, "Optimal DSP memory layout generation as a quadratic assignment problem," in *Proc. IEEE Int. Symp. on Circuits and Systems*, Hong Kong, June 1997, vol. 3, pp. 1712–1715.

2. S. Liao, S. Devadas, K. Keutzer, S. Tjiang, and A. Wang, "Storage assignment to decrease code size," in *Proc. ACM Conf. on Programming Language Design and Implementation*, June 1995, pp. 186–195.

3. D. Ottoni, G. Ottoni, G. Araujo, and R. Leupers, "Improving offset assignment through simultaneous variable coalescing," in *Proc. 7th Int. Workshop on Software and Compilers for Embedded Systems*, Vienna, September 2003, pp. 285–297.

4. C. H. Papadimitriou, "The NP-completeness of the bandwidth minimization problem," *Computing*, vol. 16, pp. 263–270, 1976.

5. J. B. Saxe, "Dynamic-programming algorithms for recognizing small-bandwidth graphs in polynomial time," *SIAM J. Alg. Disc. Meth.*, vol. 1, no. 4, pp. 363–369, December 1980.

6. M. R. Garey, R. L. Graham, D. S. Johnson, and D. E. Knuth, "Complexity results for bandwidth minimization," *SIAM J. Appl. Math.*, vol. 34, no. 3, pp. 477–495, May 1978.

7. B. Wess and M. Gotschlich, "Constructing memory layouts for address generation units supporting offset 2 access," in *Proc. IEEE Int. Conf. on Acoustics, Speech, and Signal Processing*, Munich, April 1997, vol. 1, pp. 683–686.

8. B. Wess, "Minimization of data address computation overhead in DSP programs," *Kluwer Design Automation for Embedded Systems*, vol. 4, pp. 167–185, March 1999.

9. R. Leupers and P. Marwedel, "Algorithms for address assignment in DSP code generation," in *Proc. IEEE Int. Conf. on Computer-Aided Design*, San Jose, November 1996, pp. 109–112.

10. M. C. Golumbic, *Algorithmic Graph Theory and Perfect Graphs*, Academic Press, 1980.

11. B. Wess and T. Zeitlhofer, "Optimum address pointer assignment for digital signal processors," to appear in Proc. IEEE Int. Conf. on Acoustics, Speech, and Signal Processing, 2004.

12. R. Leupers, "Offset assignment showdown: Evaluation of DSP address code optimization algorithms," in *12th International Conference on Compiler Construction (CC)*, Warsaw (Poland), April 2003, Springer Lecture Notes on Computer Science, LNCS 2622, http://www.address-code-optimization.org.

Dynamic Mapping and Ordering Tasks of Embedded Real-Time Systems on Multiprocessor Platforms

Peng Yang* and Francky Catthoor**

IMEC, Kapeldreef 75, B3001 Leuven, Belgium
{yangp,catthoor}@imec.be

Abstract. Tradeoff exploration can be found in several different areas of embedded system design. One example is task scheduling, where different task mapping and ordering choices for a target platform will lead to different performance/cost tradeoffs, which can be represented in a so-called Pareto curve. Though many scheduling algorithms have been suggested, on-line or off-line, few have been really implemented on a real platform, especially on an embedded multi-processor one. We have implemented a middleware layer to handle that problem and we have integrated a hierarchical task scheduler into it. It is compatible with most current RTOS implementations as long as they have a well defined API for task activation and synchronization. A simple DCT example demonstrates that the extra overhead is acceptable low. With a real-life test case from H.263, we demonstrate how big an impact our approach can cause. The deadline miss rate is dramatically reduced since we map and order the tasks at run-time. When voltage scaling is considered, we can save 10% more energy compared to the state-of-the-art solution. Moreover, this integration enables a novel design methodology flow, which allows further design space exploration and optimization at run time.

1 Introduction

The future of most embedded multimedia applications lies in low-power heterogeneous multi-processor platforms, which have sufficient computation and memory resources, consume extremely low energy and are flexible enough to cope with the dynamic behavior of future multi-media applications.

An up-to-date platform typically contains one or more (re-configurable) programmable components (general-purpose processor, DSP or ASIP), the analog front end, on-chip memory, I/O and other ASICs. Furthermore, it can contain power management modules, controlled by the OS, to configure the power consumption and performance of the modules in the system. Example platforms currently available for multi-media targets are TI's OMAP, Philips' Nexperia, ARM's PrimeXsys and Xilinx's Virtex-II Pro.

---

* Also PhD student of K.U. Leuven-ESAT.
** Also Professor of K.U. Leuven-ESAT.

H. Schepers (Ed.): SCOPES 2004, LNCS 3199, pp. 167–181, 2004.

Platforms obtain a high performance at a low energy cost through the exploitation of parallelism. With parallelism we can distribute the computational load of an application over several processing elements. For the same throughput, each processing element can then operate at a lower frequency, because it has less work to do. At the same time, a lower frequency implies that the CMOS circuits can operate at a lower voltage. Since in physics the dynamic energy consumption is proportional to the square of the operating voltage [2], this results in a net decrease of the energy consumption in the system, at least as long as the dynamic energy is sufficiently large compared to the static and leakage energy spent.

In multimedia applications, parallelism is typically available at different levels. The regular data processing nature of multimedia applications leads to large amounts of instruction and data-level parallelism. Advanced compilers for media processors exploit these parallelisms by software pipelining and/or VLIW techniques. However, the task-level parallelism is much more difficult to deal with and is hence less exploited today. Few systematic methodologies exist to exploit this coarse grained parallelism, especially for heterogeneous platforms, which can however only be fully exploited when applications are efficiently integrated on the platforms. Current design technologies hence fall behind the recent advances in computer architecture and processing technology. This is especially so when dealing with complex and very dynamic applications as can be found, e.g., in the MPEG4/MPEG21 standard. A consistent system design technology that can cope with such characteristics and with the ever shortening time-to-market requirements is greatly needed.

For this kind of design, one of the most critical bottlenecks is the very dynamic and concurrent behavior of many of these new applications, which are fully specified in software oriented languages (like Java, UML, SDL, C++) and still need to be executed in real-time cost/energy-sensitive ways on the usually heterogeneous SoC platforms. An effective methodology is required to map this system specification onto an embedded multi-processor platform, and normally this leads to a tradeoff among different system design objectives like energy and performance.

Pareto-based optimization is an effective way to represent and explore these tradeoffs. The Pareto-optimal concept comes from multiobjective optimization problems, where more than one conflicting optimization objectives exist. A solution is said Pareto-optimal when it is optimal in at least one optimization objective direction, compared to all the other solutions. Such a set of Pareto-optimal solution is normally called a Pareto set and can be conveniently represented by a Pareto curve. In real-world applications, a Pareto optimal set can be the result of exploring many different factors, such as architecture (CPU and/or memory) mapping, quality of service control(QoS), as long as more than one optimization objective exists.

Conventional design methodologies at best extract that Pareto optimal set and select one point from that set at design time [4]. This approach works fine for static applications. However, for modern dynamic applications, we should explore the potentially available design space at design time but defer the selection step till run time, to better tune the system to the changing environment, as we showed in [19]. Hence, our approach is to combine the advantages of the low run-time complexity of a design-time scheduling phase and the flexibility of a run-time scheduling phase. It allows to optimize the system cost function at run-time based on pre-computed cost-performance Pareto curves, and satisfies the real-time constraint at the same time.

The contributions of this paper are as follows: It provides a systematic method to handle the task scheduling problem of dynamic applications. An RTOS independent middleware layer is suggested and implemented to map and order tasks at run time. Experiments done on a real dual-processor platform have proved this approach can improve the applications' real-time and energy performance significantly.

2   Related Work

Task scheduling has been investigated overwhelmingly in the last decades. When a set of concurrent tasks – i.e. tasks that can overlap in time – have to be executed on one or more processors, a predefined method, called scheduling algorithm, must be applied to decide the order in which those tasks are executed. For a multi-processor system, another procedure, assignment, is also needed to determine on which processor one task will be executed. If a deadline, either soft or hard one, has to be met, it is called scheduling for real-time systems. A good overview of scheduling algorithms for real-time systems can be found in [13]. In our paper, the terminology *task scheduling* is used for both the task ordering and the processor assignment.

Generally speaking the scheduling algorithms can be classified as off-line and on-line algorithms. We focus here only on the latter because it provides better opportunity for run-time optimization. These algorithms are usually priority-based and are derived from Liu and Layland's classical paper [9], in which the priority of a task is either set statically, e.g. the Rate Monotonic (RM), or dynamically, e.g. the Earliest Deadline First (EDF). Nowadays, RM and EDF are still the most used algorithms.

For multi-processor systems, the scheduling algorithms can be classified in another way: migratory or nonmigratory [16]. A scheduling is called nonmigratory if a task, once it has been created and decided where to be put, stays on one processor till it terminates. It may not move, no matter how badly overloaded its processor becomes and no matter how many other processors are idle. Most current embedded systems' RTOSs are nonmigratory. Migratory scheduling is more flexible, providing more possibility for system optimizing (e.g., load balancing), but it is also more complex and difficult to design. It is proved that task migration can be very helpful in improving the system energy consumption and power density [7, 5].

Recently, Dynamic Voltage Scaling(DVS) is getting popular (see [6] for a good survey) because of its ability to reduce the unnecessary energy consumption. Our methodology can integrate and handle DVS naturally, though it is not restricted to it.

Shin and Choi [15] have extended the normal fixed-priority scheduler to implement an on-line inter-task DVS for real-time application. They slow down the processor when there is only one eligible running task and completely shut it down when that last task ends earlier than expected. To fully utilize the slack time in the on-line DVS, some new approaches are proposed recently. They can be classified as intra-task DVS, because they benefit from looking inside the boundary of a task. Lee and Sakurai [8] partition a task into several pieces, called *time-slots*, then dynamically control the supply voltage on a "time-slot by time-slot" basis, with the feedback from the software. Other approaches include checking the current code execution against data generated at compile time to find the opportunity for voltage scaling [1, 14]. To take full advantage of DVS, some authors further suggest a handshake between the content or application and the OS [3, 11].

All the above works have their limitations. Firstly, they focus mainly on the scheduling algorithm itself. Few discuss the problem of how to implement the complete system and how to integrate the scheduler with the currently available tools and middlewares. Therefore, their results are normally obtained from simulation and can not yet answer the questions as how the algorithm works in a real system and how much the overhead is. That overhead can not be ignored, especially on a multi-processor platform. Secondly, they all fix the task mapping at design time. As a result, they are less capable of handling the highly dynamic and changing multimedia applications.

3   The Design Methodology

Our design methodology comprises three stages: modeling, concurrency improving and (sub)task scheduling [19]. Here we focus only on the last one. In our model, the application are represented as a set of concurrent thread frames (TF) that exhibits a single thread of control. Each of these TFs consists of many thread nodes (TN) that can be looked at as an independent and schedulable code section.

3.1   Two-Phase Scheduling

The scheduling is done in two phases. It has been published before (see [19, 18]) but it is briefly summarized here as background information. The idea is illustrated in Fig. 1. Given a thread frame, our design-time scheduler will try to explore all the different mapping and ordering possibilities, and generate a Pareto-optimal set, where every point represents a different mapping and ordering combination. Conventional design methodologies also explore them but they select only one Pareto point and fix it, while we keep the complete Pareto set and defer the decision till run-time.

The run-time scheduler works at the granularity of thread frames. At run-time, it considers all active TFs, trying to satisfy their time constraints and minimize the system cost at the same time. The details inside a thread frame,

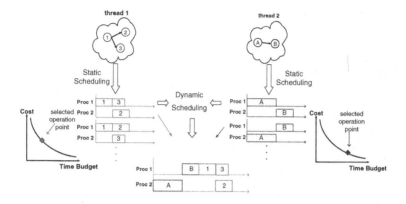

Fig. 1. A two phase scheduling method.

like the execution order or data dependency of each thread node, can remain invisible to the run-time scheduler and this reduces its complexity significantly.

We separate the task scheduling into two phases, namely design-time and run-time scheduling, for two reasons. Firstly, it gives more run time flexibility to the whole system. The system can change its behavior (e.g. minize the overall cost) according to what are running on it. Secondly, it substantially reduces the run time computation complexity because the run-time scheduler has only to handle some pre-computed results.

This methodology can in principle be applyed in many different contexts as long as Pareto-like tradeoffs exist. For example, in case of DVS, the cost can be the energy consumption. Thus our methodology results in an energy-efficient system. When the cost is energy and the horizontal axis is replaced by the quality of service (QoS), the problem becomes the energy minimization with a guaranteed QoS, as e.g. formulated in [12].

3.2   Dynamic Mapping and Ordering

After a Pareto point is selected by the run-time scheduler, the next problem is to find a systematic and generic way to map and order the TNs as decided. Consider the piece of C code in Fig. 2. This is a simple example of two TFs, which have 3 and 2 TNs respectively. Their CDFG representations can be found in Fig. 1. Notice that no dependency exists between tn_2 and tn_3 of thread frame 1 and thus they can be executed in parallel. To compile the code to a dual-processor platform, we want to achieve several goals: a) the code is written in plain ANSI C (not any concurrent C dialect); b) it should be compiled and linked by a normal compiler; c) only at run-time we will decide the execution order of the TNs and on which processor to execute them.

This is not easy remembering all the codes are compiled and linked statically, which in fact fixes the addresses of all the functions and global variables. Moreover, multiprocessor programming requires well synchronized code and protected data. It becomes even worse when we assume a dynamic and open system,

```
/* thread frame 1, video decoding */
int in[], out1[], out2[];
tf_1() {
  float c1, c2;
  tn_1(in, &c1, &c2);
  tn_2(in, c1, out1);
  tn_3(in, c2, out2);
}

/* thread frame 2, audio decoding */
int out[];
tf_2() {
  int buf[];
  tn_A(in, buf);
  tn_B(buf, out);
}
```

Fig. 2. Example 1: the virtual C code.

which allows new TFs to come and join the running applications at any moment. One obvious solution is to wrap every TF and TN in a process/thread structure provided by the RTOS and to apply the tricky and error-prone multiprocess programming method. However, this will cause frequent switches between the process space and the RTOS space and frequent context switches among processes. It also requires inter and/or remote process communication mechanisms. All these are expensive, especially for multiprocessor platforms. Therefore, we chose to run only one process on every processor and to manage the TNs by ourselves.

To handle the problems in a systematic and generic way, we have wrapped every TF into an object, which contains an initializer, a scheduler and a TF specific data structure. The scheduler keeps a set of function pointers. Every Pareto point just means a different set of values of these pointers. Whenever a new TF enters the system, its initializer is first called to register itself to the system. Then for a given Pareto point, the scheduler resets its pointers to the desired TNs in the appropriate order. Therefore, the scheduler can execute the TNs by referring to the function pointers in the given order, and map them accordingly. Fig. 3 shows the final scenario of our example assuming a scheduling decision like Fig. 1.

Our approach has a low overhead because the complete code is held in one single process space and no unnecessary context switches involved. Meanwhile, it provides an easy solution to achieve a flexible and open system.

4   Experimental System Setup

4.1   The Experimental Platform

As shown in Fig. 4, our experimental board consists of two TI C6202 DSPs, each with a 128KB on-chip memory. The on-chip memory is divided into two halves,

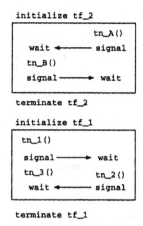

Fig. 3. The run time mapping of example 1.

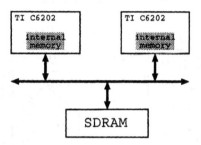

Fig. 4. The experiment board.

one for stack and the other is program addressable and free for use. An off-chip 32MB SDRAM is also available. It holds the program codes, private data and a piece of shared memory. The DSPs and the SDRAM are connected by a bus. No data cache is present, either on chip or off chip, which means: a) slower data access speed. However, we can either implement a memory allocator, handling the internal on-chip memory as a full software-controlled cache, or simply address and maintain it ourselves in the program. b) no costly overhead is paid to obtain cache consistency and coherency which are anyhow mainly useful for big multi-processor systems running general-purpose software. The embedded software designer has better knowledge and full control over his system, enabling him to avoid and manage data conflicts in a more efficient way.

On every DSP, a copy of the VSPWorks Real-Time Operating System (RTOS) [17] is running. The RTOS provides the run-time environment, memory and task management, IO control and interrupt handling. However, VSPWorks is more a stand-alone OS than a distributed OS, in the meaning that every processor runs independently, communicating and changing data with its peers only when explicitly asked to do that.

4.2   The Run-Time System

Our run-time system module runs like a middleware layer (Fig. 5). It clearly separates the application from the lower level RTOS, giving the same APIs even on different operating systems. It is compatible with most current RTOS implementations as long as they have a well defined API for task activation and synchronization. Therefore, it is easy to be ported and can be used as an integration component in a heterogeneous multi-processor platform.

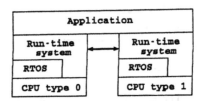

Fig. 5. The middleware.

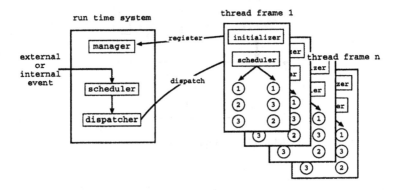

Fig. 6. The run-time system.

The run-time system performs the run-time scheduling hierarchically (Fig. 6): the system level side is responsible for managing Pareto curves, finding a Pareto point and dispatching the TFs, while the TF side does the real mapping and ordering based on the Pareto point selected by the run-time system. Whenever a new TF enters the system, it first registers itself to the run-time manager. At *specific scheduling points, triggered by a timer interrupt or other application* related events, the system side scheduler, taking into account the Pareto curves of all active TFs, finds when and which TF will be executed. Basically, this involves the ordering of the TFs, e.g. based on their priority, and selecting a Pareto point from the Pareto curve accompanying every TF, given the system restriction (e.g. the number of a specific resource) and an objective to optimize (e.g the energy consumption or quality of service). The algorithm used here to find the Pareto points can be found in [18]. Having decided the order and selected the option, the system dispatcher just calls the TF side schedulers one by one, passing the selected Pareto point. Accordingly, the TF side scheduler selects the appropriate implementation of its functions.

The hierarchical scheduling makes the system more dynamic, reusable and flexible. The run-time system does not have to know the TFs, which can be any TF, as long as they have a uniform API. The run-time system does not have to worry how to map and order the internal components of each specific TF. It is done by the TF code itself, which is generated at compile time with all the necessary details to achieve this.

Different to normal task scheduling, our implementation avoids the expensive task management service provided by the RTOS. Actually, except to the background managing thread, there is only one thread running on each processor. Meanwhile, it allows tasks to be mapped and ordered freely to accomodate the dynamic feature of future applications.

5   Experiments and Results

We have applied our methodology and implemented it for two applications on the platform introduced in section 4.1. In all of our experiments, the codes are not optimized for our TI C6000 VLIW architecture. However, we are not discussing how to optimize the code at the instruction or data size level, which is out of the scope of this paper and can be done independently. This will not reduce the effectiveness of the methodology we describe here. In this paper we consider only the task level parallelism. All the results shown later are free of instruction and data level parallelism optimization. In fact, the contents inside the bubbles on Fig. 7 are untouched compared to the original MediaBench code.

5.1   Experiment to Explore the Overhead

The first simple example we have investigated on our dual-TI platform is based on the DCT application from MediaBench [10]. This simple code has been used in an experiment designed intentionally to explore the overhead behind our run-time system.

The DCT code uses the discrete cosine transform (DCT) to compress a pixel image by a factor of 4:1 while preserving its information content. The encoder divides the image into blocks, each containing 8x8 pixels, as shown in Fig. 7. For every block, the encoder reads the image into a buffer, finds its DCT, then finally scales and packs it to the output buffer.

The original code (dct in Tab. 1) takes 1.7 million cycles to compress an image of 32x32 pixels (4x4 blocks). This number is high for several reasons. Firstly, the TI C6202 has no floating point units, while the encoder involves a lot of floating point computation. Secondly, the DSPs are configured to work without program and data cache.

Next, we have adapted the encoder to our framework. A TF wrapper is generated for every image block. As shown in that Fig. 8, every TF of dct_tf

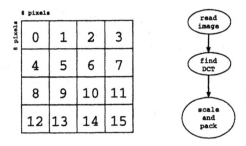

Fig. 7. A DCT encoder.

has three TNs, R, F and S (representing the three bubbles in Fig. 7). It has two possible scheduling, scheduling0 and scheduling1. If scheduling0 is selected by the system-level scheduler, the TF will first execute TN R on DSP0, then TN F on DSP1 and finally TN S on DSP0. It looks artificial but can show us the overhead. Since one image block is put into one TF, an image of size 4x4 blocks will generate 16 TF wrappers, i.e. 16 Pareto curves, each with two Pareto points. The execution time of dct_tf, including all the overhead of our framework, is 2.17 million cycles (Tab. 1) for the 4x4 image.

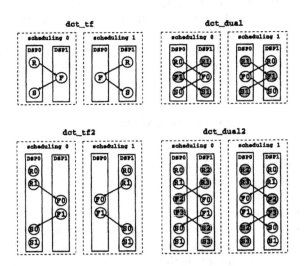

Fig. 8. Different TF compositions of the DCT encoder.

In dct_tf, at any moment, only one DSP is running the functional TN, due to the sequential feature of the block compressing. To take advantage of the multi-processor, dct_dual wraps the TNs of every two block into one TF (Fig. 8, R0 means the TN R of block 0, totally 6 TNs), which allows the TF scheduler to explore the task level parallelism and improve the performance accordingly.

For the same 4x4 image, it now takes only 1.43 million cycles, which is a 17% improvement over the original code.

As shown in Fig. 8, we have tried different compositions of the TF. We have also tried a bigger image with 8x8 blocks and the results are summarized in Tab. 1.

Table 1. Execution time of different encoders.

	4x4 blocks		8x8 blocks	
	no. of TFs	exec. time (M cycles)	no. of TFs	exec. time (M cycles)
dct	1	1.71	1	6.56
dct_tf	16	2.18	64	7.50
dct_tf2	8	2.08	32	7.16
dct_tf4	4	2.04	16	6.98
dct_tf8	2	2.02	8	6.89
dct_dual	8	1.43	32	4.52
dct_dual2	4	1.29	16	3.98
dct_dual4	2	1.26	8	3.83

From this table, we can see that the overhead of our run-time scheduling layer constantly drops with the decrease of the number of TFs, in both the dct_tf and dct_dual series for the same input image. In fact, this overhead can be decomposed into two components: the overhead per system and the overhead per TF (see Tab. 2). The former comes from the initialization and booking of the system, and it is more or less the same for every system. For every TF running on the system, we also have to pay some overhead to start it, send data to it and synchronize it. Hence, the total overhead can be expressed as $n * a + b$, where n is the number of TFs (see Tab. 2). One obvious observation from it is that the per TF overhead of dct_dual is more than two times higher than dct_tf. This can be explained by Fig. 8: dct_dual has twice the amount of data communication and synchronization as dct_tf.

Table 2. The decomposition of the overhead, in K cycles.

	dct_tf series		dct_dual series	
	4x4	8x8	4x4	8x8
a(per TF overhead)	11.19	10.88	29.11	29.50
b(per system overhead)	282	247	333	281

The per TF overhead is only 11K cycles in the dct_tf case and 29K cycles in the dct_dual case. This is acceptably low if the TF code is big enough, which is not the case here for this simple illustration but is true for any real-life application that we would consider like the H.263 test case in the next section.

Another interesting issue is the performance improvement from dct_dual cases, which take advantage of the task level parallelism exposed by our design methodology. For an image size of 4x4 blocks, the dct_dual and dct_dual4 improve the performance by 17% and 27% respectively. For an image size of 8x8, the numbers are 31% and 42%, which is already close to the 50% theoretical upperbound.

5.2 The Realistic H.263 Test Case

We have also investigated the ITU-T H.263 application, which is an international standard for video conference and other low-bit-rate communication.

We have used the Telenor C exemplary implementation code, tmn-1.7. Except to necessary changes to enable our approach, we made no more optimization, neither the algorithm level nor the instruction level. In that code, the stream can basically have 3 different kinds of video frame: I, P, and PB. The I frame is also called intra-frame because it is encoded only using the information of that video frame and does not depend on any other frame. From time to time, we have to insert an I frame because either we have a complete new video (e.g, the editing) or we have to get rid of the accumulated noise from predicting. The P frame is forwardly predicted from another I or P video frame, by using Motion Compensation. The PB frame actually contains the information of two frames. First a P frame (frame i+2) can be decoded from its previous I/P frame (frame i), then another frame, frame i+1, can be predicted forwardly from frame i and backwardly from frame i+2 and inserted between them. One sequence is that for the next period the processor can be idle because in the previous period it has already generated the video frames for both the previous and current period. For every I, P or PB frame, the code can be separated into two nodes, the decoding node and the conversion node. The decoding node does all the work related to reading in the data, entropy decoding, rescaling, idct and motion compensation, finally generating data in YUV format. To really show the video, we have to convert it from YUV format to RGB (which is understandable by the display) and store it in the display memory, which is done by the conversion node. Depending on the type of frame (I/P/PB) and the size of image, these two nodes will take a different number of processor cycles.

To simulate the dynamic behaviors of future applications (e.g. Philips' WWICE interface), we manipulate 5 video streams simultaneously where the frame size of each stream typically differs. Strm0 is the combination of different

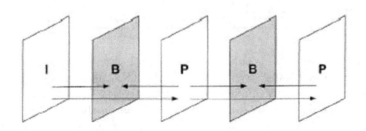

Fig. 9. The I, P, and PB frame of H.263.

CIF clips from the standard benchmark Akiyo, Coastguard, Container, Foreman and Hall video streams. Every clip lasts for 100 frames. This is used to simulate the main video stream one is watching. At the same time, we have four streams (Strm1, Strm2, Strm3 and Strm4), which are generated from shorter video clips (5-50 frames each) in QCIF format. These streams are used to simulate the user triggered events. For instance, when a user is watching TV, he may talk to another person by the video phone and browsing on line, all on the same platform. For Strm1-4, between clips we randomly inserted 2-12 idle frames, to simulate the idle time of the user.

At the beginning of every period, the application reads in the frame headers of all the five streams, to see what kind of frames it is going to handle for the current period, then maps and orders these nodes on our experimental board. We have used streams of 1000 periods and the results are summarized in Tab. 3.

We have compared the result of our dynamic mapping and ordering approach to 3 reference cases. In the first case (single in Tab. 3) we put all the nodes onto a single processor. It is used to give a reference on how a single processor performs. In the fixed_0_4 case, we put nodes of Strm0 on one processor (it is in CIF format and requires much more execution time) and Strm1-4 on another processor. In the fixed_1_3 case, we put both Strm0 and Strm1 on one processor, and Strm2-4 on another processor. When the frame rate is 20, case "single" will cause 524 deadline misses, which is more than half of the periods, while case fixed_0_4 and fixed_1_3 cause 245 and 131 deadline misses, which are better but still more than 10% of the periods are hardly usable. Under the same condition, our dynamic case will cause only 39 deadline misses, which is only 3.9% of the total periods. When the frame rate is relaxed to 15, the deadline misses caused by the fixed_0_4 and fixed_1_3 are 53 and 1, while our dynamic case meets all the deadlines. We can notice that fixed_1_3 performs much better than fixed_0_4, but the exact number of deadline misses of fixed_1_3 depends on the input streams and can be worse than what we show here. For both frame rates, our solution is always best because it can adapt to the real need of that period. In all cases, the results of our dynamic solution have already included the implementation and scheduling overhead.

Table 3. The deadline miss and energy consumption for 1000 period.

	fps=20		fps=15	
	deadline miss	energy(J)	deadline miss	energy(J)
single	524	14.71(no DVS)	265	14.71(no DVS)
fixed_0_4	245	10.75	53	9.17
fixed_1_3	131	10.14	1	8.07
dynamic	39	9.12	0	7.34

Another advantage of our dynamic mapping and ordering approach is that it can increase the energy saving impact of DVS. Since the board we use does not support DVS, we have only simulated the effects of DVS by checking the available slack time of every period. As long as a DVS-compatible processor (e.g. XScale) is on our experimental board, we can really implement it with the same approach.

According to TI's datasheet, the power consumption of the 300MHz C6202 CPU core is 300mW. We assume the working frequency can be continuously slowed down to as low as 200MHz, and the supplying voltage will proportionally scale down from 1.5V to 1.0V. This assumption is commonly taken also by other academic researchers [15]. Since the frame header of each stream is decoded first at the beginning of every period, it enables us to make an accurate estimation about the execution time of every TN to be executed in that period. With the above assumptions, we have applied DVS on fixed_0_4, fixed_1_3 and our dynamic case. The results (Tab. 3) show that our dynamic approach has 10% (fps = 20) and 9% (fps = 15) energy savings even compared to fixed_1_3, which is the best possible result if the tasks are mapped statically by the state-of-the-art DVS technique [1]. Compared to the non-DVS original case, the energy saving is 38% (fps = 20) and 50% (fps = 15).

6   Conclusion and Future Work

In this paper we have presented a systematic approach on how to insert a middleware layer between the application and the RTOS to map and order tasks dynamically for multiprocessor platforms. Two experiments have been done on a real dual-TI experimental board. This practical proof is one contribution compared to the normal simulation approach taken by other researchers. A simple DCT example is used to illustrate the overhead introduced by our middleware layer. An H.263 example shows the large impact of our approach on real-life applications, where deadline miss is dramatically reduced. When DVS is considered, an extra 10% energy saving has been achieved compared to the state-of-the-art approach.

In the near future, more applications are planned to be ported and tested. Some tools or scripts are also under development to semi-automizing the porting process. It will also be interesting to test our methodology on an heterogeneous multi-processor platform.

References

[1] A. Azevedo et al. Profile-based dynamic voltage scheduling using program checkpoints. In *DATE*, pages 168–75, 2002.
[2] A. P. Chandrakasan and R. W. Brodersen. Minimizing Power Consumption in Digital CMOS Circuits. *Proc. IEEE*, 83(4):498–523, Apr. 1995.
[3] E.-Y. Chung, L. Benini, and G. De Micheli. Contents Provider-Assisted Dynamic Voltage Scaling for Low Energy Multimedia Applications. In *ISLPED*, pages 42–47, 2002.
[4] T. Givargis, F. Vahid, and J. Henkel. System-level Exploration for Pareto-optimal Configurations in Parameterized System-on-a-Chip. *IEEE Trans. VLSI Syst.*, 10(4):579–592, Aug. 2002.

[5] S. Heo, K. Barr, and K. Asanovic. Reducing Power Density through Activity Migration. In *ISLPED*, pages 217–222, 2003.

[6] N. K. Jha. Low Power System Scheduling and Synthesis. In *ICCAD*, pages 259–63, 2001.

[7] R. Kumar, K. I. Farkas, N. P. Jouppi, P. Ranganathan, and D. M. Tullsen. Single-ISA Heterogeneous Multi-Core Architectures: The Potential for Processor Power Reduction. In *MICRO*, 2003.

[8] S. Lee and T. Sakurai. Run-Time Voltage Hopping for Low-Power Real-Time Systems. In *DAC*, pages 806–809, 2000.

[9] C. L. Liu and J. W. Layland. Scheduling Algorithms for Multiprogramming in a Hard Real-Time Environment. *J. ACM*, 20(1):46–61, Jan. 1973.

[10] MediaBench. http://cares.icsl.ucla.edu/MediaBench.

[11] J. Pouwelse, K. Langendoen, and H. Sips. Energy Priority Scheduling for Variable Voltage Processors. In *ISLPED*, pages 28–33, 2001.

[12] G. Qu and M. Potkonjak. Energy Minimization with Guaranteed Quality of Service. In *ISLPED*, pages 43–8, 2000.

[13] K. Ramamritham and J. A. Stankovic. Scheduling Algorithms and Operation Systems Support for Real-Time Systems. *Proc. IEEE*, 82(1):55–67, Jan. 1994.

[14] D. Shin, J. Kim, and S. Lee. Low-Energy Intra-Task Voltage Scheduling Using Static Timing Analysis. In *DAC*, pages 438–43, 2001.

[15] Y. Shin and K. Choi. Power Conscious Fixed Priority Scheduling for Hard Real Time Systems. In *DAC*, pages 134–139, 1999.

[16] A. S. Tanenbaum. *Distributed Operating Systems*. Prentice-Hall Inc., 1995.

[17] Windver. VSPWorks. www.windriver.com/products/vspworks/index.html.

[18] P. Yang and F. Catthoor. Pareto-Optimization-Based Run-Time Task Scheduling for Embedded Systems. In *ISSS+CODES*, pages 120–125, 2003.

[19] P. Yang, P. Marchal, C. Wong, S. Himpe, F. Catthoor, P. David, J. Vounckx, and R. Lauwereins. Managing Dynamic Concurrent Tasks in Embedded Real-Time Multimedia Systems. In *ISSS*, pages 112–9, 2002.

Integrated Intra- and Inter-task Cache Analysis for Preemptive Multi-tasking Real-Time Systems

Yudong Tan and Vincent Mooney

Center for Research on Embedded Systems and Technology
School of Electrical and Computer Engineering
Georgia Institute of Technology
Atlanta, Georgia, USA
{ydtan,mooney}@ece.gatech.edu

Abstract. In this paper, we propose a timing analysis approach for preemptive multi-tasking real-time systems with caches. The approach focuses on the cache reload overhead caused by preemptions. The Worst Case Response Time (WCRT) of each task is estimated by incorporating cache reload overhead. After acquiring the WCRT of each task, we can further analyze the schedulability of the system. Four sets of applications are used to exhibit the performance of our approach. The experimental results show that our approach can reduce the estimate of WCRT up to 44% over prior state-of-the-art.

1 Introduction

When designing a real-time system, it is of great importance that the timing of the system be predictable. While underestimating the execution time of tasks in a real-time system may cause catastrophic disasters, especially in hard real-time systems, overestimating the execution time can also lower the utilization of resources such as processors. However, processors with advanced features such as caching and pipelining are widely used in real-time systems nowadays. Using processors with these complicated architectures in real-time systems makes timing analysis more difficult.

In this paper, we propose a timing analysis approach for preemptive multi-tasking real-time systems. The approach focuses on the cache reload overhead caused by preemptions. The Worst Case Response Time (WCRT) of each task is estimated by incorporating cache reload overhead. After acquiring the WCRT of each task, we can further analyze the schedulability of the system. Four sets of applications are used to exhibit the performance of our approach. The experimental results show that our approach can reduce the estimate of WCRT up to 44% over prior state-of-the-art.

The rest of this paper is organized as follows. Section 2 investigates the previous work in this field. Section 3 states the problem and defines some terminology used in the paper. Then, an overview of our approach is given. Sections 4, 5 and 6 elaborate the details of our approach. Experimental results are presented in Section 7. The last section concludes the paper.

H. Schepers (Ed.): SCOPES 2004, LNCS 3199, pp. 182–199, 2004.

2   Previous Work

Lots of work has been done to predict the timing properties of real-time systems with caches. In general, this work can be divided into two categories. First, various methods are proposed to achieve predictable system behavior by changing some features such as cache management policies and memory mapping patterns of systems. For example, two different cache partitioning schemes are presented in [3, 4]. Each task can only use a limited portion of the cache in these two approaches. Compiler optimization and memory remapping techniques are also used to achieve predictable cache behavior [5, 6]. These approaches require either customized hardware support such as a specialized cache controller and TLB or modifications to the compilers and OS. Furthermore, utilization of resources such as cache and memory are compromised.

Static analysis is a second category of methods to predict timing properties. Such methods analyze cache behavior and make restrictive assumptions in order to predict Worst Case Execution Time (WCET) or Worst Case Response Time (WCRT) of tasks in real-time systems. Static analysis methods do not require any changes to the system under consideration. Li and Malik propose a WCET analysis approach by using an implicit path enumeration method [7]. Their approach requires path analysis at the granularity of basic blocks. Wolf and Ernst extend the concept of basic blocks to program segments and develop another framework for timing analysis, SYMTA [8]. The precision of time estimation is improved in SYMTA since the overestimate of execution time is reduced. Wilhelm et al. [11, 12] propose an abstract interpretation methodology to predict cache behavior. Stenstrom et al. [13] give another static analysis approach based on symbolic execution techniques. In both Wilhelm's and Stenstrom's approach, WCET of programs can be analyzed without knowing the exact input data. However, both of the aforementioned approaches only consider a system with a single task. They cannot handle multi-tasking systems with preemptions, in which the timing analysis becomes even more complicated.

The behavior of a multi-tasking system is affected greatly by the scheduling algorithm used in the system. In this paper, we assume that a fixed priority scheduling algorithm such as Rate Monotonic Scheduling (RMS) [14, 15] is used. We further assume a single processor with a unified (instruction plus data) set associative L1 cache and secondary memory (the secondary memory can be either on- or off-chip). However, the same method in our approach can be used to analyze timing properties in systems with more than two levels of memory hierarchy. Multiple processor systems may involve cache coherence problems which are beyond the scope of this paper. In order to analyze the schedulability of a system, we estimate the WCRT [16] of each task in the system. In preemptive multi-tasking systems, cache eviction among tasks may extend the response times of tasks. Busquests-Mataix et al. propose an approach to analyze cache-related WCRT in a multi-tasking system [17]. They conservatively assume that all cache lines used by the preempting task need to be reloaded by the preempted task when the preempted task is resumed. Tomiyama et al. give an approach to calculate Cache Related Preemption Delay (CRPD) by using

ILP [10]. However, they only consider direct mapped instruction cache. Lee et al. propose another approach for cache analysis when preemptions occur [18,19]. This approach counts the number of "useful" memory blocks by performing path analysis on the preempted task. They do not take the program structure of the preempting task into consideration. Also, the number of preemption scenarios used in their approach is exponential with the number of tasks. Negi et al. [9] refine the approach of Lee et al. in [18] by applying path analysis. However, inter-task cache eviction is not considered. Also, WCRT analysis is not mentioned in [9].

We propose an approach for inter-task cache eviction analysis in [1, 2]. This approach assumes that all cache lines used by the preempted task and evicted by the preempting task will be reloaded after the preemption. But, as presented in [18], only those cache lines used by "useful" memory blocks of the preempted task need to be reloaded.

Both the approach we present in [1, 2] and the approach of Lee et al. in [18] have their pros and cons. However, these two methods are complementary. In this paper, we focus on enhancing our approach in [1, 2] by incorporating "useful" memory block analysis in the work of Lee et al. The new approach gives the most accurate WCRT method known to date for a multi-tasking single-processor system using set-associative or direct mapped unified caches. In Section 7 we will show examples where we achieve results up to 44% better than the approach of Lee et al.

3   Overview

In this section, we first state the problem formally. Some terminology is defined for clarity. Then, we give an overview of the approach proposed in this paper.

3.1   Problem Statement

In this paper, we target uniprocessor multi-tasking preemptive real-time systems with caches. A Fixed Priority Scheduling (FPS) algorithm such as the Rate Monotonic Algorithm (RMA) is used in the system. Suppose that the system contains n tasks represented with $T_0, T_1, ..., T_{n-1}$. Each task T_i has a fixed priority p_i. We assume that the tasks are sorted in the descending order of their priorities so that we have $p_0 < p_1 < ... < p_{n-1}$. If $p_a < p_b$, T_a has a higher priority than T_b. Tasks are executed periodically. Each task T_i has a fixed period P_i. T_i arrives at the beginning of its period and must be completed by the end of its period. The Worst Case Execution Time (WCET) of task T_i is denoted with C_i. C_i can be estimated with existing analysis tools such as Cinderella [7] and SYMTA [8]. We use SYMTA to derive C_i. We use $T_{i,j}$ to represent the jth run of Task T_i. The WCET of a task is the execution time of the task in the worst case, assuming there are no preemptions or interruptions. In a preemptive multi-tasking system, WCET alone cannot reflect the schedulability of tasks in the system because of the existence of preemptions. Thus, our goal is to provide an approach to estimate the Worst Case Response Time (WCRT), which is defined as below, for every task in the system.

Definition 1. Worst Case Response Time (WCRT): WCRT is the time taken by a task from its arrival to its completion of computations in the worst case. The WCRT of task T_i is denoted by R_i. $\square$

In a multi-tasking preemptive system, a task with a low priority may be preempted by a task with a higher priority. During a preemption, the preempting task may evict some cache lines used by the preempted task. When the preempted task resumes and accesses an evicted cache line, the preempted task has to reload the cache line from memory. This cache reload overhead caused by inter-task cache evictions increases the response time of the preempted task.

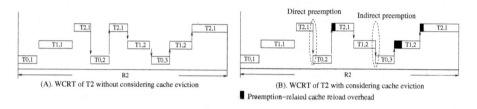

(A). WCRT of T2 without considering cache eviction   (B). WCRT of T2 with considering cache eviction

■ Preemption–related cache reload overhead

Fig. 1. Example of WCRT.

Example 1. We have three tasks T_0, T_1 and T_2. T_0 is an Inverse Discrete Cosine Transform (IDCT) extracted from an MPEG2 decoder. T_0 is invoked every 4.5ms. T_1 is an Adaptive Differential Pulse Code Modulation Decoder (ADPCMD). T_2 is an ADPCM Coder (ADPCMC). ADPCMC and ADPCMD are taken from MediaBench [23]. ADPCMC has a period of 50ms. ADPCMD has a period of 10ms. RMS is used for scheduling. T_0 has the highest priority and T_2 has the lowest priority. Figure 1 shows this example. In this example, three tasks arrive at time instant 0. However, T_2 is not executed until there are no instances of T_0 or T_1 ready to run. During the execution of T_2, it could be preempted by T_0 or T_1, which is shown in Figure 1. The response time of T_2 is the time from 0 to the time when T_2 is completed. We need to estimate the response time of such a task in the worst case. If we do not consider inter-task cache evictions, the WCRT of T_2 is shown in Figure 1(A). However, because of inter-task cache evictions, the preempted task has to reload some cache lines after preemption which imposes an overhead on the WCRT of the preempted task. Figure 1(B) shows this issue. Obviously, due to cache evictions, the WCRT of T_2 is increased, as shown in Figure 1(B). $\square$

Inter-task cache eviction(s) caused by preemption(s) affect the WCRT of a task. As shown in Example 1, there are two types of preemption, direct preemption and indirect preemption. For example, T_2 can be preempted directly by T_0 or T_1 because T_2 has the lowest priority. On the other hand, when T_2 is preempted by T_1 and T_1 is running, T_1 can be preempted further by T_0 because

T_1 has a lower priority than T_0. Although T_2 is not directly preempted by T_0, T_0 may bring a cache reload overhead to the execution time of T_1, which also extends the response time of T_2. Thus, we need to consider both indirect and direct preemptions caused by T_0 when estimating the WCRT of T_2. Figure 1 illustrates both direct and indirect preemptions.

This paper aims to incorporate inter-cache eviction cost in WCRT analysis by combining the approach of Lee et al. and the approach we presented in [1].

We perform path analysis on the preempted task and the preempting task in order to analyze the cache access pattern of the preempted task. The path analysis is based on a Control Flow Graph (CFG). A CFG is represented with a graph $G = (V, E)$, where $V = \{v_1, v_2, ..., v_m\}$ is the set of nodes and $E = \{e_1, e_2, ..., e_n\}$ is the set of edges of the graph G. Each edge $e_i = (v_k, v_j)$ represents the control dependence between two nodes, v_k and v_j. Each node v_i in a CFG represents a Single Feasible Path Program Segment (SFP-PrS) [8].

Definition 2. Single Feasible Path Program Segment (SFP-PrS): SFP-PrS is defined as a hierarchical program segment with exactly one path [8]. □

3.2   Overall Approach

Intuitively, we know that the cache lines causing reload overhead after preemptions need to satisfy two conditions.

Condition 1. These cache lines are used by both the preempted and the preempting task.

Condition 2. The memory blocks mapped to these cache lines are accessed by the preempted task before the preemption and are also required by the preempted task after the preemption (i.e., when the preempted task is resumed).

Condition 1 implies that memory blocks accessed by the preempting task conflict in the cache with memory blocks accessed by the preempted task. Thus, some of the memory blocks loaded to the cache by the preempted task before the preemption are evicted from the cache by the preempting task during the preemption. This cache eviction involves memory access patterns of both the preempted task and the preempting task. Thus, we call this type of cache eviction an inter-task cache eviction.

Condition 2 reveals that memory blocks causing cache reload overhead must have been present in the cache prior to the preemption. Furthermore, these memory blocks must be accessed again by the preempted task after the preemption, thus requiring reload to the cache. These memory blocks are called "useful memory blocks" in the work of Lee et al. [18,19]. We can use the algorithm of Lee et al. in [18] to find the maximum set of these useful memory blocks. The maximum set of useful memory blocks of the preempted task is derived from the program structure and the memory blocks accessed by the preempted task. In summary, we call this type of analysis intra-task cache eviction analysis.

Based on the two facts above, we can give an overview of our approach presented in this paper. Our approach has four steps.

First, we derive the memory trace of each task with the simulation method as used in SYMTA [8]. Here, we assume that there are no dynamic data allocations in tasks and addresses of all the data structures are fixed (e.g., any use of pointers does not result in unpredictable memory accesses). Second, we perform intra-task cache access analysis on the preempted task to find the maximum set of useful memory blocks accessed by the preempted task. Only the memory blocks in this set can possibly cause cache reload delay. Third, we use the maximum set of useful memory blocks of the preempted task to perform inter-task cache eviction analysis with the preempting tasks (i.e., all the tasks that have higher priorities than the preempted task). A low priority task might be preempted more than once by a higher priority task, depending on the period of the low priority task as compared to the period of the high priority task. As proposed in [1], path analysis is applied to the preempting task in order to tighten the estimate of cache reload overhead in this step. From the third step, we obtain an estimate of the number of cache lines that need to be reloaded after preemption. Then, we can calculate the cache reload overhead. In the fourth step, we preform WCRT analysis for all tasks based on the results from the third step.

4   Intra-task Cache Access Analysis

According to Condition 2 in Section 3.2, the memory blocks of the preempted task that can possibly cause cache reload overhead must be present in the cache before the preemption and must be accessed by the preempted task again after the preemption. Lee et al. give an approach to calculate the maximum set of such memory blocks.

A set-associative cache is defined by three parameters: the number of cache sets, the number of cache lines in a set (i.e., the number of ways) and the number of bytes/words per cache line. A direct mapped cache can be viewed as a special set associative cache which has only one way. We assume that the sets in a cache are indexed sequentially, starting from 0. All the cache lines in a cache set have the same index. A cache set with an index of i is represented with $cs(i)$. Accordingly, a memory address is divided into three parts: the tag, the index and the offset. We use $idx(a)$ to denote the index of a memory address a. When a memory block with an address of a is loaded to a set associative cache, it can only occupy a cache line with an index of $idx(a)$. In this paper, we assume that the LRU algorithm is used for cache line replacement. However, our approach can also be applied with minor modifications to caches with other replacement algorithms. For example, if a Round-Robin algorithm is used for cache line replacement, we only need to slightly change the intra-task cache eviction algorithm used in the approach of Lee et al. The inter-task cache eviction analysis algorithm can be applied to all cache line replacement policies.

As we mentioned in Section 3.1, a task can be represented with a CFG. Each node in a CFG is an SFP-PrS. A task can be preempted at any point, which is called an execution point. When a preemption happens, a task can be viewed as two parts, one part before the preemption and the other part after preemption. The pre-preemption part of the preempted task loaded memory blocks to the cache. Some of these memory blocks might be accessed again by the post-preemption part of the preempted task. These memory blocks are called useful memory blocks. Only useful memory blocks of the preempted task can possibly cause cache reload after preemptions.

For a formal description, we use the notation of *reaching memory blocks (RMB)* and *living memory blocks (LMB)* as defined in [18]. The set of *reaching memory blocks* of a cache set $cs(i)$ at an execution point s of a task is denoted by RMB_s^i. RMB_s^i contains all possible memory blocks that may reside in cache set $cs(i)$ when the task reaches execution point s. Suppose a cache set has L cache lines (i.e., a L-way set associative cache). If a memory block can reside in $cs(i)$, this memory block must have an index of i. Moreover, in order to be contained in RMB_s^i, this memory block is one of the last L distinct references to the cache set $cs(i)$ when the task runs along some execution path reaching execution point s. Otherwise, this memory would have been evicted from the cache by other memory blocks. Similarly, the set of *living memory blocks* of cache set $cs(i)$ at execution point s, denoted by LMB_s^i, contains all possible memory blocks that may be one of the first L distinct references to cache set $cs(i)$ *after* execution point s.

In [18], Lee et al. demonstrate that the intersection of RMB_s^i and LMB_s^i can be used to find a superset of the set of memory blocks in the preempted task that may cause cache line reload(s) due to preemption. The details of their algorithm can be found in [18,19]. Of course, whether those memory blocks will really cause cache line reloading still depends on the actual path the preempted task takes and the cache lines used by the preempting task.

5   Inter-task Cache Eviction Analysis

In [1, 2], we propose an approach to calculate the intersection of cache lines that are used by both the preempted task and the preempting task. In that paper, we assume that all memory blocks used by the preempted task when the preempted task runs along the longest path are useful. However, the results from the approach of Lee et al. show that this is not always true. In this paper, we focus on incorporating Lee's intra-task cache access analysis with the approach in [1, 2] in order to give a tighter estimate of cache-related preemption delay in multi-tasking preemptive systems.

As stated in Condition 1, the cache lines that may need to be reloaded must be accessed by both the preempted and preempting task. This implies that we need to calculate the intersection of cache lines used by the memory blocks found in the approach of Lee et al. and the memory blocks accessed by the preempting task.

Memory blocks that are mapped to different cache sets will never conflict in the cache. In other words, only memory blocks that have the same index can possibly evict each other because these memory blocks are loaded to the same cache set. Intuitively, we can divide memory blocks into different subsets according to their index.

Suppose we have a set of q memory block addresses, $M = \{m_0, m_1, ..., m_{q-1}\}$, and an L-way set associative cache. The index of the cache ranges from 0 to $N - 1$. We can derive N subsets of M as follows.

$$\widehat{m}_i = \{m_k \in M | idx(m_k) = i\}, \ (0 \leq i < N) \tag{1}$$

When the memory blocks in the same subset defined above are accessed, these memory blocks are loaded into the same set in the cache because they have the same index. Thus, cache evictions can happen among these memory blocks (i.e., with the same index).

If we denote $\widehat{M} = \{\widehat{m}_i | \widehat{m}_i \neq \emptyset, \ 0 \leq i < N\}$, where $\emptyset$ is the empty set and $\widehat{m}_i$ is defined as Equation 1, then $\widehat{M}$ is a partition of M [2]. Based on this conclusion, we define the Cache Index Induced Partition of a memory block address set as follows.

Definition 3. Cache Index Induced Partition (CIIP) of a memory block address set: Suppose we have a set of memory block addresses, $M = \{m_0, m_1, ..., m_{q-1}\}$, and an L-way set associative cache. The index of the cache ranges from 0 to $N - 1$. We can derive a partition of M based on the mapping from memory blocks to cache sets, which is denoted by $\widehat{M} = \{\widehat{m}_i | \widehat{m}_i \neq \emptyset, \ 0 \leq i < N\}$. Each $\widehat{m}_i = \{m_k \in M | idx(m_k) = i\}$ is a subset of M. We call $\widehat{M}$ the CIIP of M.□

The CIIP of a memory address set categorizes the memory addresses according to their indices in the cache. Cache evictions can only happen among memory blocks that are in the same subset in the CIIP. We first defined and introduced CIIP in [1].

The definition of CIIP provides a formal representation useful to analyze inter-task cache evictions. Suppose we have two tasks T_a and T_b. All the memory blocks accessed by T_a and T_b are in the set $M_a = \{m_{a,0}, m_{a,1}, ..., m_{a,k_a}\}$ and $M_b = \{m_{b,0}, m_{b,1}, ..., m_{b,k_b}\}$ respectively. T_b has a higher priority than T_a. An L-way set associative cache with a maximum index of $N - 1$ is used in the system. In the case T_a is preempted by T_b, the cache lines to be reloaded when T_a resumes are used by both the preempting task and the preempted task. Thus, we can look for the conflicting memory blocks accessed by the preempting task and the preempted task in order to estimate the number of reloaded cache lines. We can use the CIIPs of M_a and M_b to solve this problem.

We use $\widehat{M}_a = \{\widehat{m}_{a,0}, \widehat{m}_{a,1}, ..., \widehat{m}_{a,N-1}\}$ to represent the CIIP of M_a and $\widehat{M}_b = \{\widehat{m}_{b,0}, \widehat{m}_{b,1}, ..., \widehat{m}_{b,N-1}\}$ to represent the CIIP of M_b. For $\widehat{m}_{a,k_1} \in \widehat{M}_a$ and $\widehat{m}_{b,k_2} \in \widehat{M}_b$, only when $k_1 = k_2$ can memory blocks in $\widehat{m}_{a,k_1}$ possibly conflict with memory blocks in $\widehat{m}_{b,k_2}$ in the cache. Also, when the memory blocks in $\widehat{m}_{a,k_1}$ and $\widehat{m}_{b,k_2}$ are loaded into the cache, the number of conflicts in the cache cannot exceed $min(|\widehat{m}_{a,k_1}|, |\widehat{m}_{b,k_2}|, L)$, where L is the number of ways of the cache. Therefore, we can conclude that the following formula gives an upper bound for the number of cache lines that could be reloaded after Task T_a resumes following a preemption by Task T_b:

$$S(M_a, M_b) = \sum_{r=0}^{N-1} min\{|\widehat{m}_{a,r}|, |\widehat{m}_{b,r}|, L\} \tag{2}$$

where $\widehat{m}_{a,r} \in \widehat{M}_a$, $\widehat{m}_{b,r} \in \widehat{M}_b$.

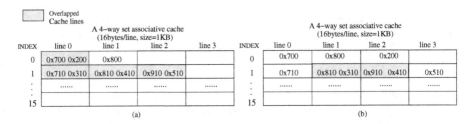

Fig. 2. Conflicts of cache lines in a set associative cache.

$S(M_a, M_b)$ denotes an upper bound on the number of cache lines that conflict when the memory blocks in M_a and M_b are loaded into the cache. This number can be used to estimate the cache lines to be reloaded due to T_b preempting T_a.

Example 2. Suppose we have a a 4-way set associative cache with 16 sets. Each cache line has 16 bytes. Two tasks T_1 and T_2 run with this cache. The memory block addresses accessed by T_1 and T_2 are contained in $M_1 = \{0x700, 0x800, 0x710, 0x810, 0x910\}$ and $M_2 = \{0x200, 0x310, 0x410, 0x510\}$ respectively. The CIIP of M_1 and M_2 are $\widehat{M_1} = \{\{0x700, 0x800\}, \{0x710, 0x810, 0x910\}\}$ and $\widehat{M_2} = \{\{0x200\}, \{0x310, 0x410, 0x510\}\}$ respectively.

If we map the memory blocks in M_1 and M_2 to the cache as shown in Figure 2(a), we find that the maximum number of overlapped cache lines, which is 4, is the same as the result derived from Equation 2. Note that the memory blocks can be mapped to cache lines in other ways (e.g., $0x800$ can possibly be mapped to line 0 instead of line 1, but in this case $0x800$ would kick out $0x700$ or vice versa). In any case, the mapping given in Figure 2 gives a case in which the largest amount of cache line overlaps occur. Let us consider another case: if we map the memory blocks in M_1 and M_2 to the cache as shown in the Figure 2(b), only two cache lines overlap. Therefore, Equation 2 only gives an upper bound (as opposed to an exact count) for the number of overlapped cache lines. □

Now, we can calculate the intersection of useful memory blocks of the preempted task as derived from the approach of Lee et al. and the memory blocks used by the preempting task in order to estimate the cache reload overhead.

Suppose we have two tasks, T_a and T_b. T_b has a higher priority than T_a, thus, T_b can preempt T_a. In the case that T_b preempts T_a, we want to know the number of cache lines that need to be reloaded by T_a after T_a resumes from the preemption.

Definition 4. The Maximum Useful Memory Blocks Set (MUMBS): The maximum intersection set of LMB and RMB over all the execution points of a task T_a is called the maximum set of useful memory blocks of this task. It is represented with $\tilde{M}_a$. $\widehat{\tilde{M}_a}$ is the CIIP of $\tilde{M}_a$.

We use the approach of Lee et al. to calculate the MUMBS of the preempted task. Only the memory blocks in this set can possibly be reloaded by the preempted task.

The simulation method in SYMTA is used to obtain all the memory blocks that can possibly accessed by the preempting task [8]. All these memory blocks are contained in a set M_b. $\widehat{M_b}$ is the CIIP of M_b. Only the memory blocks in M_b can possibly evict the cache lines used by the preempted task. Note that we can apply path analysis techniques proposed in [1, 2] to the preempting task in order to tighten the estimate of cache reload overhead by reducing the number of memory blocks in M_b.

Then, we apply Equation 2 to calculate the intersection of memory block set $\tilde{M_a}$ and M_b, which is shown in Equation 3. This result gives an upper bound on the number of cache lines that can possibly need to be reloaded after T_b preempts T_a.

$$S(\tilde{M_a}, M_b) = \sum_{r=0}^{N-1} min\{|\widehat{m}_{a,r}|, |\widehat{m}_{b,r}|, L\} \tag{3}$$

where $\widehat{m}_{a,r} \in \widetilde{M_a}$, $\widehat{m}_{b,r} \in \widehat{M_b}$.

We use $C_{pre}(T_a, T_b)$ to represent the cache reload cost imposed on task T_a when T_a is preempted by task T_b. Suppose the penalty for a cache miss is a constant, C_{miss}. Then, $C_{pre}(T_a, T_b)$ can be calculated with the following equation:

$$C_{pre}(T_a, T_b) = S(\tilde{M_a}, M_b) \times C_{miss} \tag{4}$$

6   WCRT Analysis

We can use the Worst Case Response Time (WCRT) to analyze schedulability of a multi-tasking real-time analysis as shown in [17]. The approach uses the following recursive equations to calculate the WCRT R_i of the task T_i.

$$R_i = C_i + \sum_{j \in hp(i)} \lceil \frac{R_i}{P_j} \rceil \times (C_j + \gamma_j) \tag{5}$$

where $hp(i)$ is the set of tasks whose priorities are higher than T_i. Because we assume that all tasks are sorted in the descending order of their priorities in this paper, we have $hp(i) = \{k|0 \le k < i\}$. γ_j is the cache reload cost related to preemptions caused by T_j (indirect or direct). Recall that C_j is the WCET of T_j and P_j is the period of Task T_j as defined in Section 3.1. In this equation, the term $\sum_{j \in hp(i)} \lceil \frac{R_i}{P_j} \rceil \times (C_j + \gamma_j)$ reflects the interference of preempting tasks during the execution time of T_i. This equation can be calculated iteratively. The iteration can be terminated when R_i converges or R_i is greater than the deadline of T_i. If R_i is greater than its deadline, task T_i cannot be guaranteed to be scheduled successfully.

In [17], the authors assume that all the cache lines used by the preempting task need to be reloaded after the preemption. As we pointed out in Section 4 and 5, this assumption exaggerates the cache reload cost for each preemption. We can apply inter-task and intra-task cache eviction analysis techniques above to reduce the overestimation in Equation 5.

When we estimate the WCRT of task T_i, we need to consider all possible preemptions caused by each task, T_k, $0 \le k < i$, which has a higher priority than T_i. T_k can preempt T_i directly, which brings a cache reload overhead of $C_{pre}(T_i.T_k)$ to the WCRT of T_i. T_i can also be preempted by T_k indirectly. Let us consider Example 3.

Example 3. Consider two cases in Figure 1(B). T_2 is preempted by T_0 twice. At the first time, T_2 is preempted by T_0 directly, thus, the cache reload overhead is $C_{pre}(T_2, T_0)$. In the second case, T_2 is preempted by T_1 first, then T_1 is preempted by T_0 further. Thus, T_2 is preempted by T_0 indirectly in this case. The cache reload overhead caused by this indirect preemption is $C_{pre}(T_1, T_0)$. In practice, it is difficult to know if T_0 preempts T_2 directly or indirectly. In order to avoid underestimating the WCRT of T_2, we use $max(C_{pre}(T_1, T_0), C_{pre}(T_2, T_0))$ as the cache reload overhead caused by T_0 preempting T_2 (i.e., either indirectly or directly).□

Example 3 shows that when one or more than one task has a priority higher than T_i and lower than T_k, the cache reload overhead caused by T_k preempting T_i depends on the actual preemption scenarios, which is difficult to predict in practice. Thus, in order to avoid underestimating WCRT, we use an upper bound, $max_{l=k+1}^{i}\{C_{pre}(T_l, T_k)\}$, to uniformly estimate the cache reload cost caused by T_k preempting T_i.

In Equation 5, C_j is the WCET estimate of T_j without considering preemption. We use SYMTA [8] to estimate WCET. Note that the cost of context switch caused by preemptions is not included in Equation 5. Here, we focus on cache reload overhead analysis and assume the cost of a context switch is a constant, C_{cs}, which is equal to the WCET of a context switch. The context switch function cannot be preempted, so the context switch cost is not affected by inter-task cache eviction. Therefore, it is reasonable to assume the context switch cost is a constant, which is its WCET. The context switch function is called twice in every preemption, once for switching to the preempting task and once for resuming the preempted task.

When preemptions are allowed in a multi-tasking system, the WCRT of tasks that can be preempted may be increased because of cache reload overhead. By considering the cache reload overhead, Equation 5 can be modified as follows:

$$R_i = C_i + \sum_{j=0}^{i-1} \lceil \frac{R_i}{P_j} \rceil \times (C_j + max_{l=j+1}^{i}\{C_{pre}(T_l, T_j)\} + 2C_{cs}) \qquad (6)$$

Based on Equation 6, we can estimate the WCRT for each task T_i with the following iteration:

$R_i^0 = C_i;$

$R_i^1 = C_i + \sum_{j=0}^{i-1} \lceil \frac{R_i^0}{P_j} \rceil \times (C_j + max_{l=j+1}^{i}\{C_{pre}(T_l, T_j)\} + 2C_{cs})$

...

$R_i^k = C_i + \sum_{j=0}^{i-1} \lceil \frac{R_i^{k-1}}{P_j} \rceil \times (C_j + max_{l=j+1}^{i}\{C_{pre}(T_l, T_j)\} + 2C_{cs})$

This iteration terminates when R_i converges or R_i is greater than the deadline of T_i. After the iteration is terminated, we compare the value of R_i with the deadline of T_i. Only if R_i is less than the deadline of T_i can T_i be guaranteed to be successfully scheduled. Hence, we can analyze the schedulability of the system based on the WCRT estimate of each task.

In Equation 6, every preemption is tied to an invocation of a task. Thus, no infeasible preemptions are introduced to the WCRT estimate. A preemption is included in our estimate only when a task with a higher priority than the running task arrives (i.e., the condition for preempting is satisfied). However, in the approach of Lee et al., the number of preemptions are estimated separately from the number of invocations of tasks. Due to this separate estimation of the number of preemptions, Lee et al. [19] suffer from a problem that our approach as presented in this paper does not have: infeasible preemptions that cannot happen in any real case could potentially be included in the WCRT estimate. To eliminate this possibility, Lee et al. use an ILP formulation to remove infeasible preemptions.

Now, let us consider the computational complexity of this iteration procedure. Because we conclude that R_i converges and $R_i = R_i^k$ if R_i^k is equal to R_i^{k+1}, R_i has to increase monotonically before the iteration is terminated. R_i has to be increased by $min_{j=0}^{j=i-1}(C_j)$ at least in each iteration. On the other hand, R_i cannot exceed P_i. Thus, the number of iterations is limited by $\frac{P_i}{min_{j=0}^{j=i-1}(C_j)}$. This implies that the number of iterations has a constant upper bound when the periods and the WCET of tasks are determined. In each iteration, we have to calculate $max_{l=j+1}^{i}\{C_{pre}(T_l, T_j)\}$. This can be done by calculating all possible preemption scenarios $C_{pre}(T_b, T_a)$, where $a < b$, $0 \leq a \leq n-2$ and $1 \leq b \leq n-1$. n is the number of tasks. So the number of preemption-related cache reload cost is $O(n^2)$, where n is the number of tasks. Note that in [19], in order to estimate the WCRT for one task, all the preemption scenarios have to be investigated. The total number of preemption scenarios is exponential in the number of tasks. Thus, our method is more feasible and scalable than [19] when there are a large amount of tasks in the system.

7   Experimental Results

Our experiments are run on an ARM9TDMI processor with a 4-way set associative unified cache, the size of which is 32KB. Each line in the cache is 16 bytes; thus, there are 512 lines in each "way" of the cache in total. The instruction set is simulated with XRAY [22]. The whole system is integrated with Seamless CVE provided by Mentor Graphics [21]. The tasks are supported by the Atalanta RTOS developed at Georgia Tech [20].

First, we have two experiments each with three tasks. The tasks in the first experiment, IDCT, ADPCMD and ADPCMC, are described in Example 1. The tasks in the second experiment are a Mobile Robot control program (MR), an Edge Detection algorithm (ED) and an OFDM transmitter (OFDM). We use

Table 1. Tasks.

Tasks in Experiment I				Tasks in Experiment II			
Task	WCET(us)	Period(us)	Pri.	Task	WCET(us)	Period(us)	Pri.
ADPCMC	7675	50,000	4	OFDM	2830	40,000	4
ADPCMD	2839	10,000	3	ED	1392	6,500	3
IDCT	1580	4,500	2	MR	830	3,500	2

Table 2. Number of cache lines to be reloaded.

Experiment I					Experiment II				
Preemptions	A1	A2	A3	A4	Preemptions	A1	A2	A3	A4
ADPCMC by IDCT	249	68	64	56	OFDM by MR	245	134	118	88
ADPCMC by ADPCMD	220	114	92	64	OFDM by ED	254	172	135	98
ADPCMD by IDCT	183	58	55	46	ED by MR	245	87	85	81

SYMTA to estimate the WCET of each task in the experiments. The periods, priorities and WCET of tasks in each experiment are listed in Table 1.

In the experiment, we compare four approaches to estimate cache reload overhead caused by preemptions. Furthermore, we calculate the WCRT of each task by using Equation 6.

Approach 1 (A1): All cache lines used by preempting tasks are reloaded for a preemption. Note that this approach is proposed by [17].

Approach 2 (A2): Only lines in the intersection set of lines used by the preempting task and the preempted task are reloaded for a preemption. The inter-task cache eviction method proposed in [1] is used here.

Approach 3 (A3): Intra-task cache access analysis for the preempted task proposed by Lee et al. in [19] is used here. Note that no path analysis is applied in this approach. This approach can potentially include infeasible preemptions in the WCRT estimate (which does not exist in our approach).

Approach 4 (A4): Both inter-task cache eviction analysis and intra-task cache access analysis are used to estimate the cache reload cost. Also, path analysis proposed in [1] is applied to the preempting task. Approach 4 is the approach described in this paper.

The estimates of the number of cache lines to be reloaded in each type of preemption derived with these fours approaches are listed in Table 2.

Table 3. Comparison of WCRT estimate.

C_{miss}	Experiment I						Experiment II					
	Task	A1	A2	A3	A4	ART	Task	A1	A2	A3	A4	ART
10	ADPCMC	35743	29392	29172	28836	23512	OFDM	9847	9350	9279	6456	6113
	ADPCMD	6565	6315	6309	6291	6190	ED	2567	2409	2407	2403	2382
20	ADPCMC	48528	35607	35079	29420	23867	OFDM	12510	10096	9954	9524	6211
	ADPCMD	6931	6431	6419	6383	6223	ED	2812	2496	2492	2484	2400
30	ADPCMC	88606	38997	38139	35175	24101	OFDM	23501	12174	11964	99844	6255
	ADPCMD	7297	6547	6529	6475	6278	ED	3057	2583	577	2565	2426
40	ADPCMC	359239	48146	39335	35843	24353	OFDM	45216	16700	12774	10444	6362
	ADPCMD	7663	6663	6639	6567	6354	ED	3302	2670	2662	2646	2525

We use SYMTA [8] to obtain the WCET of a context switch, which implies that the instructions of the context switch function and the memory blocks where contexts of the preempted and the preempting tasks are saved are not in the L1 cache when the context switch function is called. In this case, the WCET of a single context switch estimated with SYMTA is 1049 cycles.

In the first experiment, the WCRT of ADPCMC and ADPCMD can be calculated based on the results shown in Table 2. Notice that IDCT has the highest priority and thus cannot ever be preempted. As a result, the WCRT of IDCT is just equal to its WCET. We also vary the C_{miss} from 10 cycles to 40 cycles to investigate the influence of cache miss penalty on the WCRT. The estimate results (Approach 1 through Approach 4) and the Actual Response Times (ART) – which is the WCRT as observed in simulation – are listed in Table 3. (Please note that as we did not exhaust all possible input data in our simulations, the observed ART may underpredict WCRT; nonetheless, for our experiments the ART should be quite close to the WCRT considering the fact that the tasks in the experiments do not have complicated control flows and the size of the input data is fixed). Table 4 lists the improvement of our approach (Approach 4) over all other approaches (Approach 1, Approach 2 and Approach 3) in these first two experiments.

Approach 1 assumes that all cache lines used by the preempting task will be accessed by the preempted task after the preempted task is resumed. Obviously, this may not be true. Some cache lines will never be used by the preempted task no matter which path the preempted task takes. Thus, by calculating the set of cache lines that can possibly be accessed by both the preempting and the preempted task, we can further reduce the estimate of the number of cache lines to be reloaded by the preempted task, as shown in Approach 2.

Approach 3 calculates the maximum set of memory blocks in the preempted task that can potentially cause cache reload. Inter-task cache evictions are also considered in this approach. However, there is no path analysis in this approach. As compared with Approach 3, Approach 4, in which we apply path analysis techniques on the preempting task, achieves a significant reduction of up to 30% in the WCRT estimate of OFDM.

Table 4. Comparison of results for different approaches.

Comparison	Experiment I				Experiment II				
	Cache Penalty (cycles)					Cache Penalty (cycles)			
	Task	10	20	30	40	Task	10	20	30	40
A4 vs. A1	ADPCMC	19%	39%	60%	92%	OFDM	34%	23%	57%	77%
	ADPCMD	4%	8%	11%	14%	ED	6%	12%	16%	20%
A4 vs. A2	ADPCMC	2%	17%	10%	26%	OFDM	31%	6%	18%	38%
	ADPCMD	1%	1%	1%	1%	ED	0.2%	0.5%	1%	1%
A4 vs. A3	ADPCMC	1.4%	16%	8%	9%	OFDM	30%	4%	17%	18%
	ADPCMD	0.2%	0.3%	0.5%	0.6%	ED	0.3%	0.6%	0.8%	1%

We also executed a third experiment with a larger number of tasks. In this experiment, we have six tasks, OFDM, ADPCMC, ADPCMD, IDCT, ED and MR. The priority and period of each task is listed in Table 5. Note that, in order to satisfy the necessary condition of schedulability of a real-time system (i.e., the total utilization of all tasks must be less than 100% [14, 15]), we increase the periods of some tasks as compared to the same tasks in experiment 1 and experiment 2. ADPCMC has the lowest priority and MR has the highest prority. The WCET of each task stays the same.

Table 5. Tasks in Experiment III.

	T_1(MR)	T_2(IDCT)	T_3(ED)	T_4(ADPCMD)	T_5(OFDM)	T_6(ADPCMC)
Period(us)	7,000	9,000	13,000	20,000	40,000	50,000
Priority	2	3	4	5	6	7
WCET(us)	830	1580	1392	2839	2830	7675

We use the four different approaches described earlier to estimate the WCRT of the two tasks with the lowest priorities, OFDM and ADPCMC, which may be preempted more frequently than other tasks. Table 6 gives the WCRT estimates of OFDM and ADPCMC with the different approaches.

Table 6. WCRT estimates in Experiment III.

	WCRT estimates of ADPCMC					WCRT estimates of OFDM				
C_{miss}	A1	A2	A3	A4	A4 vs.A3	A1	A2	A3	A4	A4 vs. A3
10	51572	34837	34336	33781	2%	16901	16217	15948	15643	2%
20	75585	58646	51990	38235	27%	25904	17531	16993	16383	4%
30	258814	75673	69025	57496	18%	50831	25756	24697	17123	31%
40	6837328	152023	76729	68599	11%	116464	33690	31834	17863	44%

Approach 3 and Approach 4 are compared in Table 6. By applying path analysis, the WCRT estimate is reduced by up to 44%. Thus, we demonstrate that our approach can tighten WCRT estimate significantly by using path analysis technique, which is missing in the enhanced approach of Lee et al. [19].

As stated in Section 6, the approach of Lee et al. cannot guarantee removal of all infeasible preemptions. We have one last (actually, fourth) experiment to show the effect of infeasible preemptions. For example, consider the following scenario based on the experiment in Lee et al. [19].

The four tasks listed in Table 7 are used in the experiment in [19]. When the cache reload penalty is 100 cycles (this is the penalty used by Lee et al. in [19]), the WCRT of FIR (i.e., the task with the lowest priority) given by the approach of Lee et al. is 5,323,620 cycles. However, the WCRT estimate resulting from the iteration we proposed in Section 6 is 3,297,383 cycles, which shows a reduction of 38%. Note that we use the preemption related cache reload cost as

Table 7. Tasks in the paper of Lee et al. [19].

Task	Period	WCET
FFT	$320,000$	$60,234 + 280 \times C_{miss}$
LUD	$1,120,000$	$255,998 + 364 \times C_{miss}$
LMS	$1,920,000$	$365,893 + 474 \times C_{miss}$
FIR	$25,600,000$	$557,589 + 405 \times C_{miss}$

reported in [19]. Since we use the same cache reload cost for each preemption, the difference in WCRT estimate is caused by the the number of preemptions used in WCRT estimate. Apparently, the approach of Lee et al. cannot remove all the infeasible preemptions.

8   Conclusion

We propose a method to analyze the preemption cost caused by cache eviction in a multi-tasking real-time system. The method first analyzes the maximum set of memory blocks in the preempted task that can possibly cause cache reload. Then, the method incorporates the inter-task cache eviction behavior by calculating the intersection set of cache lines used by the preempting task and the preempted task. By combining these two approaches, we achieve over prior state-of-the-art up to 44% reduction in WCRT estimate in our experiments.

For future work, we plan to expand our analysis approach for systems with more than two-level memory hierarchy. Also, we will research the cache eviction problem in multi-processor systems.

Acknowledgment

This research is funded by NSF under INT-9973120, CCR-9984808 and CCR-0082164. We acknowledge donations received from Denali, Hewlett-Packard, Intel, LEDA, Mentor Graphics, Sun and Synopsys. We also thank Jan Staschulat and Prof. Dr. Rolf Ernst for their help in using SYMTA.

References

1. Y. Tan and V. Mooney, "Timing Analysis for Preemptive Multi-tasking Real-Time Systems," *Proceedings of Design, Automation and Test in Europe (DATE'04)*, pp. 1034-1039, February 2004.
2. Y. Tan and V. Mooney, "Timing Analysis for Preemptive Multi-tasking Real-time Systems with Caches," Technical Report, GIT-CC-04-02, Georgia Institute of Technology, February 2004.
3. D. Kirk, "SMART (Strategic Memory Allocation for Real-Time) Cache Design", *Proceedings of IEEE 10th Real-Time System Symposium*, pp. 229-237, December 1989.

4. G. Suh, L. Rudolph and S. Devadas, "Dynamic Cache Partitioning for Simultaneous Multithreading Systems," *Proceedings of the IASTED International Conference on Parallel and Distributed Computing and Systems*, pp. 116-127, September 2001.

5. J. Liedtke, H.Härtig and M. Hohmuth, "OS-Controlled Cache Predictability for Real-Time Systems," *Proceedings of the Third IEEE Real-Time Technology and Applications Symposium (RTAS'97)*, pp. 213-227, June 1997.

6. F. Muller, "Compiler Support for Software-based Cache Partitioning," *Proceedings of ACM SIGPLAN Workshop on Languages, Compliers and Tools for Real-Time Systems*, pp. 125-133, June 1995.

7. Y. Li and S. Malik, *Performance Analysis of Real-Time Embedded Software*, Kluwer Academic Publishers, Boston, 1999.

8. F. Wolf, *Behavioral Intervals in Embedded Software*, Kluwer Academic Publishers, Norwell, MA, 2002.

9. H. Negi, T. Mitra and A. Roychoudhury, "Accurate Estimation of Cache-related Preemption Delay," *Proceedings of ACM Joint Symposium CODES+ISSS*, pp. 201-206, October 2003.

10. H. Tomiyama and N. Dutt, "Program path analysis to bound cache-related preemption delay in preemptive real-time systems," *Proceedings of the Eighth International Workshop on Hardware/software Codesign*, pp. 67-71, May 2000.

11. C. Ferdinand, R. Heckmann, M. Langenbach, F. Martin, M. Schmidt, H. Theiling, S. Thesing and R. Wilhelm, "Reliable and Precise WCET Determination for a Real-Life Processor," *Proceedings of the First International Workshop on Embedded Software, (EMSOFT 2001)*, pp. 469-485, Volume 2211 of LNCS, Springer-Verlag (2001).

12. M. Alt, C. Ferdinand, F. Martin and R. Wilhelm, "Cache behavior prediction by abstract interpretation," *Proceedings of Static Analysis Symposium (SAS'96)*, pp. 52-66, September 1996.

13. T. Lundqvist and P. Stenstrom, "An Integrated Path and Timing Analysis Method based on Cycle-Level Symbolic Execution," *Real-Time Systems*, Volume 17, Issue 2-3, pp. 183-207, November 1999.

14. J. Lehoczky, L. Sha and Y. Ding, "The Rate Monotonic Scheduling Algorithm:Exact Characterization and Average Case Behavior," *Proc. IEEE 10th Real-Time System Symposium*, pp. 166-171, 1989.

15. C. Liu and J. Layland, "Scheduling Algorithms for Multiprogramming in a Hard Real-Time Environment," *Journal of ACM*, Vol. 20, No. 1, pp. 26-61, January 1973.

16. K. Tindell, A. Burns, A. Wellings, "An Extendible Approach for Analyzing Fixed Priority Hard Real-Time Tasks," *Real-Time Systems* Vol.6, No.2, pp. 133-151, March 1994.

17. J. Busquets-Mataix, J. Serrano, R. Ors, P. Gil and A. Wellings, "Adding instruction cache effect to schedulability analysis of preemptive real-time systems," *Real-Time Technology and Applications Symposium*, pp. 204-212, June 1996.

18. C. Lee, J. Hahn, Y. Seo, S. Min, R. Ha, S. Hong, C. Park, M. Lee and C. Kim. "Analysis of Cache-related Preemption Delay in Fixed-priority Preemptive Scheduling," *IEEE Transactions on Computers*, Vol. 47, No. 6, pp. 700-713, 1998.

19. C. Lee, J. Hahn, Y.-M. Seo, S. Min, R. Ha, S. Hong, C. Park, M. Lee and C. Kim, "Enhanced Analysis of Cache-related Preemption Delay in Fixed-priority Preemptive Scheduling," *IEEE Real-Time Systems Symposium*, pp. 187-198, December 1997.

20. D. Sun, D. Blough and V. Mooney, "Atalanta: A New Multiprocessor RTOS Kernel for System-on-a-Chip Applications," Technical Report GIT-CC-02-19, Georgia Institute of Technology, April 2002.
21. Mentor Graphics, Seamless Hardware/Software Co-Verification, http://www.mentor.com/seamless/.
22. Mentor Graphics XRAY Debugger, http://www.mentor.com/embedded/xray/.
23. MediaBench, http://cares.icsl.ucla.edu/MediaBench/.
24. Berkeley MPEG2 decoder, http://bmrc.berkeley.edu/frame/research/mpeg/.

A Fuzzy Adaptive Algorithm
for Fine Grained Cache Paging

Susmit Bagchi and Mads Nygaard

Department of Computer and Information Science
Norwegian University of Science and Technology (NTNU)
Trondheim, Norway
{susmit,mads}@idi.ntnu.no

Abstract. The performance of page replacement algorithms used by the virtual memory management system and file system of operating systems is important because of the higher disk access latency. The situation complicates further under the limitation of memory. There exists a set of page replacement algorithms, however, a majority of them are based on static policies. In this paper, a novel Fuzzy Adaptive Page Replacement algorithm (FAPR) is proposed. The FAPR algorithm applies fuzzy inference technique based on an adaptive rule-base and online priority control. The algorithm is simulated in a highly memory-constrained environment under various load distributions. The results demonstrate that the FAPR algorithm enhances the performance in comparison to the commonly used algorithms such as, LRU and LFU. In the worst-case execution model, FAPR algorithm averages the performance of the LRU and LFU algorithms. This paper describes the design and simulation of the FAPR algorithm along with the results.

Keywords: LRU/LFU, fuzzy logic, reference string, lookahead, cache, normal/uniform distributions, paging algorithms.

1 Introduction

The disk access latency is significantly larger than the access latency of RAM. As the performance gap between microprocessors and secondary storage media increases, the disk cache management becomes increasingly important for the file system performance. The efficiency of the page replacement algorithm is important to the virtual memory manager, the file system of operating systems and the other subsystems such as MDVM [28]. An efficient page replacement algorithm should have three qualities [20]. First, the algorithm should be capable of distinguishing the hot and cold pages in cache aiming to reduce page faults. Secondly, the algorithm should have efficient implementation meaning that it should use a constant and small amount of memory to store the history per page in the cache. Specially, in the memory-constrained systems such as, mobile handheld devices, the algorithm does not have the luxury to consume large space to store history of pages enhancing memory waste. Thirdly, a smart page replacement algorithm should be free from any unrealistic assumptions and must adapt to the dynamics of the reference string in order to reduce page faults. Although the cache paging algorithms have been studied extensively, most of the page replacement algorithms are based on a set of static policies and assumptions about the page access probability

H. Schepers (Ed.): SCOPES 2004, LNCS 3199, pp. 200–213, 2004.

[8][11]. We argue that a realistic and efficient approach to employ dynamic adaptation in cache paging algorithms should be free from strict assumptions about the probability distribution of reference string and may employ fuzzy inference technique. According to the fuzzy inference theory, we say that there should be much fine-grained and multilevel in between hot and cold categories of pages. Hence, the page replacement decisions should also be based on multilevel adaptive strategies and not on any fixed scheme. This paper proposes a novel algorithm for cache paging named Fuzzy Adaptive Page Replacement (FAPR), which employs adaptive rule-based fuzzy inference technique. We are interested in the systems having very low cache to disk capacity ratio meaning memory constrained environments. It is shown that the FAPR algorithm performs significantly better than the other commonly used algorithms under memory constraints. The main distinguishing characteristics of the FAPR algorithm are given below.

- *FAPR does not assume any condition on the reference string distribution.*
- *It is independent of any predetermined and empirically tuned control parameters such as, page size, segment size, eviction point etc.*
- *FAPR does not statically segment the cache space with fixed logical boundaries.*
- *The algorithm allows pages to move across segments in any direction depending on access pattern.*
- *It uses page replacement decision based on fuzzy inference based on an adaptive rule-base comprised of multiple parameters.*
- *FAPR does not restrict the page replacement decision within any particular segment in the cache. Hence FAPR is not a biased algorithm while doing page replacements.*
- *The algorithm maintains the history of pages in a small (in order of few bytes) and constant amount of memory. FAPR does not store voluminous history of expired pages.*
- *The FAPR algorithm performs significantly better than the other conventional algorithms under a very low cache to disk capacity ratio.*

We have simulated the FAPR algorithm for varying cache sizes under a set of different input reference string patterns. We have imposed a fairly tight memory restriction on the algorithm (cache to disk capacity ratio varies from 0.0002 to 0.03). It is observed that FAPR algorithm utilizes the cache memory more efficiently exploiting the reference string patterns under memory constraints. In a uniprocess model, the FAPR algorithm performs 3%-5% better than LRU and LFU for largely varying reference string distributions. Specially, when the reference string is comprised of a combination of asymmetrically distributed data reference locality patterns over the entire disk space, the FAPR algorithm successfully reduces the page fault rate by 4%, 15% and 19% when the cache to disk capacity ratios are 0.01, 0.02 and 0.03 respectively. Hence, the overall performance improvement in FAPR is significant, and the algorithm effectively realizes an adaptive behaviour for different kinds of string patterns denoting page access localities. However, the worst-case execution performance of FAPR is close to the performance of the LRU and LFU algorithms because of the lack of any program locality patterns. We are currently investigating the response of the FAPR algorithm using trace driven analysis methods and block prefetching. This paper is organized as follows. Section 2 outlines the background works. Section 3 explains the FAPR algorithm. A high-level pseudo code representation of the algorithm is included. Section 4 depicts the comparative analysis of the algorithm. Section 5 describes the simulation methods and the obtained results. Graphical representations of the response of FAPR, LRU and LFU algorithms are presented. Section 6 concludes the paper.

2 Background Works

A number of algorithms are developed for the cache and buffer managements in operating systems and in database systems. LRU and LFU are the two most widely used algorithms because of simplicity and performance [17][20][21]. In real life, different processes may have different disk block access patterns [7]. The LRU policy is well adaptable to the changes in workload [20]. It is observed that the LRU and LFU gradually reduce page faults with increased cache sizes under the narrow regions of program locality. But, LRU performs poorly if processes have a clear reference string pattern in a wide range [7]. A frequency based FSB algorithm is proposed to overcome the poor performance of LFU [14]. The FSB partitions entire cache into three segments and replaces pages from the "old" segment of the cache. The drawbacks of FSB are its dependency of performance on the size of "middle" segment of the cache [16] and its insensitivity to exploit the "hotness" of a page indicated by the access frequency [14]. Hence, the true dynamics of the reference string get missed in the course of time. The IRM and LRUSM algorithms are based on the program locality patterns [8]. It is noted that LRUSM is an LRU-stack model and does not capture the true dynamics of the reference string [8]. The statistical estimation based LRU-K algorithm takes the page replacement decision depending upon the time of K th-to-last non-correlated reference to the block [18][20]. However, LRU-K algorithm is not very adaptive and does not combine page access frequency along with the recency in a unified manner [20]. It is noted that LRU-K does not work well for the pages without significant differences of reference frequencies [21]. Moreover, LRU-K is computationally expensive and enhances memory waste by keeping voluminous history of expired pages nonresident in the cache [20][21]. The LRU-K algorithm uses Bayesian statistical estimations, which is controversial in proving the validity of results [22]. The ARC cache replacement scheme tries to adapt to the workload by using two LRU lists (L1, L2) and learning techniques [27]. The list L2 maintains pages that are twice frequently accessed within a short interval as compared to L1. However, ARC scheme enhances the memory consumption twice that of the actual number of cache pages in memory. This is because ARC needs to maintain two lists each having the lengths equal to the actual cache size [27]. In addition, ARC does not try to detect the dynamics of the reference string by applying multilevel decision threshold. The ARC scheme is dependent on the "recency" and "frequency" parameters while controlling the cache replacement strategy. The 2Q algorithm [19], like LRU-K, quickly removes cold pages from the cache when K is small [20]. The downside of the 2Q is the empirically tuned static values of the control parameters "Kin" and "Kout" [21]. These empirically tuned static values are also sensitive to the types of workloads [21]. The EELRU is based on the recency of a page access and uses LRU policy by default keeping MRU pages in a fixed cache partition [17]. The drawbacks of EELRU are the static assignment of LRU region and empirically tuned eviction point. In addition, EELRU keeps the history of evicted pages in main memory [17], enhancing memory waste. The performance gain by EELRU is not significant as compared to LRU and performs poorly in some cases. The LIRS algorithm [21] is based on the strict assumptions that there exists stability on the IRR block over certain time, and empirically chooses 1% of the total cache size as LIR hoping that there is no cache-miss on the LIR segment. In a similar manner, the LRFU algorithm [20] is based on a static weighing function and empirically selects the control parameters λ and c. The performance of LRFU is only 3% better than 2Q. For the larger cache size and $\lambda = 1$, the performance of LRFU degenerates to the LRU policy. However, aforesaid algorithms do not employ the elegant approach of fuzzy rule-based adaptive strategy. The fuzzy inference technique would be an attractive approach while applying dynamic adaptive strategy in the cache paging algorithms.

3 Developing the Algorithm

3.1 The Model

In this section, we establish a basic model considering a set of processes and associated reference strings. It is assumed that disk blocks are cached in a finite amount of pages in main memory. The executing processes generate a sequence of references to disk blocks known as a reference string. Let us consider a set of active processes, $A=\{P_i : 1\leq i \leq d\}$ during the interval time t, in which the level of multiprocessing is defined by [d=d(t)][8]. The reference string generated by A in a variable time space T is, $\omega(T)=\{a_j(t) : 1\leq j \leq n , 1\leq t \leq T \}$ where n is the number of elements in the input string. In a practical situation the reference string sequence is not known a priori. Hence, it is assumed that $\omega(T)$ will be generated online. We segment $\omega(T)$ into equal intervals of Δt denoted by $\omega_i[\Delta t]$ such that, $\cup_{i=0, T-1} \omega_i[\Delta t] = \omega(T)$. Hence, for any $\omega_j[\Delta t]$, $\omega_k[\Delta t]\in \omega(T)$, either $\omega_j[\Delta t]\cap\omega_k[\Delta t] = \phi$ or $\omega_j[\Delta t]\cap\omega_k[\Delta t] \subset \omega(T)$. The pages in the disk cache are considered as a set of elements V such that $n >> |V|$ for a sufficiently large t. At any instant $t \leq T$, V may consist of three partitions π_0, π_1, π_2 such that, $\pi_i=\{v_k\in V: 1\leq k \leq |V|\}$, i=0,1,2 and $\pi_0 \cup \pi_1 \cup \pi_2=V$ and $\pi_0 \cap \pi_1=\pi_0 \cap \pi_2=\pi_1 \cap \pi_2=\phi$. The π_0, π_1 and π_2 are formed dynamically at any instant $t \leq T$ whenever there will be a page reference made by a process. For every $v_k\in V$, there exists an ordered tuple representing the properties associated with v_k. Two such property sets are, $Q=\{q_i : q_i \in N\}$ and $S=\{s_j : s_j \in N , s_j>0\}$, where N is a set of natural numbers, representing dynamic priority or weight assigned to v_k at any $t \leq T$ and the total number of references made to v_k in $\omega(T)$ respectively. A relation Γ is defined as, $\Gamma:V\rightarrow Q \times S$ such that for any ordered tuple $X\in Q\times S$ and $\forall v_k\in V$, if $\langle v_k, X\rangle \in \Gamma$ then, $\forall Y\in Q\times S$, $\{\Gamma(v_k) - \langle v_k, X\rangle\}\cap\{\langle v_k, Y\rangle\}= \phi$ within any Δt and $X\neq Y$. We impose no restriction on cardinalities of π_0, π_1 and π_2. If a function, represented as $h(\omega_i[\Delta t])$, evaluates the cache hit for some $\omega_i[\Delta t]$ and q_i is the priority in $\omega_i[\Delta t]$, then the value of q_{i+1} for the newly incoming page in $\omega_{i+1}[\Delta t]$ is governed by the following function definitions:

> If $h(\omega_i[\Delta t]) \geq h(\omega_{i-1}[\Delta t])$: $q_{i+1} = (q_i + 1)$;
> If $h(\omega_{i-1}[\Delta t]) > h(\omega_i[\Delta t])$ and $q_i > 0$: $q_{i+1} = (q_i - 1)$;
> Otherwise: $q_{i+1} = C$, where $C > 0$ is a constant.

The performance of the FAPR, LRU and LFU algorithms are measured in terms of a normalized page fault rate referred to as "%page fault".

3.2 The Adaptive Rule-Base

In this section we develop the fuzzy logic based adaptive rule-base. Fuzzy logic is a part of fuzzy set theory, and has proven industrial applications. The fuzzy inference technique is an attractive solution and beneficial for the systems characterized by uncertainty and vagueness [23][24]. In our case, the probability distribution of the randomly varying reference string is not well known in advance. Hence, application of the fuzzy logic based adaptive inference technique in the cache paging algorithm would be an attractive approach. For the sake of simplicity of understanding, let the symbols H, M and L denote π_0, π_1 and π_2 and B = {H, M, L}. The input vector to the fuzzyfier is represented by I = {α, $\Gamma(v_k)$, b} where, α = {0, 1}, $v_k \in$ V and b$\in$ B. We call "cache hit" if α = 1 and "cache miss" if α = 0. Let, $\langle q_k, s_k \rangle = \Gamma(v_k)$. The fuzzy membership function is defined as, μ_α: I$\rightarrow$ [0, 1]. The two sets of fuzzyfied output of I are shown in Figure 1.1 and Figure 1.2. The characteristic of the fuzzy membership function is shown in Figure 2. Rather than marking the binary "hot" and "cold" states of the pages, the fuzzyfier distinguishes five different states of the pages in cache such as, "very cold", "cold", "medium", "hot" and "very hot" states.

$\mu_{\alpha=0}$	$q_k>0$, $s_k>1$	$q_k=0$, $s_k>1$	$q_k>0$, $s_k=1$	$q_k=0$, $s_k=1$
H	0.3	0.5	0.3	0.9
M	0.3	0.9	0.3	0.9
L	0.6	0.1	0.3	0.1

$\mu_{\alpha=1}$	$q_k>0$, $s_k>1$	$q_k=0$, $s_k>1$	$q_k>0$, $s_k=1$	$q_k=0$, $s_k=1$
H	0.1	0.3	0.3	0.6
M	0.9	0.3	0.9	0.3
L	0.9	0.6	0.3	0.6

Fig. 1.1. Membership Table for α=0.   **Fig. 1.2.** Membership Table for α=1.

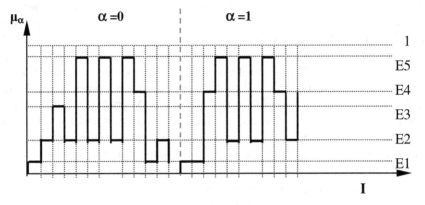

Fig. 2. Characteristics of the Fuzzy Membership Functions.

The linguistic variables denoting the five states of a page, to formulate the fuzzy implications, are defined as, E1=0.1, E2=0.3, E3=0.5, E4=0.6 and E5=0.9 representing the states of cache pages varying from "very cold" to "very hot" respectively. The values of

E1, E2 and E3 increase in the step of 0.2 denoting increasing membership of a page to the "hotness". However, the value of E4 is chosen with a lower incremental step of 0.1 putting the "medium" and "hot" pages in a close proximity. Otherwise, the membership of "very hot" pages is valued at E5 = 0.9 having a highest step increment of 0.3. For all v_k in V, the set of actions performed by the algorithm is defined as, A1$\rightarrow$ ϕ, A2$\rightarrow$ (q_k= q_k+1), A3$\rightarrow$ (A2 $\wedge$ M=M$\cup${v_k}), A4$\rightarrow$ (H=H$\cup${v_k}), A5$\rightarrow$ (M=M$\cup${v_k}), A6$\rightarrow$ (q_k= q_k-1), A7$\rightarrow$ (L=L$\cup${v_k}) and A8$\rightarrow$ (A6 $\wedge$ M=M$\cup${v_k}). The adaptive rule-base created by the fuzzy implications based on actions A1 to A8, state of α and linguistic variable values (E1 to E5) is shown in Figure 3.

if α = 1 AND E1 then A1	if α = 0 AND E1 then A1
if α = 1 AND E2 then A2	if α = 0 AND E2 then A6
if α = 1 AND E3 then A1	if α = 0 AND E3 then A5
if α = 1 AND E4 then A3	if α = 0 AND E4 then A8
if α = 1 AND E5 then A4	if α = 0 AND E5 then A7

Fig. 3. The Adaptive Rule-Base.

The FAPR algorithm uses the adaptive rule-base while doing cache update and page replacement operations. On the events of cache hit and cache miss, the cache is repartitioned and priority values are updated according to the rules described in the rule-base. In the next section, the high level description of the algorithm is presented.

3.3 Description of the Algorithm

In this section, the description of FAPR algorithm is presented. We have divided the entire cache space (C) into three dynamic and logical partitions named H, M and L as shown in Figure 4. The reference string is logically divided into sequence of intervals. The length of an interval is chosen as $\lfloor$cache_length/4$\rfloor$, where "cache_length" represents the cache size. Every page in the cache is assigned three parameters such as, "Priority", "Partition" and "Count". The "Priority" value is one of the page replacement decision parameters dynamically calculated according to the function described in section 3.1.

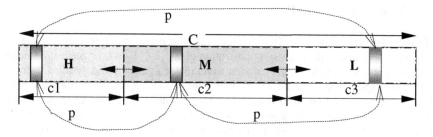

Fig. 4. General Structure of Cache and Page (p) Movements.

The "Priority" value of a page indicates the "hotness" of a page based on recency and determines the resident partition of the page in cache. The duration of an interval is chosen 25% of the cache size to incorporate fast adaptation by recalculating "Priority" values periodically. The "Partition" and "Count" represent the current partition and access frequency of a page. The algorithm keeps track of the number of cache hits ("cur_hit" and "prev_hit") in two consecutive intervals and determines the priority of pages ("boost") in the next interval through online approximation. The default value of the page priority is set to 1/3 of cache size because the cache has three partitions. A newly incoming page is placed in the partition H to allow it to stay in the cache for the next interval, and assigned the priority value as calculated at that point of time. If this page is not re-accessed in the next sequence interval then it becomes an aging page. The priority and partition of residency of aging pages change according to the adaptive rule-base while doing cache update and page replacement operations. Based on the state of a page, the movement of a page (p) across the dynamic partitions can be in both directions as shown in Figure 4. A page (p) can move between segments H, M and L, as shown by dotted arrows in Figure 4, depending on the page access patterns. The cardinalities of H, M and L may vary over time based on the page population dynamics in those segments. In other words, depending on the movement of pages, the length c_1, c_2 and c_3 may vary over time. The aging pages are repartitioned and the priority values are modified following the adaptive rule-base. The page replacement decision is hierarchical based on Priority, Partition and Count values of pages. The FAPR algorithm is not confined to any particular partition for the page replacement operation. It tries to find a victim page with the minimum priority and count in partition L, M and H. The order of selecting a victim for replacement decreases according to its residency in L, M and H partitions respectively. Hence, depending on the dynamics of the reference string, the page replacement can happen in one of the three partitions depending on the availability of a victim. If multiple pages have the same access frequency (priority) then the page with the minimum priority (access frequency) is selected for replacement. Otherwise, the tie is broken arbitrarily in case of the equality in all respect amongst two pages. In the pseudo code representation of FAPR algorithm, the "CacheSearchUpdate(Page)", "Select-Page(L, M, H)", "FireRule(Page, Cache_Event)" and "InsertPage(Page, Count, Partition, Priority)" procedures implement cache search/update, page replacement, firing fuzzy adaptive rules and the new page insertion operations respectively. In the worst-case execution, the entire cache search and partitioning can be done in O(V) without committing a costly cache rearrangement for every request as necessary in the case of LRU [13]. The algorithm is presented in pseudo code shown in Figure 7.

4   Comparative Analysis

It should be noted that the buffer management algorithms in database area make use of information deduced from query optimization plans [20]. However, such information is not applicable in virtual memory systems and disk caching by file systems. Hence, the buffer management algorithms are only comparable in the domain of database systems [20] and not in the domain of operating systems. The LRU and LFU are the two most widely used paging algorithms because of simplicity and performance [17][20][21]. LFU suffers from a misleading temporary program locality indicated by the reference string. Although FSB overcomes such problem, but FSB is prone to the performance unpredictability due to its assumption of a large middle segment in the cache and the dependence of its performance on the block size. The FSB policy does not fully exploit the reference locality information provided by the page count. The LRU-SP combines access recency and frequency information of a page to take replacement decision, but does not provide adaptive replacement scheme. The EELRU applies LRU policy by default without significant performance improvement and sometime performs poorly in comparison to LRU [17]. The pitfalls of EELRU are the assumptions of the static page-access recency behaviour over time and the maintenance of a static LRU segment in the cache. Hence, EELRU algorithm can be viewed as a blind or unfair adaptive policy, which is unrealistic in multiprocess execution. Another drawback of EELRU is that the early eviction point (e) and late region (M) are chosen statically. In another case, the 2Q algorithm employs LRU policy in the "Am" queue [19]. The experiments on real data from DB2 trace show that the performance difference between LRU, 2Q and LRU-2 are often below 5% [19] and the performances become comparable with large cache size. The "Kin" and "Kout" control parameters of 2Q algorithm are predetermined, empirically tuned, and are sensitive to the types of workloads [21]. Hence, 2Q is not an adaptive algorithm. Additionally, the 2Q algorithm is memory intensive and complex [21]. The LRU-K replacement policy is based on the time of the K th-to-last non-correlated reference to a page in cache. The LRU-K uses Bayesian statistical estimation to calculate the probability of accessing a page but the validity of estimation is a subject of controversy because Bayesian estimation depends on the prior distribution, which cannot be estimated statistically [22]. The LRU-K, K>2, is less responsive to the changes in page access patterns [18]. Hence, LRU-K may not adapt in a highly dynamic multiprocessing system where the reference string variation is not stable. The LRU-K algorithm uses strict assumptions about the unchanged page access probability over the length of the reference string, and that each disk page has a well-defined probability determining the next reference [18]. Additionally, LRU-K algorithm does not admix the page access recency and frequency values in a unified manner [20]. It retains voluminous history of removed pages in the main memory [18]. Hence, LRU-K is the memory intensive, non-adaptive algorithm, and do not improve performance consistently [20][21]. Similarly, the LRFU algorithm is also based on a static weighing function and empirically chosen controlling parameters such as, λ and c. In a same way, the LIRS algorithm assumes the stability on the IRR of a block over time and statically allocates 1% of the cache space as LIR [21]. The ARC cache replacement scheme tries to employ adaptive strategy based on two LRU lists and enhances the memory-resource consumption twice that of the actual cache size [27]. In addition, the cache replacement decision in ARC is dependent on "recency" and "frequency" parameters. The ARC does not employ fine-grained page replacement scheme by employing multi-valued logic and fuzzy inference technique.

The majority of the algorithms discussed above do not use dynamic adaptation free from any assumptions. Unlike static policy based LRU, LFU, LRFU, 2Q, FSB and others, the proposed FAPR algorithm employs an adaptive rule-based fuzzy inference technique. The page replacement decision is hierarchical based on multiple parameters. In contrast to the EELRU, 2Q and FSB algorithms, FAPR algorithm does not assume any restriction or condition on the segment sizes, block sizes, eviction point and permanent-page-residency in the cache. Unlike LRFU, LRU-K, 2Q and EELRU policies, the FAPR algorithm does not employ any pre-estimated and empirically tuned control parameters. The FAPR algorithm modifies a set of controlling parameters online based on reference string patterns. In contrast to EELRU, FSB and 2Q, the page replacement decision in FAPR algorithm is not confined in any particular segment in cache. Hence, FAPR is not an unfair or blind adaptation. In contrast to FSB and EELRU algorithms, the FAPR algorithm allows the pages in the cache to move in different partitions in any direction depending on their history. The FAPR algorithm employs an opportunistic adaptive strategy while determining the priority value of a page. The algorithm later, while taking the page replacement decision, uses the priority value. Unlike LRU-K, ARC and EELRU, the FAPR algorithm maintains the history of pages in a small (in order of few bytes) and constant amount of memory. FAPR does not store the voluminous history of expired pages and unlike ARC, the FAPR algorithm does not need the memory space twice that of actual cache size. In contrast to the LRU-K algorithm, which uses strict assumptions on the page access probability distribution, FAPR does not depend on any such assumptions. In contrast to ARC, the FAPR algorithm categorizes cache pages into five different states and applies adaptive strategy based on fuzzy inference technique. It is worth mentioning that maintaining histories for the individual pages in the cache only requires $(n|V|)$ amount of memory, where n is in the order of a few bytes. In addition, the worst-case computational complexity for the search and update operations is $O(V)$.

5   Simulations and Results

LRU is one of the most popular caching algorithms [8]. It is widely used in virtual memory system and file cache because of the efficiency and simplicity [17][21]. The advantage of LRU algorithm is that it adapts well to the workload variations compared to other algorithms [20]. In a complementary case, LFU is non-adaptive. We have simulated the LRU, LFU and FAPR algorithms in C language under Windows 2000 for comparative studies. We have investigated the performance of the FAPR algorithm under a large variety of load distributions in a memory-constrained environment. The environment of the simulation experiment consists of a 20 MB hard disk and a variable cache size having 600KB at maximum. The disk cache consists of 4KB pages in main memory. This means that the disk contains 5000 blocks, and the cache contains 150 pages at maximum. We have used a fairly low cache to disk capacity ratio to emulate a memory constrained environment. The cache to disk capacity ratio hence varies from 0.0002 to 0.03. In our experiments, the cache length varies from 1 to 150, representing different memory constraint phases. Often it happens that some of the disk blocks are frequently referenced due to program locality, whereas some of the disk blocks are rarely accessed in any execution. In other cases the access pattern may appear to be very random. The property of normal probability distribution function is that it is a good approximation of a random variable having no specifically known distribution pattern [25]. In addition, the normal distribution function is used when the randomness is caused by independent sources acting additively [26]. The probability distribution of the disk block access pattern would not be known in any given form a priori and hence, any particularly chosen probability distribution function might not be suitable. However, the central limit theorem indicates that the normal distribution may act as a good approximation for the random variable with unknown distribution [25]. Hence, in a very long-term execution scenario, the entire reference string generated by processes over the disk space can be approximately modeled using a normal probability distribution function.

The input reference strings having small, medium and large variances respectively within normal distribution represent different locality patterns of block access. The reference string generated by multiple processes will exhibit asymmetrically distributed locality patterns over the disk space. Hence, we have modeled such scenarios using a combination of normal distributions with a set of different means and variances. The simulation is accomplished in two phases. The first phase depicts a single process execution scenario as described below and it uses an input reference string length equal to 50000:

1. **Experiment I(a):** This experiment tries to catch the responses of the algorithms under a narrow region of program locality. We have used an input string with a small mean/variance equal to 2500/50.

2. **Experiment I(b):** This experiment is designed to understand the algorithmic responses under moderately and widely varying program locality patterns. The mean/variance is set to 2500/150.

3. **Experiment I(c):** In this experiment we have used very widely varying program locality patterns with the mean/variance equal to 2500/750.

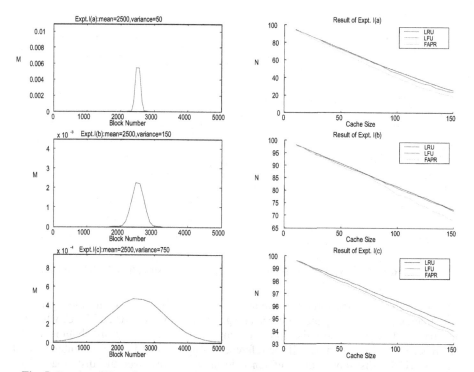

Fig. 5. Results of Experiments I(a), (b) and (c). M: Probability distribution. N: %Page fault.

The responses of the FAPR, LRU and LFU algorithms are given in Figure 5. The right hand side figures compare the page fault percentage of FAPR with LRU and LFU, while the left hand side figures show the corresponding probability density distributions of the reference string. It is evident from the results shown in Figure 5 that the FAPR algorithm performs better than LRU and LFU by reducing the page faults by 3%-5% on average over considerably large reference string sizes. It indicates that FAPR is more successful in adapting to the reference string pattern than the other candidates under a low cache to disk capacity ratio. In a more practical situation, the execution environment will be multiprocessing. Hence, the reference string pattern would exhibit multiple program localities asymmetrically distributed over the disk space along with some sequential access patterns. In yet another case the entire disk access pattern would be very random with no program locality pattern available. The second phase of our experiment simulates these situations under the same memory constraints as described above. This set of experiments is described below:

4. **Experiment II:** In this experiment we have combined four different normal probability distribution functions to simulate multiple program localities of various degrees. The reference string size is 200000. The combinations of mean and variance are: 1000/25; 2000/150; 3000/250; 4000/50.

5. **Experiment III:** This experiment simulates the worst case where the reference string is very random and scattered over the entire disk space. We have used a uniformly distributed reference string of size 50000.

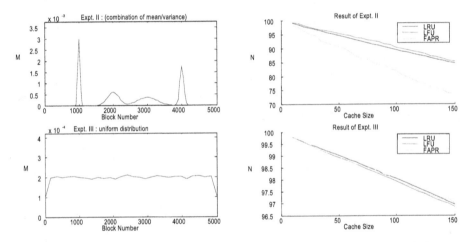

Fig. 6. Results of Experiments II and III. M: Probability distribution. N: %Page fault.

The responses of the three algorithms are given in Figure 6. Again, the right hand side figures compare the page fault percentage of FAPR with LRU and LFU, while the left hand side figures show the corresponding probability density distributions of the reference string. In experiment II the reference string is comprised of a combination of asymmetrically distributed data reference locality patterns over the disk space. The FAPR algorithm successfully reduces the page fault rate by 4%, 15% and 19% compared to LRU and LFU when the cache to disk capacity ratios are 0.01, 0.02 and 0.03 respectively. Hence, the overall performance improvement of FAPR is significant. It is demonstrated through our simulation that the FAPR algorithm efficiently utilizes the available disk cache under a low cache to disk capacity ratio. It is evident from the result of experiment II that, in the tight memory constraint environment, FAPR outperforms the other algorithms. As experiment III shows, the worst-case execution performance of FAPR is close to the performances of LRU and LFU due to of the lack of any true program locality patterns to be adapted to.

```
init: current_length ← 0; cur_hit ← 0; prev_hit ← 0; boost ← ⌈cache_length/3⌉;
Proc InsertPage(Page, Count, Partition, Priority):
        begin
                CachePageList ← Page;
                ⟨Page.Count, Page.Partition, Page.Priority⟩ ← ⟨Count, Partition, Priority⟩;
        end begin

Proc CacheSearchUpdate(Page):
        begin
                if(current_length < ⌊cache_length/4⌋) current_length ← current_length+1;
                else {    current_length ← 0;
                          switch(prev_hit) {
                                        case(prev_hit = 0):
                                                prev_hit ← cur_hit; break;
                                        case(prev_hit < cur_hit):
                                                boost ← boost+1; prev_hit ← cur_hit;
                                                break;
                                        case(prev_hit > cur_hit):
                                                if(boost != 0) boost ← boost-1; break;
                                                else boost ← ⌈cache_length/3⌉; break;
                                        case(prev_hit = cur_hit):
                                                boost ← boost+1; break;
                                        }
                          cur_hit ← 0; }
                if(CACHE_HIT) { Page.Count ← Page.Count+1;
                                FireRule(Page, CACHE_HIT);
                                cur_hit ← cur_hit+1; }
                else {    if(!CACHE_FULL) InsertPage(Page, 1, H, boost);
                          else {    FireRule(NULL, CACHE_MISS);
                                    ReplacePage ← SelectPage(L, M, H);
                                    ReplacePage ← Page;
                                    InsertPage(ReplacePage, 1, H, boost); }
                      }
        end begin

Proc SelectPage(L, M, H):
        begin
                i ← 0; ⟨p₀, p₁, p₂⟩ ← ⟨L, M, H⟩;
                ⟨m₀, m₁, m₂⟩ ← minimum page Count in ⟨ p₀, p₁, p₂⟩;
                while(i < 3)
                        {   if (( page in pᵢ) & ( Priority = 0 ) & ( Count = mᵢ)) return page;
                            else if(( page in pᵢ) & ( Count = mᵢ)) return page;
                            i++;
                        }
        end begin
```

Fig. 7. The Pseudo Code of the FAPR Algorithm.

6 Conclusions

This paper has presented the design and simulation of a novel page replacement algorithm, called FAPR. The FAPR algorithm is designed as a history based adaptive algorithm incorporating a fuzzy rule-base. The FAPR algorithm is independent of any predetermined internal parameters such as, cache segment size or block size etc. The FAPR algorithm does not assume any unrealistic external conditions such as, specific probability distribution of reference string and empirically tuned control parameters having static values. The page replacement decision in FAPR is hierarchical, and is dependent on three parameters denoting the reference string pattern. In cases where memory is limited, the FAPR algorithm utilizes the available cache memory more effectively than other commonly used page replacement algorithms. We have considered a low range of cache to disk capacity ratio, varies from 0.0002 to 0.03. In the case of largely varying data access locality patterns in a uniprocess model, the FAPR algorithm performs 3%-5% better than the LRU and LFU algorithms over a range of cache sizes. In the case of multiple access locality patterns asymmetrically distributed over the disk space, the FAPR outperforms the LRU and LFU algorithms by reducing page faults by 4%, 15% and 19% when the cache to disk capacity ratios are 0.01, 0.02 and 0.03 respectively. Hence, the overall performance improvement in FAPR is significant, and the algorithm effectively realizes adaptation for different kinds of string patterns denoting access localities. In addition, the worst-case execution performance of FAPR is approximately equal to the average performance of the conventional algorithms like LRU and LFU due to the lack of any pattern embedded within the reference string. The FAPR algorithm is comparatively inexpensive because it does not try to compute expensive statistical estimations or lengthy numerical calculations on a long sequence on every access. The memory requirement of FAPR to store the history per page in the cache is constant and considerably smaller than the other algorithms. We are currently investigating the response of the FAPR algorithm using trace driven analysis methods and block prefetching.

References

1. Cao, P., 1995. Application-controlled file caching and prefetching, Ph.D. thesis, Princeton University, (CSRT-522-95).
2. Cormen, T. H., Leiserson, C. E., Rivest, R. L., 1995. Introduction to Algorithms, MIT press, pp. 77-91.
3. Ehrig, H., Kreowski, H-J., Montanari, U., Rozenberg, G., Hand book of graph grammars and computing by graph transformation, World Scientific, Vol. 3, pp. 80-86.
4. Fait, A., Rosen, Z., 1997. Experimental studies of access graph based heuristics: Beating the LRU standard?, In SIAM symposium on discrete mathematics, New York.
5. Felten, E. W., Cao, P., Li, K., 1994. Application controlled file caching policies, In conference proc. of USENIX, Berkeley, CA, pp. 171-182.
6. Gallier, J. H., 1987. Logic for Computer Science, John Wiley & Sons, pp. 4-12, 39-50.
7. Gidoen, G., Cao, P., 1996. Adaptive page replacement based on memory reference behaviour, In TOCS, Washington.
8. Hwang, K., Faye, A. B., 1985. Computer architecture and parallel processing, McGraw-Hill, pp. 60-113.
9. Itzkovitz, A., Schuster, A., 1999. Multiview and milipage fine grain sharing in page-based DSMs, In proc. of 3rd Symposium on OSDI (USENIX), New Orleans.

10. Karlin, A. R., Felten, E. W., Cao, P., Li, K., 1996. Implementation and performance of integrated application-controlled file caching, prefetching and disk scheduling, In TOCS, New York.
11. Karlin, A. R., Felten, E. W., Cao, P., Li, K., 1995. A study of integrated prefetching and caching strategies, In Proc. ACM SIGMETRICS, pp. 188-197.
12. Liu, C. L., 1977. Elements of discrete mathematics, McGraw-Hill, pp. 59-72, 82-113.
13. Lubomir, B., Alan, C. S., 1988. The logical design of Operating Systems, Prentice-Hall, pp. 216-232.
14. Robinson, J., Devarakonda, M., 1990. Data Cache Management using Frequency-Based Replacement, ACM SIGMETRICS Conference on Measurement and Modeling of Computer Systems, Colorado.
15. Vivek, P. S., Druschel, P., Zwaenepoel, W., 1999. IO-Lite: A unified I/O buffering and caching system, In Proc. of 3rd Symposium on OSDI (USENIX), New Orleans.
16. William, S., 2001. Operating Systems, Prentice Hall, pp. 502-505.
17. Yannis, S., Scott, K., Paul, W., EELRU: Simple and Effective Adaptive Page Replacement, ACM SIGMETRICS International Conference on Measurement and Modeling of Computer Systems, Vol. 27, 1999, pp. 122-133.
18. Elizabeth, J. O., Patrick, E. O., Gerhard, W., The LRU-K Page Replacement Algorithm for Database Disk Buffering, ACM SIGMOD International Conference on Management of Data, Washington D.C., 1993, pp. 297-306.
19. Johnson, T., Shasha, D., 2Q: A Low Overhead High Performance Buffer Management Algorithm, Proc. of the 20th International Conference on Very Large Databases, 1994, pp. 439-450.
20. Lee, D., Choi, J., Kim, J., Noh, S., Min, S., Cho, Y., Kim, C., LRFU: A Spectrum of Policies that Subsumes the Least Recently Used and Least Frequently Used Policies, IEEE Transaction on Computers, 2001, pp. 1352-1361.
21. Jiang, S., Zhang, X., LIRS: An Efficient Low Inter-reference Recency Set Replacement Policy to Improve Buffer Cache Performance, In Proc. ACM SIGMETRICS Conf., 2002.
22. Eirc, W. W., Bayesian Analysis, MathWorld, CRC Press LLC., Wolfram Research Inc., 1999, http://mathworld.wolfram.com/BayesianAnalysis.html.
23. Sonja, P. L., Amy, W., Fuzzy Control Model in the Hospitality Industry, International Journal of Agile Management Systems, Bradford, Vol. 2, pp. 156, 2000.
24. Bannatyne, R., Development of Fuzzy Logic in Embedded Control, Sensor Review, Bradford, Vol. 14, pp. 11-15, 1994.
25. Eric, W. W., Probability Distributions, MathWorld, CRC Press LLC., Wolfram Research Inc., 1999, http://mathworld.wolfram.com/NormalDistribution.html.
26. Jain, R., The Art of Computer Systems Performance Analysis, John Wiley Inc., 1991, pp. 492-495.
27. Nimrod M., Modha S. D., ARC: A Self-Tuning, Low Overhead Replacement Cache, USENIXFAST 2003, San Francisco, March 2003.
28. Susmit B., Mads N., On the Concept of Mobile Distributed Virtual Memory System, IEEE DSN, The International Conference on Dependable Systems and Networks, IEEE CS Press, Italy, 2004.

DSP Code Generation
with Optimized Data Word-Length Selection

Daniel Menard and Olivier Sentieys

Reconfigurable and Retargetable Digital Device Group (R2D2) IRISA
6 rue de Kerampont, F-22300 Lannion, France
menard@irisa.fr
http://www.irisa.fr/R2D2/

Abstract. Digital signal processing applications are implemented in
embedded systems with fixed-point arithmetic to minimize the cost and
the power consumption. To reduce the application time-to-market,
methodologies for automatically determining the fixed-point specification are required. In this paper, a new methodology for optimizing the
fixed-point specification in the case of software implementation is described. Especially, the technique proposed to select the data word-length
under a computation accuracy constraint is detailed. Indeed, the latest
DSP generation allows to manipulate a wide range of data types through
sub-word parallelism and multiple-precision instructions. In comparison with the existing methodologies, the DSP architecture is completely
taken into account to optimize the execution time under accuracy constraint. Moreover, the computation accuracy evaluation is based on an
analytical approach which allows to minimize the optimization time of
the fixed-point specification. The experimental results underline the efficiency of our approach.

1 Introduction

Most digital signal processing algorithms are specified with floating-point data
types but they are finally implemented into fixed-point architectures to satisfy
the cost and the power consumption constraints of embedded systems. To reduce
the embedded system time-to-market, high-level development tools are required
to automate some tasks. The manual transformation of floating-point data into
fixed-point data is a time-consuming and error prone task. Indeed, some experiments [8] have shown that this manual conversion can represent up to 30% of the
global implementation time. Thus, methodologies for the automatic transformation of floating-point data into fixed-point data have been proposed [12][26].

For Digital Signal Processors (DSP), the aim is to define the optimal fixed-
point specification which maximizes the accuracy and minimizes the size and the
execution time of the code. Existing methodologies [13][26] achieve a floating-
point to fixed-point conversion leading to an ANSI-C code with integer data
types. Nevertheless, the different elements of the target DSP are not taken into
account for the process of fixed-point data coding. The analysis of the architecture influence on the computation accuracy underlines the necessity to take into

H. Schepers (Ed.): SCOPES 2004, LNCS 3199, pp. 214–228, 2004.

account the DSP architecture to obtain an optimized fixed-point specification. Particularly, the different data types supported by the latest DSP generation offer an opportunity to make a trade-off between the computation accuracy and the code execution time.

In this paper, a new global methodology for the implementation of floating-point algorithms into fixed-point processors under accuracy constraint is presented, and especially, the stage of data word-length selection is detailed. Firstly, the available methodologies for the fixed-point conversion are presented in section two. After a review of the different datapath elements in a DSP which influence the computation accuracy, the fixed-point conversion methodology is presented in section four. In section five, the data word-length determination stage is detailed. Finally, some experimental results obtained on different applications are given.

2   Related Work

In this section the different available methodologies for the automatic implementation of floating-point algorithms into fixed-point architectures are presented. These methodologies achieve the floating-point to fixed-point transformation at a high-level (source code).

The FRIDGE [11] methodology developed at the Aachen University achieves a transformation of the floating-point C source code into a C code with fixed-point data types. In the first step called *annotations*, the user defines the fixed-point format of some variables which are critical in the system or for which the fixed-point specification is already known. Moreover, global annotations can be defined to specify some rules for the entire system (maximal data word-length, casting rules). The second step called *interpolation* [25][11] corresponds to the determination of the integer and fractional part word-length for each data. The fixed-point data formats are obtained from a propagation rule set and the program control flow analysis. This step leads to an entire fixed-point specification of the application. This description is simulated to verify if the accuracy constraint is fulfilled. The commercial tool *CoCentric Fixed-point Designer* proposed by Synopsys is based on this approach.

In [26], a method called *embedded approach* is proposed for generating an ANSI-C code for a DSP compiler from the fixed-point specification obtained previously. The data (source data) for which the fixed-point formats have been obtained with the technique presented previously, are specified with the available data types (target data) supported by the target processor. The freedom degrees due to the source data position in the target data allow to minimize the scaling operations. This methodology allows to achieve a bit-true implementation in a DSP of a fixed-point specification. But the fixed-point data formats are not optimized according to the target processor and especially according to the different data types supported by this processor.

The aim of the tool presented in [13] is to transform a floating-point C source code into an ANSI-C code with integer data types to be independent of the target architecture. Moreover, a fixed-point format optimization is done to minimize the number of scaling operations. Firstly, the floating-point data types are replaced by fixed-point data types and the scaling operations are included in the code. The scaling operations and the fixed-point data formats are determined from the dynamic range information. The reduction of scaling operation number is based on the assignation of a common format to several relevant data allowing the minimization of the scaling operation cost function. This cost function depends on the processor scaling capacities. For processor with a barrel shifter, the scaling operation cost is equal to one cycle, otherwise the number of cycles required for a shift of n bits is equal to n cycles.

In this methodology, the scaling operations are minimized. But, the code execution time is not optimized under a global accuracy constraint. The accuracy constraint is only specified through the definition of a maximal accuracy degradation allowed for each data. Moreover, the architecture model used for the scaling operation minimization does not lead to an accurate estimation of the scaling operation execution time. For processor based on a specialized architecture, the scaling operation execution time depends on the data location in the datapath. Furthermore, for processors with instruction-level parallelism capacities, the overhead due to scaling operations depends on the scheduling step and can not be easily evaluated before the code generation process.

These two methodologies achieve a floating-point to fixed-point transformation leading to an ANSI-C code with integer data types. Nevertheless, the different target DSP elements are not taken into account for the fixed-point conversion. Especially, the opportunities offered by DSPs, able to manipulate a wide variety of data types, are not exploited.

3   Digital Signal Processor Architecture

DSP architectures are designed to compute efficiently the arithmetic operations involved in digital signal processing applications. Different elements of the datapath influence the computation accuracy as described in [17]. The most important element is the data word-length. Each processor is defined by its native data word-length which is the word-length of the data that the processor buses and datapath can manipulate in a single instruction cycle [14]. For most of the fixed-point DSPs, the native data word-length is equal to 16 bits. For ASIP (Application Specific Instruction-set Processor) or some DSP cores like the CEVA-X and the CEVA-Palm [20](CEVA), this native data word-length is customizable to fit better the architecture to the target application. The computation accuracy is linked to the word-length of the data which are manipulated by the operations and depends on the kind of instructions which are used for implementing the operation.

DSPs allow through classical instructions, the achievement of a multiply accumulate (MAC) operation without lost of information, by providing a double precision result. The adder and the multiplier output word-lengths are equal to the double of the native data word-length. Nevertheless, the data dynamic

Table 1. Word-length of the data which can be manipulated by different DSP for arithmetic operations (multiplication, addition, shift).

Processor	Data Types (bits)
TMS320C64x (T.I.) [23]	8, 16, 32, 40, 64
TigerSHARC (A.D.) [2]	8, 16, 32, 64
SP5, UniPhy (3DSP) [1]	8, 16, 24, 32, 48
CEVA-X1620 (CEVA) [3]	8, 16, 32, 40
ZSP500 (LSI Logic) [24]	16, 32, 40, 64
OneDSP (Siroyan)	8, 16, 32, 44, 88

range increase due to successive accumulations can lead to an overflow. Thus, some DSPs extend the accumulator word-length by providing guard bits. These supplementary bits allow the storage of the additional bits generated during successive accumulations.

Many DSPs support multiple-precision arithmetic to increase the computation accuracy. In this case, the data are stored in memory with a more important precision. The data word-length is a multiple of the natural data word-length. Given that multiple-precision operations manipulate greater data word-length, a multiple-precision operation is achieved with several classical operations. Consequently, the execution time of this operation is greater than the one of a classical operation.

To reduce the code execution time, some recent DSPs allow the exploitation of the data-level parallelism by providing SWP (Sub-Word Parallelism) capacities. An operator (multiplier, adder, shifter) of word-length N is split to execute k operations in parallel on sub-word of word-length N/k. This technique can accelerate the code execution time up to a factor k. Thus, these processors can manipulate a wide diversity of data types as shown in table 1. In [6], this technique has been used for implementing a CDMA synchronisation loop in the TigerSharc DSP [2]. The SWP capacities allow to achieve 6,6 MAC per cycle with two MAC units.

4   Fixed-Point Conversion

A new methodology for the implementation of floating-point algorithms into fixed-point DSPs under accuracy constraint has been proposed in [15]. In our methodology, the determination and the optimization of the the fixed-point specification are directed by the accuracy constraint. Moreover, the DSP architecture is completely taken into account. The code generation and the fixed-point conversion process are coupled to obtain an optimized fixed-point specification. The different phases of our methodology are presented in figure 1.

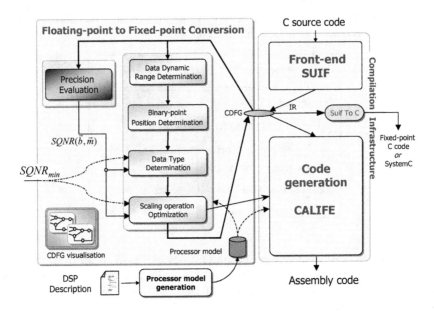

Fig. 1. Framework structure.

First, the floating-point C source algorithm is transformed with the SUIF front-end, into an intermediate representation (IR) described as a Control Data Flow Graph (CDFG). The first stage of the methodology, corresponding to the data dynamic range evaluation, is based on an analytical approach. A combination of the L1 and Chebychev norms [21] and the results of the arithmetic interval theory [9] allows to determine the data dynamic range in non-recursive systems and in recursive linear time-invariant systems.

The results obtained are used for the determination of the data binary-point position to avoid overflows. For the different application DFGs (Data Flow Graph), the binary-point positions are determined during the DFG traversal from the sources to the sinks. For each data and operator, a rule is applied for determining the position of the binary-point. This approach enables to manage adder with guard bits. In this stage, the scaling operations required to obtain a valid fixed-point specification are inserted.

The third stage corresponds to the data word-length determination to obtain a complete fixed-point format for each data. It is detailed in section five.

Finally, the scaling operation localization are optimized to minimize the code execution time as long as the accuracy constraint is fulfilled. The execution time is modified through the scaling operation moving. This stage aim is to find the scaling operation location which allows to minimize the execution time and to fulfill the accuracy constraint. Given that the instruction level parallelism is limited for conventional DSPs, the scaling operation execution time can be estimated from the execution time of the instructions used for implementing this operation. For processors with instruction level parallelism, the execution time estimation must be coupled with the scheduling stage to take account of the partial instructions which are executed in parallel. The back-end of the compilation infrastructure is based on a retargetable code generation tool [4].

The determination and the optimization of the fixed-point specification are made under accuracy constraint. The accuracy is evaluated trough the Signal to Quantization Noise Ratio (SQNR) metric. An analytical method [18] that enables to obtain automatically the SQNR expression from the application CDFG is used in this flow.

5   Data Type Determination

In the fixed-point conversion design flow, each data type (word-length) is determined to obtain a complete fixed-point format for each data of the CDFG. This module must allow to explore the diversity of the data types available in recent DSPs as explained in section three. To increase the computation accuracy, multiple-precision operations can be used. Nevertheless, the execution time is more important. To reduce the computation execution time, data parallelism can be exploited trough Sub-Word Parallelism operations in recent DSPs. Consequently, the precision of the computation is reduced.

The main goal of the code generation process is to minimize the code execution time under a given accuracy constraint. Thus, our methodology selects the instructions which will respect the global accuracy constraint and minimize the code execution time. The methodology structure is presented in figure 2. Before to start the optimization process, different stages must be achieved. They correspond to the accuracy evaluation, the instruction selection and the application execution time estimation.

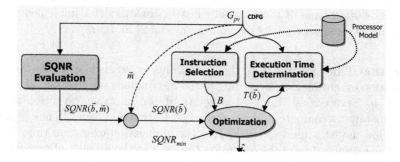

Fig. 2. Structure of the data type determination process. This process is applied to the CDFG (G_{pv}) obtained after the determination of the data binary-point positions.

5.1   Accuracy Evaluation

The most common used criteria for evaluating the computation accuracy is the Signal to Quantization Noise Ratio (SQNR) [12][10]. Traditional methods [5][12] are based on fixed-point simulations. But these techniques lead to huge fixed-point optimization time. Indeed, multiple simulations are needed for this optimization process, since a new fixed-point simulation is required when any fixed-point data format is modified. Thus, the methodology based on an analytical method and proposed in [18], is used. It allows to determine automatically the analytical expression of the Signal to Quantization Noise Ratio for a CDFG. In a fixed-point system, the output quantization noise is due to the propagation of the different noise sources generated during cast operations. The output noise power expression is computed from the noise source statistical parameters and the gain between the output and each noise source. For linear time-invariant systems, these gains are determined with the help of the transfer function concept.

The CDFG is made up of N_o operations o_i. Let b_i and m_i be the word-length and binary-point position of the operation o_i operands. Let $\overrightarrow{b} = [b_1, b_2, \ldots, b_i, \ldots b_{N_o}]$ and $\overrightarrow{m} = [m_1, m_2, \ldots, m_i, \ldots m_{N_o}]$ be the vectors specifying respectively the word-length and the binary-point position of all CDFG operation operands. The SQNR expression is obtained according to the vector $\overrightarrow{b}$ and $\overrightarrow{m}$.

5.2   Estimation of the Code Execution Time

DSP Processor Modelization. The processor is modelized by a Data Flow (DF) instruction set. These instructions implement arithmetic operations and data transfers between the memory and the processing unit. The instructions are obtained from one or several instructions of the processor instruction set. Each DF instruction j_k is characterized by its function γ_k, by its operand word-length b_k and by its execution time t_k. This execution time is obtained from the processor model. For SWP instructions, the execution time is set to the processor instruction execution time divided by the number of operations achieved in parallel. For the multiple-precision instructions, the execution time is the sum of the execution time of the processor instructions used for implementing this operation. A processor model example is presented in figure 3.a.

Execution Time Estimation. The aim of this section is to estimate the global application execution time according to the instructions selected for each CDFG operation. Nevertheless, the goal is not to obtain an exact execution time estimation but to compare and to select two instruction series. Thus, a simple estimation model is used for evaluating the application execution time T. This time T is computed from the execution time t_i and the number of executions n_i of each operation o_i as follows

$$T = \sum_i t_i . n_i \tag{1}$$

This estimation method is based on the sum of the instruction execution times and leads to accurate results for DSPs without instruction parallelism. For DSPs with instruction level parallelism (ILP), this method does not take account of the instructions executed in parallel. Nevertheless, this estimation gives results which allow to compare efficiently two instruction series in the case of processor with ILP.

For classical and SWP instructions, the gains due to the transformation (code parallelization) of the vertical code into an horizontal one are closed. Indeed, the two instruction series use the same functional units at the same clock cycles. The difference lies in the functionality of the processor unit. For SWP instructions, the functional units manipulate fractions of word instead of the entire word.

A multiple-precision instruction corresponds to a serie of classical instructions. Thus, in the best case and after the scheduling stage, the multiple-precision instruction execution time can be equal to the execution time of the classical precision instructions. In this case, the classical operations must be favored if the precision constraint is fulfilled to reduce the data memory size. Therefore, the multiple-precision instruction execution time is set to the maximal value to select these multiple-precision instructions only if the classical instructions can not fulfill the precision constraint.

This approach for the code execution time estimation can be improved with more accurate techniques such as those presented in [7][22].

5.3   Data Word-Length Optimization

For each CDFG operation o_i, the different instructions, which allow to achieved o_i, are selected. Let I_i, be the set specifying the instructions selected for the operation o_i. Let B_i, be the set specifying all the word-lengths which can be taken by the operation o_i operands. Thus, for each operation o_i, the optimal word-length $\widehat{b}_i$ ($\widehat{b}_i \in B_i$) which allows to minimize the global execution time $T(\overrightarrow{b})$ and to respect the minimal precision constraint must be selected. Consequently, the application execution time $T(\overrightarrow{b})$ is minimized as long as the accuracy constraint ($SQNR_{min}$) is fulfilled as described in equation 2. This optimization process is illustrated with a FIR filter example in figure 3.

$$\min_{\overrightarrow{b} \in B} \left(T(\overrightarrow{b}) \right) \quad \text{such as} \quad SQNR(\overrightarrow{b}) \geq SQNR_{min} \tag{2}$$

Given that the number of values for each variable b_i is limited, the optimization problem can be modelized with a tree and a *branch and bound* algorithm can be used to obtain the optimized solution. This technique leads to an exponential optimization time. Consequently, the success of this approach is based on the limitation of the search space. Four techniques presented in the next section are used for limiting the search space.

5.4   Search Space Limitation

Instruction Combination Restriction. The modelization of this optimization problem with a tree allows to enumerate exhaustively all the solutions. Nevertheless, all the instruction combinations are not valid. For illustrating this problem, an example is presented in figure 4. The operation inputs and output

Instruction	Function	Execution	I/O operand word-length		
J_k	γ_k	time t_k	b^{in1}	b^{in2}	b^{out}
J_1	MULT	0.25	8	8	16
J_2	MULT	0.5	16	16	32
J_3	MULT	1	32	32	64
J_4	ADD	0.25	16	16	16
J_5	ADD	0.5	32	32	32
J_6	ADD	1	64	64	64

(a) **Data Flow instruction set**

(b) **Application DFG**

(c) **Solution modelization with a tree**

Fig. 3. Modelization of the data word-length optimization process for a FIR filter. (a) Modelization of the processor data flow instructions (b) FIR filter Data Flow Graph (c) Modelization with a tree of the different solutions of the optimization problem.

are annotated with their fixed-point format. Given that the operation o_l input is the result of the operation o_k, the number of bits for the fractional part of the o_l input can not be strictly greater than the number of bit for the fractional part of the o_k output. Thus, the instruction tested for the operation o_l is valid if the following conditions are fulfilled

$$
\begin{aligned}
n_k^s &\geq n_l^e \\
n_l^s &\geq n_h^e
\end{aligned}
\tag{3}
$$

If the conditions 3 are not respected, the exploration of the subtree is stopped and a new instruction is tested for the operation o_l. This technique allows to reduce significantly the search space.

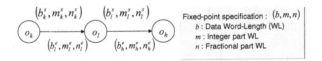

Fig. 4. Data flow example.

Partial Solution Evaluation. In the *branch-and-bound* algorithm, the partial solutions are evaluated to stop the tree exploration, if they can not lead to the best solution.

At the tree level l, the exploration of the subtree induced by the node representing $\widehat{b}_l$ can be stopped if the minimal execution time which can be obtained during the exploration of this subtree is greater than the minimal execution time which has already been obtained. Given that only the word-lengths b_0 to b_l are defined, the minimal execution time is determined by selecting for the operation o_j ($j \in [l+1, N_o]$), the instruction with the minimal execution time t_j. In most of the case, it is equivalent to select for the operation o_j, the instruction with the minimal operand word-length ($\underline{b}_j$). In this case, for each tree level l, the following relation is obtained

$$T([\widehat{b}_0, \ldots, \widehat{b}_{l-1}, \widehat{b}_l, \underline{b}_{l+1}, \ldots, \underline{b}_{N_o}]) \leq T([\widehat{b}_0, \ldots, \widehat{b}_{l-1}, \widehat{b}_l, b_{l+1}, \ldots, b_{N_o}]) \tag{4}$$

At the tree level l, the exploration of the subtree induced by the node representing $\widehat{b}_l$ can be stopped if the maximal SQNR which can be obtained during the exploration of this subtree is lower than the precision constraint ($SQNR_{min}$). The SQNR maximal value is obtained by fixing the word-lengths b_j ($j \in [l+1, N_o]$) to their maximal values. Indeed, given that the SQNR is a monotonous and rising function, the SQNR maximal value is obtained for the maximal operand word-length ($\overline{b}_j$). Thus, for each tree level l, the following relation is obtained

$$SQNR([\widehat{b}_0, \ldots, \widehat{b}_{l-1}, \widehat{b}_l, \overline{b}_{l+1}, \ldots, \overline{b}_{N_o}]) \geq SQNR([\widehat{b}_0, \ldots, \widehat{b}_{l-1}, \widehat{b}_l, b_{l+1}, \ldots, b_{N_o}]) \tag{5}$$

Node Evaluation Order. This optimization technique based on a tree exploration is sensitive to the node evaluation order. To find quickly a good solution for reducing the search space, the variables with the most influence on the optimization process must be evaluated first. The variables are sorted by their influence on the global execution time and the SQNR.

Reduction of the Number of Values per Variable. For applications with a great number of variables, the optimization time can become huge. To obtain reasonable optimization time, the optimization is achieved in two steps. Firstly, the variables corresponding to the data word-length are considered as positive integer numbers and a classical optimization technique is used for minimizing the code execution time under accuracy constraint. Let $\widetilde{b}_i$ be the optimized solution obtained with this technique for the variable b_i. Secondly, the technique based on the *branch-and-bound* algorithm presented previously is applied with a reduced number of values per variable. For each variable b_i, only the values which are member of B_i and immediately higher and lower than $\widetilde{b}_i$ are retained. Thus only, two values are tested for each variable and the search space is dramatically reduced.

6   Experiments

6.1   Complex Correlator

The complex correlator application is used for the de-spreading operation in a CDMA receiver [19]. It achieves the correlation between a complex signal x

and a complex code c. In this experiment, the complex correlator characteristic $T_{opt} = f(SQNR_{min})$ is determined for the TMS320C64x architecture model. This characteristic defines the optimized execution time obtained for a given SQNR constraint. It allows to analyse the trade-off between the execution time and the computation accuracy offered by the processor. The results are presented in figure 5. This characteristic is obtained by applying our word-length optimization method for different SQNR constraints. Each point (ρ_o, T_o) of the curve $T_{opt} = f(SQNR_{min})$ represents the optimized execution time (T_o) obtained for the SNQR constraint ρ_o. This experiment has been achieved with no constraint on the data types for the application input and output. The execution time is normalized with the execution time obtained with a classical implementation called implementation 2.

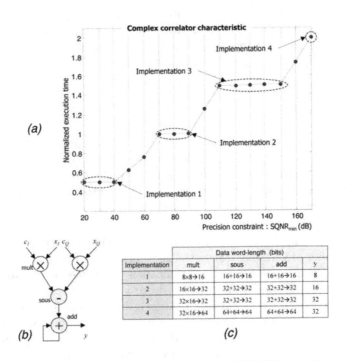

Fig. 5. (a) Complex correlator characteristic $T_{opt} = f(SQNR_{min})$. For each SQNR constraint $(SQNR_{min})$, the optimized execution time T_{opt} is reported. (b) Data Flow Graph for the correlator real part computation (c) Details of the different particular implementations obtained for the complex correlator characteristic.

The curve evolves by stage. The fixed-point specifications associated with each particular implementation are detailed in the table presented in figure 5.c. The implementations 1, 2 and 4 are based on the same structure. The data are stored in memory with b_n bits. The multiplication leads to a result with $2.b_n$ bits and the addition operand word-length is equal to $2.b_n$. For the implementations

1, 2 and 4, the word-length b_n is respectively equal to 8, 16 and 32 bits. For the implementation 3, the data are stored in memory with 32 bits and the addition operand word-length is equal to 32 bits. Thus, the computations are achieved on single precision with this implementation. It allows to reduce the application execution time compare to the implementation 4. This characteristic underlines the trade-off between the execution time and the computation accuracy obtained for new DSP generation with SWP capacities. For the different implementations, the optimization time is less than 8 seconds.

6.2   Second Order IIR Filter

The previous example underlines our methodology interest for DSPs with SWP capacities. Nevertheless, this methodology can be used to implement applications which require high precision into conventional DSPs. Indeed, this methodology allows to select classical or multiple-precision instructions. For illustrating these aspects, a second order Infinite Impulse Response (IIR) filter is implemented into the DSP TMS320C54x.

The SQNR obtained with an implementation based on classical operations is low (50 dB). To increase the computation accuracy, double precision operations are used. The characteristic $T_{opt} = f(SQNR_{min})$ obtained with the TMS320C54x architecture model is presented in figure 6. The execution time is normalized with the classical implementation (implementation 1) execution time.

The implementation 2 leads to an interesting trade-off. For the implementations 1 and 2, the input and output filter word-lengths are equal to 16 bits. Thus, the input and output fixed-point specifications of implementation 1 and 2 are identical. Nevertheless, the implementation 2 allows to increase the output SQNR of 40 dB and leads to an execution time growth of only 60% compared to implementation 1. For this solution, the recursive part of the filter uses double precision operations and the data z_y are stored in memory with 32 bits to limit the accuracy loss. For the different implementations, the optimization time is less than 5 seconds.

6.3   WCDMA Receiver

A more complex application, corresponding to a WCDMA rake receiver, has been tested. This application is integrated into third-generation radio communication systems (UMTS) [19]. This rake receiver is made up of a symbol estimation part and a synchronization part [16]. Before to start the fixed-point conversion process, the minimal precision constraint $(SQNR_{min})$ must be defined. The SQNR minimal value is obtained with the technique detailed in [16] according to the receiver performances evaluated through the Bit Error Rate (BER).

The methodology has been used to obtain the application fixed-point specification. The target processor is the TMS320C64x high performance VLIW DSP. The different scaling operations are moved towards the coefficients to reduce the code execution time. The opportunities offered by the SWP instructions allow to

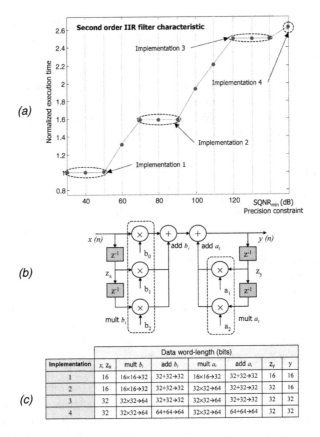

Fig. 6. (a) IIR filter characteristic $T_{opt} = f(SQNR_{min})$. For each SQNR constraint ($SQNR_{min}$), the optimized execution time T_{opt} is reported. (b) Data Flow Graph for the IIR filter (c) Details of the different particular implementations obtained for the IIR filter characteristic.

decrease significantly the code execution time. For the symbol estimation part, the execution time is reduced from a factor of 3.5 compared to a solution based only on classical instructions. For the synchronization part, the execution time is divided by a factor of 3.1. The different techniques proposed for the limitation of the search space allow to obtain an optimization time lower than 3 minutes for this application.

7   Conclusion

In this paper, a new methodology for the implementation of floating-point algorithms into fixed-point architectures under accuracy constraint has been presented. Compared to a manual based approach, this kind of tool enables to reduce significantly the application time-to-market. The stage for the data word-length selection has been detailed. The aim of this phase is to select the set of instructions which allows to respect the global accuracy constraint and to minimize the code execution time. The different techniques used to limite the search space to obtain reasonable optimization time have been presented. The experiment results show the different possible trade-offs between the accuracy and the execution time. Our method underlines the different opportunities offered by DSPs with SWP capacities.

References

1. 3DSP. *SP-5 Fixed-point Signal Processor Core*. 3DSP Corporation, July 1999.
2. Analog Device. *TigerSHARC Hardware Specification*. Analog Device, December 1999.
3. CEVA. *CEVA-X1620 Datasheet*. CEVA, 2004.
4. F. Charot and V. Messe. A Flexible Code Generation Framework for the Design of Application Specific Programmable Processors. In *7th international workshop on Hardware/Software Codesign, CODES'99*, Rome, Italy, May 1999.
5. M. Coors, H. Keding, O. Luthje, and H. Meyr. Fast Bit-True Simulation. In *Design Automation Conference 2001 (DAC-01)*, Las Vegas, US, June 2001.
6. D. Esftathiou, J. Fridman, and Z. Zvonar. Recent developpements in enabling technologies for the software-defined radio. *IEEE Communication Magazine*, pages 112–117, August 1999.
7. N. Ghazal, R. Newton, and J. Rabaey. Predicting performance potential of modern dsps. In *DAC 00*, 2000.
8. T. Grötker, E. Multhaup, and O.Mauss. Evaluation of HW/SW Tradeoffs Using Behavioral Synthesis. In *7th International Conference on Signal Processing Applications and Technology (ICSPAT 96)*, Boston, October 1996.
9. R. Kearfott. Interval Computations: Introduction, Uses, and Resources. *Euromath Bulletin*, 2(1):95–112, 1996.
10. H. Keding, F. Hurtgen, M. Willems, and M. Coors. Transformation of Floating-Point into Fixed-Point Algorithms by Interpolation Applying a Statistical Approach. In *9th International Conference on Signal Processing Applications and Technology (ICSPAT 98)*, 1998.
11. H. Keding, M. Willems, M. Coors, and H. Meyr. FRIDGE: A Fixed-Point Design And Simulation Environment. In *Design, Automation and Test in Europe 1998 (DATE-98)*, 1998.
12. S. Kim, K. Kum, and S. Wonyong. Fixed-Point Optimization Utility for C and C++ Based Digital Signal Processing Programs. *IEEE Transactions on Circuits and Systems II*, 45(11), November 1998.
13. K. Kum, J. Kang, and W. Sung. AUTOSCALER for C: An optimizing floating-point to integer C program converter for fixed-point digital signal processors. *IEEE Transactions on Circuits and Systems II - Analog and Digital Signal Processing*, 47:840–848, September 2000.
14. P. Lapsley, J. Bier, A. Shoham, and E. A. Lee. *DSP Processor Fundamentals: Architectures and Features*. Berkeley Design Technology, Inc, Fremont, CA, 1996.
15. D. Menard, D. Chillet, F.Charot, and O. Sentieys. Automatic Floating-point to Fixed-point Conversion for DSP Code Generation. In *International Conference on Compilers, Architectures and Synthesis for Embedded Systems 2002 (CASES 2002)*, Grenoble, October 2002.

16. D. Menard, M. Guitton, S. Pillement, and O. Sentieys. Design and Implementation of WCDMA Platforms : Challenges and Trade-offs. In *nternational Signal Processing Conference (ISPC 03)*, Dallas, April 2003.

17. D. Menard, P. Quemerais, and O. Sentieys. Influence of fixed-point DSP architecture on computation accuracy. In *XI European Signal Processing Conference (EUSIPCO 2002)*, Toulouse, September 2002.

18. D. Menard and O. Sentieys. Automatic Evaluation of the Accuracy of Fixed-point Algorithms. In *Design, Automation and Test in Europe 2002 (DATE-02)*, Paris, March 2002.

19. T. Ojanper and R. Prasad. *WCDMA : Towards IP mobility and mobile internet.* Artech House Universal Personal Communications Series, 2002.

20. B. Ovadia and G. Wertheizer. PalmDSPCore - Dual MAC and Parallel Modular Architecture. In *10th International Conference on Signal Processing Applications and Technology (ICSPAT 99)*, Orlando, November 1999. Miller Freeman Inc.

21. T. Parks and C. Burrus. *Digital Filter Design.* Jhon Willey and Sons Inc, 1987.

22. A. Pegatoquet, E. Gresset, M. Auguin, and L. Bianco. Rapid Development of Optimized DSP Code from a High Level Description through Software Estimations. In *DAC 99*, 1999.

23. Texas Instruments. *TMS320C64x Technical Overview.* Texas Instruments, February 2000.

24. S. Wichman and N. Goel. *The Second Generation ZSP DSP*, 2002.

25. M. Willems, V. Bursgens, H. Keding, and H. Meyr. System Level Fixed-Point Design Based On An Interpolative Approach. In *Design Automation Conference 1997 (DAC 97)*, June 1997.

26. M. Willems, V. Bursgens, and H. Meyr. FRIDGE: Floating-Point Programming of Fixed-Point Digital Signal Processors. In *8th International Conference on Signal Processing Applications and Technology (ICSPAT 97)*, 1997.

Instruction Selection for Compilers
that Target Architectures with Echo Instructions

Philip Brisk, Ani Nahapetian, and Majid Sarrafzadeh

Computer Science Department
University of California, Los Angeles,
Los Angeles, California, 90095
{philip,ani,majid}@cs.ucla.edu

Abstract. Echo Instructions have recently been introduced to allow embedded processors to provide runtime decompression of LZ77-compressed programs at a minimal hardware cost compared to other recent decompression schemes. As embedded architectures begin to adopt echo instructions, new compiler techniques will be required to perform the compression step. This paper describes a novel instruction selection algorithm that can be integrated into a retargetable compiler that targets such architectures. The algorithm uses pattern matching to identify repeated fragments of the compiler's intermediate representation of a program. Identical program fragments are replaced with echo instructions, thereby compressing the program. The techniques presented here can easily be adapted to perform procedural abstraction, which replaces repeated program fragments with procedure calls rather than echo instructions.

1 Introduction

For embedded system designers, the mandate to minimize costs such as memory size and power consumption trumps any desire to optimize performance. For these reasons, one approach that has prevailed in recent years has been to store the program in compressed form on-chip, thereby reducing the size of on-chip memory. Decompression in this context may be performed either software or hardware. Software decompression severely limits performance, whereas decompression in hardware requires custom circuitry. If the goal is to minimize the total transistor count on the chip while providing runtime decompression, then the savings in storage cost must dominate the cost of the decompression circuitry. Echo Instructions [1] [2], introduced in 2002, provide architectural support for the execution of LZ77-compressed programs while requiring considerably less physical area than comparable hardware-based decompression schemes. Echo instructions are therefore likely to become standard features in embedded architectures within the next few years. To exploit echo instructions for the purpose of reducing code size, new compiler techniques will be necessary.

This paper presents a novel instruction selection algorithm for retargetable compilers that target architectures featuring echo instructions. This algorithm identifies recurring patterns in a program's intermediate representation and replaces them with

H. Schepers (Ed.): SCOPES 2004, LNCS 3199, pp. 229–243, 2004.
© Springer-Verlag Berlin Heidelberg 2004

echo instructions, thereby compressing the program. Echo instructions, unlike procedure calls, do not require stack frame manipulation and parameter passing, and thus allow a higher rate of compression. At the same time, replacement of identical code sequences with echo instructions imposes additional constraints on the register allocator, which must assign registers, perform coalescing, and insert spill code in such a way that the program fragments identified by the instruction selection algorithm are mapped to identical code sequences in the final program. Identical code fragments may then be replaced with echo instructions during final code emission.

The paper is organized as follows. Section 2 discusses related work. Section 3 describes our contribution: an instruction selection algorithm that is tailored to the task of code compression using echo instructions. Section 4 describes our experimental results and analysis, which we believe justifies our algorithms and approach. Section 5 concludes the paper.

2   Related Work

2.1   Echo Instructions and LZ77 Compression

Fraser [1] proposed the echo instruction to allow the runtime execution of programs compressed using a variant of the LZ77 algorithm [3] that analyzes assembly code as opposed to sequential data. The LZ77 algorithm compresses a character string by identifying recurring substrings, which are replaced by pointers to the first occurrence of the substring. Each pointer contains two fields expressed as a pair (offset, length), which is assumed to be equivalent to a single character. Offset is the distance from the pointer to the beginning of the first instance of the substring. Length is the number of characters in the substring. An example of LZ77 compression is shown in Figure 1.

An echo instruction contains two immediate (constant-valued) fields: offset and length, exactly like LZ77 compression. The basic sequence of control operations for a sequential echo instruction is described as follows.

1. Branch to PC – offset
2. Execute the next length instructions
3. Return to the original call point

| Original String: | **ABCDBCABCDBACABCDBDAABCDBABC** |
| Compressed String: | **ABCDBC(6, 5)AC(9, 5)DA(12, 5)(13, 3)** |

Fig. 1. A string compressed using the LZ77 algorithm. Each pair (offset, length) is assumed to comprise one character. In practice, the actual number of bits required to encode each pair depends on the number of bits required to express the pointer and offset, as well as the number of bits required to encode each specific character

Echo instructions are quite similar to procedure calls, however there are several stark differences. First and foremost, an echo instruction may branch to any arbitrary location in instruction memory; procedure calls explicitly branch to the first statement of the procedure body. Secondly, an echo instruction explicitly encodes the number of instructions that will execute before execution returns to the call point; a procedure call, in contrast, will continue to execute instructions until a return instruction that terminates the body of the procedure is encountered. Third, the code sequences referenced by two echo instructions may overlap. For example, repeated patterns may overlap, as exemplified by patterns ABCDE and ABC in Figure 1. Under procedural abstraction, these two patterns, despite their redundancy, require two separate subroutine bodies; it should be noted that ABCDE could call ABC as a subroutine itself. Finally, the echo instruction is a single branch, whereas each procedure call will inevitably be coupled with instructions that pass parameters, save and restore register values, and manipulate the stack frame.

Lau et. al. [2] described the bitmasked echo instruction, which combined the sequential echo instruction with predicated execution. The length field is replaced with a bitmask field. If the ith bit of bitmask is set, then the ith instruction from the beginning of the sequence is executed; otherwise, a NOP is executed. The primary advantage of bitmasked echo instructions is that they allow non-identical code fragments to reference a common code sequence. Unfortunately, they do not scale well to large instruction sequences. If we assume that the length and bitmask fields of the sequential and bitmasked echo instructions both require n bits, then a sequential echo may reference patterns containing as many as 2^n instructions; the bitmasked echo, however, can only reference sequences containing at most n instructions.

Lau et. al. described an approach for architectural support for echo instructions for embedded processors. To do this required two registers – one to hold the address of the original call point, and the other to hold the value length. As each of the length instructions in step 2 above is executed, length is decremented. When the value of length reaches zero, control is transferred back to the call point. In addition to the two registers, a reverse counter, a comparator, and a multiplexer are the only datapath components required. Of course, hardware corresponding to the appropriate new controller states must also be accounted for. The issue of hardware cost will be revisited in Section 2.3, when we compare echo instructions to other hardware-based decompression techniques.

2.2 Procedural Abstraction

Procedural abstraction is a compile-time code-size optimization that identifies repeated sequences of instructions in an assembly-level program and replaces them with procedure calls. The body of each procedure is identical to the sequence it replaces. Procedural abstraction requires no special hardware, but entails significant overhead due to parameter passing, saving and restoring registers, and stack frame manipulation. A substring matching approach based on suffix trees proposed by Fraser et. al. [4] has been a widely recognized algorithm for procedural abstraction. Two instructions are mapped to the same character if and only if all fields in the instruction are equal. Fraser's algorithm performed procedural abstraction at link time, following register allocation and instruction scheduling. Consequently, it was unable to identify semantically equivalent instruction sequences that were identical to one another within a rescheduling of instructions and/or a renaming of registers. The basic algorithm has since been updated with register renaming [5] [6] and instruction reordering [2] to match a wider variety of patterns. Runeson [7] recently advocated an approach by which procedural abstraction is performed prior to register allocation, which is similar to our work in spirit. Register renaming is not applicable here because register allocation has not yet been performed, nor is instruction reordering applied.

Our approach differentiates itself from these previous techniques by using graph isomorphism rather than substring matching to identify repeated code fragments. Like Runeson, our algorithm is performed prior to both register allocation and instruction scheduling. Therefore, our algorithm detects equivalent patterns based on the dependence structure of operations rather than an arbitrary ordering of quadruples. Another distinction is that previous approaches operate on the granularity of basic blocks. If two basic blocks are semantically equivalent, they are replaced with procedure calls; otherwise, they are not. Our approach identifies recurring patterns within blocks that may differ only by a few instructions.

2.3   Code Compression in Hardware

Lefurgy et. al. [8] proposed a form of dictionary compression which assigns variable-length codewords to sequences based on the frequency with which each sequence occurs. Each codeword is translated into an index value, which is used to access a dictionary that holds a decompressed instruction sequence corresponding to each codeword. The dictionary access is incorporated into the processor's instruction fetch mechanism. The Call Dictionary (CALD) instruction, introduced by Liao et. al. [9], exploits repeated code fragments in a similar manner to echo instructions. The instruction sequences are placed into an external cache, which is referenced by CALD instructions. Echo instructions, alternatively, always refer to the main instruction stream, thereby eliminating the need for the external cache.

The Compressed Code RISC Processor (CCRP) [10] [11] allows a compiler to divide a program into blocks, which are then compressed using Huffman encoding. Blocks are decompressed when they are brought into the instruction cache, requiring a Huffman decoder circuit to be placed between memory and cache. The CPU remains oblivious to the runtime decompression mechanism; only the cache is redesigned. A similar approach was taken by IBM's CodePack [12] [13] [14], which divided 32-bit instructions into 16-bit halves that are compressed independently. A decompression circuit is similarly placed between memory and cache.

In the above examples, the cost of the hardware that performs the decompression is a potential limiting factor. Echo instructions require considerably less hardware that dictionaries – which are essentially memory elements – and Huffman decoders. We do not argue that echo instructions provide the highest quality compression compared to these schemes. The key to the future success of echo instructions is their low physical cost, which translates to a lower price paid by the consumer.

3 Instruction Selection for Echo Instructions

The traditional problem of instruction selection in compiler theory involves transforming a program represented in the intermediate representation (IR) to a linear list of machine instructions. An echo instruction, in contrast, is a placeholder that represents a finite-length linear sequence of instructions. The technique presented here decouples the traditional instruction selection and the detection of code sequences to be replaced with echo instructions. We present an algorithm that identifies repeating patterns within the IR. Each instance of each pattern is replaced by an echo instruction. The algorithm is placed between the traditional instruction selection and register allocation phases of a compiler. This work, it should be noted, does not consider bitmasked echo instructions [2].

A basic block is a maximal-length instruction sequence that begins with the target of a branch and contains no interleaving branch or branch target instructions. We represent each basic block with a Dataflow Graph (DFG). Vertices represent machine instructions, and edges represent dependencies between instructions. The advantage of the DFG representation is no explicit ordering is imposed on the set of the instructions. The only scheduling constraints are imposed by dependencies in the DFG. DFGs are directed acyclic graphs, where vertices represent operations and edges represent direct data dependencies between operations. Two graphs $G_1 = (V_1, E_1)$ and $G_2 = (V_2, E_2)$ are isomorphic if there exists a function f: $V_1 \rightarrow V_2$ satisfying

$$(v_1, v_2) \in E_1 \Leftrightarrow (f(v_1), f(v_2)) \in E_2 \qquad (1)$$

The graph isomorphism problem has not been proven NP-Hard; however, no polynomial-time solution has been found either [15]. To perform isomorphism testing, we used the publicly available VF2 algorithm [16], which has a worst-case time complexity of $O(nn!)$, but runs efficiently for the majority of DFGs we tested.

A pattern is defined to be a subgraph of any DFG. Patterns are assigned integer labels such that two patterns have equal labels if and only if they are isomorphic. To reduce the number of isomorphism tests required to label a pattern, we store the set of patterns in a hash table. For pattern p, a hash function h(p) is computed over some combination of invariant properties of p. Invariant properties are numeric properties of the graph that must be equal if the two graphs are isomorphic. For example, we consider the number of vertices and edges in p, the critical path length of p, and the frequency distribution of vertex and/or edge labels in p. Using this approach, we must only test p for isomorphism against patterns p' satisfying h(p') = h(p).

Any non-overlapping set of patterns that are isomorphic may be replaced by echo instructions. Our intuition is that patterns that occur with great frequency throughout the IR are the best candidates to be replaced by echo instructions. The most frequently occurring patterns will most likely be small – containing just one or two operations, but may be embedded within larger patterns that occur less frequently. A competent scheduling algorithm could account for this fact when scheduling the instruction sequences referenced by echo instructions to maximize pattern overlap.

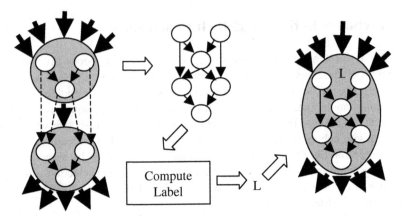

Fig. 2. Generating, Labeling, and Clustering a Pattern Between Two Supernodes

The algorithm described in the next section generates patterns in terms of smaller sub-patterns. The process of labeling, and clustering a pattern composed of subpatterns is shown in Figure 2. The bold edge shows that there are data dependencies between the sub-patterns, and the dashed edges represent the actual dependencies. The resulting pattern is assigned a uniquely identifying integer label, which is computed using the isomorphism testing technique described above.

3.1 Algorithm Description

The instruction selection algorithm presented here is based on a framework for regularity extraction described in [17]. The algorithm, shown in Figure 3, is applied between an instruction selection pass that is unaware of echo instructions and a register allocation pass that ensures reusability among pattern instances. To avoid complications due to control flow, the pattern detection algorithm ignores branches. The input to the algorithm is a set of DFGs G*. A local variable, M, is a function that maps vertices, edges, and patterns to a set of integer labels. These labels are used to identify semantically equivalent operations. Since register allocation has not been performed, it is unnecessary to consider register usage in our definition of operation equivalence.

The algorithm begins by calling **Label_Vertices_and_Edges(...)**. This function assigns integer labels to vertices such that two vertices are assigned equal labels if and only if their opcodes match, and all immediate operands – if any – have the same value. Edges are assigned labels to distinguish whether or not they are the left or right inputs to a commutative operator. These edge labels allow us distinguish the seemingly dissimilar instructions $c = a - b$ and $c = b - a$. Note that for a commutative operation $\circ$, $a \circ b$ and $b \circ a$ are semantically equivalent.

Next, the algorithm enumerates a set of patterns using the function **Generate_Edge_Patterns(...)**. For each edge $e = (u, v)$, the subgraph $G_e = (\{u, v\}, \{e\})$ is generated as a candidate pattern. Each candidate pattern is assigned a label as described in the previous section.

```
Algorithm:         Echo_Instr_Select(G*, Threshold, Limit)

Parameters:        G* := {Gi = (Vi, Ei)} : set of n DFGs
                   Threshold, Limit : integer

Variables:         M : mapping from vertices, edges, and  pat-
                       terns to labels.
                   Pi : set of patterns
                   Conflict(Gi, p) : conflict graph
                   MIS(Gi, p) : independent set
                   gain(p), best_gain : integer
                   best_ptrn : pattern (DFG)

1.   For i = 1 to n
2.       Label_Vertices_and_Edges(M, Gi)
3.       Generate_Edge_Patterns(M, Gi)
4.   EndFor
5.   For each pattern p in M
6.       gain(p) := 0
7.       For i := 1 to n
8.           Pi := Generate_Overlapping_Patterns(Gi, p)
9.           If Pi is not empty
10.              Conflict(Gi, p) :=
                     Compute_Conflict_Graph(Pi)
11.              MIS(Gi, p) := Compute_MIS(G, Limit)
12.              gain(p) := gain(p) + |MIS(Gi, p)|
13.          EndIf
14.      EndFor
15.  EndFor
16.  best_gain := max{gain(p)}
17.  best_ptrn := p s.t. gain(p) = best_gain
18.  While best_gain > Threshold
19.      For i := 1 to n
20.          Cluster_Indep_Patterns(M, Gi, MIS(Gi, best_ptrn))
21.          Update_Patterns(M, Gi, MIS(Gi, best_ptrn))
22.      EndFor
23.      best_gain := max{gain(p)}
24.      best_ptrn := p s.t. gain(p) = best_gain
25.  EndWhile
```

Fig. 3. Echo Instruction Selection Algorithm

The next step is to identify the pattern that offers the greatest gain in terms of compression. Lines 5-17 of the algorithm accomplish this task. Given a pattern p and a DFG G, the gain associated with p, denoted gain(p) is the number of subgraphs of G that can be covered by instances of pattern p, under the assumption that overlapping patterns are not allowed.

An example of a DFG with a set of overlapping patterns is shown in Figure 4 (a). Given a set of overlapping patterns, determining the largest set of non-overlapping patterns is akin to finding a maximum independent set (MIS), a well-known NP-Complete Problem [15]. An overlap graph for the example in Figure 4 (a) is shown in Figure 4 (b). The shaded vertices in Figure 4 (b) represent one of several MISs. The resulting set of non-overlapping patterns is shown in Figure 4 (c).

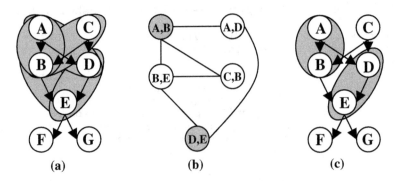

Fig. 4. Overlapping patterns (a), a Conflict Graph (b), and Independent Set (c)

The function **Compute_Conflict_Graph(…)** creates the conflict graph, and the function **Compute_MIS(…)** computes its MIS. To compute the MIS, we use a randomized iterative improvement algorithm described in [18]. The algorithm begins with a randomly generated independent set (IS). During each iteration, the algorithm randomly adds and removes vertices to and from the independent set. The algorithm terminates after it undergoes a fixed number (Limit) of iterations without improving the size of the largest MIS. Limit is set to 500 for our experiments.

The cardinality of the MIS is the gain associated with pattern p for DFG G. This is because each pattern instance combines two nodes and/or patterns into a single pattern, for a net reduction in code size of one. The best gain is computed by summing the gain of each pattern over all DFGs. The pattern with the largest net gain is the best pattern, p_{best}. Each pattern instance is replaced with a supernode that maintains the internal input-output connectivity of the original pattern. Furthermore, all of the original data dependencies must be maintained. We refer to the process of replacing a pattern instance with a supernode as *clustering*. Once all instances of a given pattern are clustered, we update the set of patterns and adjust their respective gains. Then, we can once again identify the best pattern, and decide whether or not to continue.

Clustering is performed by the function **Cluster_Independent_Patterns(…)** and is illustrated in Figure 5 (a) and (b). The dashed edges in Figure 5 (b) indicate data dependencies that must be maintained across pattern boundaries; these edges are technically removed from the graph and replaced with bold edges that represent dependencies between patterns. Figure 5 (b) illustrates this process. Each addition operation has been subsumed into a supernode. Technically, each dashed edge is removed from the graph, and replaced with a bold edge between supernodes. Bold edges are characterized by the fact that at least one of their incident vertices is a supernode; they are also used to generate larger patterns from smaller ones in future iterations of the algorithm, as illustrated in Figure 2.

Now that an initial set of patterns has been generated, we must update the frequency count for all remaining patterns in G. The function **Update_Patterns(…)** performs this task. In particular, the bold edges enable several different 3 and 4-node patterns to be generated. The most favorable pattern is then selected for clustering, and the algorithm repeats again. The algorithm terminates when the best gain is less-than-or-equal-to a user-specific parameter, *Threshold*; we set threshold to 1.

Figure 5 (c) shows a second iteration of the algorithm. The resulting patterns subsume the patterns generated previously during the algorithm, yielding larger pattern instances. At this point, no further patterns can be generated that occur more than once in the DFG, so the algorithm terminates. One of the two resulting pattern instances is replaced with an echo instruction, which references the other instance as shown in Figure 5 (d). At least one instance of each uniquely identifiable pattern must be left in the program; otherwise, it simply couldn't execute. For example, if an instance existed elsewhere in the program, both instances could be replaced with echo instructions, as illustrated in Figure 5 (e). Ideally, the pattern that is left intact should reside in a portion of the program that executes frequently – namely a loop body.

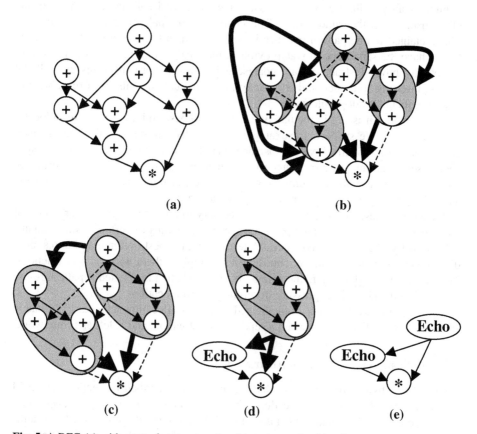

Fig. 5. A DFG (a) with a set of patterns replaced by supernodes (b), after a second iteration (c), and with one of the supernodes replaced with an echo instruction (d). If the pattern existed elsewhere in the program, both could be replaced with echo instructions (e)

3.2   Implications for Register Allocation

The algorithm presented in the previous section identifies patters that occur throughout the compiler's intermediate representation of the program; it does not, however, ensure that these patterns will be mapped to identical code sequences in the final program. In particular, the compiler must enforcing identical register usage among instances of identical patterns.

A register allocator performs three primary functions: mapping live ranges to physical registers, inserting spill code, and coalescing redundant move instructions, effectively eliminating them. To the best of our knowledge, no existing register allocation techniques maximize reuse of previously identified code fragments.

To ensure pattern reuse, corresponding live ranges in instances of identical patterns must be mapped to the same physical register. Inserting spill code into a fragment eliminates all possibilities for its re-use, unless identical spill code is inserted into other instances of the same pattern. The same goes for coalescing: if a move instruction contained in one pattern instance is coalesced, then that pattern instance will no longer have the same topology as previously identical pattern instances – unless corresponding move instructions are coalesced in those pattern instances as well. Of course, inserting spill code and coalescing move instructions outside of reusable program fragments is not problematic.

At this point, it is not immediately clear how to best optimize a register allocator for code reuse. We suspect, for example, that strictly enforcing register assignment constraints for all identical pattern instances may lead to an inordinate amount of spill code inserted around pattern boundaries, which may lead to sub-optimal results in terms of code size. Similarly, enforcing all-or-none constraints for spill code insertion and coalescing within patterns may be problematic as well.

Because of these problems, it may be necessary to instantiate several non-identical code sequences for each unique pattern; each instance must therefore be made identical to exactly one of these sequences. Alternatively, the best option may be to simply discard certain pattern instance, choosing not to replace them with echo instructions. This approach could alleviate the amount of spill code that is inserted if pattern re-use leads to inordinate register pressure in certain program locations.

At this point, we have not implemented a register allocation scheme; this issue is sufficiently complicated to warrant a separate investigation, and is left as future work.

3.3   Application to Procedural Abstraction

It should be obvious to the reader that the algorithm described in Section 3.1 could easily be adapted to perform procedural abstraction. Pattern instances are replaced by procedure calls rather than echo instructions. Procedure calls, however, have additional overhead associated with them: parameter passing, stack frame allocation and deallocation, and saving and restoring register values to memory. This will entail a different approach to estimating the potential gain of each pattern, which must incorporate the number of inputs and outputs to each pattern as well as the number of nodes in the pattern. Since this work focuses on architectures supporting echo instructions, we leave this investigation as an open avenue for future work.

4 Experimental Methodology and Results

4.1 Motivation and Goals

In this section, we evaluate the effectiveness of the instruction selection algorithm described in Section 3. Since we have not yet implemented a register allocation scheme, a complete evaluation of our compression technique is impossible. The results presented in this section therefore count the number of IR operations that have been subsumed by patterns; they do not reflect actual final code sizes. In particular, we cannot know, a priori, exactly how many move instructions will be coalesced by the register allocator; moreover, we cannot immediately determine how much spill code the allocator will introduce, or where it will be introduced. Finally, we cannot determine whether or not our pattern re-use will lead to the introduction of additional move instructions (or spill code) that the allocator would otherwise not have inserted.

Instead, we decouple our evaluation of the instruction selection technique from the register allocator. The purpose of the experiments presented here are twofold. First, we wish to show that the instruction selection algorithm is capable of achieving favorable compression under an ideal register allocator. This is necessary to justify a future foray into register allocation. Secondly, we recognize that our demands for pattern reuse may impede the register allocator's ability to reduce code size by coalescing move instructions. Admittedly, we cannot explore this tradeoff without a register allocator in place. To compensate, we measure the effectiveness of our instruction selection technique under both ideal and less-than-ideal assumptions regarding the allocator.

Ideally, we would like to compare the results of our technique with Lau et. al. [2]; unfortunately, this comparison is inappropriate at the present time. Our analysis has been integrated into a compiler, whereas Lau's is built into Squeeze [5], a binary optimization tool. Squeeze performs many program transformations on its own in order to compress the resulting program. Lau's baseline results used Squeeze to compress the program in absence of echo instructions. Because the back end of our compiler has not been completed, we cannot yet interface with a link-time optimizer such as Squeeze. Therefore, the transformations that yielded Lau's baseline results are unavailable to us at the present time.

4.2 Framework and Experimental Methodology

We implemented our instruction selection algorithm into the Machine SUIF compiler framework [19]. Machine SUIF includes passes that target the Alpha and x86 architectures. We selected the Alpha as a target, primarily because Lau et. al. [2] did the same, and this will enable future comparisons between the two techniques. The Machine SUIF IR is a CFG, with basic blocks represented as lists of quadruples – similar to the IR used by Runeson [7]. We performed a dependence analysis on the instruction lists, and generated a DFG for each basic block. Instruction selection was performed for the alpha target using the do_gen pass, provided with Machine SUIF. Following this pass, we applied our instruction selection algorithm.

The Machine SUIF compiler considers only one source code file at a time. We apply the instruction selection algorithm to all DFGs in each input file, but we do not attempt to detect patterns across multiple files. Considering every DFG in an entire program at once would yield superior compression results; however, we believe that the results presented here are sufficient to justify our algorithmic contributions.

Finally, we do not attempt to measure the performance overhead that arises due to echo instructions. Although we could have generated some preliminary estimates by using profiling to determine the execution frequency for each basic block, we believe that these numbers would be inaccurate. One side effect of compressing a program is that a greater portion of it can fit into cache at any given time, thereby reducing the miss rate [20]. This can often mitigate the performance penalty due to additional branching that arises due to compression. Profiling alone cannot experimentally capture these nuances; cycle-accurate simulation would be more appropriate. We cannot perform this type of simulation until the register allocator is complete.

4.3   Approximating the Effects on Register Allocation

Machine SUIF liberally sprinkles move instructions throughout its IR as it is constructed. An effective register allocator must aggressively coalesce these moves in order to compress the program. We performed experiments under two sets of assumptions: *optimistic*, and *pessimistic*. The optimistic model assumes that all move instructions will be coalesced by the allocator; the pessimistic model, in contrast, assumes that none are coalesced. In practice, most register allocators will coalesce the majority of move instructions, but certainly not all of them.

The majority of graph coloring register allocators (e.g. Briggs [21] and George-Appel [22]) coalesce as many move instructions as possible. We call these allocators Pessimistic Allocators, because they do not coalesce move instructions until it is provably safe to do so – in other words, no spill code will be inserted as a result. A recent Optimistic Allocator, developed by Park and Moon [23], reverses this paradigm. Their allocator initially coalesces all move instructions. Following this, the optimistic allocator only inserts moves as an alternative to spill code.

The pessimistic assumption approximates a lower bound on the size number of moves coalesced by the allocator; the optimistic assumption provides an upper bound. These bounds, however, do not include estimates of code size increases due to spill code insertion. If a live range existing in on pattern instance is spilled, we can safely spill the corresponding live range in all other instances of the same pattern, although this will likely hurt performance. More significantly, we cannot estimate whether move instructions will be inserted at pattern boundaries. Despite these inaccuracies, we believe that the experiments detailed in section 4.5 validate the effectiveness of our instruction selection technique.

4.4   Benchmark Applications

We selected a set of eight applications from the MediaBench [24] and MiBench [25] benchmark suites. These benchmarks are summarized in Table 1.

Table 1. Summary of Benchmark Applications

Benchmark	Description
ADPCM	Adaptive Differential Pulse Code Modulation
Blowfish	Symmetric Block Cipher with Variable Key Length
Epic	Experimental Image Data Compression Utility
G721	Voice Compression
JPEG	Image Compression and Decompression
MPEG2 Dec	MPEG2 Decoder
MPEG2 Enc	MPEG2 Encoder
Pegwit	Public Key Encryption and Authentication

Upon inspecting the source code for several of these benchmarks, we observed that many were written in a coding style with loops manually unrolled. Loop unrolling exposes instruction-level parallelism to a processor, but at the expense of code size. An embedded system designer who wished to minimize code size would not unroll loops. To mimic this coding style, we rewrote the programs ourselves, which reduced both the size of the program and the size of certain basic blocks within the program. The latter, in turn, reduced the overall runtime of our compiler as well.

4.5   Results and Elaboration

The experimental results for our set of benchmarks under both pessimistic and optimistic assumptions are shown in Table 2. The pessimistic results assume that the register allocator is unable to coalesce any move instructions. The optimistic results assume that all move instructions are coalesced, except for those used for parameter passing during procedure calls. The columns entitled Uncompressed and Compressed show the number of DFG operations in each benchmark before and after our instruction selection algorithm, which effectively compresses the program. Each move instruction that is coalesced reduces program size as well.

Under pessimistic assumptions, our instruction selection technique the net code size reduction across all benchmarks was 36.25%; under optimistic assumptions, the net code size reduction was 25.00%. Taking pessimistic uncompressed code size as a baseline, compression under optimistic assumptions reduced net code size by 45.29%. Although the optimistic results yield a greater net reduction in code size than the pessimistic results, the fraction of the code size reduction attributable to instruction selection is considerably less for the optimistic results than the pessimistic results.

For all applications other than APDCM – which is considerably smaller than every other benchmark – the compressed pessimistic results yield a smaller code size than the uncompressed optimistic results. If the opposite were true, then echo instructions might not be an appropriate form of compression; instead, focusing on coalescing as a code size reduction technique might have been a better strategy. Altogether, our results empirically verify the effectiveness of our instruction selection strategy.

Table 2. Experimental Results showing the code size of each program before and after compression. The Pessimistic Results assume that the register allocator is unable to coalesce any move instructions; the Optimistic Results assume that all move instructions are coalesced

Benchmark	Pessimistic		Optimistic	
	Uncompressed	Compressed	Uncompressed	Compressed
ADPCM	1273	954	839	764
Blowfish	5822	3137	3909	2515
Epic	11320	7459	7646	6070
G721	4445	3067	3122	2527
JPEG	83036	52992	61484	46342
MPEG2 Dec.	18248	11939	13487	10328
MPEG2 Enc.	24710	15925	18494	13510
Pegwit	17718	10720	12531	9082

5 Conclusion

This paper describes an instruction selection algorithm for compilers that target architectures featuring echo instructions. The instruction selection algorithm identifies replaces repeated patterns in the compiler's IR with echo instructions, thereby compressing the program. The instruction selection algorithm must be coupled with a register allocator to ensure identical register usage among isomorphic patterns. Under a set of pessimistic assumptions, our instruction selection algorithm reduced code size by 36.25% on average. A more realistic study, under more optimistic assumptions showed an average reduction in code size of 25.00%.

References

1. Fraser, C. W.: An Instruction for Direct Interpretation of LZ77-compressed Programs. In: Microsoft Technical Report TR-2002-90 (2002)
2. Lau, J., Schoemackers, S., Sherwood, T., and Calder, B.: Reducing Code Size With Echo Instructions. In: CASES. (2003)
3. Ziv, J., and Lempel, A.: A Universal Algorithm for Sequential Data Compression. In: IEEE Trans. on Information Theory, 23(3) (1977) 337-343
4. Fraser, C. W., Myers, E. W., and Wendt, A.: Analyzing and Compressing Assembly Code. In ACM Symposium on Compiler Construction. (1984)
5. Debray, S., Evans, W., Muth, R., and De Sutter, B.: Compiler Techniques for Code Compaction. In: ACM Trans. Programming Languages and Systems, 22(2) (2000) 378-415
6. Cooper, K. D., and McIntosh, N. Enhanced Code Compression for Embedded RISC Processors. In: International Conference on Programming Language Design and Implementation (1999).
7. Runeson, J.: Code Compression Through Procedural Abstraction before Register Allocation. Masters Thesis, University of Uppsala (1992)
8. Lefurgy, C. Bird, P., Chen, I., and Mudge, T.: Improving Code Density Using Compression Techniques. In: 30th International Symposium on Microarchitecture (1997)

9. Liao, S., Devadas, S., and Keutzer, K.: A Text-compression-based Method for Code Size Minimization in Embedded Systems. In: ACM Trans. Design Automation of Embedded Systems, 4(1) (1999) 12-38

10. Wolfe, A., and Chanin, A.: Executing Compressed Programs on an Embedded RISC Architecture. In 25th International Symposium on Microarchitecture (1992)

11. Kozuch, M., and Wolfe, A.: Compression of Embedded System Programs. In: IEEE Int. Conf. Computer Design (1994)

12. Kemp, T. M., Montoye, R. K., Harper, J. D., Palmer, J. D., and Auerbach, D. J.: A Decompression Core for PowerPC. In: IBM Journal of Research and Development, 42(6) (1998) 807-812

13. Game, M, and Booker, A.: CodePack: Code Compression for PowerPC Processors, Version 1.0. In: Technical Report, IBM Microelectronics Division.

14. Lefurgy, C., Piccininni, E., and Mudge, T.: Evaluation of a High Performance Data Compression Method. In: 32nd International Symposium on Microarchitecture (1999).

15. Garey, M. R., and Johnson, D. S.: Computers and Intractability: A Guide to the Theory of NP-Completeness. W. H. Freeman and Co. (1979)

16. Cordella, L. P., Foggia, P., Sansone, C., and Vento, M.: An Improved Algorithm for Matching Large Graphs. In: The 3rd IAPR-TC15 Workshop on Graph-based Representations (2001)

17. Kastner, R., Kaplan, A., Memik, S. O., and Bozorgzadeh, E.: Instruction Generation for Hybrid Reconfigurable Systems. In: ACM Trans. Design Automation of Embedded Systems, 7(4) (2002) 605-627.

18. Kirovski, D., and Potkonjak, M.: Efficient Coloring of a Large Spectrum of Graphs. In: Design Automation Conference (1997).

19. http://www.eecs.harvard.edu/hube/research/machsuif.html

20. Kunchithapadam, K., and Larus, J. R.: Using Lightweight Procedures to Improve Instruction Cache Performance. In: University of Wisconsin-Madison Technical Report CS-TR-99-1390 (1999)

21. Briggs, P., Cooper, K. D., and Torczon, L.: Improvements to Graph Coloring Register Allocation. In: ACM Trans. Programming Languages and Systems, 16(3) (1994) 428-455

22. George, L., and Appel, A. W.: Iterated Register Coalescing. In: ACM Trans. Programming Languages and Systems, 18(3) (1996) 300-324

23. Park, J., and Moon, S. M.: Optimistic Register Coalescing. In: International Conference on Parallel Architectures and Compilation Techniques (1998)

24. Lee, C., Potkonjak, M., and Mangione-Smith, W.: MediaBench: A Tool for Evaluating and Synthesizing Multimedia and Communications Applications. In: 30th International Symposium on Microarchitecture (1997)

25. Guthaus, M. R., Ringenberg, J. S., Ernst, D., Austin, T. M., Mudge, T., and Brown, R. B.: MiBench: A free, commercially representative embedded benchmark suite. In: IEEE 4th Annual Workshop on Workload Characterization (2001)

A Flexible Tradeoff Between Code Size and WCET Using a Dual Instruction Set Processor[*]

Sheayun Lee[1], Jaejin Lee[1], Chang Yun Park[2], and Sang Lyul Min[1]

[1] School of Computer Science and Engineering
Seoul National University
Seoul 151-742, Korea
sylee@archi.snu.ac.kr, jlee@cse.snu.ac.kr, symin@dandelion.snu.ac.kr
[2] Department of Computer Science and Engineering
Chungang University
Seoul 156-756, Korea
cypark@cau.ac.kr

Abstract. Embedded systems are often constrained in terms of both code size and execution time, due to a limited amount of available memory and real-time nature of applications. A dual instruction set processor, which supports a reduced instruction set (16 bits/instruction) in addition to a full instruction set (32 bits/instruction), allows an opportunity for a tradeoff between these two performance criteria. Specifically, while the reduced instruction set can be used to reduce code size by providing smaller instructions, a program compiled into the reduced instruction set typically runs slower than the same program compiled into the full instruction set. Motivated by this observation, we propose a code generation technique that exploits this tradeoff relationship by selectively using the two instruction sets for different sections in the program. The proposed technique not only provides a mechanism to enable a flexible tradeoff between a program's code size and its execution time, but also optimizes the program towards enhancing its WCET (worst case execution time). The results from our experiments show that our proposed technique can be effectively used to fine-tune an application program on a spectrum of code size and worst case performance, which in turn enables a system-wide optimization on memory space and execution speed involving multiple applications.

1 Introduction

Embedded systems are characterized by complex requirements due to the diversity of application areas and tight cost constraint. For example, in a cost-sensitive

---

[*] This work was supported in part by the Ministry of Education under the Brain Korea 21 Project in 2004, by the Ministry of Science and Technology under the National Research Laboratory program, and by the IT SoC Promotion Group of the Korean IT Industry Promotion Agency under the Human Resource Development Project for IT SoC Key Architects. The ICT at Seoul National University provided research facilities for this study. An earlier version of this paper appeared in the Proceedings of the 3rd International Workshop on Worst-Case Execution Time Analysis, 2003.

H. Schepers (Ed.): SCOPES 2004, LNCS 3199, pp. 244–258, 2004.

system with a limited amount of memory, application code size is of utmost importance. On the other hand, real-time embedded systems have stringent constraints on the execution times of application programs, to meet deadlines even in the worst case. In many systems both constraints are present, where the code size and the execution time should be considered at the same time in order to build cost-effective systems.

A *dual instruction set processor* offers a challenging problem in code generation, where we should consider a tradeoff between code size and execution speed. Such processors have been developed to provide a method to generate compact code by supporting both a full (normal) instruction set and a reduced instruction set, in which an instruction has a smaller number of bits [1]. Examples include the 16-bit Thumb instruction set in addition to the 32-bit ARM instruction set [2], the MIPS 32/16-bit TinyRISC [3], and the ARC Tangent [4] processors. When such a processor is employed, the code size can be reduced by using the reduced instruction set. However, in general, a program compiled into the reduced instruction set typically runs slower than its full instruction set counterpart. The main reason behind this performance gap is that the full instruction set program executes fewer instructions, since a single full instruction can perform more operations than a single reduced instruction.

This motivates us to exploit the tradeoff relationship between the code size and the WCET (worst case execution time) for real-time embedded systems, where the amount of available memory is limited and tasks must meet timing requirements. We propose a code generation technique that enables a flexible tradeoff between a program's code size and its WCET by selectively using the two instruction sets for different sections within a single program. The technique is based on selective code transformation [5], where a given program is first compiled into the reduced instruction set, and later a selected subset of basic blocks are transformed into the full instruction set. The selection of blocks to be transformed is made in such a way that the reduction of WCET is maximized within a given code size budget.

The main contributions of our technique are the following. First, by providing a quantitative analysis on the tradeoff relationship between a program's code size and WCET, it facilitates the development of a system-level design framework that optimizes a system with multiple application programs on memory space and execution speed. Second, unlike traditional compiler techniques that aim at optimizing programs for average case performance, the proposed technique guides the program optimization towards improving the worst case performance by incorporating a WCET analysis technique in the code generation process.

The rest of the paper is organized as follows. In the next section, we give an overview of related work. Section 3 describes the overall framework of our proposed approach. In Section 4, we detail the selective code transformation algorithm for optimizing a given program for enhanced WCET. Then, we describe the implementation of our technique and present the results in Section 5. Finally, Section 6 concludes the paper.

2   Related Work

Halambi *et al.* [1] developed a method to reduce code size by using a dual instruction set processor. In their approach, a given program is first compiled into generic instructions, and then translated into different instruction sets. The technique groups consecutive generic instructions that may be translated into the reduced instruction set, and decides whether to translate these instructions depending on the estimated size of the resulting code. This approach focuses mainly on minimizing the code size by generating mixed instruction set code, largely ignoring the impacts on performance.

Another technique for generating code for a dual instruction set processor has been proposed by Krishnaswamy and Gupta [6]. They propose four heuristic methods to improve instruction cache performance by using different instruction sets for different functions. In addition to this function-level approach, they developed a fine-grained approach, where the program is first compiled into the reduced instruction set, and certain predefined sequences of instructions are replaced by full instructions that accomplish the same operations. For this purpose, they apply a pattern matching algorithm to identify the sequences of instructions that are better executed in the full instruction set.

The selective code transformation technique [5] was proposed as an approach to generate mixed instruction set code by determining the instruction set to be used for each basic block. In this approach, the program is first compiled into the reduced instruction set, and then a selected subset of basic blocks are transformed into the full instruction set. In order to select the blocks to be transformed, a detailed cost-benefit model has been developed based on the execution profile information of the program.

Our approach is distinguished from the previous techniques in that we aim to optimize the program for its worst case performance instead of average case execution time. A few attempts have been made to build a link between program optimization and WCET analysis. Lim *et al.* [7] describe a WCET analysis technique for optimized programs, focusing on the correspondence between a program's control structure and the optimized machine code. They propose a compiler-assisted approach, where the timing analysis relies on an optimizing compiler that provides a consistent hierarchical representation and a source-level correspondence.

Another approach to WCET analysis for optimized programs has been proposed by Kirner [8]. In this technique, the author proposes a method to transform the flow facts required in the timing analysis in parallel with compiler optimizations. That is, whenever the compiler performs a code enhancing transformation, the information needed to search for the longest execution path is updated accordingly, and then used for the WCET analysis of the optimized program.

While the above mentioned approaches focus on analyzing the WCET of optimized programs, a recent study by Zhao *et al.* [9] describes a method to facilitate an environment to tune the WCET of a program by using an interactive compilation system. The approach aims at finding a program transformation sequence that yields good worst case performance, by allowing the user to gauge

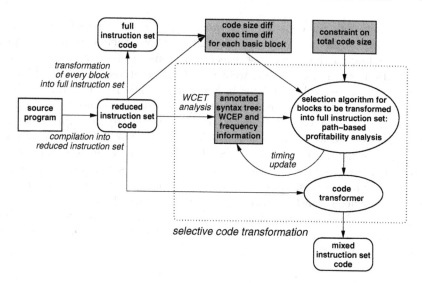

Fig. 1. The proposed code generation framework. By incorporating a WCET analysis technique, the code transformation is guided towards optimizing the WCET within the code size limit of the whole program.

the progress of reducing the WCET during the compilation process. In addition, they propose a technique to automatically search for an effective optimization sequence using a genetic algorithm.

3   Overall Approach

Our code generation technique consists of three steps. First, we compile the entire program into the reduced instruction set. The resulting code serves as the baseline for the code size, i.e., the smallest code possible for the given program. Second, we determine the set of basic blocks to be transformed into the full instruction set that gives the maximum reduction of WCET while maintaining the code size under a given upper bound. Finally, the selected blocks are transformed into the full instruction set and a mixed instruction set code is generated as a result.

This procedure is illustrated in Figure 1. In order to decide which blocks to transform, we need information regarding the code size and execution time of each block when it is compiled into the reduced instruction set or the full instruction set. The code size of each block in either instruction set can be estimated in a straightforward manner by examining the instruction sequence. On the other hand, the (worst case) execution time of each block is analyzed using an architecture description that models pipelined execution of instructions. We obtain the code size and execution time information of basic blocks in the full instruction set by performing the transformation on each basic block.

In addition to the code size and execution time differences for basic blocks, the selection algorithm requires information about their execution frequency corresponding to the worst case execution scenario. To derive this frequency information, we perform a hierarchical WCET analysis. The WCET analysis technique will be explained later in Section 4.3. The result of this analysis is given as an annotated syntax tree that encodes the worst case timing information as well as the WCEP (worst case execution path) including basic block execution counts, as will be explained later in Section 4.3. The execution frequency information in the WCEP, combined with the code size and execution time differences, is input to the selection algorithm that determines the set of basic blocks to be transformed into the full instruction set. The algorithm selects the blocks whose transformation is estimated to give the most WCET savings within the code size budget. Based on its results, a code transformer performs transformation of the selected blocks into the full instruction set to generate the final mixed instruction set code.

4   Selective Code Transformation for WCET Optimization

This section details the selective code transformation framework used in our proposed code generation technique for dual instruction set processors. Intuitively, it is desirable to transform the blocks that are frequently executed under the worst case execution scenario, and that have large execution time differences in the two instruction set modes. We cannot, however, consider the basic blocks individually, since transforming a single block will usually degrade the WCET due to the mode switching overhead while nonetheless increasing the total code size. Specifically, transition between the two instruction set modes is typically triggered by executing a special instruction or sequence of instructions. Therefore, when the two instruction sets are used within a single program in a mixed manner, the code generator must insert mode switch instructions at appropriate program points. A fair amount of attention needs to be paid to these mode switch instructions, since inserting many of them can significantly increase the code size. Moreover, frequent transitions between the two modes by executing the mode switch instructions generally degrade the overall performance of the program by incurring a large execution time overhead.

To address this problem, our selective code transformation incorporates a profitability analysis based on the concept of *acyclic subpaths* [10], which are defined as the maximal subpaths that do not traverse any back edge of a loop. Since the acyclic subpaths capture the set of basic blocks that are likely to be executed together, we define a cost-benefit model based on them as the selection criteria for blocks to be transformed, as will be explained in Section 4.1.

Using this profitability analysis, an iterative selection algorithm is applied to determine the set of blocks to be transformed. The algorithm incrementally improves the WCET of the program by selecting in each iteration the set of blocks whose transformation will give the most WCET savings per unit increase in the code size. A detailed description of the algorithm will be given in Section 4.2.

In order to steer the code transformation towards enhancing the program's WCET in each iteration of the selection algorithm, we need a mechanism to detect a possible change in the WCEP resulting from transforming the selected basic blocks. To this end, we propose a method to update the timing information on the annotated syntax tree by propagating the effect of changes in the transformed blocks' execution times. The propagation is done in such a way that only the portions of the program whose execution times have changed are re-analyzed. This timing update scheme will be described in Section 4.3.

4.1   Path-Based Profitability Analysis

A program is given by a control flow graph $P = \langle V, E \rangle$, where $V = \{v_i \mid i = 1, 2, \ldots, n\}$ is the set of basic blocks and $E = \{e_{ij} = \langle v_i, v_j \rangle\}$ is the set of edges which represent the control flow in the program. Assume that a subset of basic blocks are in the full instruction set mode and the remaining blocks are in the reduced instruction set mode. That is, the set of blocks V is partitioned into two disjoint subsets F and R, which denote the set of blocks in the full and the reduced instruction sets, respectively.

We define a set of notations for the code size and execution time of a basic block compiled into the two different instruction sets. Let $s_F(v)$ and $s_R(v)$ denote the code size of a block v compiled into the full and the reduced instruction sets, respectively. Similarly, we denote by $t_F(v)$ and $t_R(v)$ the (worst case) execution times of block v compiled into the full and the reduced instruction sets, respectively.

Given a path p, the cost of its transformation is defined as the increase in the code size by transforming the blocks on that path into the full instruction set, taking the mode switching overhead into account. It can be calculated by first summing the code size differences for the blocks being transformed, and then adding the mode switching overhead to the sum. Note that transforming a set of basic blocks not only causes insertion of new mode switch instructions but also possibly results in removal of certain mode switch instructions that were previously needed. Specifically, when a block is transformed from the reduced instruction set into the full instruction set, the mode switch instructions should be removed from the edges connecting the block with other blocks that are already in the full instruction set mode.

To account for the insertion and removal of mode switch instructions due to transforming a path p, we define $E^M(p)$ to be the set of edges where mode switch instructions are newly introduced, and $E^m(p)$ to be the set of edges from which existing mode switch instructions are removed. These two sets can be computed by analyzing the control flow graph of the program. In addition, we let $V(p)$ denote the set of all the basic blocks on p. Then the set of blocks to be transformed is given by $V(p) \cap R$, which contains only the blocks on p that have not yet been transformed. Then the cost $c(p)$ of transforming p can be calculated by

$$c(p) = \sum_{v \in V(p) \cap R} (s_F(v) - s_R(v)) + o_s \times \left(|E^M(p)| - |E^m(p)| \right) , \qquad (1)$$

where o_s is the total size of instructions required for a single mode switch.

On the other hand, the benefit $b(p)$ associated with path p is defined to be the reduction in the WCET of the whole program by transforming the blocks on that path, taking the mode switching overhead into account. It can be computed by first summing the execution time difference for each block multiplied by its execution frequency, and then subtracting the mode switching overhead. That is,

$$b(p) = \sum_{v \in V(p) \cap R} (c_V(v) \times (t_R(v) - t_F(v)))$$

$$- o_t \times \left(\sum_{e \in E^M(p)} c_E(e) - \sum_{e \in E^m(p)} c_E(e) \right), \qquad (2)$$

where o_t denotes the execution time overhead incurred by a single mode switch, while $c_V(v)$ and $c_E(e)$ give the execution counts of a block v and an edge e, respectively.

Now we define a reward function $r(p)$ for a subpath p to be the ratio of its benefit to its cost. That is, $r(p) = b(p)/c(p)$ gives the expected amount of WCET reduction for the unit increase in the code size. Using this profitability analysis based on the cost-benefit model, a greedy algorithm determines which blocks are to be transformed in order to maximize the WCET reduction within a given code size limit, as will be explained in the following section.

4.2   Selection Algorithm

Based on the path-based profitability analysis described in the previous section, the algorithm for selecting blocks to be transformed proceeds as follows. First, we set the code size budget to equal the difference between the upper bound on the code size and the total code size of the program compiled entirely into the reduced instruction set. We begin by enumerating all the acyclic subpaths of the program's WCEP, and add them to the set of candidate subpaths. For each of the candidate subpaths, we evaluate the reward function $r(p)$ by calculating the cost and benefit associated with it. Then we apply a simple heuristic that iteratively selects among the candidate subpaths the one with the maximum value of the reward function, provided that its cost does not exceed the remaining code size budget. The blocks on the selected subpath are (assumed to be) transformed into the full instruction set. In each iteration of the algorithm, the code size budget is adjusted accordingly, as well as the set of candidate subpaths.

The selection procedure is repeated until no more transformation can be done because either one of the following conditions hold: (1) selection of any of the remaining subpaths would violate the code size limit, or (2) no further reduction of the WCET is possible by transforming more blocks. The algorithm described above is illustrated in Figure 2.

Note that, in each iteration, when a subpath is selected and the blocks on it are transformed, the cost and benefit associated with other candidate subpaths may change, since (1) the transformed blocks may be shared by other subpaths, and (2) inserting or removing mode switch instructions possibly affects the cost

V: set of all the basic blocks in the program
U_s: upper bound on the total code size
S_R: code size of the program when compiled entirely
 into the reduced instruction set

$B \leftarrow U_s - S_R$
$R \leftarrow V$
$F \leftarrow \phi$
$P \leftarrow \{\text{acyclic subpaths of the WCEP}\}$

while (there exists a path $p \in P$ s. t. $c(p) \leq B$ and $b(p) \geq 0$) {
 for each $p \in P$, calculate $r(p) = b(p)/c(p)$
 select $p \in P$ with maximum $r(p)$ with $c(p) \leq B$
 $B \leftarrow B - c(p)$
 $F \leftarrow F \cup V(p)$
 $R \leftarrow R - V(p)$
 if (change in the WCEP)
 $P \leftarrow \{\text{acyclic subpaths of the new WCEP}\}$
 else
 $P \leftarrow P - \{p \mid V(p) \cap R = \phi\}$
}

Fig. 2. Algorithm for selection of blocks to be transformed. After the algorithm is finished, F will contain the blocks to be transformed from the reduced instruction set into the full instruction set.

and benefit of other subpaths. Therefore, we adjust the cost and benefit of transforming each of the remaining subpaths as we iterate the selection procedure.

Moreover, since the execution time of the WCEP is reduced by transforming the selected subpath, it is no longer guaranteed to have the largest execution time among all the possible execution paths in the program. When the WCEP changes due to the transformation, we should enumerate the acyclic subpaths of the new WCEP and resume the selection procedure. Therefore, we need a method to determine whether or not the WCEP of the program has changed due to the transformation. We should do this without re-analyzing the whole program every time a subpath is selected and transformed, since analyzing a program's WCET has a substantial complexity. This can be done by updating the timing information on the annotated syntax tree generated in the initial analysis of WCET, as will be detailed in the next section.

4.3 Timing Update Using an Annotated Syntax Tree

Hierarchical analysis of a program's WCET works with a syntax tree of the program and a set of timing formulas operating on each node in the tree. The syntax tree of a program is a hierarchical representation of its control structure, where intermediate nodes correspond to program constructs and leaf nodes are the basic blocks. To estimate the WCET of a program, nodes in its syntax tree are recursively visited, while different timing formulas are applied to different types of program constructs (sequential statements, conditional statements, loops, etc) to calculate the WCET of the corresponding program construct.

To enable the timing information update resulting from transformation of a subset of blocks, we propose an extension to the basic timing schema [11], similar to the ETS (extended timing schema) [12] that was originally developed as a technique to take into account pipelining and caching effects in hierarchical WCET analysis. Specifically, each node in the syntax tree is associated with a data structure called WCTA (worst case timing abstraction) instead of a single execution time bound. A WCTA of a program construct contains timing information of every execution path that *might* be the worst case execution path for that program construct. Each element in a WCTA is called a PA (path abstraction), which encapsulates the information regarding the execution path that it represents. In addition to the path's WCET, a PA holds the pipeline information about a sufficient number of leading and trailing instructions of the path. This information is used to model the pipelined sequential execution of this path preceded or succeeded by other paths in evaluating a parent node's timing formula. Besides, this information allows us to account for the mode switching overhead incurred by sequential execution of two basic blocks in different instruction set modes.

With this extension, analyzing a program's WCET effectively enumerates all the possible execution paths in the program. Note, however, that the set of all the possible execution paths can be substantially large, making the time and space complexity of the analysis too high to be practical. Therefore, in applying a timing formula for a program construct, we prune the PAs for paths that are guaranteed not to be part of the WCEP of the whole program [12]. With this pruning operation, such paths are not considered in analyzing the program constructs that are at higher levels in the program's hierarchical structure.

For the purpose of updating the timing information as basic blocks are incrementally transformed, we annotate the syntax tree with the WCTA associated with each node when the whole program's WCET is initially analyzed. Afterwards, when a subpath is selected for transformation, we first identify the leaf nodes that correspond to the basic blocks being transformed. Then we propagate the execution time changes from those leaf nodes upwards in the annotated syntax tree by updating the WCTAs of the nodes being encountered until we reach the root node. Since the nodes are visited in a bottom-up manner when we propagate the timing updates, we analyze the nodes in an order according to their depths. That is, instead of recursively traversing the entire tree, we process the nodes at the same distance from the root node at the same time, so that no node is visited more than once. This way, the timing update re-analyzes only the intermediate nodes on the path from the root node to leaf nodes corresponding to the blocks being transformed, while the recorded WCTAs are reused for all the other nodes.

Figure 3 gives an example of the timing update explained above. Assume that the selection algorithm has decided to transform an acyclic subpath *c-d-*

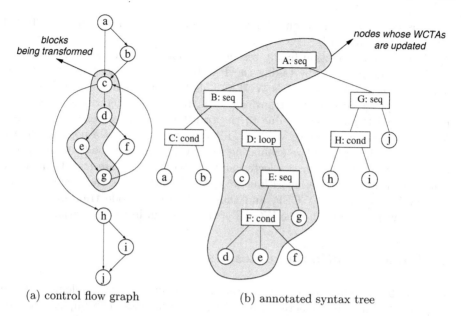

(a) control flow graph   (b) annotated syntax tree

Fig. 3. Timing update example. Only the portion of the program affected by the transformation is re-analyzed to detect a possible change in the WCEP.

e-g in the loop. Then, beginning from the leaf nodes that correspond to the transformed basic blocks, the timing update is propagated on the annotated syntax tree. When we compute the WCTA for a conditional statement node F, it has two PAs in it: one for path d-e and the other for path d-f. Since we know that blocks d and f are in different instruction set modes, we let the PA for path d-f account for the mode switch that occurs when control flows from block d to block f.

Then the timing information continues to propagate to node E, and the WCTA for the node is updated. This node's WCTA has two distinct execution paths: d-e-g and d-f-g. In analyzing the execution time of the path d-f-g, a mode switch from block f to block g is taken into account. Similarly, all other mode switches are accounted for when a program construct implies a sequential execution of blocks in different instruction set modes.

As the timing update information continues to propagate on the annotated syntax tree, nodes D, B, and A are visited in that order, and their WCTAs are updated. Note that the WCTAs for nodes C and G that have been recorded in the initial WCET analysis are reused when we update the WCTAs for nodes B and A, respectively. Also note that node H is not visited in the timing update process, since it belongs to a subtree for the program portion that is not affected by the transformation. In summary, although we essentially re-enumerate all the possible execution paths in the program for the timing update, the timing analysis needs to be done only for the segments of the paths that are affected by the transformation[1].

When the propagation finally reaches the root node, we determine the new WCET of the program by taking the PA that has the largest execution time among those in the root node's WCTA. This PA corresponds to the WCEP of the whole program after the transformation. In order to determine whether or not the WCEP has changed due to the transformation, we compare this new WCEP against the previous WCEP. This way, we can detect a possible change in execution time without re-evaluating the WCTA for every node in the syntax tree every time a subpath is selected and the blocks on it are transformed. By using this timing update algorithm, we can efficiently track the changes in the program's WCET and WCEP, and thus the selective code transformation is guided towards improving the WCET of the program in each iteration.

5   Implementation and Results

To validate the effectiveness of our proposed approach, we implemented the proposed technique and performed a set of experiments. The implementation is targeted to the ARM7TDMI [13] processor, which supports both a 32-bit ARM instruction set and a 16-bit Thumb instruction set. We implemented the algorithm for selecting basic blocks to be transformed, using the path-based profitability analysis described in Section 4.1. For the hierarchical WCET analysis, we implemented a timing analyzer that can handle both of the two instruction set architectures, which can calculate the WCET of a given program even when the two instruction sets are used in conjunction. The absence of cache memory and the simple pipeline structure of the target processor allow us to calculate tight WCET bounds for programs using a simple pipeline model. We also implemented the code generator for the target architecture that can generate a mixed instruction set code, by modifying the VPO [14] code generation interfaces.

We extracted a set of benchmark programs from the SNU-RT benchmark suite [15], which is a collection of benchmark programs representing typical applications for real-time embedded systems. The `fir` benchmark implements a finite impulse response filter algorithm, and `matmul` computes a multiplication of two 5×5 integer matrices. The `ludcmp` program solves 10 simultaneous linear equations by the LU decomposition method. Finally, `jfdctint` benchmark implements an integer discrete cosine transform for the JPEG image compression algorithm.

To demonstrate the tradeoff between code size and WCET, we applied our selective code transformation to the set of benchmarks, generating ten different versions of code for each program. Among the different versions, code T refers to the program compiled entirely into the Thumb instruction set, while code A

---

[1] The number of intermediate nodes whose WCTAs are re-evaluated over all the iterations of the selection algorithm is bound by $O(n^2)$, where n is the number of basic blocks in the program. A rigorous complexity analysis of the timing update algorithm has been omitted due to the space limitation of the paper.

is generated by transforming all the basic blocks into the ARM instruction set. The other versions M_1, M_2, ..., and M_9 are generated by gradually increasing the code size limit. That is, we set the code size budget to 10 %, 20 %, ..., and 90 % of the difference between the sizes of A and T. For each generated code M, we calculated the relative code size by

$$relative\_size(M) = \frac{size(M) - size(T)}{size(A) - size(T)} , \qquad (3)$$

where $size(x)$ denotes the total size of code x. Similarly, we calculated the relative WCET of each generated code by

$$relative\_WCET(M) = \frac{WCET(M) - WCET(A)}{WCET(T) - WCET(A)} , \qquad (4)$$

where $WCET(x)$ denotes the estimated WCET of code x.

Figure 4 shows the relative code size and the relative WCET for each benchmark program. For comparison purposes, the vertical axis of each graph is labeled with the actual code size and WCET of code T and code A. The results verify that there exists a clear tradeoff relationship between the code size and WCET of programs, and that our selective code transformation can effectively exploit this tradeoff. The size of each program grows as we increase the code size budget, while the curve remains below the diagonal line. This indicates that our selective code transformation framework successfully maintained the size of the resulting code under the size limit. On the other hand, with the increase of the code size, the WCET decreases and the amount of the WCET reduction according to the code size budget differs from one program to another.

For the `fir` benchmark program, the code size increase is virtually linear to the increase of the code size budget. This is because the program has a number of small nested loops, and the selection algorithm was able to successfully find code sections whose transformation cost could fit into respective code size budgets. On the other hand, the WCET of the program is reduced significantly even for a modest increase in the code size. When the code size budget is 30 % of the size difference between code A and code T, as much as 94 % of total achievable WCET reduction was made.

For the `matmul` program, the WCET reduction is not remarkable for small code size budgets. However, when the code size budget reaches 30 %, the WCET sharply decreases by up to 84 % of the total achievable WCET savings. This is the point where the innermost loop of the three-level nested loop of the matrix multiplication algorithm is transformed into the ARM instruction set. As we further increase the code size budget, the code for the outer loops begins to be transformed and the WCET gradually approaches that of code A.

In the results for `ludcmp`, the code size increases in a stepwise manner, whereas the WCET becomes close to that of code A even with a small code size budget. Specifically, for only 10 % code size budget, the WCET reduction is more than 99 % of the total achievable savings. This behavior results from the fact that this particular benchmark program has a number of basic blocks that

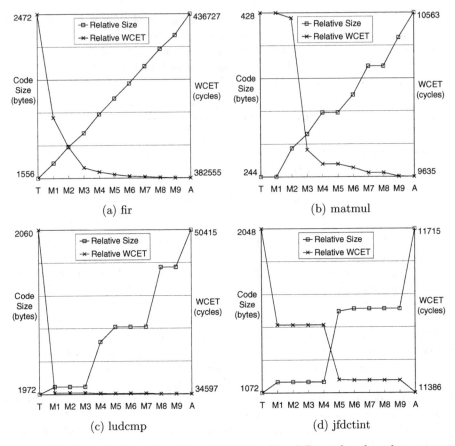

Fig. 4. Relative code size and relative WCET for four different benchmark programs. The code size increases while the WCET is reduced as we gradually increase the code size limit.

are smaller in ARM mode than in Thumb mode. After a careful investigation of the generated assembly code, we discovered that this is because of large constants used in the program source. Due to Thumb's limited instruction encoding space, several Thumb instructions are required to form a large constant, while a single ARM instruction is sufficient. When such large constants are used extensively as is the case for the ludcmp benchmark program, certain basic blocks compiled into the ARM instruction set have smaller execution times as well as smaller code sizes than the same blocks compiled into the Thumb instruction set. Such blocks are favored for transformation in the early phases of the incremental selection algorithm, resulting in a small total code size with the WCET close to that of code A.

Finally, the tradeoff relationship between the code size and WCET of the jfdctint program is notably different from those of the above mentioned programs. For this benchmark, code T is as much as 48 % smaller than code A, while its WCET is only 3 % larger than that of code A. This large difference in the code size and small difference in the WCET results from the fact that the jfdctint algorithm mainly performs simple arithmetic operations which are implemented by single instructions both in the ARM mode and in the Thumb mode. Therefore, while the size of code A is nearly double that of code T, both versions of the program execute approximately the same number of instructions. However, even in such a case, our selective code transformation technique tries to reduce the WCET as much as possible for a given code size limit, and approximately 50 % budget was needed to reduce the WCET by 92 % of the total achievable savings.

6   Conclusions

We have presented a code generation technique for a dual instruction set processor that enables a flexible tradeoff between a program's code size and its WCET. By selectively using the two instruction sets for different sections within a single program, the proposed technique tries to minimize the program's WCET while maintaining the total code size under a given upper bound. Our approach first compiles the whole program into the reduced instruction set, and then selectively transforms a subset of basic blocks into the full instruction set. The selection algorithm combines a greedy heuristic and a path-based profitability analysis, which accurately estimates the code size increase and the WCET reduction by transforming the blocks on a path. During the selection procedure, changes in the program's timing behavior due to the transformation are updated on the annotated syntax tree, so that the selective code transformation can be steered towards improving the WCET.

The proposed technique has been implemented for the ARM7TDMI target processor, which supports a 16-bit Thumb instruction set in addition to a 32-bit ARM instruction set. The validity and effectiveness of our approach has been demonstrated by experiments using a set of benchmark programs. The results show that the technique can effectively balance the tradeoff between a program's code size and its WCET. This tradeoff data can be used in a system-level design framework that tries to optimize the entire system with multiple applications that have both code size constraint and timing requirements. In addition, unlike traditional compiler optimization techniques that try to optimize programs for average case execution time, our code generation framework is geared towards improving the program's worst case performance by incorporating a hierarchical WCET analysis technique.

The future directions of our research will focus on the following. First, the practicality of the proposed approach can be improved by incorporating instruction cache in the WCET analysis and selective code transformation. Since altering the sizes of basic blocks affects the instruction cache behavior, a code placement technique should be employed to reflect the caching effect. Second, the execution time of transformed code can be improved by enabling program optimization techniques that operate across basic block boundaries. Especially, a global register re-allocation is expected to reduce the WCET of transformed basic blocks by using the registers that are only available in the full instruction set mode.

References

1. A. Halambi, A. Shrivastava, P. Biswas, N. Dutt, and A. Nicolau. An efficient compiler technique for code size reduction using reduced bit-width ISAs. In *Proceedings of the DATE (Design, Automation and Test in Europe)*, Paris, France, March 2002.
2. S. Furber. *ARM System Architecture*. Addison-Wesley, 1996. ISBN 0-201-40352-8.
3. K. Kissel. MIPS16: High-density MIPS for the embedded market. Technical report, Silicon Graphics MIPS Group, 1997.
4. ARC Cores (http://www.arc.com). *The ARCtangent-A5 Processor*.
5. S. Lee, J. Lee, S. L. Min, J. Hiser, and J. W. Davidson. Code generation for a dual instruction set processor based on selective code transformation. In *Proceedings of the 7th International Workshop on Software and Compilers for Embedded Systems (SCOPES)*, pages 33–48, Vienna, Austria, September 2003.
6. A. Krishnaswamy and R. Gupta. Profile guided selection of ARM and Thumb instructions. In *Proceedings of LCTES/SCOPES*, Berlin, Germany, June 2002.
7. S.-S Lim, J. Kim, and S. L. Min. A worst case timing analysis technique for optimized programs. In *Proceedings of the 5th International Conference on Real-Time Computing Systems and Applications (RTCSA)*, pages 151–157, Hiroshima, Japan, October 1998.
8. R. Kirner. *Extending Optimising Compilation to Support Worst-Case Execution Time Analysis*. PhD thesis, Vienna University of Technology, May 2003.
9. W. Zhao, P. Kulkarni, D. Whalley, C. Healy, F. Mueller, and G.-R. Uh. Tuning the WCET of embedded applications. In *Proceedings of the 10th IEEE Real-Time and Embedded Technology and Applications Symposium (RTAS)*, pages 472–481, Toronto, Canada, May 2004.
10. T. Ball and J. R. Larus. Efficient path profiling. In *Proceedings of the 29th Annual IEEE/ACM Symposium on Microarchitecture*, pages 46–57, Paris, France, 1996.
11. C. Y. Park and A. C. Shaw. Experiments with a program timing tool based on source-level timing schema. In *Proceedings of the 11th Real-Time Systems Symposium*, pages 72–81, December 1990.
12. S.-S. Lim, Y. H. Bae, G. T. Jang, B.-D. Rhee, S. L. Min, C. Y. Park, H. Shin, K. Park, S.-M. Moon, and C. S. Kim. An accurate worst case timing analysis for RISC processors. *IEEE Transactions on Software Engineering*, 21(7):593–694, 1995.
13. Advanced RISC Machines Ltd. *ARM7TDMI Data Sheet*, August 1995.
14. M. E. Benitez and J. W. Davidson. Target-specific global code improvement: Principles and applications. Technical Report CS-94-42, Department of Computer Science, University of Virginia, April 1994.
15. SNU Real-Time Benchmark Suite. http://archi.snu.ac.kr/realtime/benchmark.

Author Index

Ascheid, Gerd 33

Bagchi, Susmit 200
Bekooij, Marco 77
Bhattacharyya, Shuvra S. 47
Brisk, Philip 229

Cascini Peixoto, Daniela Cristina 2
Catthoor, Francky 122, 167
Ceng, Jianjiang 33

da Silva Júnior, Diógenes Cecílio 2
Deprettere, Ed 62
Dimitroulakos, Grigoris 122

Falk, Heiko 137

Galanis, Michalis D. 122
Goutis, Costas 122

Hohenauer, Manuel 33
Huss, Sorin Alexander 107

Ienne, Paolo 17

Jain, Diviya 17
Johnstone, Adrian 92
Jung, Michael 107

Kammler, David 33
Karuri, Kingshuk 33
Kienhuis, Bart 62
Ko, Ming-Yung 47
Kumar, Anshul 17

Lee, Jaejin 244
Lee, Sheayun 244
Leupers, Rainer 33

Menard, Daniel 214
Mesman, Bart 77
Meyr, Heinrich 33
Milidonis, Athanasios 122
Min, Sang Lyul 244
Mooney, Vincent 182
Moreira, Orlando 77
Murthy, Praveen K. 47

Nahapetian, Ani 229
Nygaard, Mads 200

Park, Chang Yun 244
Pastrnak, Milan 77
Poplavko, Peter 77
Pozzi, Laura 17

Sarrafzadeh, Majid 229
Scharwaechter, Hanno 33
Scott, Elizabeth 92
Sentieys, Olivier 214

Tan, Yudong 182
Theodoridis, George 122
Turjan, Alexandru 62

Uhler, Michael 1

van Meerbergen, Jef 77
Verma, Manish 137

Wess, Bernhard 152
Wieferink, Andreas 33

Yang, Peng 167

Zeitlhofer, Thomas 152

Author Index

Lecture Notes in Computer Science

For information about Vols. 1–3099

please contact your bookseller or Springer

Vol. 3232: R. Heery, L. Lyon (Eds.), Research and Advanced Technology for Digital Libraries. XV, 528 pages. 2004.

Vol. 3220: J.C. Lester, R.M. Vicari, F. Paraguaçu (Eds.), Intelligent Tutoring Systems. XXI, 920 pages. 2004.

Vol. 3208: H.J. Ohlbach, S. Schaffert (Eds.), Principles and Practice of Semantic Web Reasoning. VII, 165 pages. 2004.

Vol. 3207: L.T. Jang, M. Guo, G.R. Gao, N.K. Jha, Embedded and Ubiquitous Computing. XX, 1116 pages. 2004.

Vol. 3206: P. Sojka, I. Kopecek, K. Pala (Eds.), Text, Speech and Dialogue. XIII, 667 pages. 2004. (Subseries LNAI).

Vol. 3205: N. Davies, E. Mynatt, I. Siio (Eds.), UbiComp 2004: Ubiquitous Computing. XVI, 452 pages. 2004.

Vol. 3203: J. Becker, M. Platzner, S. Vernalde (Eds.), Field Programmable Logic and Application. XXX, 1198 pages. 2004.

Vol. 3199: H. Schepers (Ed.), Software and Compilers for Embedded Systems. X, 259 pages. 2004.

Vol. 3198: G.-J. de Vreede, L.A. Guerrero, G. Marín Raventós (Eds.), Groupware: Design, Implementation and Use. XI, 378 pages. 2004.

Vol. 3194: R. Camacho, R. King, A. Srinivasan (Eds.), Inductive Logic Programming. XI, 361 pages. 2004. (Subseries LNAI).

Vol. 3193: P. Samarati, P. Ryan, D. Gollmann, R. Molva (Eds.), Computer Security – ESORICS 2004. X, 457 pages. 2004.

Vol. 3192: C. Bussler, D. Fensel (Eds.), Artificial Intelligence: Methodology, Systems, and Applications. XIII, 522 pages. 2004. (Subseries LNAI).

Vol. 3189: P.-C. Yew, J. Xue (Eds.), Advances in Computer Systems Architecture. XVII, 598 pages. 2004.

Vol. 3186: Z. Bellahsène, T. Milo, M. Rys, D. Suciu, R. Unland (Eds.), Database and XML Technologies. X, 235 pages. 2004.

Vol. 3184: S. Katsikas, J. Lopez, G. Pernul (Eds.), Trust and Privacy in Digital Business. XI, 299 pages. 2004.

Vol. 3183: R. Traunmüller (Ed.), Electronic Government. XIX, 583 pages. 2004.

Vol. 3182: K. Bauknecht, M. Bichler, B. Pröll (Eds.), E-Commerce and Web Technologies. XI, 370 pages. 2004.

Vol. 3181: Y. Kambayashi, M. Mohania, W. Wöß (Eds.), Data Warehousing and Knowledge Discovery. XIV, 412 pages. 2004.

Vol. 3180: F. Galindo, M. Takizawa, R. Traunmüller (Eds.), Database and Expert Systems Applications. XXI, 972 pages. 2004.

Vol. 3179: F.J. Perales, B.A. Draper (Eds.), Articulated Motion and Deformable Objects. XI, 270 pages. 2004.

Vol. 3178: W. Jonker, M. Petkovic (Eds.), Secure Data Management. VIII, 219 pages. 2004.

Vol. 3177: Z.R. Yang, H. Yin, R. Everson (Eds.), Intelligent Data Engineering and Automated Learning – IDEAL 2004. XVIII, 852 pages. 2004.

Vol. 3175: C.E. Rasmussen, H.H. Bülthoff, B. Schölkopf, M.A. Giese (Eds.), Pattern Recognition. XVIII, 581 pages. 2004.

Vol. 3174: F. Yin, J. Wang, C. Guo (Eds.), Advances in Neural Networks - ISNN 2004. XXXV, 1021 pages. 2004.

Vol. 3172: M. Dorigo, M. Birattari, C. Blum, L. M.Gambardella, F. Mondada, T. Stützle (Eds.), Ant Colony, Optimization and Swarm Intelligence. XII, 434 pages. 2004.

Vol. 3170: P. Gardner, N. Yoshida (Eds.), CONCUR 2004 - Concurrency Theory. XIII, 529 pages. 2004.

Vol. 3166: M. Rauterberg (Ed.), Entertainment Computing – ICEC 2004. XXIII, 617 pages. 2004.

Vol. 3163: S. Marinai, A. Dengel (Eds.), Document Analysis Systems VI. XII, 564 pages. 2004.

Vol. 3162: R. Downey, M. Fellows, F. Dehne (Eds.), Parameterized and Exact Computation. X, 293 pages. 2004.

Vol. 3160: S. Brewster, M. Dunlop (Eds.), Mobile Human-Computer Interaction – MobileHCI 2004. XVIII, 541 pages. 2004.

Vol. 3159: U. Visser, Intelligent Information Integration for the Semantic Web. XIV, 150 pages. 2004. (Subseries LNAI).

Vol. 3158: I. Nikolaidis, M. Barbeau, E. Kranakis (Eds.), Ad-Hoc, Mobile, and Wireless Networks. IX, 344 pages. 2004.

Vol. 3157: C. Zhang, H. W. Guesgen, W.K. Yeap (Eds.), PRICAI 2004: Trends in Artificial Intelligence. XX, 1023 pages. 2004. (Subseries LNAI).

Vol. 3156: M. Joye, J.-J. Quisquater (Eds.), Cryptographic Hardware and Embedded Systems - CHES 2004. XIII, 455 pages. 2004.

Vol. 3155: P. Funk, P.A. González Calero (Eds.), Advances in Case-Based Reasoning. XIII, 822 pages. 2004. (Subseries LNAI).

Vol. 3154: R.L. Nord (Ed.), Software Product Lines. XIV, 334 pages. 2004.

Vol. 3153: J. Fiala, V. Koubek, J. Kratochvíl (Eds.), Mathematical Foundations of Computer Science 2004. XIV, 902 pages. 2004.

Vol. 3152: M. Franklin (Ed.), Advances in Cryptology – CRYPTO 2004. XI, 579 pages. 2004.

Vol. 3150: G.-Z. Yang, T. Jiang (Eds.), Medical Imaging and Augmented Reality. XII, 378 pages. 2004.

Vol. 3149: M. Danelutto, M. Vanneschi, D. Laforenza (Eds.), Euro-Par 2004 Parallel Processing. XXXIV, 1081 pages. 2004.

Vol. 3148: R. Giacobazzi (Ed.), Static Analysis. XI, 393 pages. 2004.

Vol. 3146: P. Érdi, A. Esposito, M. Marinaro, S. Scarpetta (Eds.), Computational Neuroscience: Cortical Dynamics. XI, 161 pages. 2004.

Vol. 3144: M. Papatriantafilou, P. Hunel (Eds.), Principles of Distributed Systems. XI, 246 pages. 2004.

Vol. 3143: W. Liu, Y. Shi, Q. Li (Eds.), Advances in Web-Based Learning – ICWL 2004. XIV, 459 pages. 2004.

Vol. 3142: J. Diaz, J. Karhumäki, A. Lepistö, D. Sannella (Eds.), Automata, Languages and Programming. XIX, 1253 pages. 2004.

Vol. 3140: N. Koch, P. Fraternali, M. Wirsing (Eds.), Web Engineering. XXI, 623 pages. 2004.

Vol. 3139: F. Iida, R. Pfeifer, L. Steels, Y. Kuniyoshi (Eds.), Embodied Artificial Intelligence. IX, 331 pages. 2004. (Subseries LNAI).

Vol. 3138: A. Fred, T. Caelli, R.P.W. Duin, A. Campilho, D.d. Ridder (Eds.), Structural, Syntactic, and Statistical Pattern Recognition. XXII, 1168 pages. 2004.

Vol. 3137: P. De Bra, W. Nejdl (Eds.), Adaptive Hypermedia and Adaptive Web-Based Systems. XIV, 442 pages. 2004.

Vol. 3136: F. Meziane, E. Métais (Eds.), Natural Language Processing and Information Systems. XII, 436 pages. 2004.

Vol. 3134: C. Zannier, H. Erdogmus, L. Lindstrom (Eds.), Extreme Programming and Agile Methods - XP/Agile Universe 2004. XIV, 233 pages. 2004.

Vol. 3133: A.D. Pimentel, S. Vassiliadis (Eds.), Computer Systems: Architectures, Modeling, and Simulation. XIII, 562 pages. 2004.

Vol. 3132: B. Demoen, V. Lifschitz (Eds.), Logic Programming. XII, 480 pages. 2004.

Vol. 3131: V. Torra, Y. Narukawa (Eds.), Modeling Decisions for Artificial Intelligence. XI, 327 pages. 2004. (Subseries LNAI).

Vol. 3130: A. Syropoulos, K. Berry, Y. Haralambous, B. Hughes, S. Peter, J. Plaice (Eds.), TeX, XML, and Digital Typography. VIII, 265 pages. 2004.

Vol. 3129: Q. Li, G. Wang, L. Feng (Eds.), Advances in Web-Age Information Management. XVII, 753 pages. 2004.

Vol. 3128: D. Asonov (Ed.), Querying Databases Privately. IX, 115 pages. 2004.

Vol. 3127: K.E. Wolff, H.D. Pfeiffer, H.S. Delugach (Eds.), Conceptual Structures at Work. XI, 403 pages. 2004. (Subseries LNAI).

Vol. 3126: P. Dini, P. Lorenz, J.N.d. Souza (Eds.), Service Assurance with Partial and Intermittent Resources. XI, 312 pages. 2004.

Vol. 3125: D. Kozen (Ed.), Mathematics of Program Construction. X, 401 pages. 2004.

Vol. 3124: J.N. de Souza, P. Dini, P. Lorenz (Eds.), Telecommunications and Networking - ICT 2004. XXVI, 1390 pages. 2004.

Vol. 3123: A. Belz, R. Evans, P. Piwek (Eds.), Natural Language Generation. X, 219 pages. 2004. (Subseries LNAI).

Vol. 3122: K. Jansen, S. Khanna, J.D.P. Rolim, D. Ron (Eds.), Approximation, Randomization, and Combinatorial Optimization. IX, 428 pages. 2004.

Vol. 3121: S. Nikoletseas, J.D.P. Rolim (Eds.), Algorithmic Aspects of Wireless Sensor Networks. X, 201 pages. 2004.

Vol. 3120: J. Shawe-Taylor, Y. Singer (Eds.), Learning Theory. X, 648 pages. 2004. (Subseries LNAI).

Vol. 3118: K. Miesenberger, J. Klaus, W. Zagler, D. Burger (Eds.), Computer Helping People with Special Needs. XXIII, 1191 pages. 2004.

Vol. 3116: C. Rattray, S. Maharaj, C. Shankland (Eds.), Algebraic Methodology and Software Technology. XI, 569 pages. 2004.

Vol. 3115: P. Enser, Y. Kompatsiaris, N.E. O'Connor, A.F. Smeaton, A.W.M. Smeulders (Eds.), Image and Video Retrieval. XVII, 679 pages. 2004.

Vol. 3114: R. Alur, D.A. Peled (Eds.), Computer Aided Verification. XII, 536 pages. 2004.

Vol. 3113: J. Karhumäki, H. Maurer, G. Paun, G. Rozenberg (Eds.), Theory Is Forever. X, 283 pages. 2004.

Vol. 3112: H. Williams, L. MacKinnon (Eds.), Key Technologies for Data Management. XII, 265 pages. 2004.

Vol. 3111: T. Hagerup, J. Katajainen (Eds.), Algorithm Theory - SWAT 2004. XI, 506 pages. 2004.

Vol. 3110: A. Juels (Ed.), Financial Cryptography. XI, 281 pages. 2004.

Vol. 3109: S.C. Sahinalp, S. Muthukrishnan, U. Dogrusoz (Eds.), Combinatorial Pattern Matching. XII, 486 pages. 2004.

Vol. 3108: H. Wang, J. Pieprzyk, V. Varadharajan (Eds.), Information Security and Privacy. XII, 494 pages. 2004.

Vol. 3107: J. Bosch, C. Krueger (Eds.), Software Reuse: Methods, Techniques and Tools. XI, 339 pages. 2004.

Vol. 3106: K.-Y. Chwa, J.I. Munro (Eds.), Computing and Combinatorics. XIII, 474 pages. 2004.

Vol. 3105: S. Göbel, U. Spierling, A. Hoffmann, I. Iurgel, O. Schneider, J. Dechau, A. Feix (Eds.), Technologies for Interactive Digital Storytelling and Entertainment. XVI, 304 pages. 2004.

Vol. 3104: R. Kralovic, O. Sykora (Eds.), Structural Information and Communication Complexity. X, 303 pages. 2004.

Vol. 3103: K. Deb, e. al. (Eds.), Genetic and Evolutionary Computation – GECCO 2004. XLIX, 1439 pages. 2004.

Vol. 3102: K. Deb, e. al. (Eds.), Genetic and Evolutionary Computation – GECCO 2004. L, 1445 pages. 2004.

Vol. 3101: M. Masoodian, S. Jones, B. Rogers (Eds.), Computer Human Interaction. XIV, 694 pages. 2004.

Vol. 3100: J.F. Peters, A. Skowron, J.W. Grzymała-Busse, B. Kostek, R.W. Świniarski, M.S. Szczuka (Eds.), Transactions on Rough Sets I. X, 405 pages. 2004.